CRANKSHAFT™

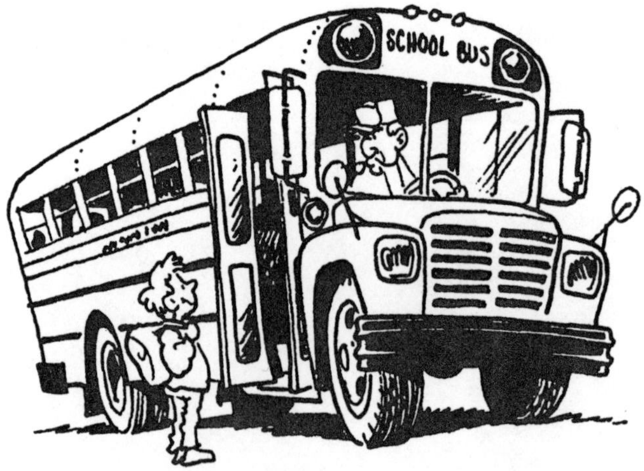
SCHOOL BUS

CRANKSHAFT®

by Tom Batiuk and Chuck Ayers

Andrews and McMeel
A Universal Press Syndicate Company
Kansas City

ISBN: 0-8362-1889-2

Library of Congress Catalog Card Number: 92-70023

ATTENTION: SCHOOLS AND BUSINESSES ───

Andrews and McMeel books are available at quantity discounts with bulk purchase for educational, business, or sales promotional use. For information, please write to: Special Sales Department, Andrews and McMeel, 4900 Main Street, Kansas City, Missouri 64112.

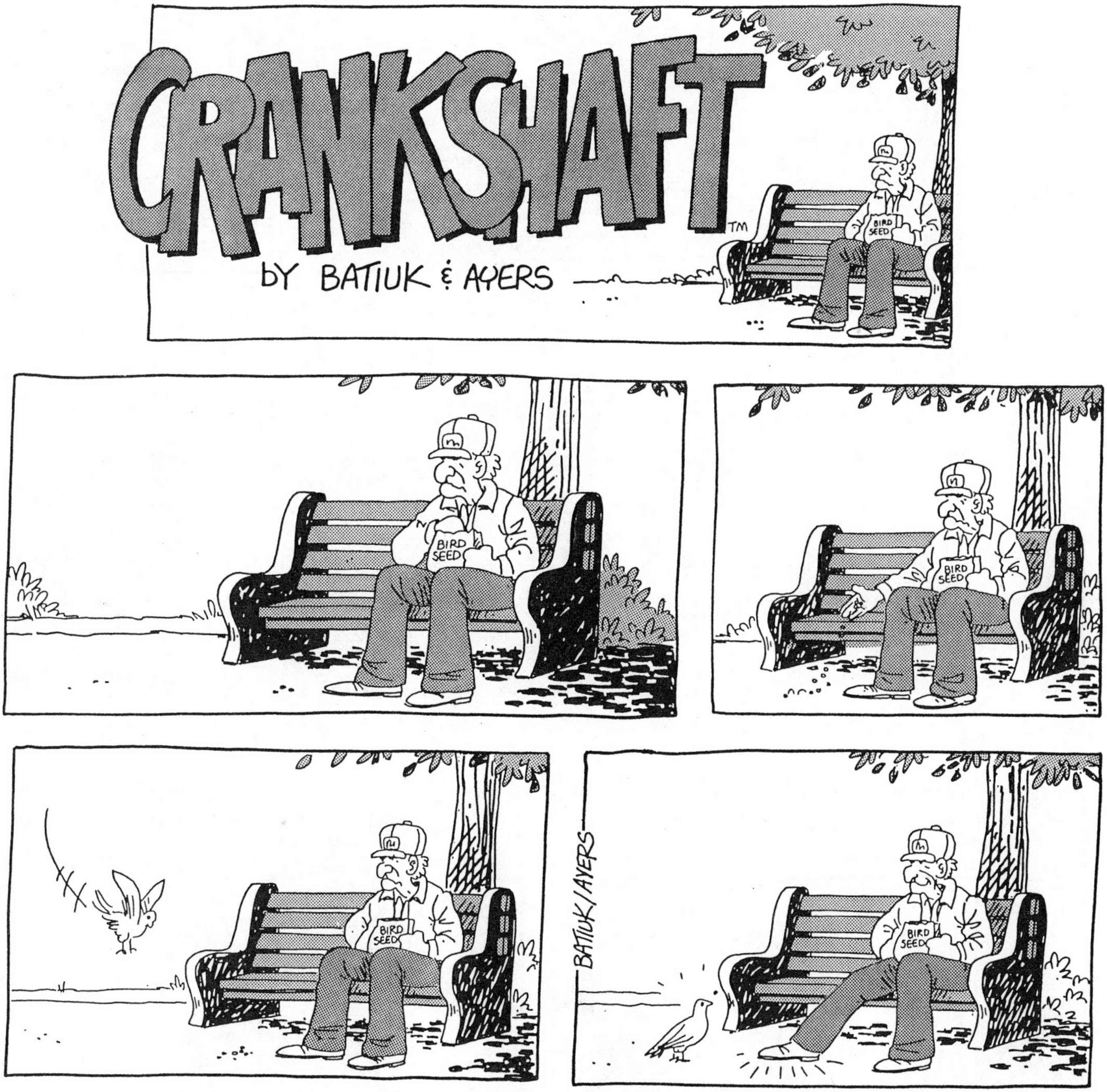
CRANKSHAFT
TM
BY BATIUK & AYERS
BIRD SEED
BIRD SEED
BIRD SEED
BIRD SEED
BATIUK/AYERS
BIRD SEED

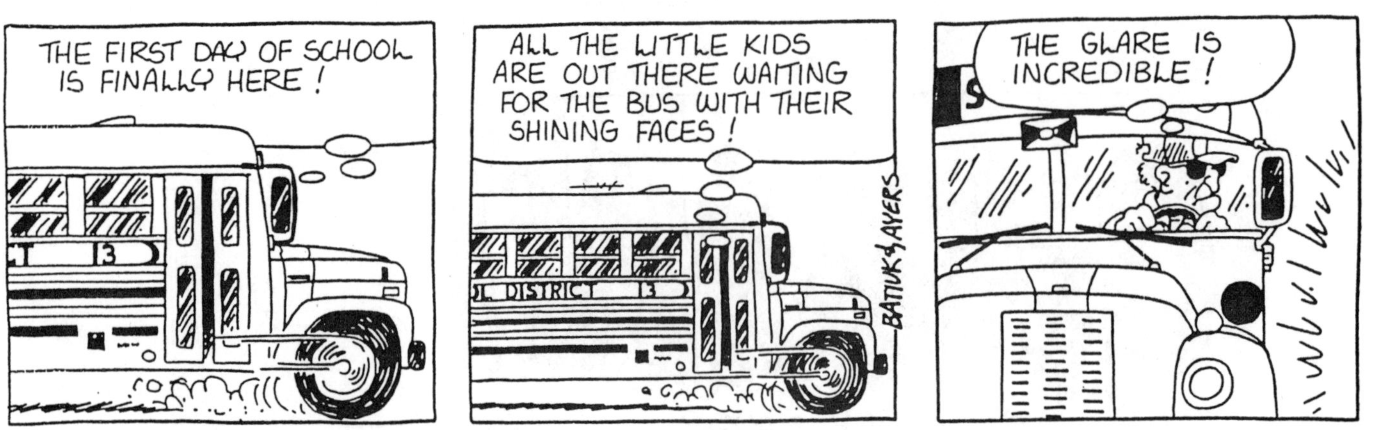

THE FIRST DAY OF SCHOOL IS FINALLY HERE!
ALL THE LITTLE KIDS ARE OUT THERE WAITING FOR THE BUS WITH THEIR SHINING FACES!
DISTRICT 13
BATIUK & AYERS
THE GLARE IS INCREDIBLE!

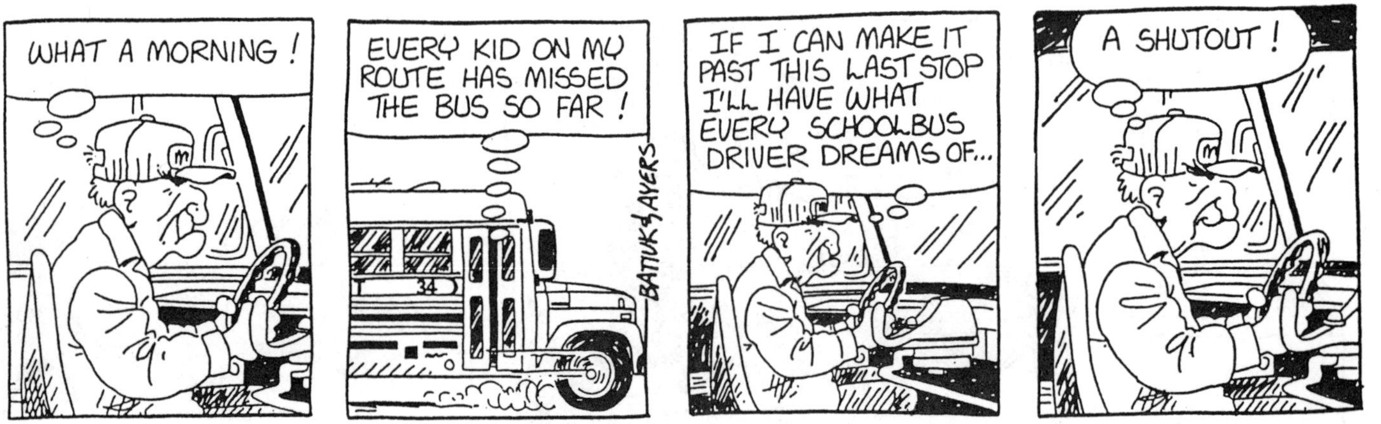

WHAT A MORNING!
EVERY KID ON MY ROUTE HAS MISSED THE BUS SO FAR!
34
BATIUK & AYERS
IF I CAN MAKE IT PAST THIS LAST STOP I'LL HAVE WHAT EVERY SCHOOLBUS DRIVER DREAMS OF...
A SHUTOUT!

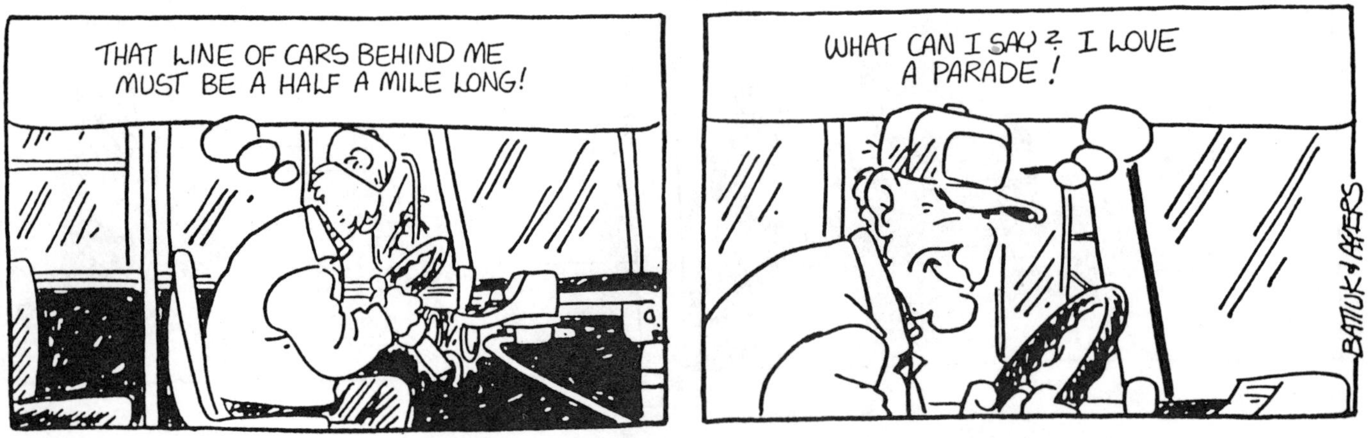

THAT LINE OF CARS BEHIND ME MUST BE A HALF A MILE LONG!
WHAT CAN I SAY? I LOVE A PARADE!
BATIUK & AYERS

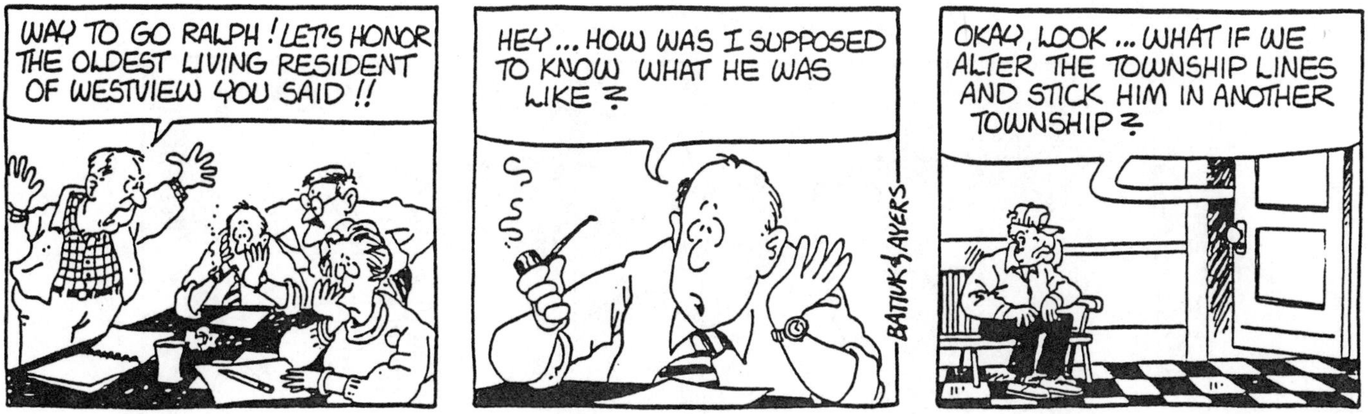

WAY TO GO RALPH ! LET'S HONOR THE OLDEST LIVING RESIDENT OF WESTVIEW YOU SAID !!
HEY ... HOW WAS I SUPPOSED TO KNOW WHAT HE WAS LIKE ?
BATIUK & AYERS
OKAY, LOOK ... WHAT IF WE ALTER THE TOWNSHIP LINES AND STICK HIM IN ANOTHER TOWNSHIP ?

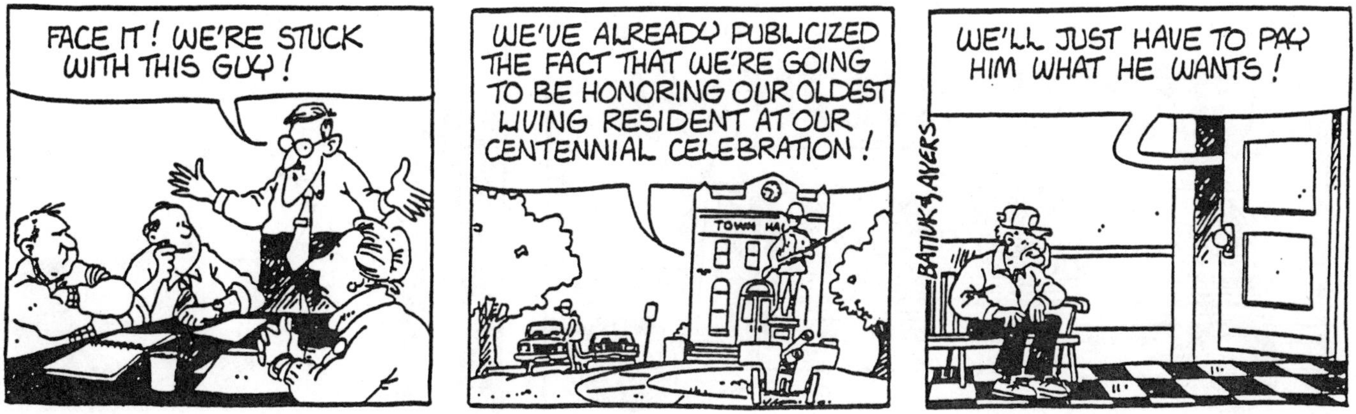

FACE IT ! WE'RE STUCK WITH THIS GUY !
WE'VE ALREADY PUBLICIZED THE FACT THAT WE'RE GOING TO BE HONORING OUR OLDEST LIVING RESIDENT AT OUR CENTENNIAL CELEBRATION !
BATIUK & AYERS
WE'LL JUST HAVE TO PAY HIM WHAT HE WANTS !

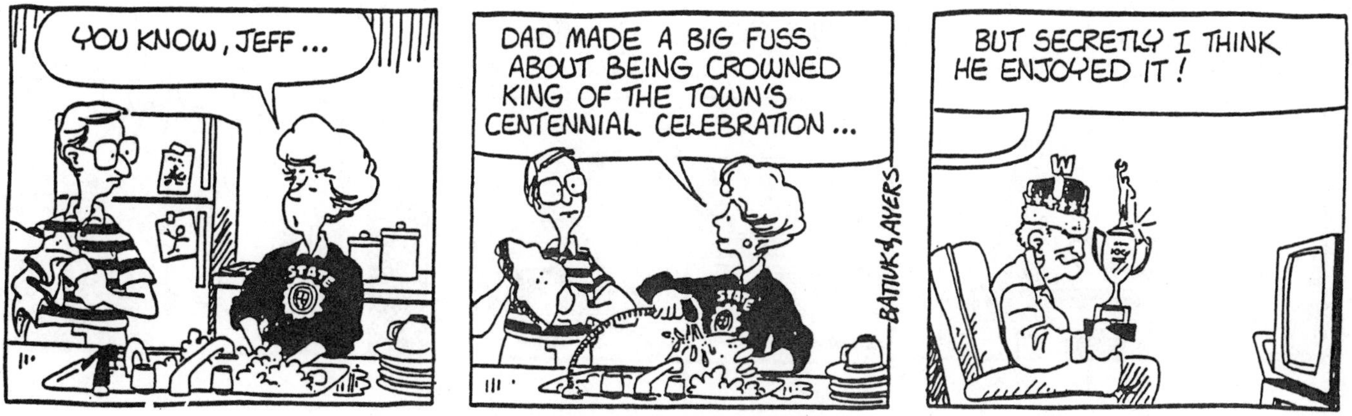

YOU KNOW, JEFF ...
STATE
DAD MADE A BIG FUSS ABOUT BEING CROWNED KING OF THE TOWN'S CENTENNIAL CELEBRATION ...
BATIUK & AYERS
BUT SECRETLY I THINK HE ENJOYED IT !
W

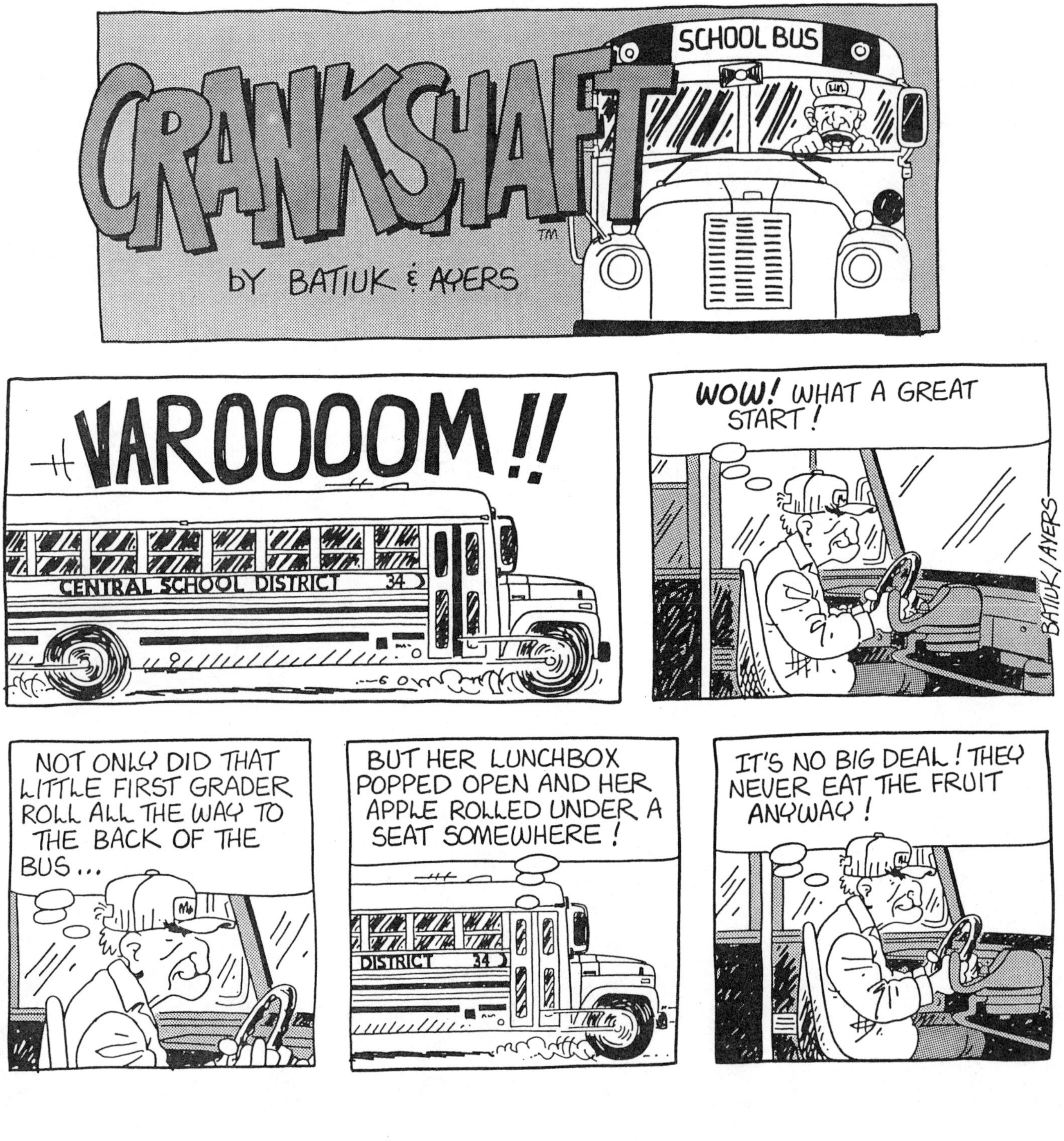
CRANKSHAFT™
SCHOOL BUS
BY BATIUK & AYERS
VAROOOOM!!
CENTRAL SCHOOL DISTRICT 34
WOW! WHAT A GREAT START!
BATIUK/AYERS
NOT ONLY DID THAT LITTLE FIRST GRADER ROLL ALL THE WAY TO THE BACK OF THE BUS...
BUT HER LUNCHBOX POPPED OPEN AND HER APPLE ROLLED UNDER A SEAT SOMEWHERE!
DISTRICT 34
IT'S NO BIG DEAL! THEY NEVER EAT THE FRUIT ANYWAY!

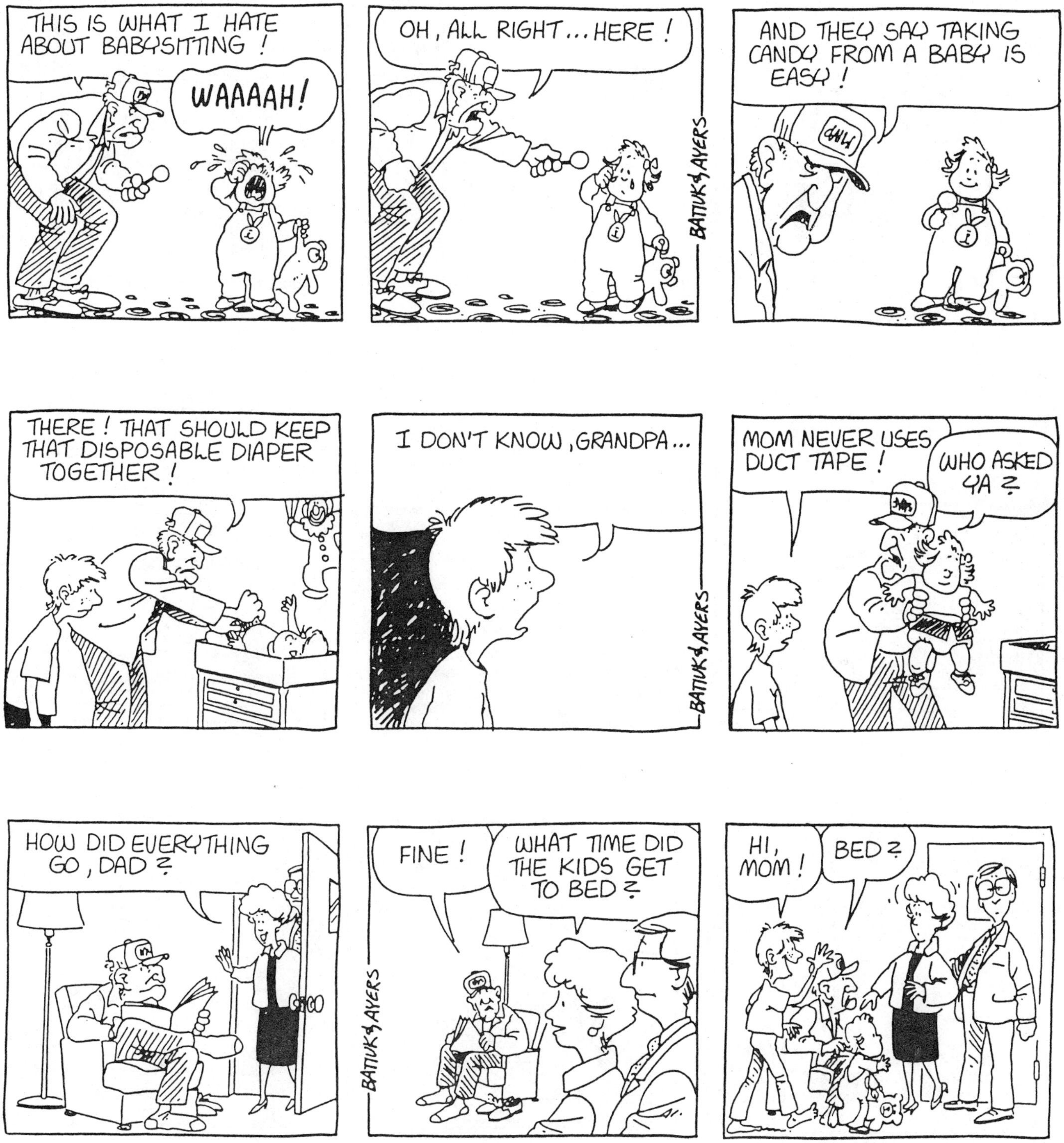
THIS IS WHAT I HATE ABOUT BABYSITTING !
WAAAAH!
OH, ALL RIGHT... HERE !
BATIUK & AYERS
AND THEY SAY TAKING CANDY FROM A BABY IS EASY !
THERE ! THAT SHOULD KEEP THAT DISPOSABLE DIAPER TOGETHER !
I DON'T KNOW, GRANDPA...
BATIUK & AYERS
MOM NEVER USES DUCT TAPE !
WHO ASKED YA ?
HOW DID EVERYTHING GO, DAD ?
BATIUK & AYERS
FINE !
WHAT TIME DID THE KIDS GET TO BED ?
HI, MOM !
BED ?

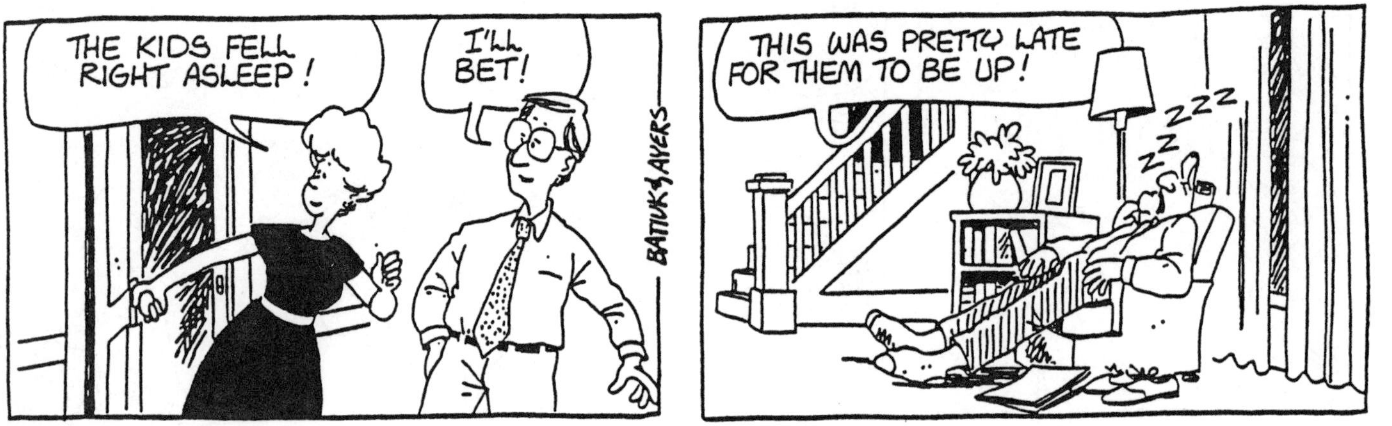
THE KIDS FELL RIGHT ASLEEP!
I'LL BET!
BATIUK & AYERS
THIS WAS PRETTY LATE FOR THEM TO BE UP!
ZZZZZ

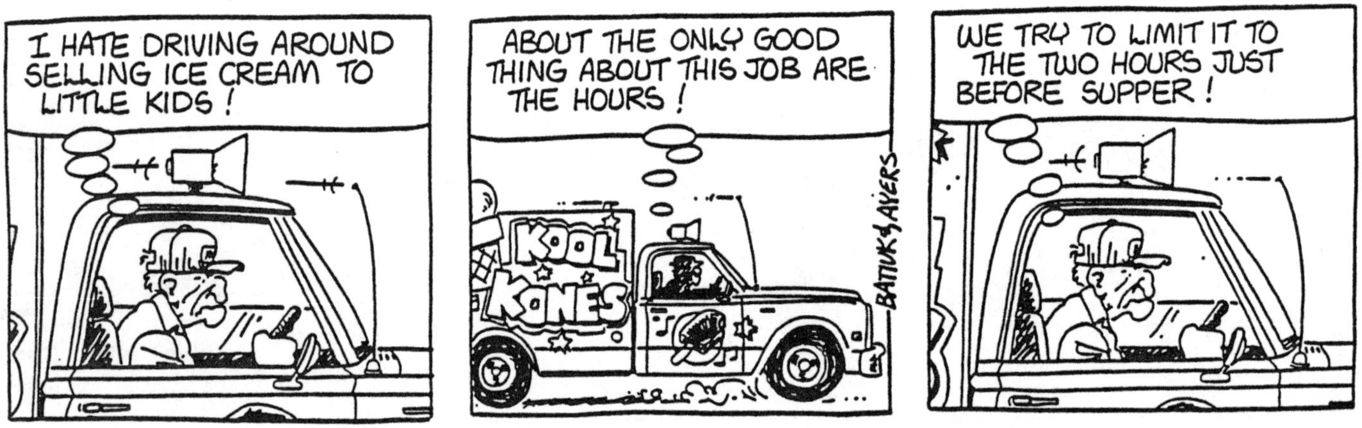
I HATE DRIVING AROUND SELLING ICE CREAM TO LITTLE KIDS!
ABOUT THE ONLY GOOD THING ABOUT THIS JOB ARE THE HOURS!
KOOL KONES
BATIUK & AYERS
WE TRY TO LIMIT IT TO THE TWO HOURS JUST BEFORE SUPPER!

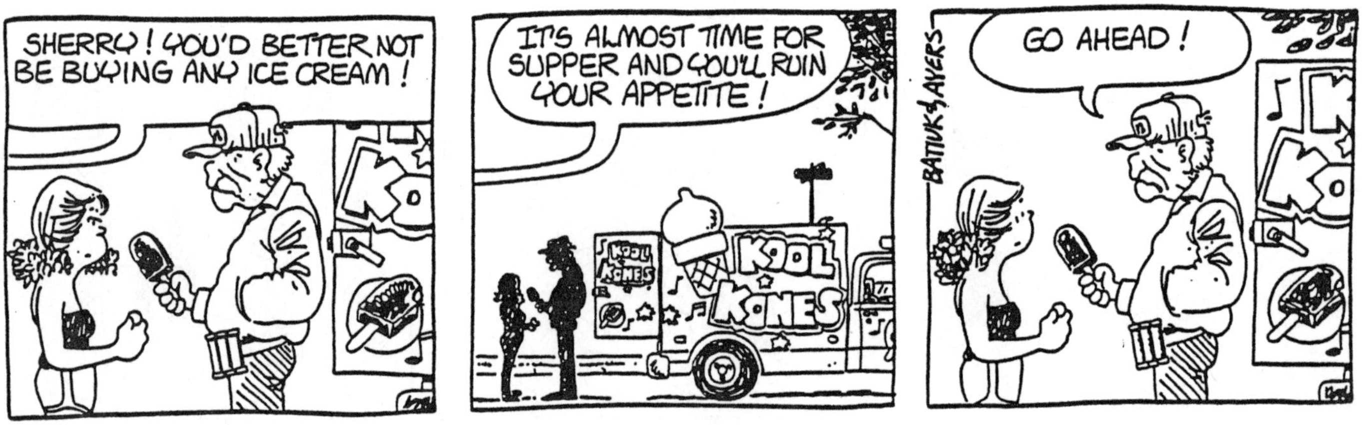
SHERRY! YOU'D BETTER NOT BE BUYING ANY ICE CREAM!
IT'S ALMOST TIME FOR SUPPER AND YOU'LL RUIN YOUR APPETITE!
KOOL KONES
BATIUK & AYERS
GO AHEAD!

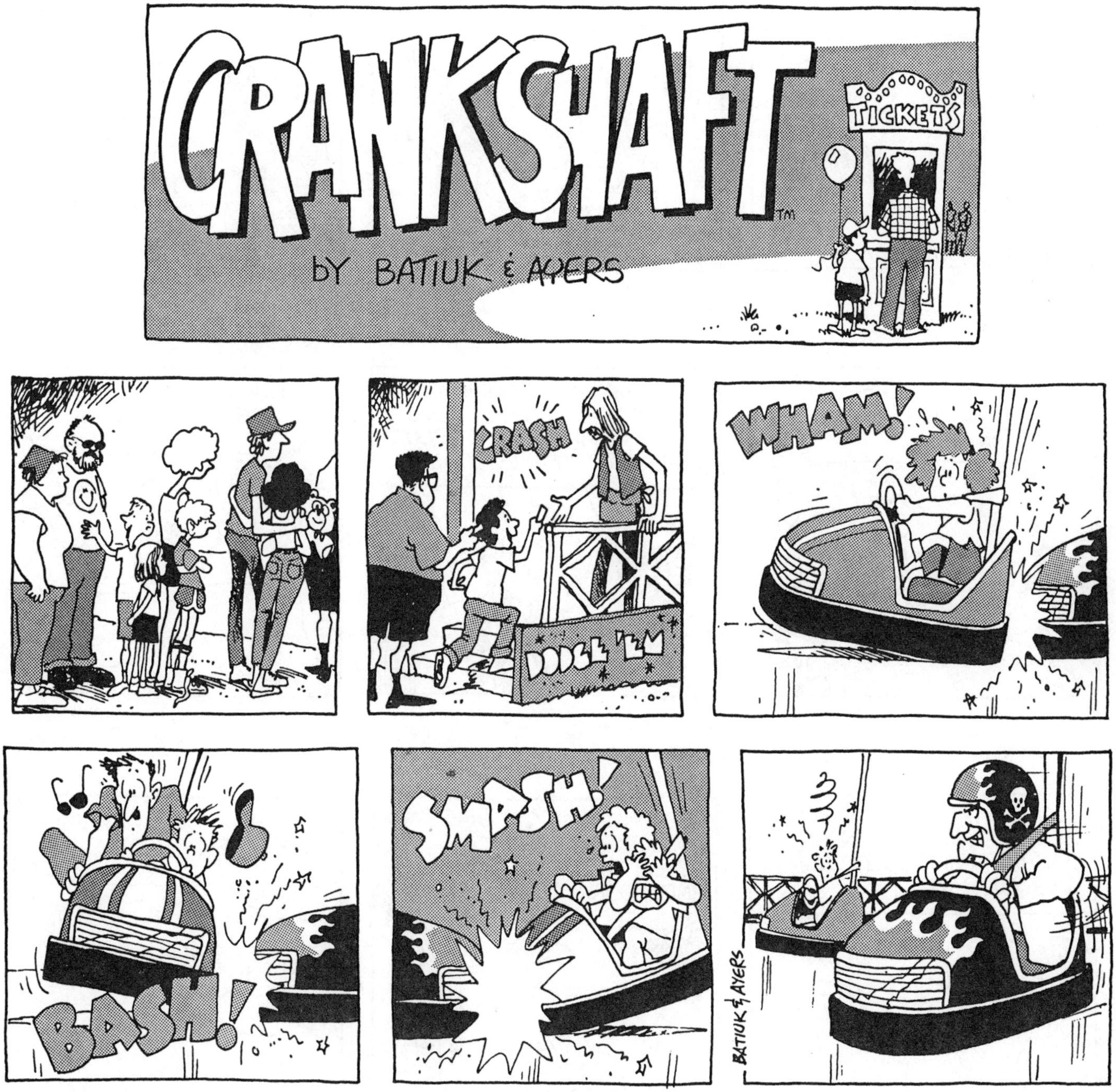
CRANKSHAFT
TM
BY BATIUK & AYERS
TICKETS
CRASH
DODGE 'EM
WHAM!
BASH!
SMASH!
BATIUK & AYERS

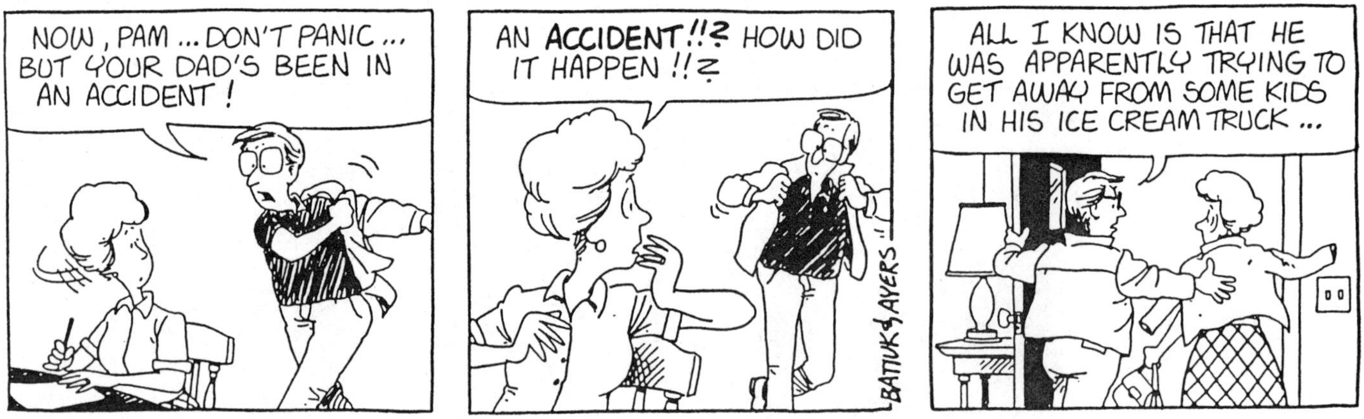
NOW, PAM ... DON'T PANIC ... BUT YOUR DAD'S BEEN IN AN ACCIDENT!
AN ACCIDENT!!? HOW DID IT HAPPEN!!?
BATIUK & AYERS
ALL I KNOW IS THAT HE WAS APPARENTLY TRYING TO GET AWAY FROM SOME KIDS IN HIS ICE CREAM TRUCK ...

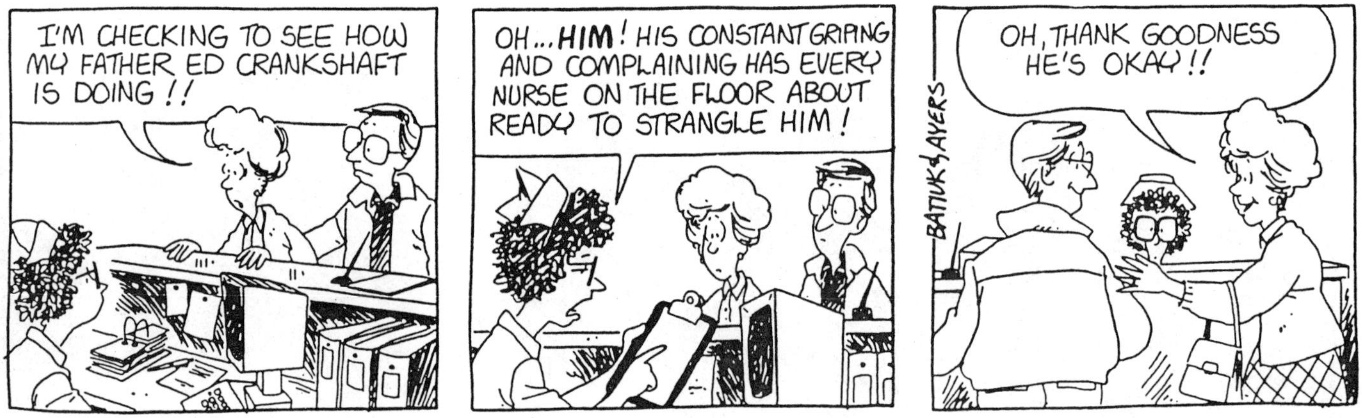
I'M CHECKING TO SEE HOW MY FATHER ED CRANKSHAFT IS DOING!!
OH... HIM! HIS CONSTANT GRIPING AND COMPLAINING HAS EVERY NURSE ON THE FLOOR ABOUT READY TO STRANGLE HIM!
BATIUK & AYERS
OH, THANK GOODNESS HE'S OKAY!!

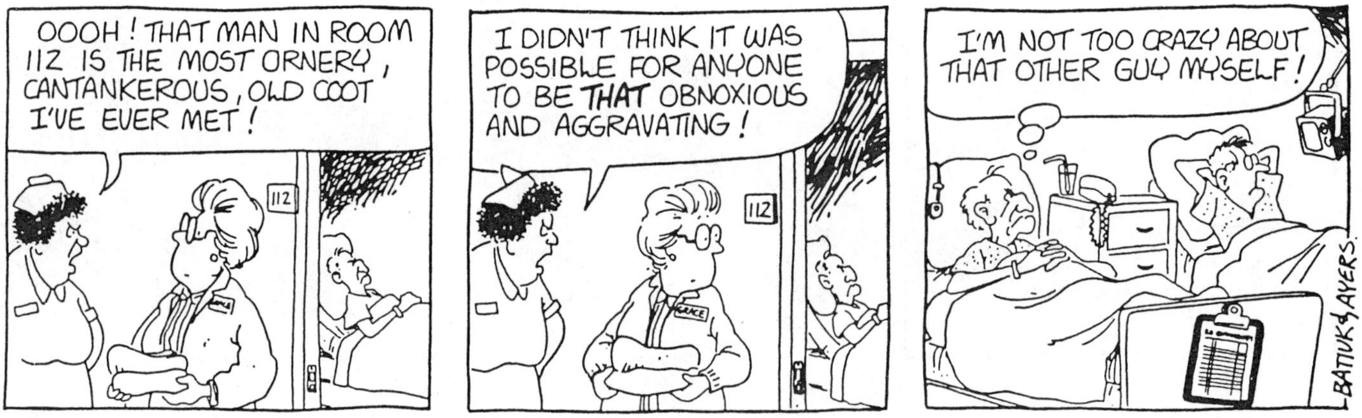
OOOH! THAT MAN IN ROOM 112 IS THE MOST ORNERY, CANTANKEROUS, OLD COOT I'VE EVER MET!
112
I DIDN'T THINK IT WAS POSSIBLE FOR ANYONE TO BE THAT OBNOXIOUS AND AGGRAVATING!
112
GRACE
I'M NOT TOO CRAZY ABOUT THAT OTHER GUY MYSELF!
BATIUK & AYERS

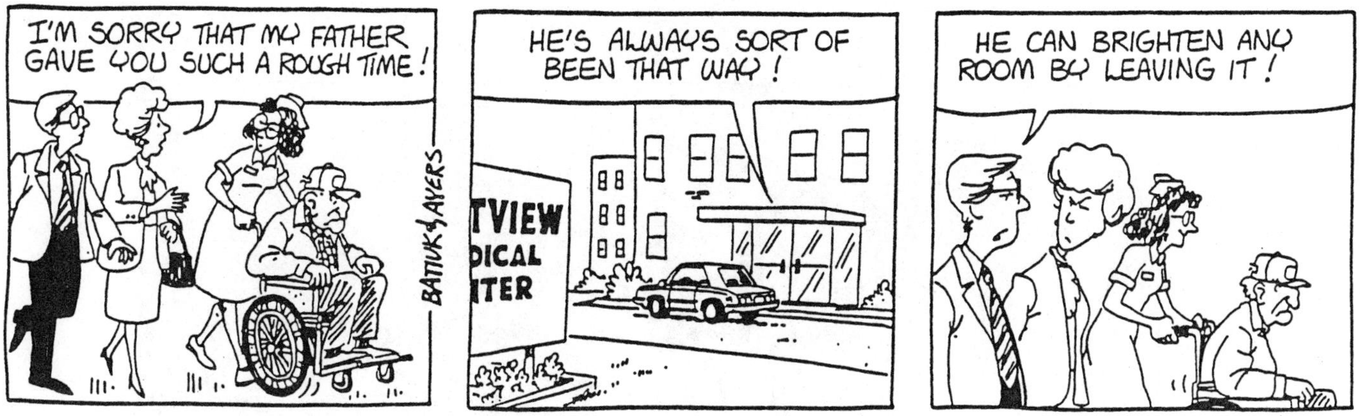

I'M SORRY THAT MY FATHER GAVE YOU SUCH A ROUGH TIME!
HE'S ALWAYS SORT OF BEEN THAT WAY!
TVIEW
DICAL
TER
HE CAN BRIGHTEN ANY ROOM BY LEAVING IT!
BATIUK & AYERS

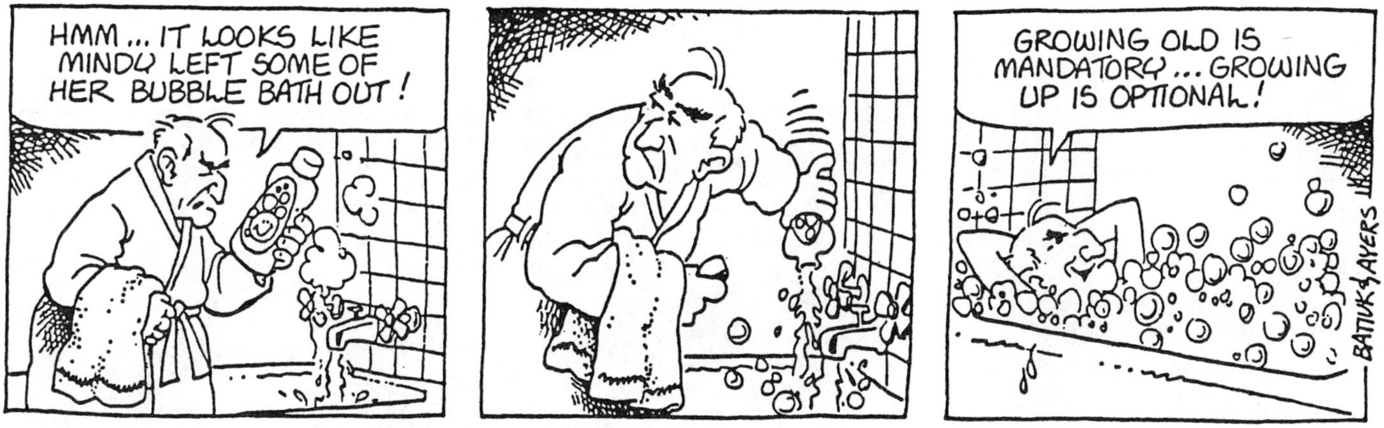

HMM ... IT LOOKS LIKE MINDY LEFT SOME OF HER BUBBLE BATH OUT!
GROWING OLD IS MANDATORY ... GROWING UP IS OPTIONAL!
BATIUK & AYERS

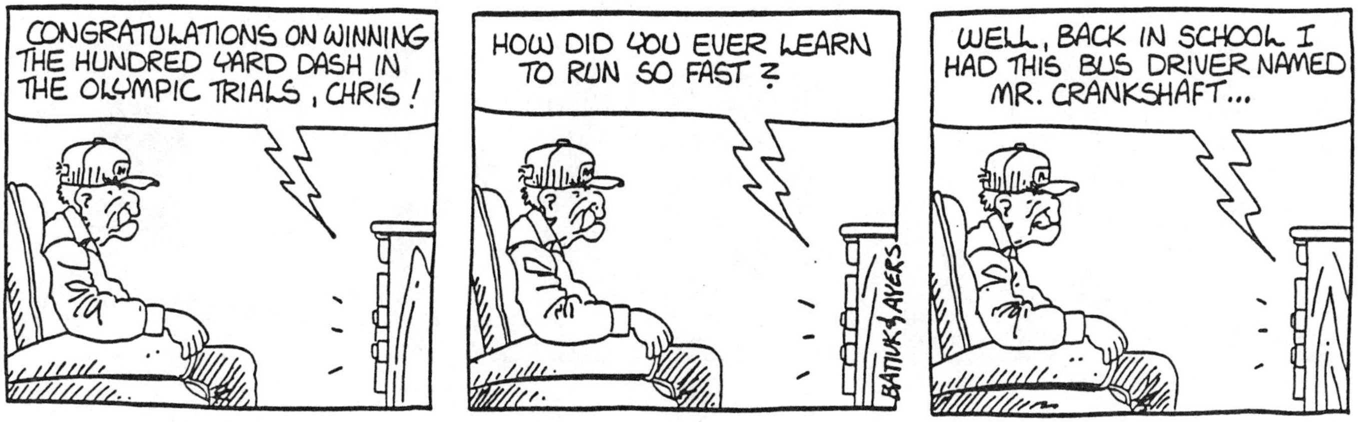

CONGRATULATIONS ON WINNING THE HUNDRED YARD DASH IN THE OLYMPIC TRIALS, CHRIS!
HOW DID YOU EVER LEARN TO RUN SO FAST?
WELL, BACK IN SCHOOL I HAD THIS BUS DRIVER NAMED MR. CRANKSHAFT...
BATIUK & AYERS

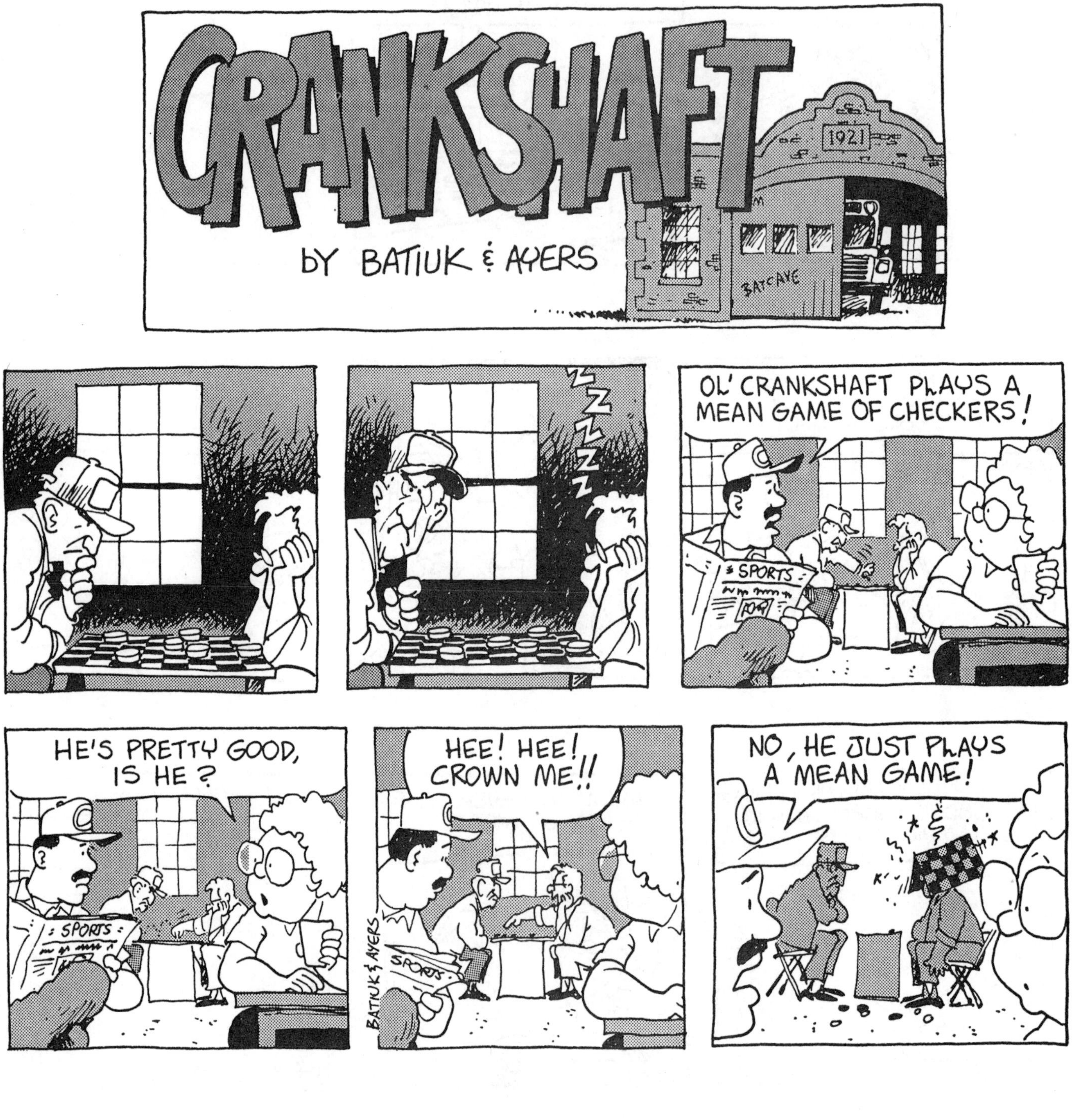
CRANKSHAFT
by BATIUK & AYERS
1921
BATCAVE
Z Z Z Z Z
OL' CRANKSHAFT PLAYS A MEAN GAME OF CHECKERS!
SPORTS
HE'S PRETTY GOOD, IS HE?
SPORTS
HEE! HEE! CROWN ME!!
BATIUK & AYERS
SPORTS
NO, HE JUST PLAYS A MEAN GAME!

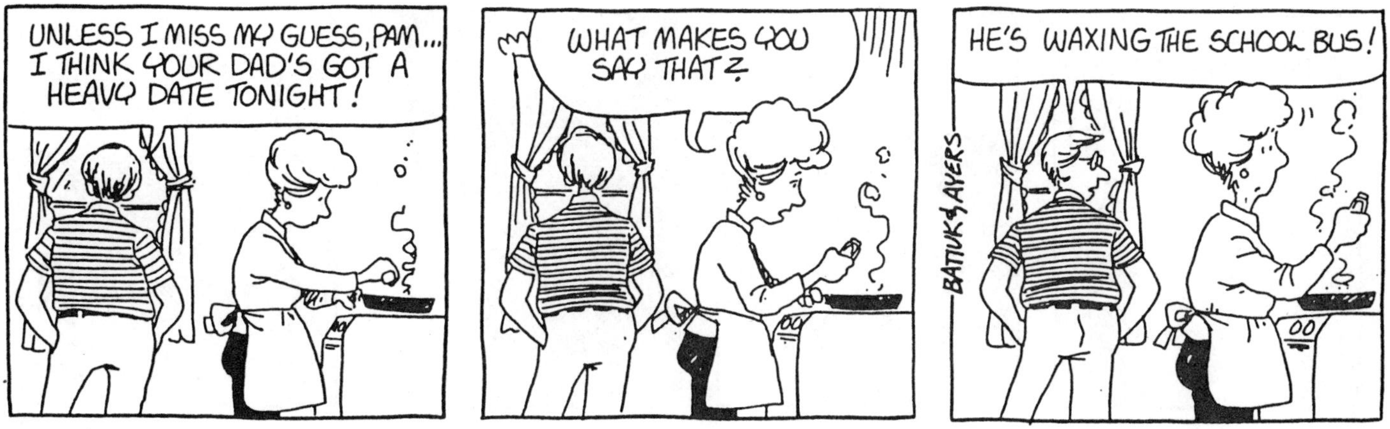
UNLESS I MISS MY GUESS, PAM... I THINK YOUR DAD'S GOT A HEAVY DATE TONIGHT!
WHAT MAKES YOU SAY THAT?
HE'S WAXING THE SCHOOL BUS!
BATIUK & AYERS

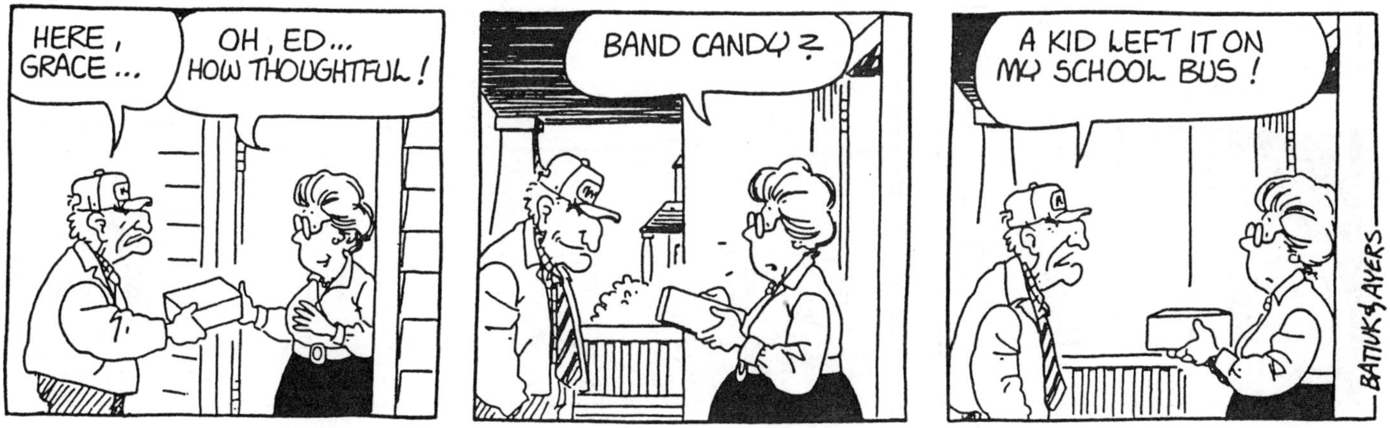
HERE, GRACE...
OH, ED... HOW THOUGHTFUL!
BAND CANDY?
A KID LEFT IT ON MY SCHOOL BUS!
BATIUK & AYERS

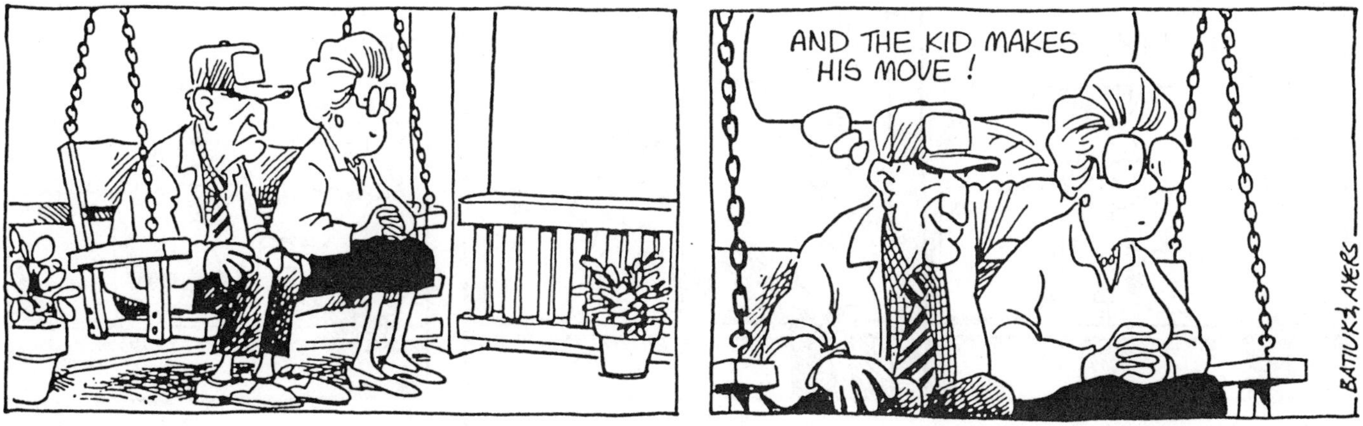
AND THE KID MAKES HIS MOVE!
BATIUK & AYERS

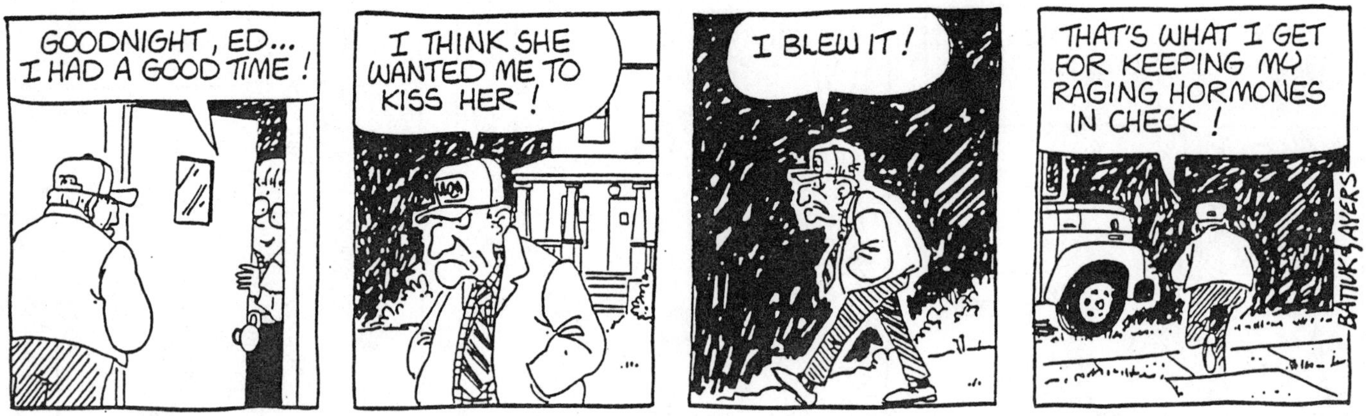
GOODNIGHT, ED... I HAD A GOOD TIME!
I THINK SHE WANTED ME TO KISS HER!
I BLEW IT!
THAT'S WHAT I GET FOR KEEPING MY RAGING HORMONES IN CHECK!
BATIUK & AYERS

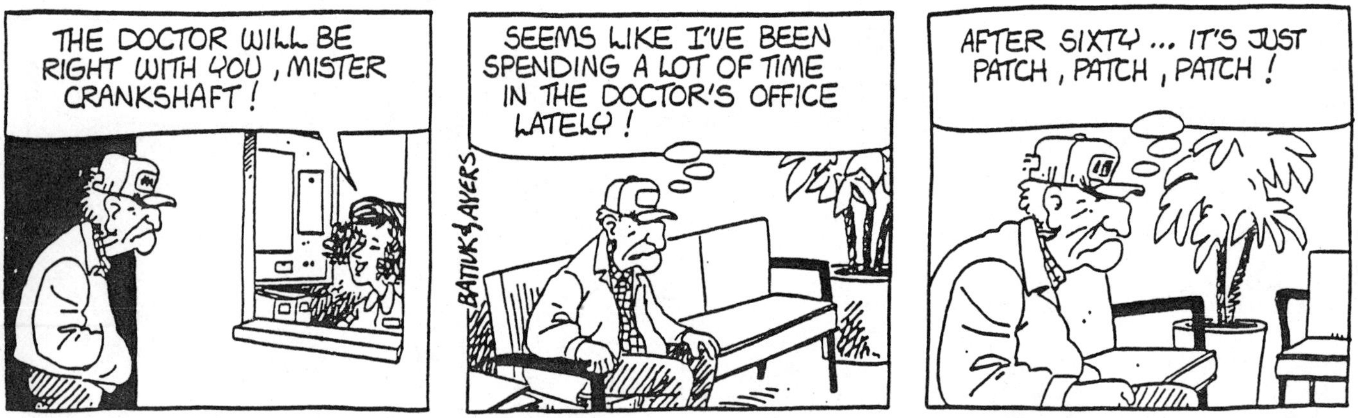
THE DOCTOR WILL BE RIGHT WITH YOU, MISTER CRANKSHAFT!
SEEMS LIKE I'VE BEEN SPENDING A LOT OF TIME IN THE DOCTOR'S OFFICE LATELY!
AFTER SIXTY... IT'S JUST PATCH, PATCH, PATCH!
BATIUK & AYERS

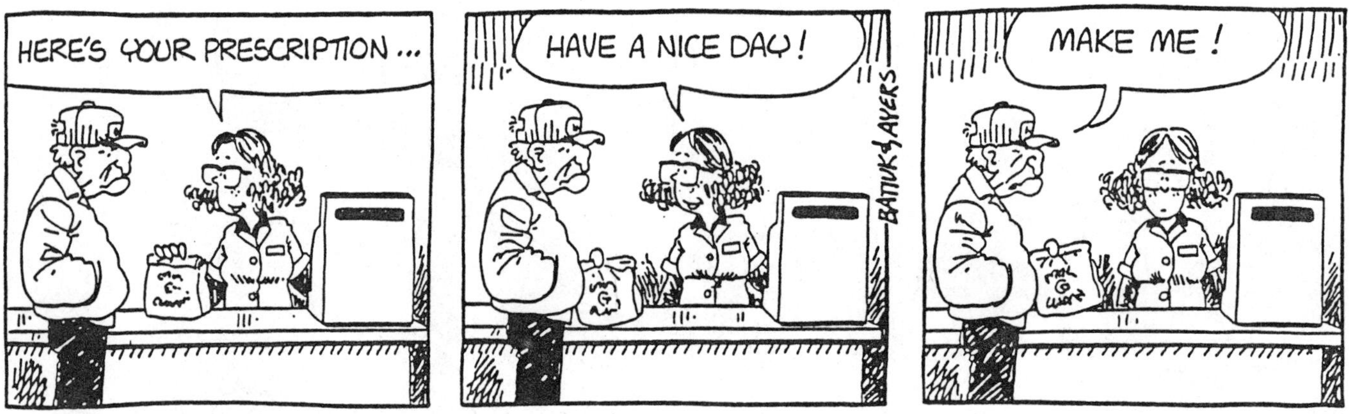
HERE'S YOUR PRESCRIPTION...
HAVE A NICE DAY!
MAKE ME!
BATIUK & AYERS

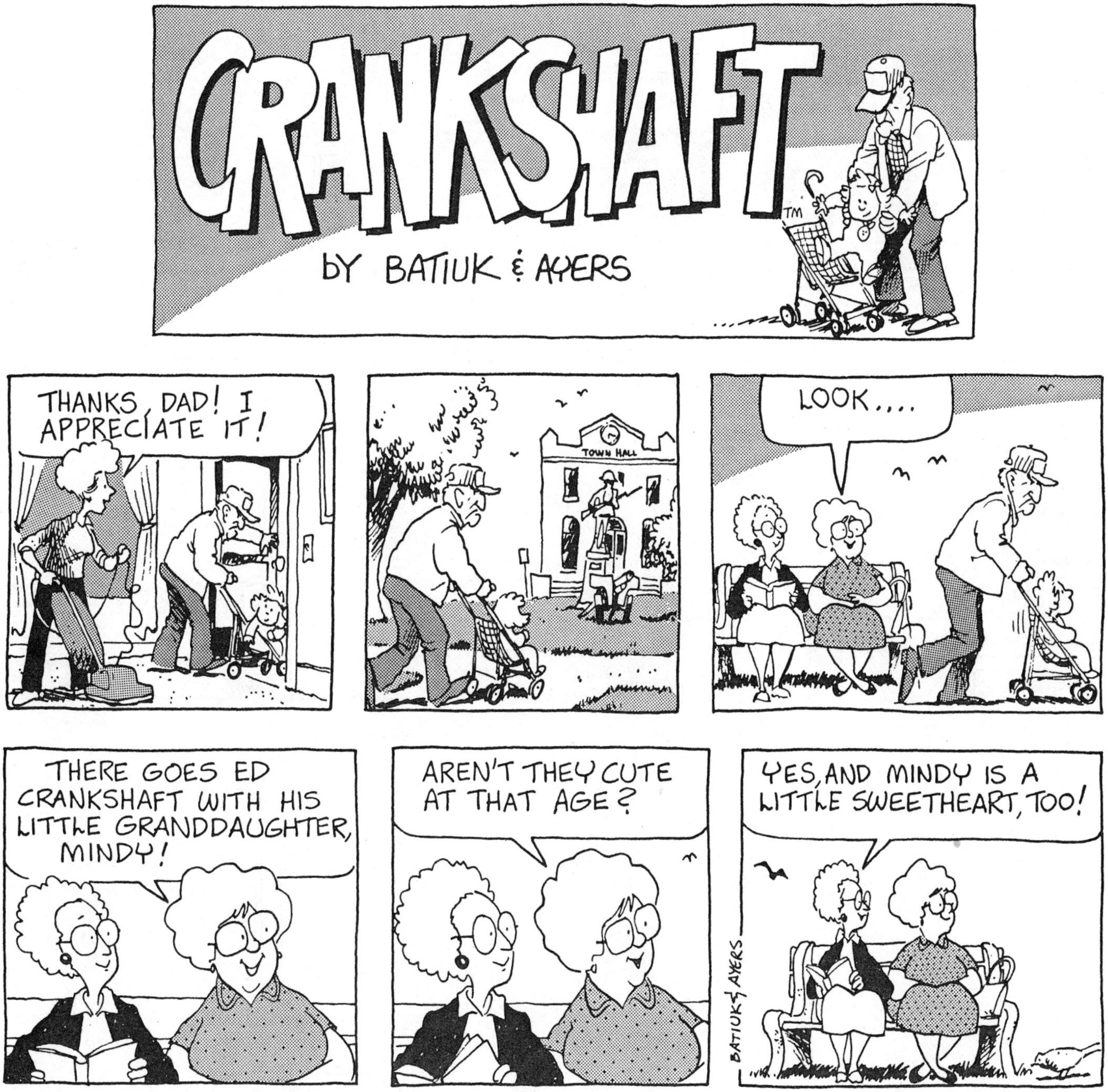
CRANKSHAFT
TM
BY BATIUK & AYERS
THANKS, DAD! I APPRECIATE IT!
TOWN HALL
LOOK....
THERE GOES ED CRANKSHAFT WITH HIS LITTLE GRANDDAUGHTER, MINDY!
AREN'T THEY CUTE AT THAT AGE?
YES, AND MINDY IS A LITTLE SWEETHEART, TOO!
BATIUK & AYERS

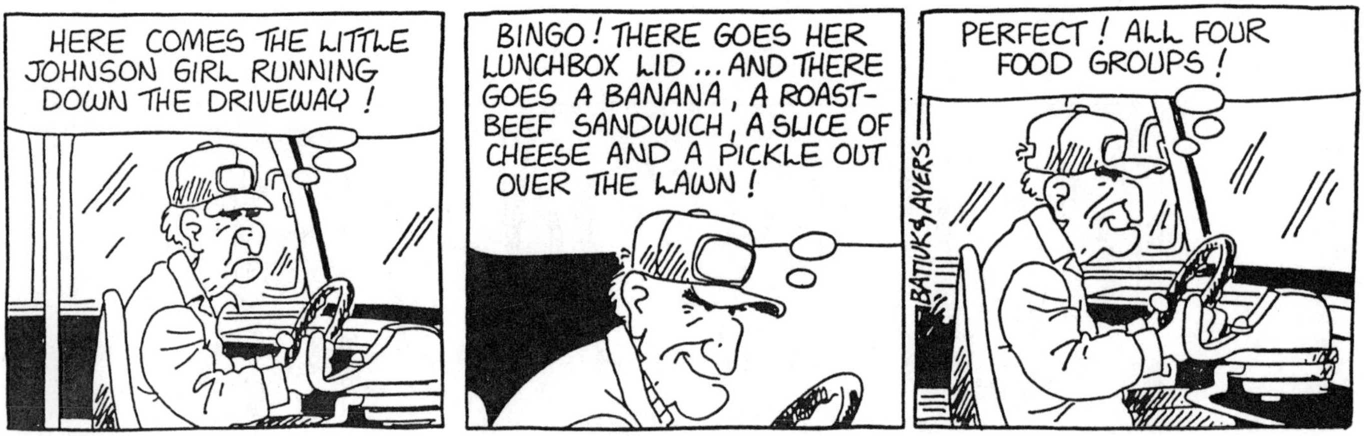
HERE COMES THE LITTLE JOHNSON GIRL RUNNING DOWN THE DRIVEWAY!
BINGO! THERE GOES HER LUNCHBOX LID... AND THERE GOES A BANANA, A ROAST-BEEF SANDWICH, A SLICE OF CHEESE AND A PICKLE OUT OVER THE LAWN!
BATIUK & AYERS
PERFECT! ALL FOUR FOOD GROUPS!

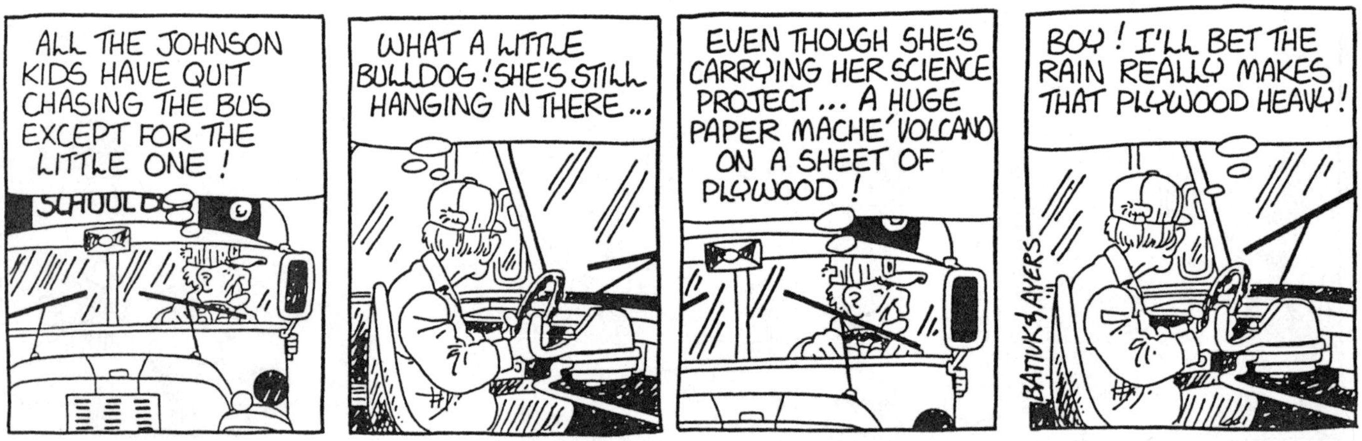
ALL THE JOHNSON KIDS HAVE QUIT CHASING THE BUS EXCEPT FOR THE LITTLE ONE!
SCHOOL BU
WHAT A LITTLE BULLDOG! SHE'S STILL HANGING IN THERE...
EVEN THOUGH SHE'S CARRYING HER SCIENCE PROJECT... A HUGE PAPER MACHE' VOLCANO ON A SHEET OF PLYWOOD!
BATIUK & AYERS
BOY! I'LL BET THE RAIN REALLY MAKES THAT PLYWOOD HEAVY!

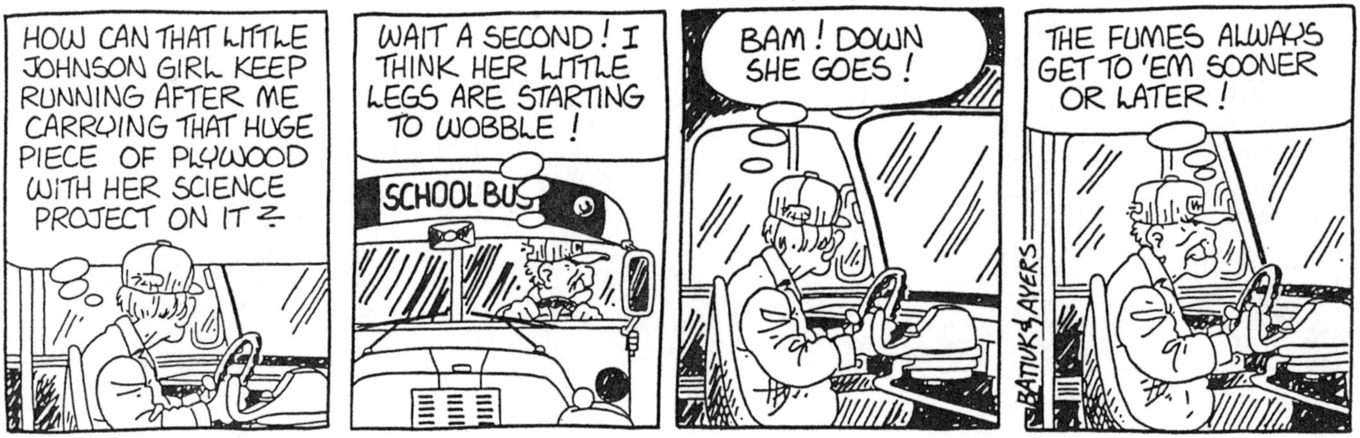
HOW CAN THAT LITTLE JOHNSON GIRL KEEP RUNNING AFTER ME CARRYING THAT HUGE PIECE OF PLYWOOD WITH HER SCIENCE PROJECT ON IT?
WAIT A SECOND! I THINK HER LITTLE LEGS ARE STARTING TO WOBBLE!
SCHOOL BUS
BAM! DOWN SHE GOES!
BATIUK & AYERS
THE FUMES ALWAYS GET TO 'EM SOONER OR LATER!

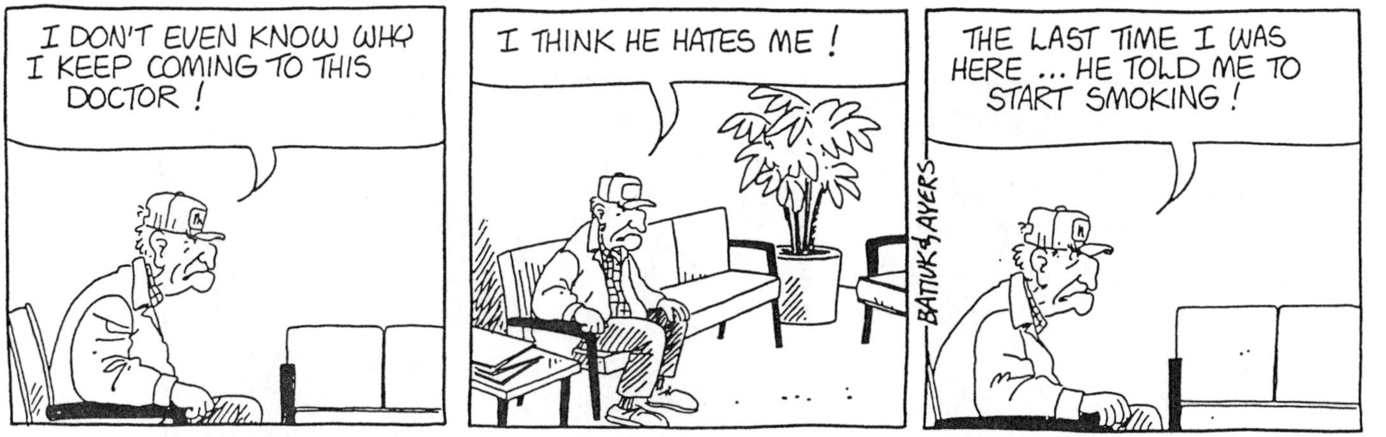
I DON'T EVEN KNOW WHY I KEEP COMING TO THIS DOCTOR !
I THINK HE HATES ME !
THE LAST TIME I WAS HERE ... HE TOLD ME TO START SMOKING !
BATIUK & AYERS

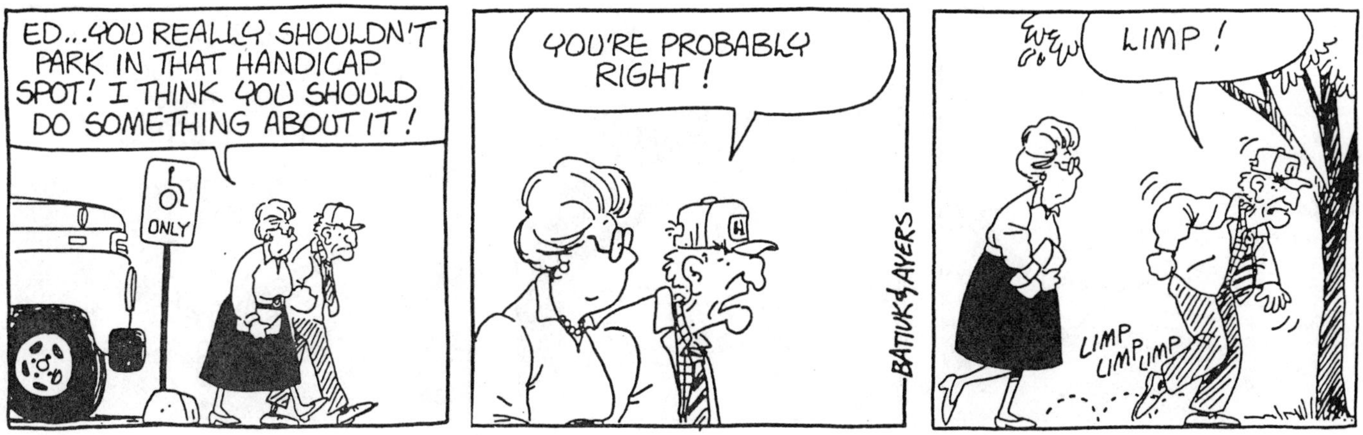
ED...YOU REALLY SHOULDN'T PARK IN THAT HANDICAP SPOT! I THINK YOU SHOULD DO SOMETHING ABOUT IT !
ONLY
YOU'RE PROBABLY RIGHT !
BATIUK & AYERS
LIMP !
LIMP
LIMP
LIMP

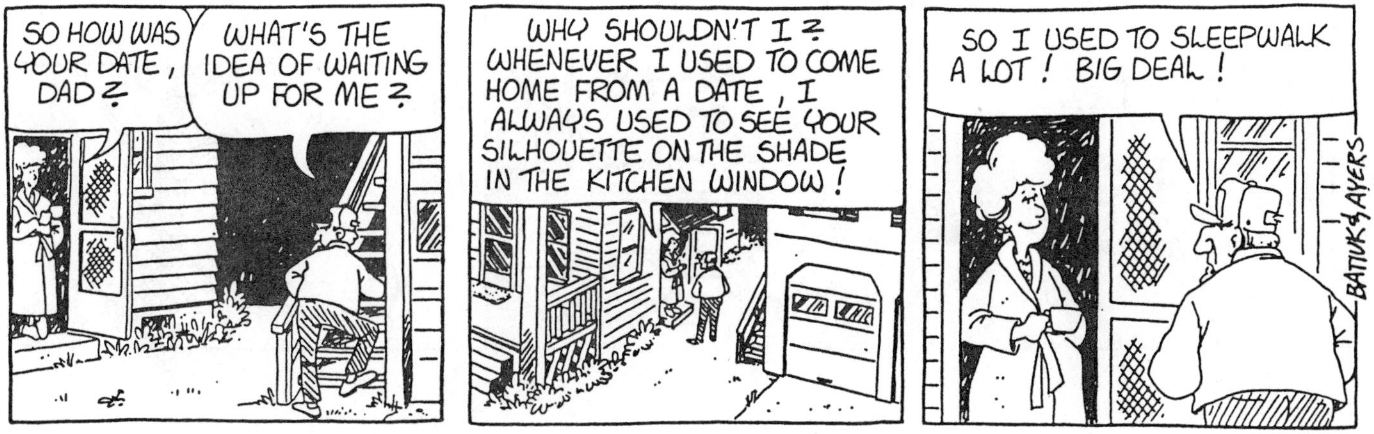
SO HOW WAS YOUR DATE, DAD ?
WHAT'S THE IDEA OF WAITING UP FOR ME ?
WHY SHOULDN'T I ? WHENEVER I USED TO COME HOME FROM A DATE, I ALWAYS USED TO SEE YOUR SILHOUETTE ON THE SHADE IN THE KITCHEN WINDOW !
SO I USED TO SLEEPWALK A LOT ! BIG DEAL !
BATIUK & AYERS

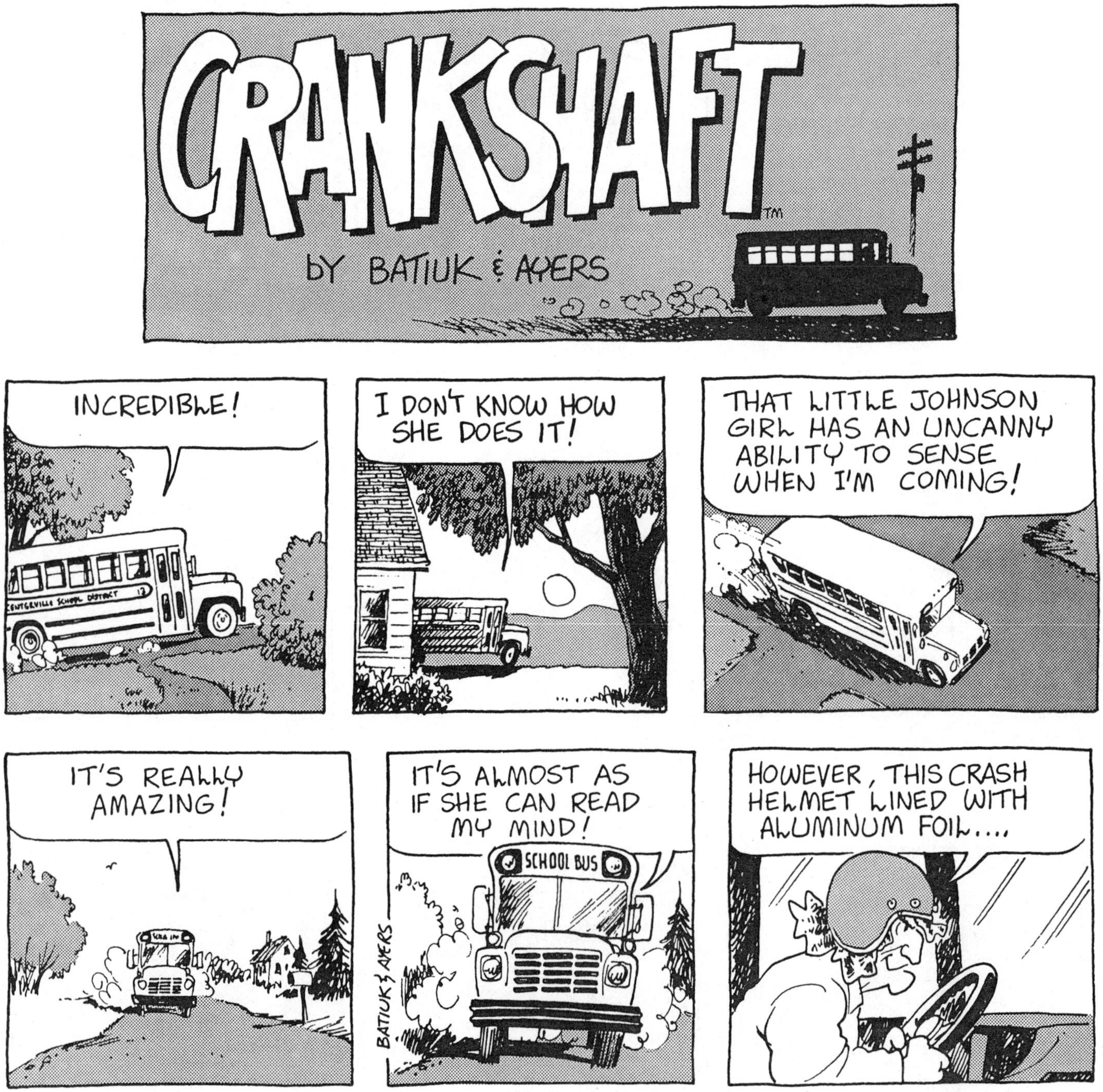
CRANKSHAFT
BY BATIUK & AYERS
CENTERVILLE SCHOOL DISTRICT
INCREDIBLE!
I DON'T KNOW HOW SHE DOES IT!
THAT LITTLE JOHNSON GIRL HAS AN UNCANNY ABILITY TO SENSE WHEN I'M COMING!
IT'S REALLY AMAZING!
IT'S ALMOST AS IF SHE CAN READ MY MIND!
SCHOOL BUS
BATIUK & AYERS
HOWEVER, THIS CRASH HELMET LINED WITH ALUMINUM FOIL....

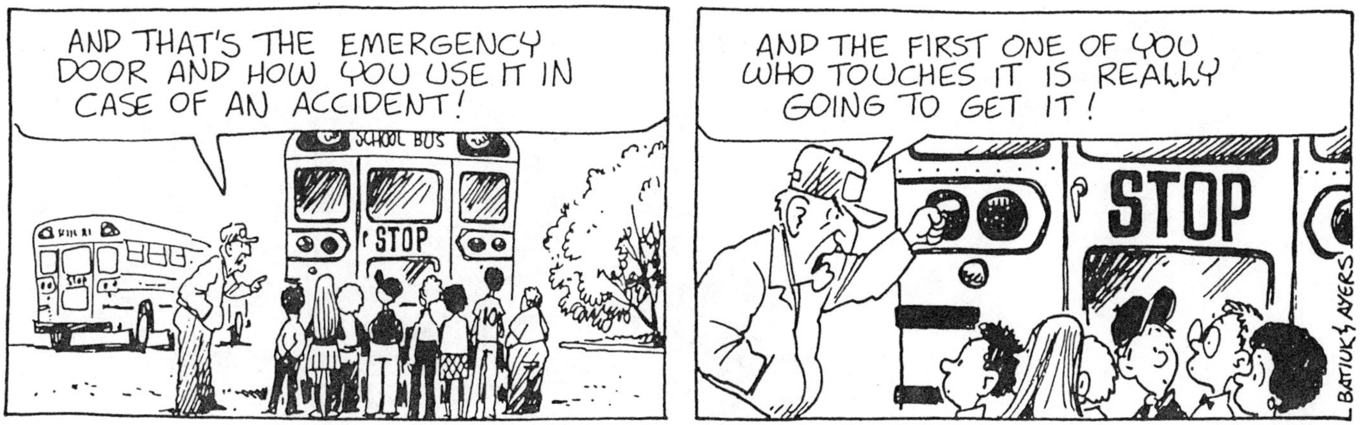
AND THAT'S THE EMERGENCY DOOR AND HOW YOU USE IT IN CASE OF AN ACCIDENT!
SCHOOL BUS
STOP
AND THE FIRST ONE OF YOU WHO TOUCHES IT IS REALLY GOING TO GET IT!
STOP
BATIUK & AYERS

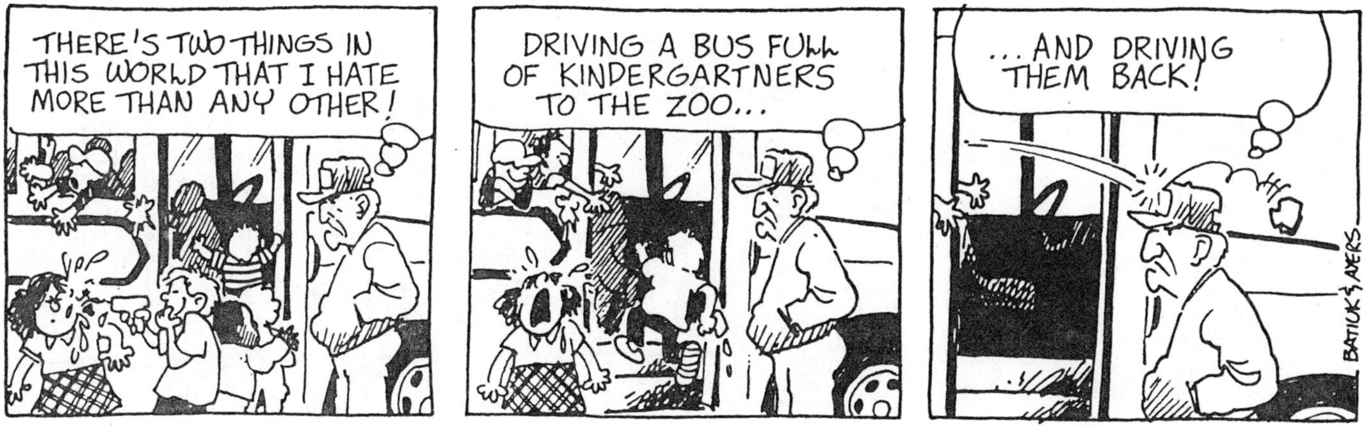
THERE'S TWO THINGS IN THIS WORLD THAT I HATE MORE THAN ANY OTHER!
DRIVING A BUS FULL OF KINDERGARTNERS TO THE ZOO...
...AND DRIVING THEM BACK!
BATIUK & AYERS

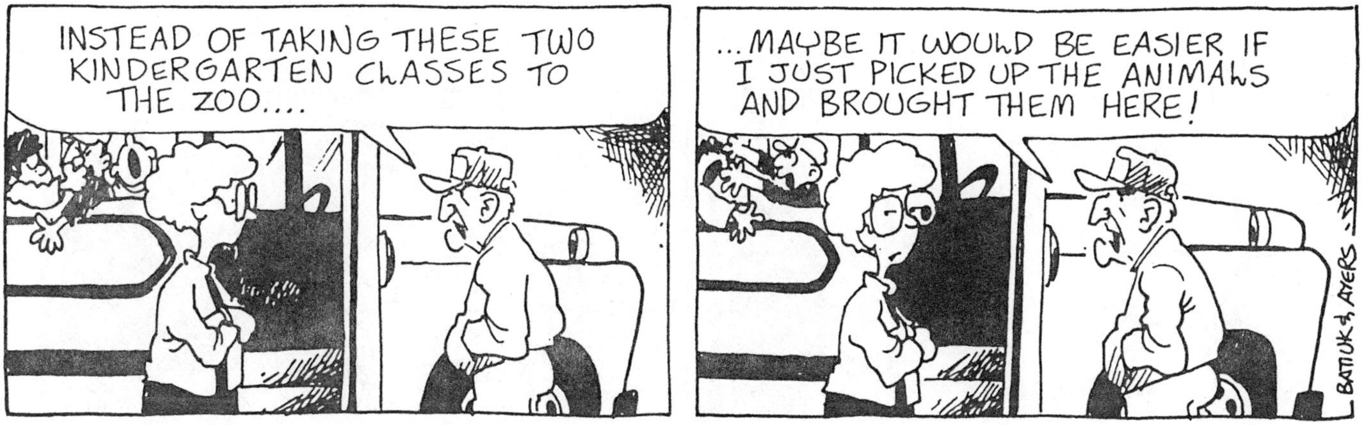
INSTEAD OF TAKING THESE TWO KINDERGARTEN CLASSES TO THE ZOO....
...MAYBE IT WOULD BE EASIER IF I JUST PICKED UP THE ANIMALS AND BROUGHT THEM HERE!
BATIUK & AYERS

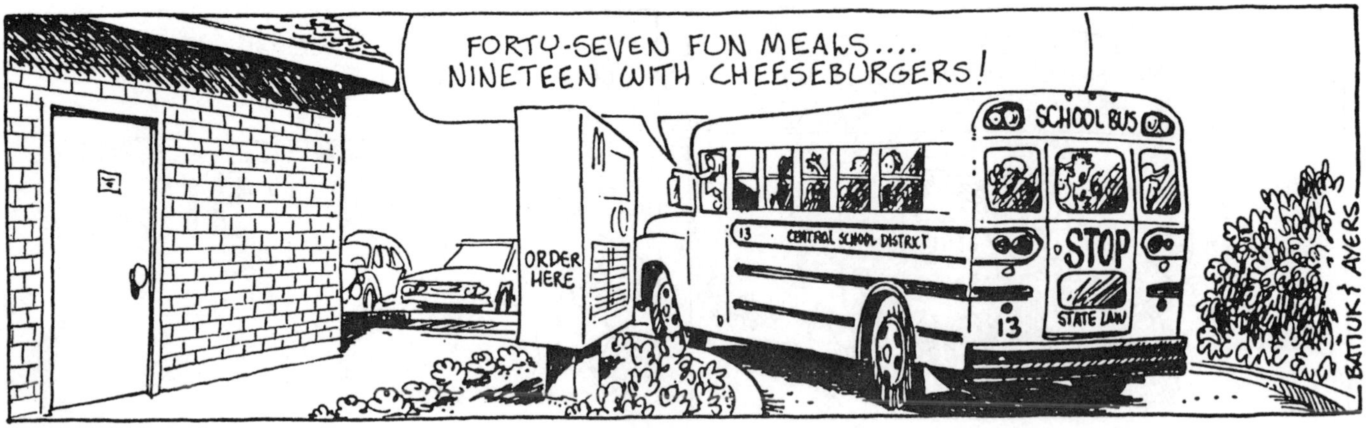
FORTY-SEVEN FUN MEALS.... NINETEEN WITH CHEESEBURGERS!
ORDER HERE
SCHOOL BUS
13 CENTRAL SCHOOL DISTRICT
STOP
STATE LAW
13
BATIUK & AYERS

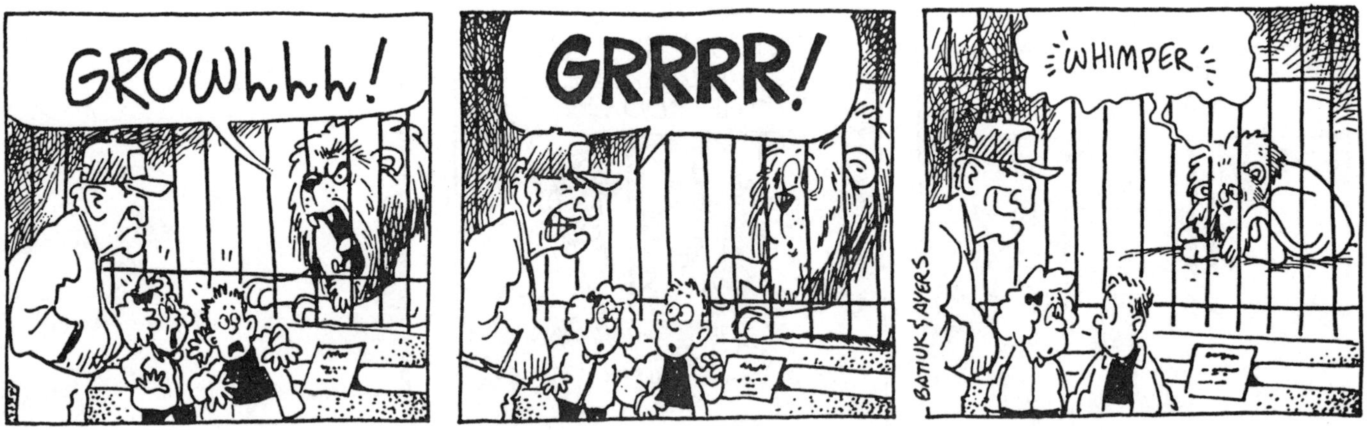
GROWhhh!
GRRRR!
WHIMPER
BATIUK & AYERS

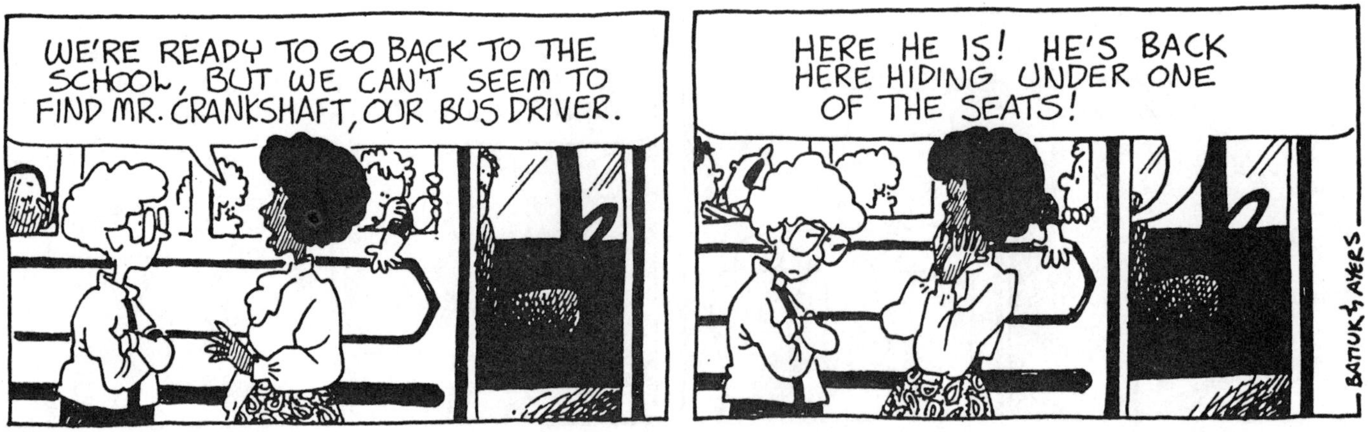
WE'RE READY TO GO BACK TO THE SCHOOL, BUT WE CAN'T SEEM TO FIND MR. CRANKSHAFT, OUR BUS DRIVER.
HERE HE IS! HE'S BACK HERE HIDING UNDER ONE OF THE SEATS!
BATIUK & AYERS

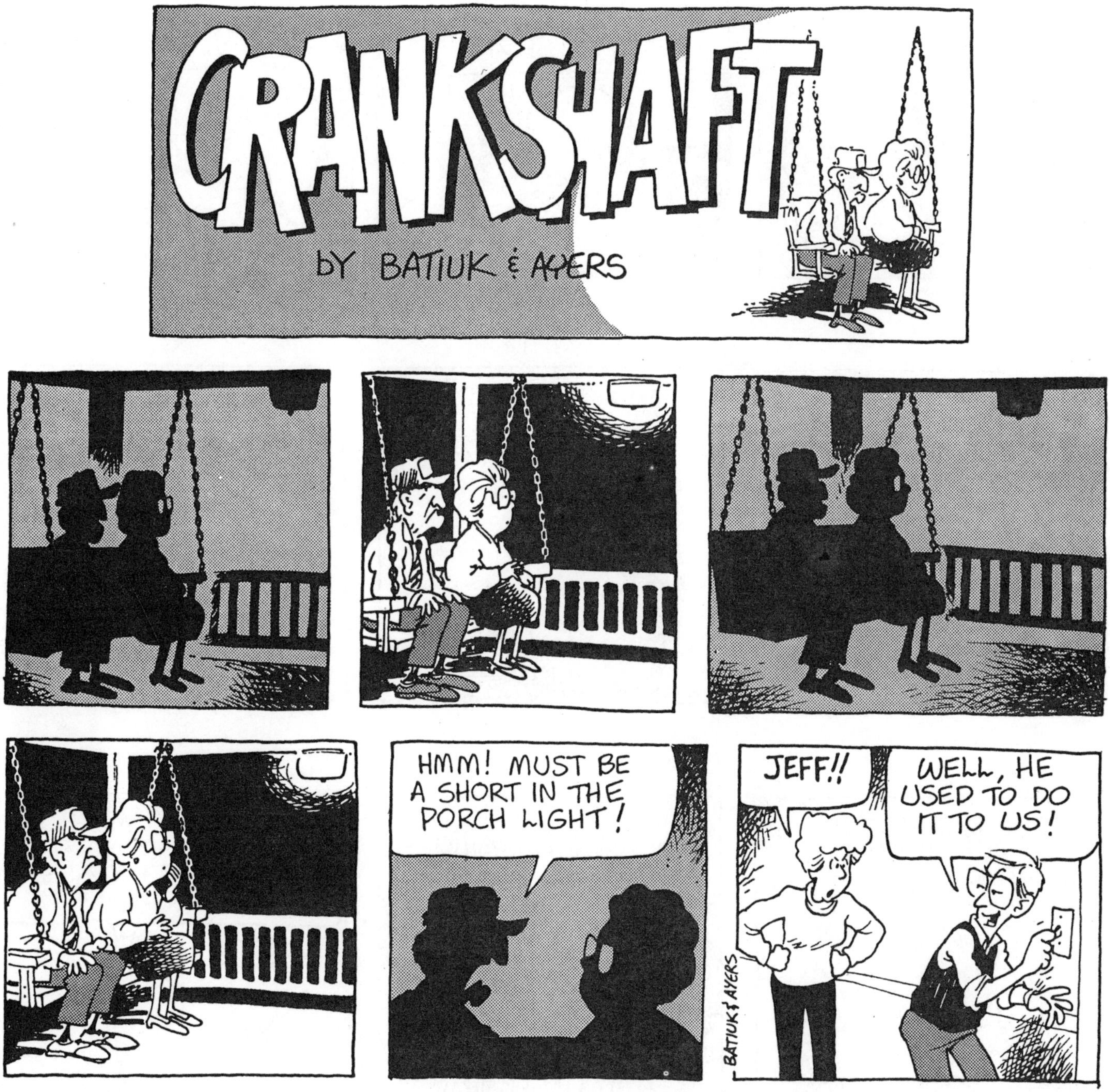
CRANKSHAFT
TM
BY BATIUK & AYERS
HMM! MUST BE A SHORT IN THE PORCH LIGHT!
BATIUK & AYERS
JEFF!!
WELL, HE USED TO DO IT TO US!

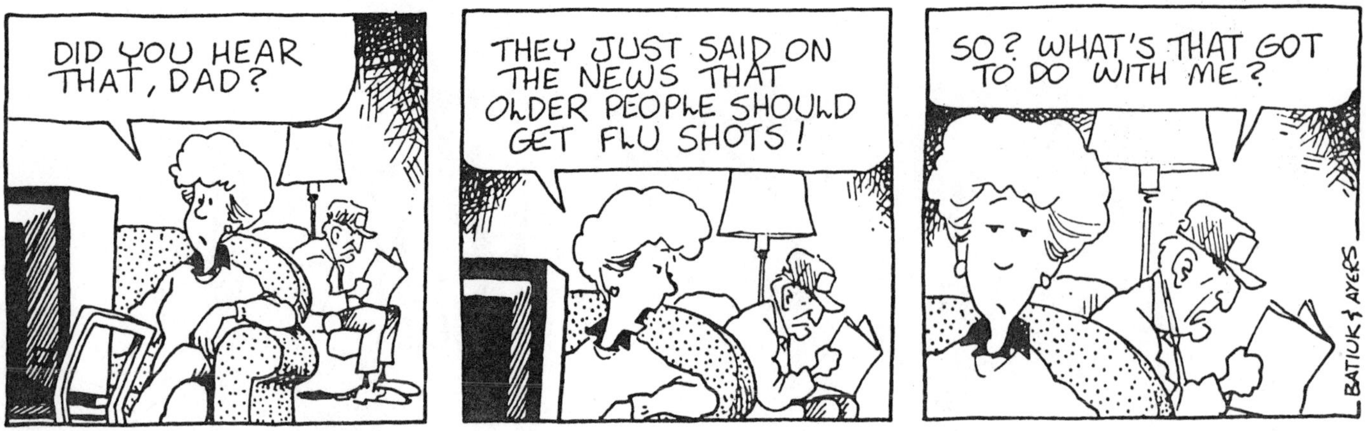
DID YOU HEAR THAT, DAD?
THEY JUST SAID ON THE NEWS THAT OLDER PEOPLE SHOULD GET FLU SHOTS!
SO? WHAT'S THAT GOT TO DO WITH ME?
BATIUK & AYERS

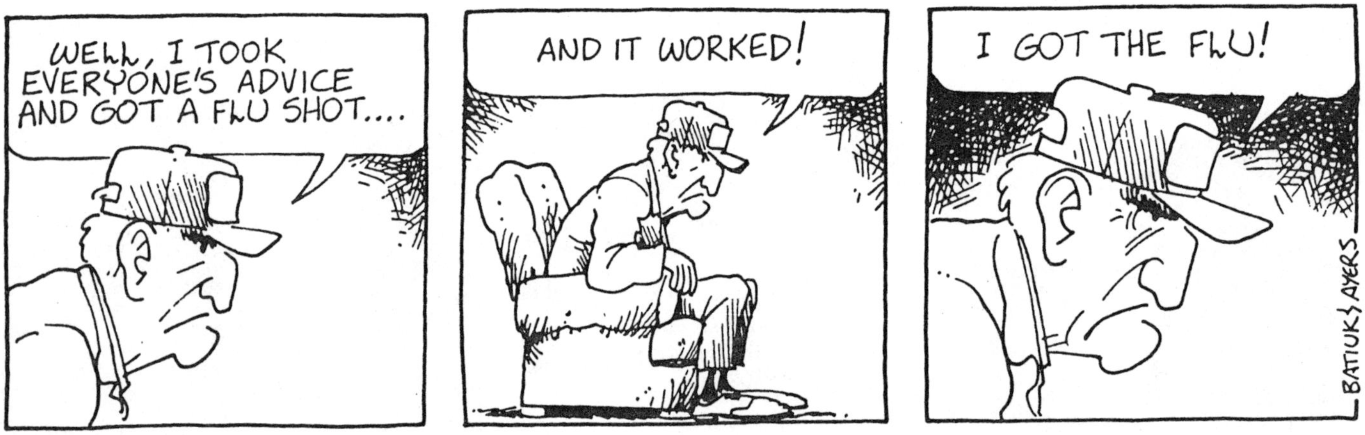
WELL, I TOOK EVERYONE'S ADVICE AND GOT A FLU SHOT....
AND IT WORKED!
I GOT THE FLU!
BATIUK & AYERS

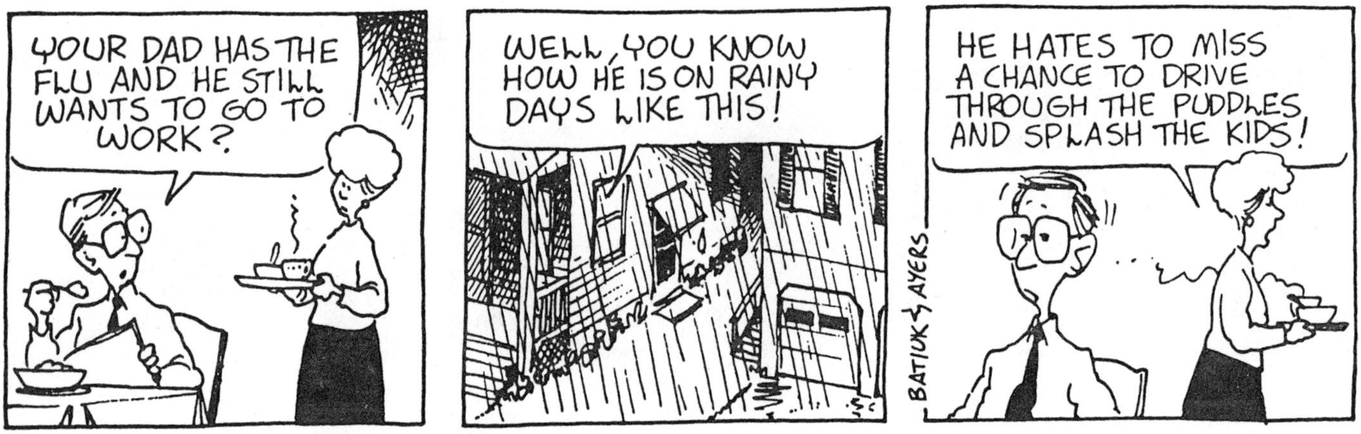
YOUR DAD HAS THE FLU AND HE STILL WANTS TO GO TO WORK?
WELL, YOU KNOW HOW HE IS ON RAINY DAYS LIKE THIS!
BATIUK & AYERS
HE HATES TO MISS A CHANCE TO DRIVE THROUGH THE PUDDLES AND SPLASH THE KIDS!

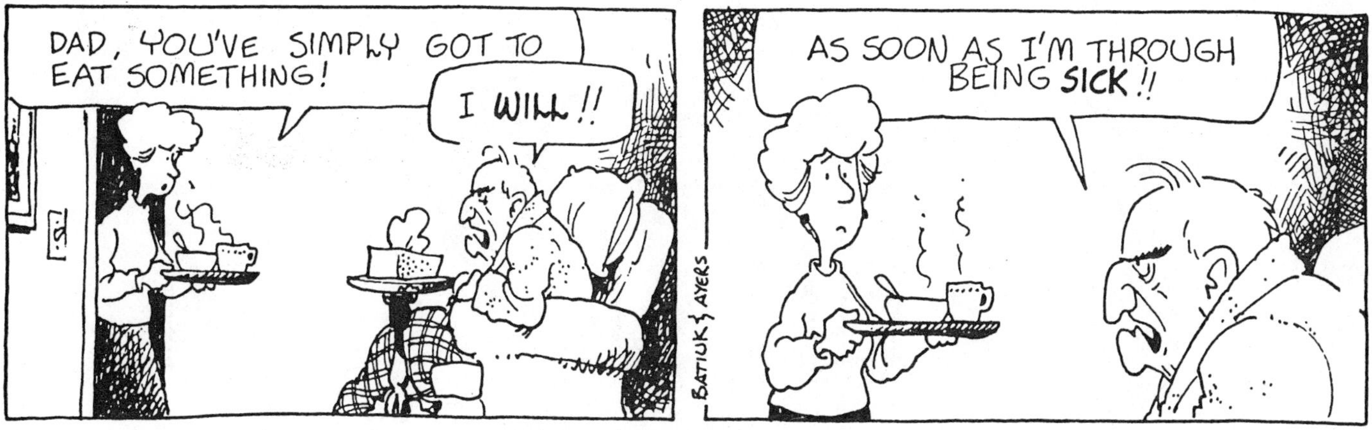
DAD, YOU'VE SIMPLY GOT TO EAT SOMETHING!
I WILL!!
AS SOON AS I'M THROUGH BEING SICK!!
BATIUK & AYERS

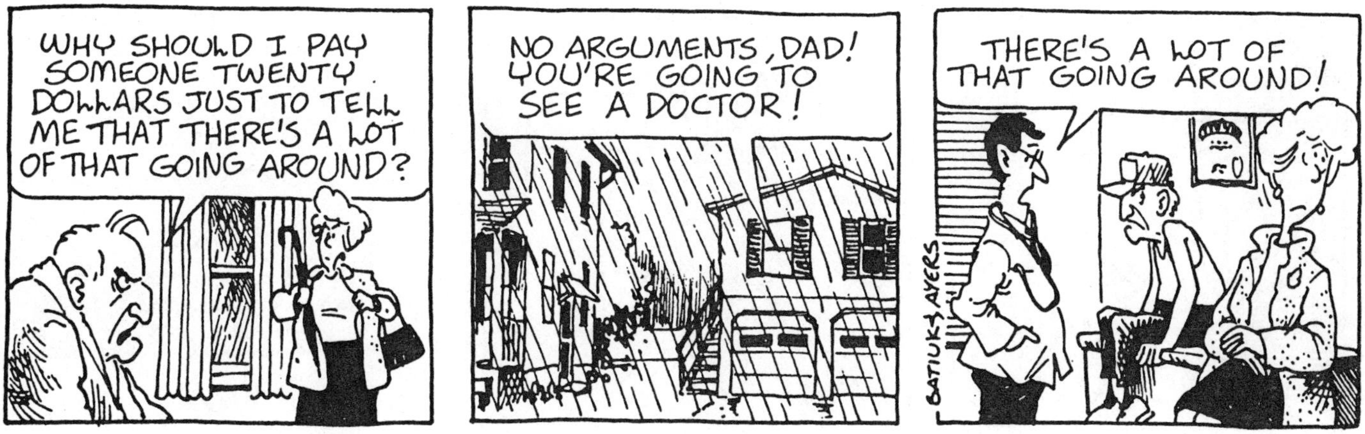
WHY SHOULD I PAY SOMEONE TWENTY DOLLARS JUST TO TELL ME THAT THERE'S A LOT OF THAT GOING AROUND?
NO ARGUMENTS, DAD! YOU'RE GOING TO SEE A DOCTOR!
THERE'S A LOT OF THAT GOING AROUND!
BATIUK & AYERS

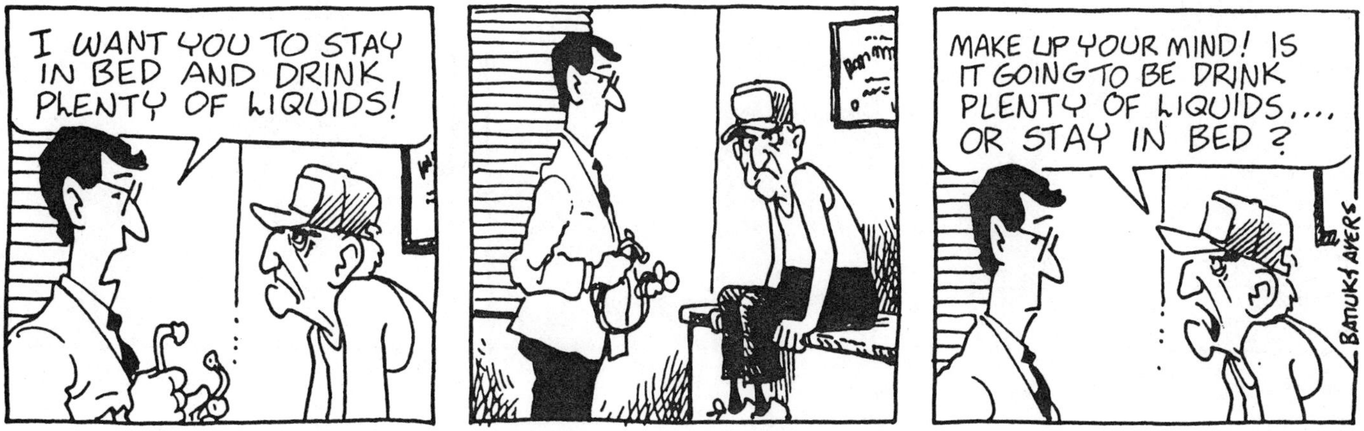
I WANT YOU TO STAY IN BED AND DRINK PLENTY OF LIQUIDS!
MAKE UP YOUR MIND! IS IT GOING TO BE DRINK PLENTY OF LIQUIDS.... OR STAY IN BED?
BATIUK & AYERS

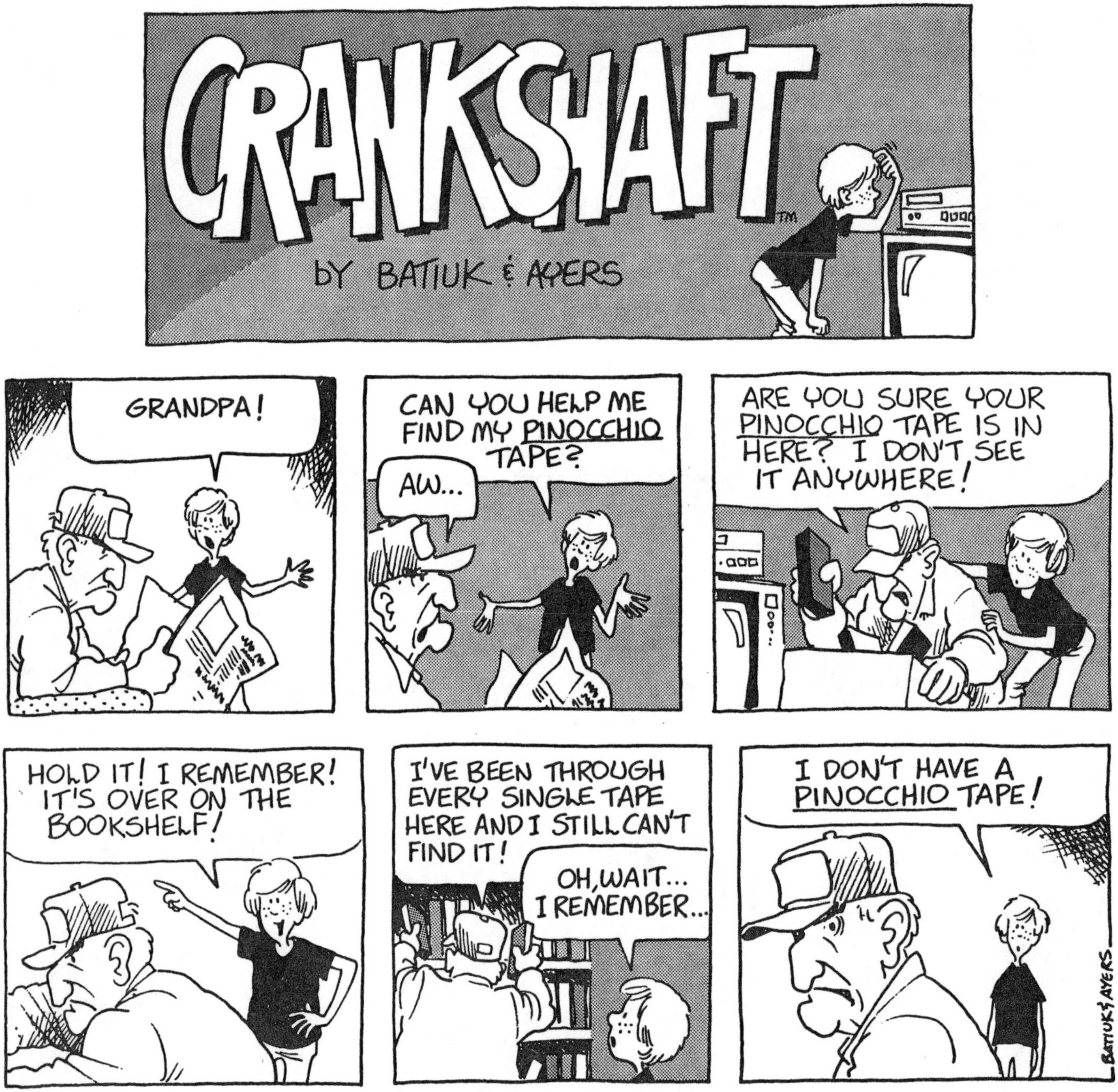

CRANKSHAFT
BY BATIUK & AYERS
GRANDPA!
CAN YOU HELP ME FIND MY PINOCCHIO TAPE?
AW...
ARE YOU SURE YOUR PINOCCHIO TAPE IS IN HERE? I DON'T SEE IT ANYWHERE!
HOLD IT! I REMEMBER! IT'S OVER ON THE BOOKSHELF!
I'VE BEEN THROUGH EVERY SINGLE TAPE HERE AND I STILL CAN'T FIND IT!
OH, WAIT... I REMEMBER...
I DON'T HAVE A PINOCCHIO TAPE!
BATIUK & AYERS

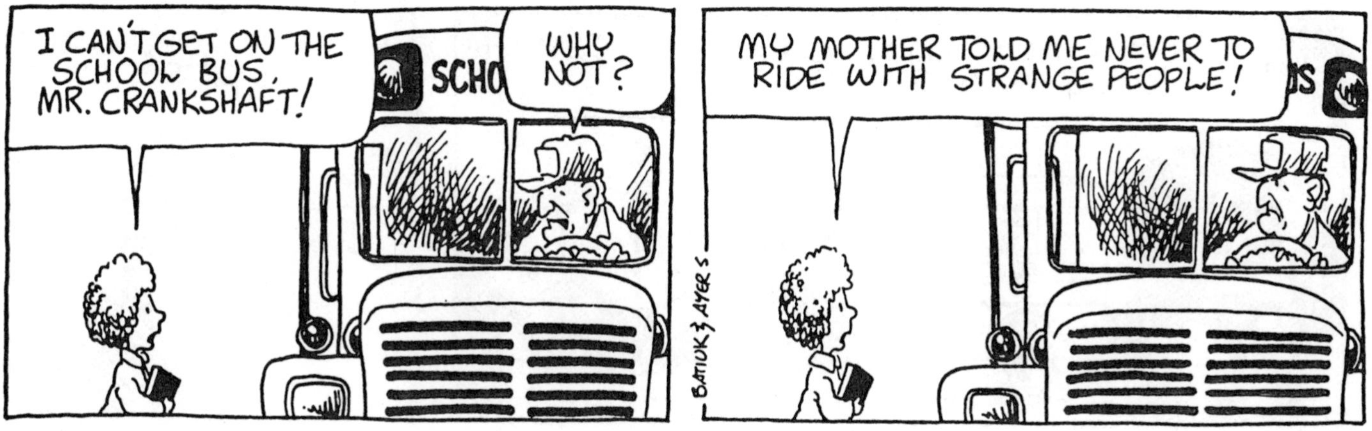
I CAN'T GET ON THE SCHOOL BUS, MR. CRANKSHAFT!
WHY NOT?
SCHO
BATIUK & AYERS
MY MOTHER TOLD ME NEVER TO RIDE WITH STRANGE PEOPLE!

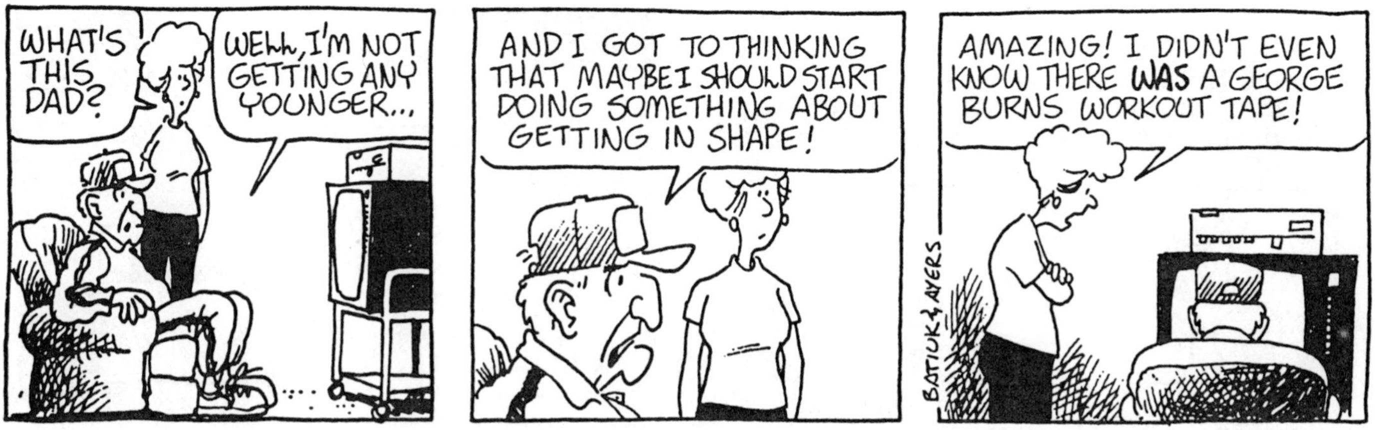
WHAT'S THIS, DAD?
WELL, I'M NOT GETTING ANY YOUNGER...
AND I GOT TO THINKING THAT MAYBE I SHOULD START DOING SOMETHING ABOUT GETTING IN SHAPE!
BATIUK & AYERS
AMAZING! I DIDN'T EVEN KNOW THERE **WAS** A GEORGE BURNS WORKOUT TAPE!

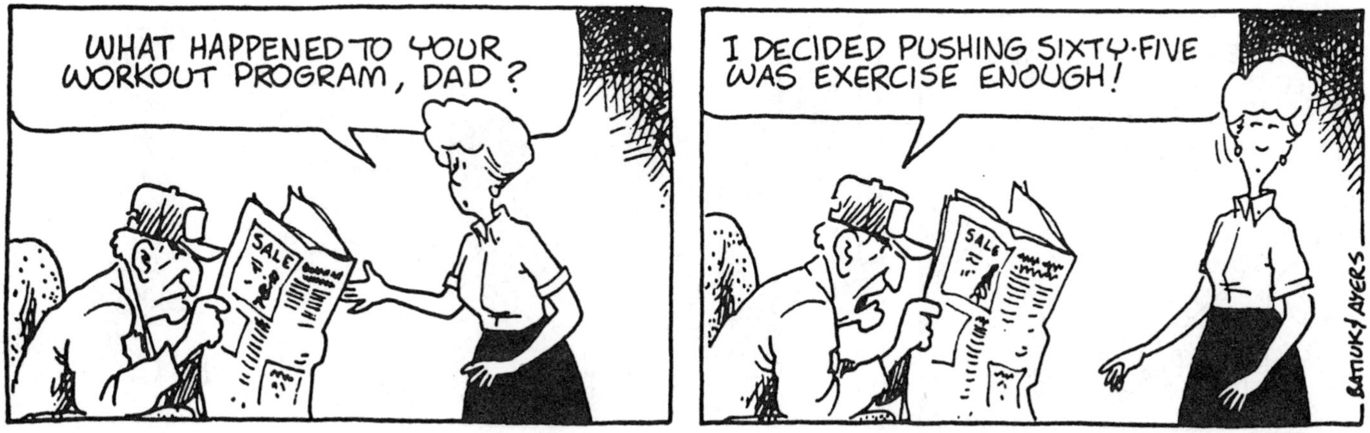
WHAT HAPPENED TO YOUR WORKOUT PROGRAM, DAD?
SALE
I DECIDED PUSHING SIXTY-FIVE WAS EXERCISE ENOUGH!
BATIUK & AYERS

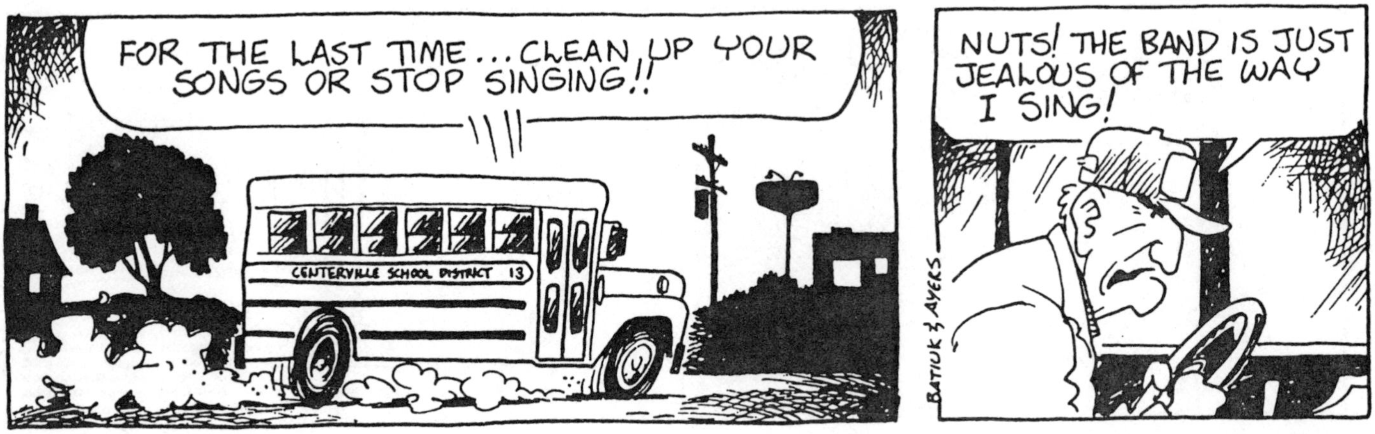
FOR THE LAST TIME... CLEAN UP YOUR SONGS OR STOP SINGING!!
CENTERVILLE SCHOOL DISTRICT 13
NUTS! THE BAND IS JUST JEALOUS OF THE WAY I SING!
BATIUK & AYERS

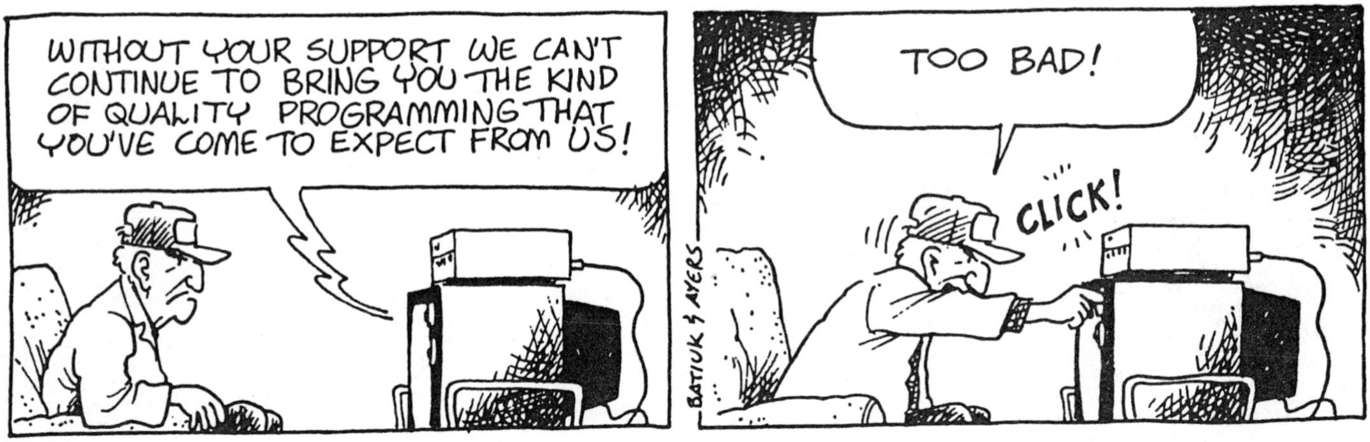
WITHOUT YOUR SUPPORT WE CAN'T CONTINUE TO BRING YOU THE KIND OF QUALITY PROGRAMMING THAT YOU'VE COME TO EXPECT FROM US!
BATIUK & AYERS
TOO BAD!
CLICK!

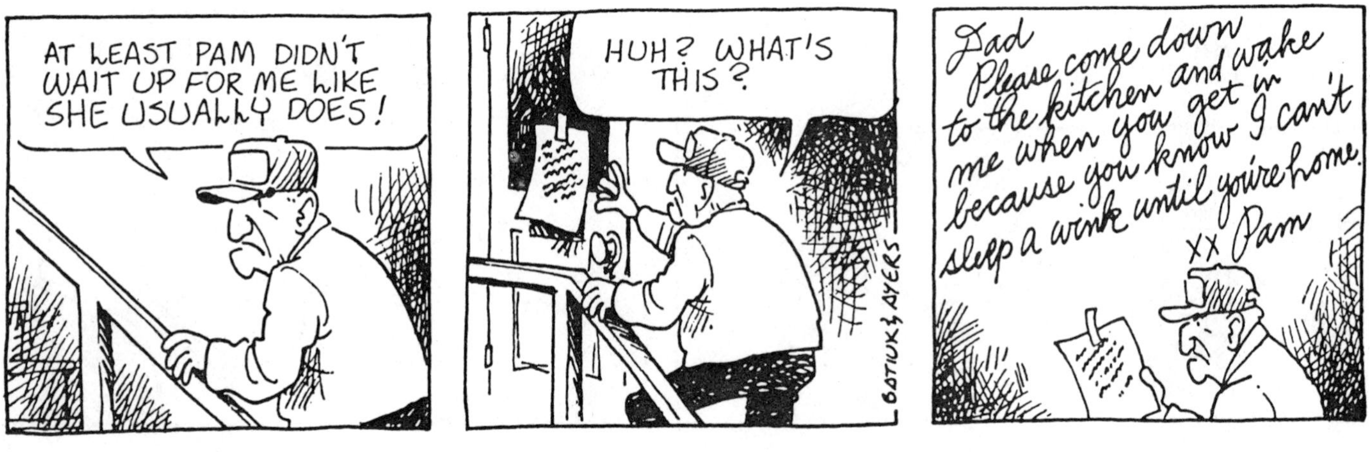
AT LEAST PAM DIDN'T WAIT UP FOR ME LIKE SHE USUALLY DOES!
HUH? WHAT'S THIS?
BATIUK & AYERS
Dad
Please come down to the kitchen and wake me when you get in because you know I can't sleep a wink until you're home.
XX Pam

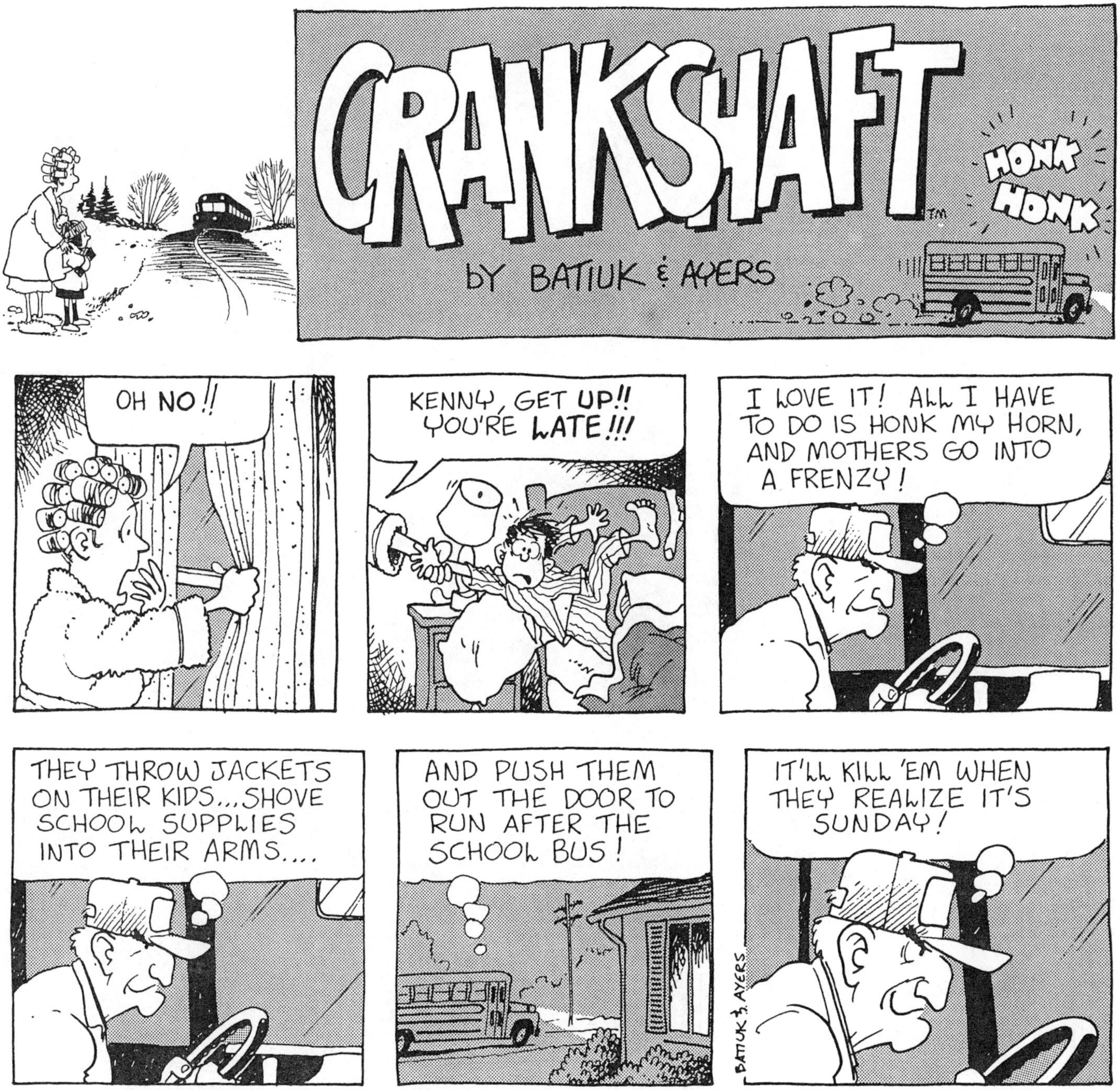
CRANKSHAFT
BY BATIUK & AYERS
HONK HONK
OH NO!!
KENNY, GET UP!! YOU'RE LATE!!!
I LOVE IT! ALL I HAVE TO DO IS HONK MY HORN, AND MOTHERS GO INTO A FRENZY!
THEY THROW JACKETS ON THEIR KIDS... SHOVE SCHOOL SUPPLIES INTO THEIR ARMS....
AND PUSH THEM OUT THE DOOR TO RUN AFTER THE SCHOOL BUS!
IT'LL KILL 'EM WHEN THEY REALIZE IT'S SUNDAY!
BATIUK & AYERS

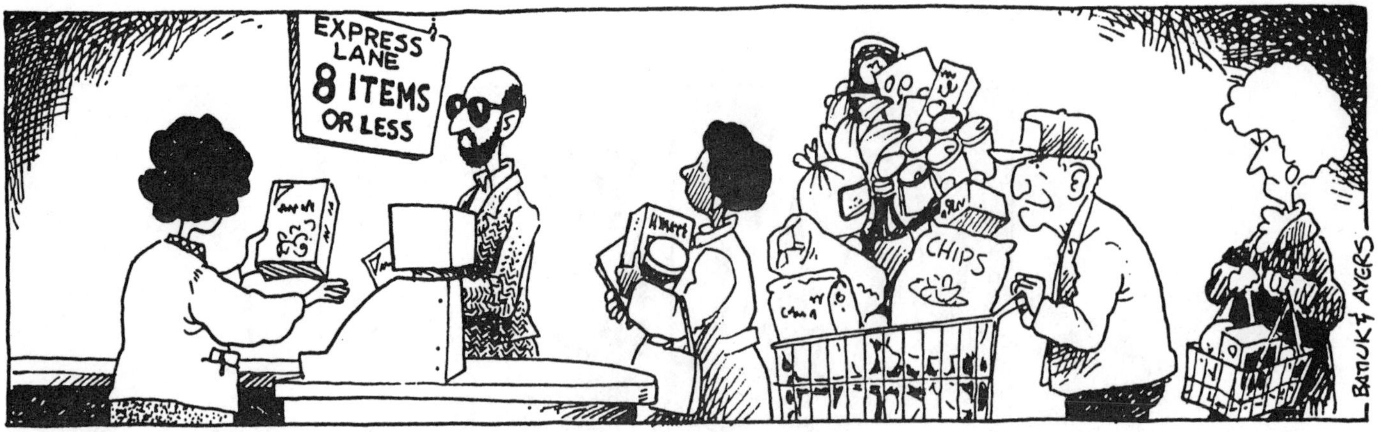
EXPRESS LANE
8 ITEMS OR LESS
CHIPS
BATIUK & AYERS

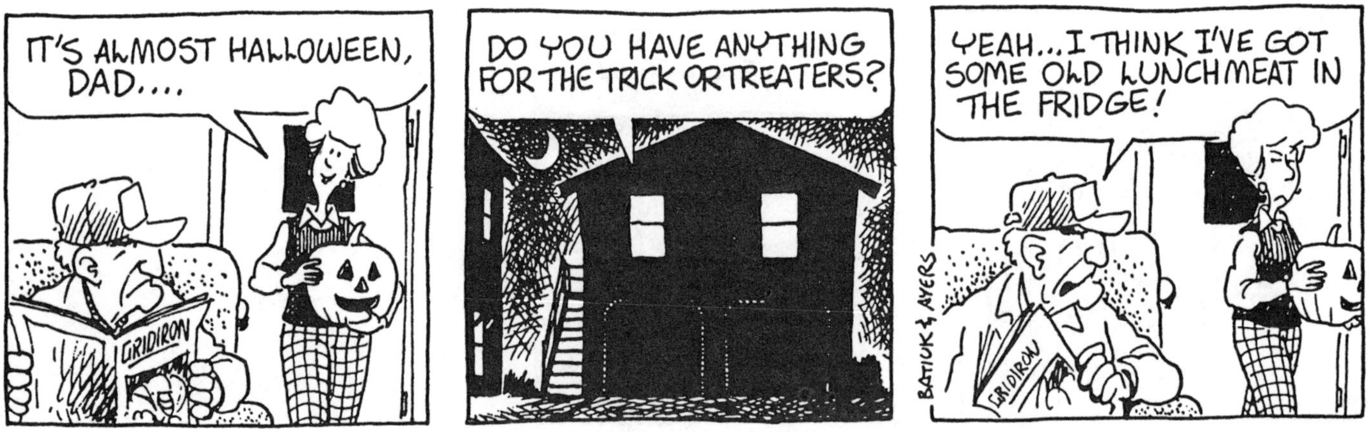
IT'S ALMOST HALLOWEEN, DAD....
GRIDIRON
DO YOU HAVE ANYTHING FOR THE TRICK OR TREATERS?
YEAH... I THINK I'VE GOT SOME OLD LUNCHMEAT IN THE FRIDGE!
BATIUK & AYERS
GRIDIRON

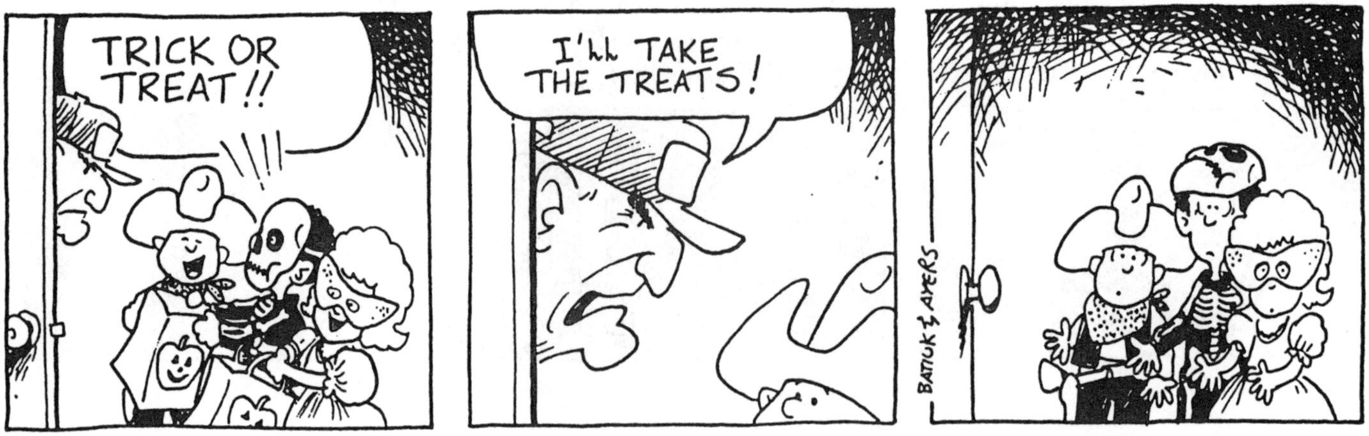
TRICK OR TREAT!!
I'LL TAKE THE TREATS!
BATIUK & AYERS

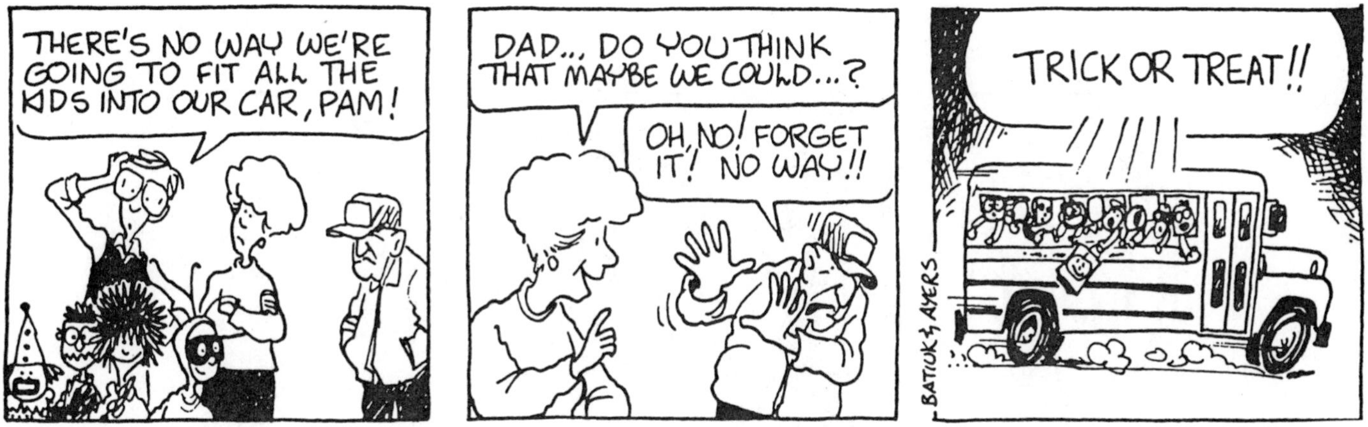
THERE'S NO WAY WE'RE GOING TO FIT ALL THE KIDS INTO OUR CAR, PAM!
DAD.., DO YOU THINK THAT MAYBE WE COULD...?
OH, NO! FORGET IT! NO WAY!!
TRICK OR TREAT!!
BATIUK & AYERS

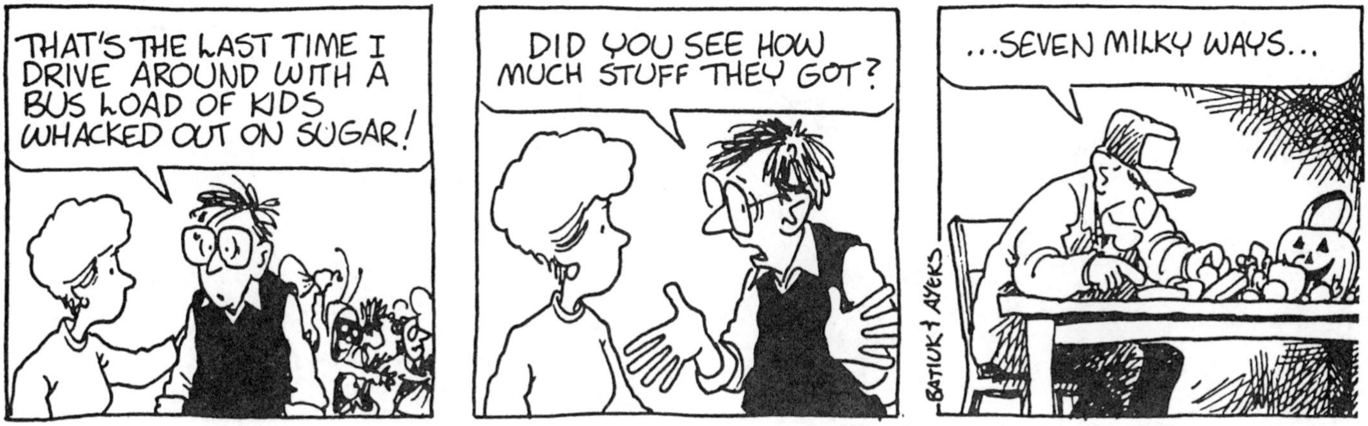
THAT'S THE LAST TIME I DRIVE AROUND WITH A BUS LOAD OF KIDS WHACKED OUT ON SUGAR!
DID YOU SEE HOW MUCH STUFF THEY GOT?
...SEVEN MILKY WAYS...
BATIUK & AYERS

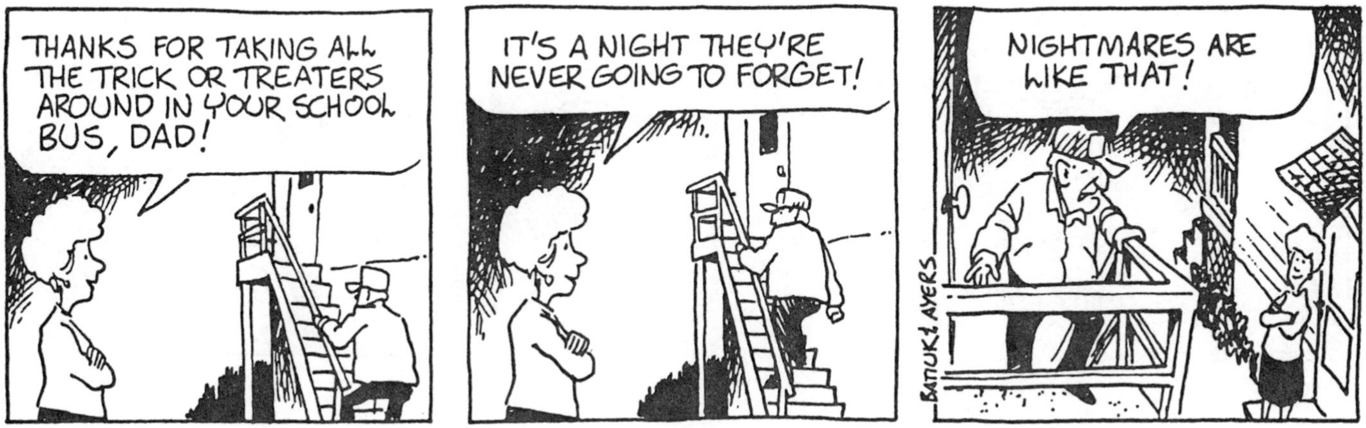
THANKS FOR TAKING ALL THE TRICK OR TREATERS AROUND IN YOUR SCHOOL BUS, DAD!
IT'S A NIGHT THEY'RE NEVER GOING TO FORGET!
NIGHTMARES ARE LIKE THAT!
BATIUK & AYERS

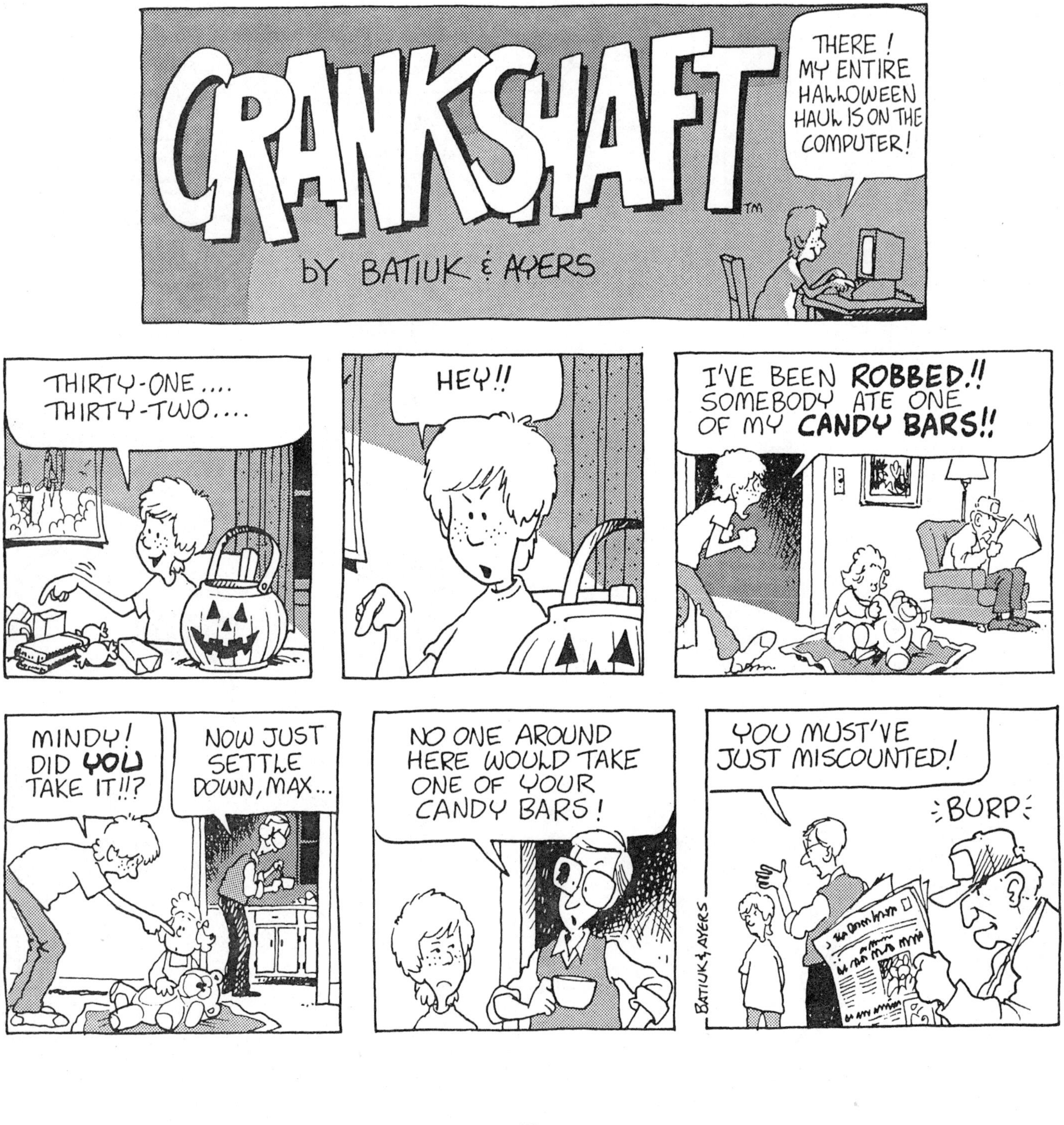
CRANKSHAFT
BY BATIUK & AYERS
THERE! MY ENTIRE HALLOWEEN HAUL IS ON THE COMPUTER!
THIRTY-ONE.... THIRTY-TWO....
HEY!!
I'VE BEEN ROBBED!! SOMEBODY ATE ONE OF MY CANDY BARS!!
MINDY! DID YOU TAKE IT!!?
NOW JUST SETTLE DOWN, MAX...
NO ONE AROUND HERE WOULD TAKE ONE OF YOUR CANDY BARS!
YOU MUST'VE JUST MISCOUNTED!
BURP
BATIUK & AYERS

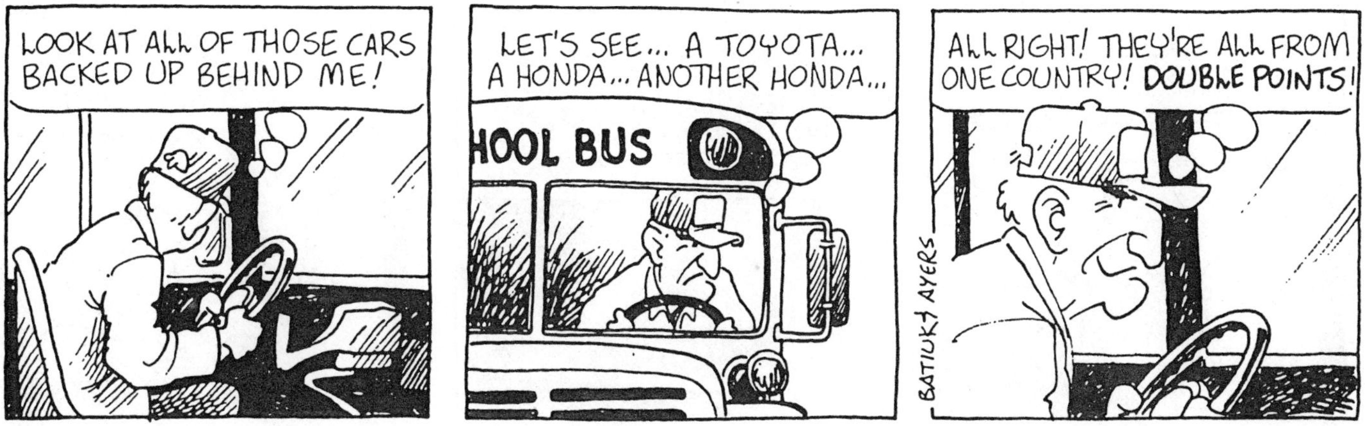
LOOK AT ALL OF THOSE CARS BACKED UP BEHIND ME!
LET'S SEE... A TOYOTA... A HONDA... ANOTHER HONDA...
HOOL BUS
ALL RIGHT! THEY'RE ALL FROM ONE COUNTRY! **DOUBLE POINTS!**
BATIUK + AYERS

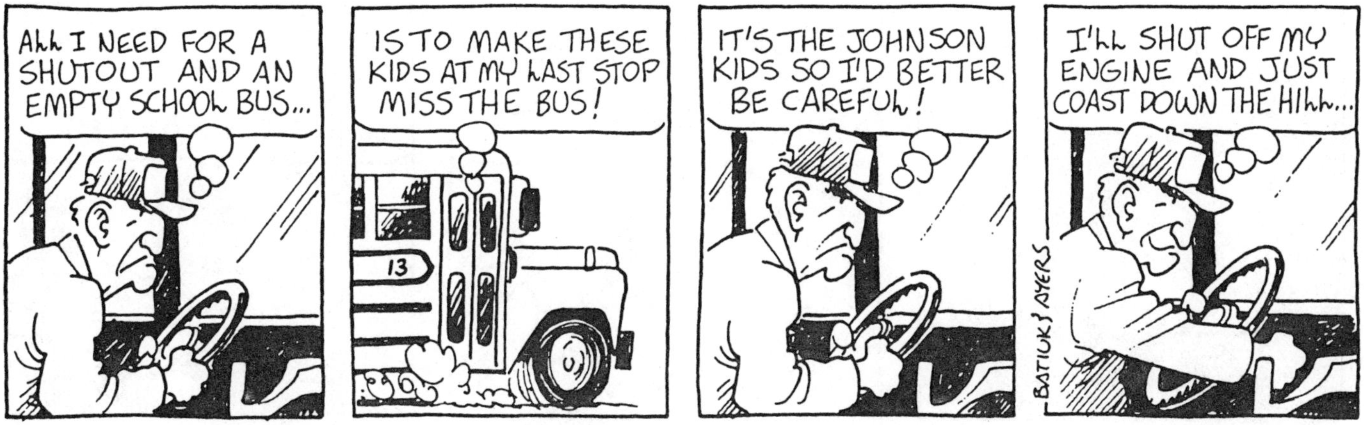
ALL I NEED FOR A SHUTOUT AND AN EMPTY SCHOOL BUS...
IS TO MAKE THESE KIDS AT MY LAST STOP MISS THE BUS!
13
IT'S THE JOHNSON KIDS SO I'D BETTER BE CAREFUL!
I'LL SHUT OFF MY ENGINE AND JUST COAST DOWN THE HILL...
BATIUK + AYERS

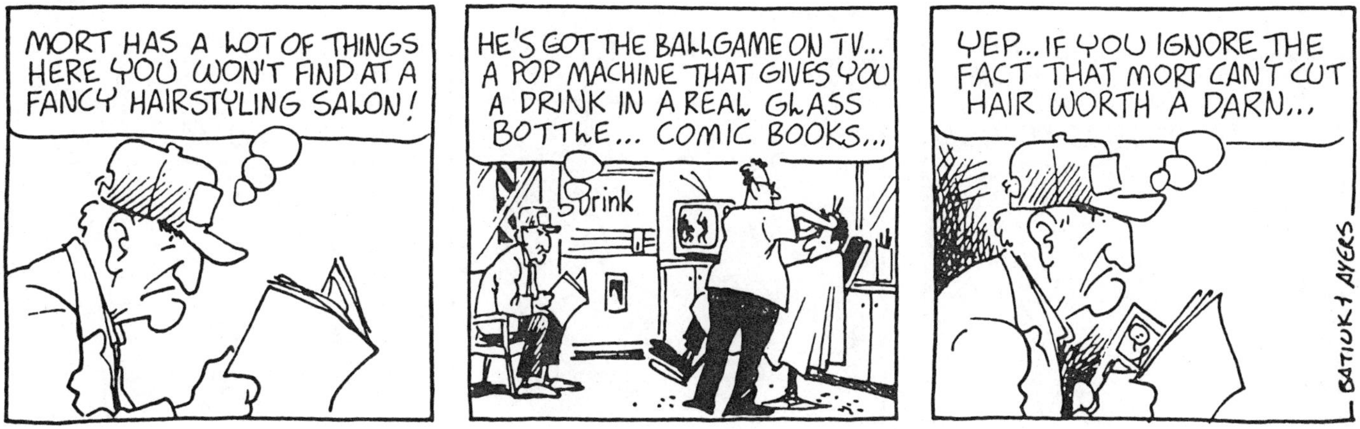
MORT HAS A LOT OF THINGS HERE YOU WON'T FIND AT A FANCY HAIRSTYLING SALON!
HE'S GOT THE BALLGAME ON TV... A POP MACHINE THAT GIVES YOU A DRINK IN A REAL GLASS BOTTLE... COMIC BOOKS...
Drink
YEP... IF YOU IGNORE THE FACT THAT MORT CAN'T CUT HAIR WORTH A DARN...
BATIUK + AYERS

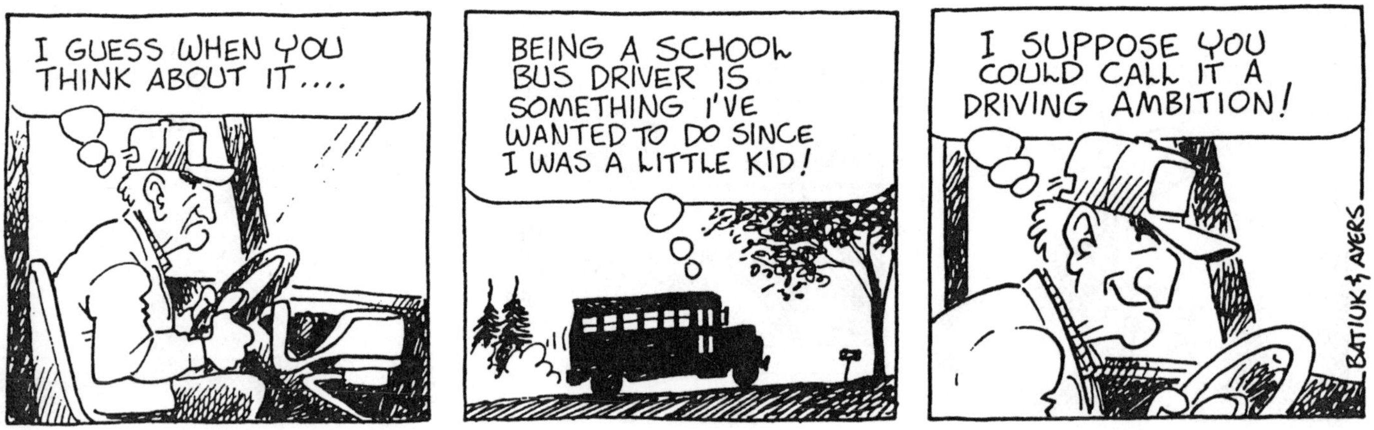
I GUESS WHEN YOU THINK ABOUT IT....
BEING A SCHOOL BUS DRIVER IS SOMETHING I'VE WANTED TO DO SINCE I WAS A LITTLE KID!
I SUPPOSE YOU COULD CALL IT A DRIVING AMBITION!
BATIUK & AYERS

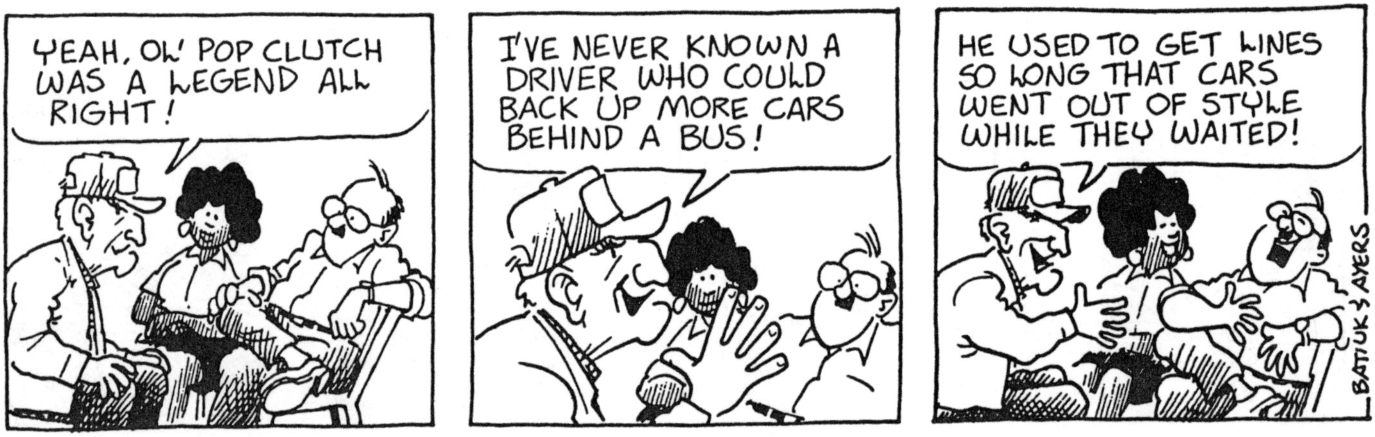
YEAH, OL' POP CLUTCH WAS A LEGEND ALL RIGHT!
I'VE NEVER KNOWN A DRIVER WHO COULD BACK UP MORE CARS BEHIND A BUS!
HE USED TO GET LINES SO LONG THAT CARS WENT OUT OF STYLE WHILE THEY WAITED!
BATIUK & AYERS

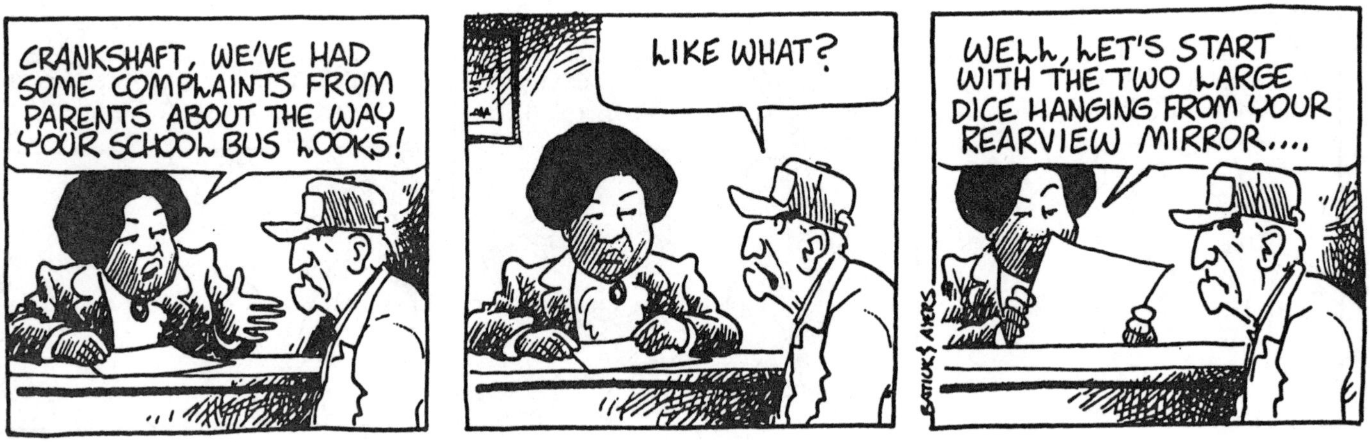
CRANKSHAFT, WE'VE HAD SOME COMPLAINTS FROM PARENTS ABOUT THE WAY YOUR SCHOOL BUS LOOKS!
LIKE WHAT?
WELL, LET'S START WITH THE TWO LARGE DICE HANGING FROM YOUR REARVIEW MIRROR....
BATIUK & AYERS

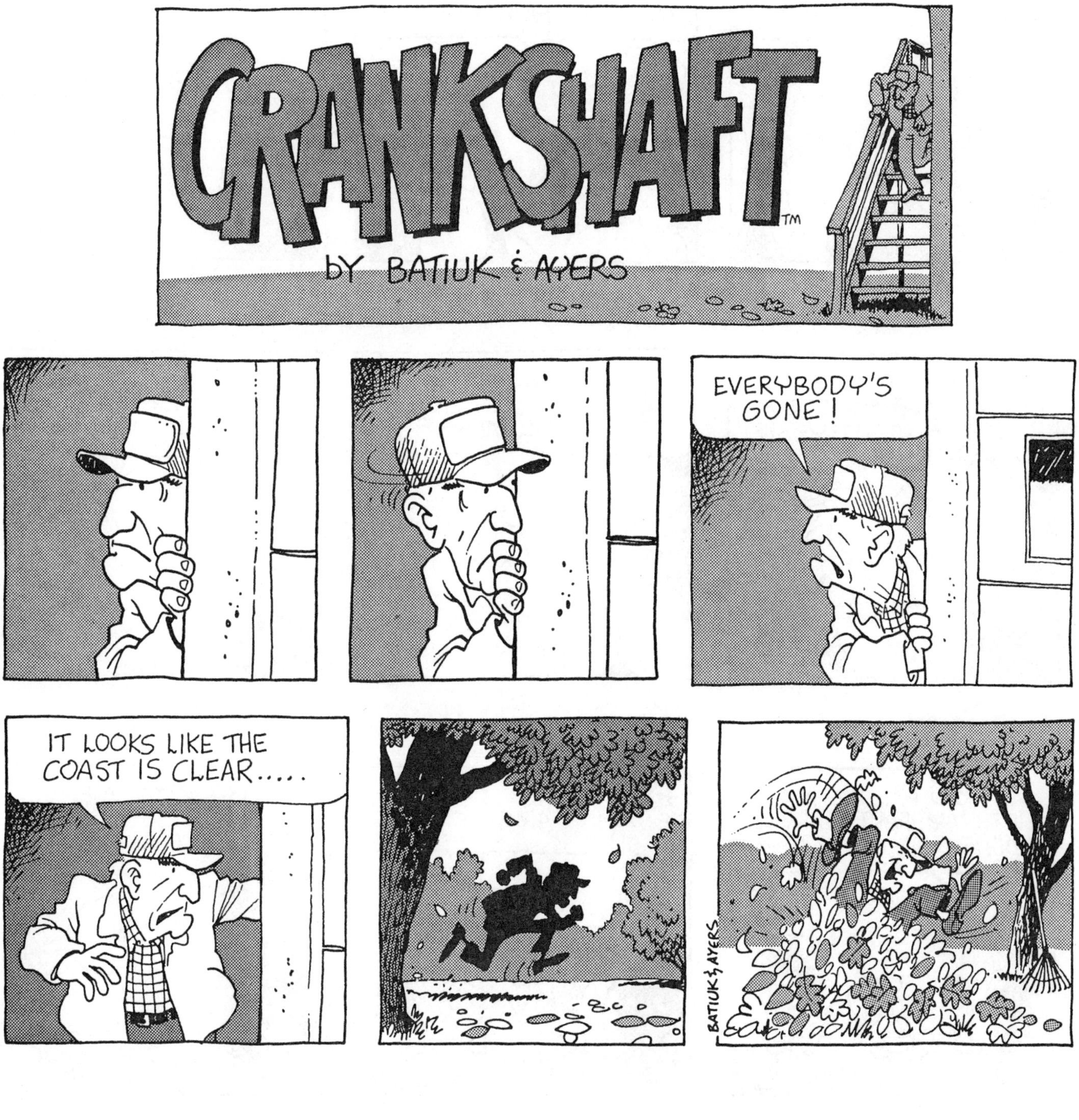
CRANKSHAFT
TM
BY BATIUK & AYERS
EVERYBODY'S GONE!
IT LOOKS LIKE THE COAST IS CLEAR.....
BATIUK & AYERS

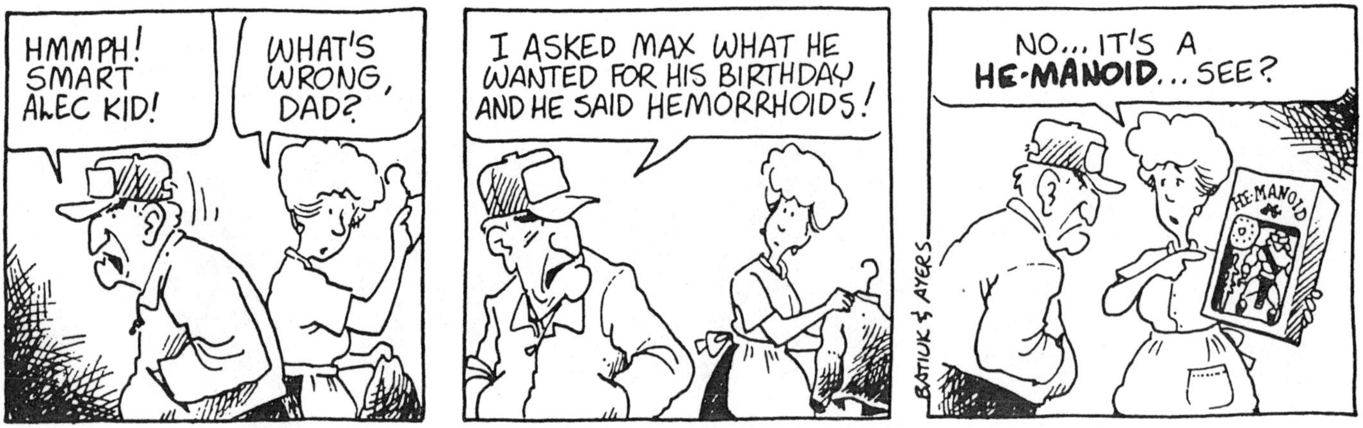
HMMPH! SMART ALEC KID!
WHAT'S WRONG, DAD?
I ASKED MAX WHAT HE WANTED FOR HIS BIRTHDAY AND HE SAID HEMORRHOIDS!
NO... IT'S A **HE-MANOID**... SEE?
HE-MANOID
BATIUK & AYERS

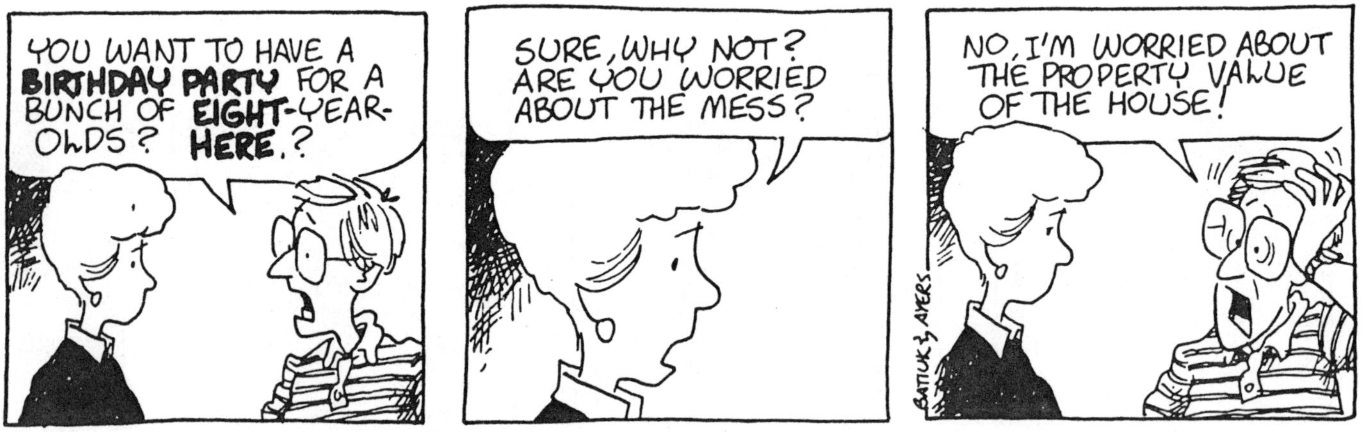
YOU WANT TO HAVE A **BIRTHDAY PARTY** FOR A BUNCH OF **EIGHT**-YEAR-OLDS? **HERE**.?
SURE, WHY NOT? ARE YOU WORRIED ABOUT THE MESS?
NO, I'M WORRIED ABOUT THE PROPERTY VALUE OF THE HOUSE!
BATIUK & AYERS

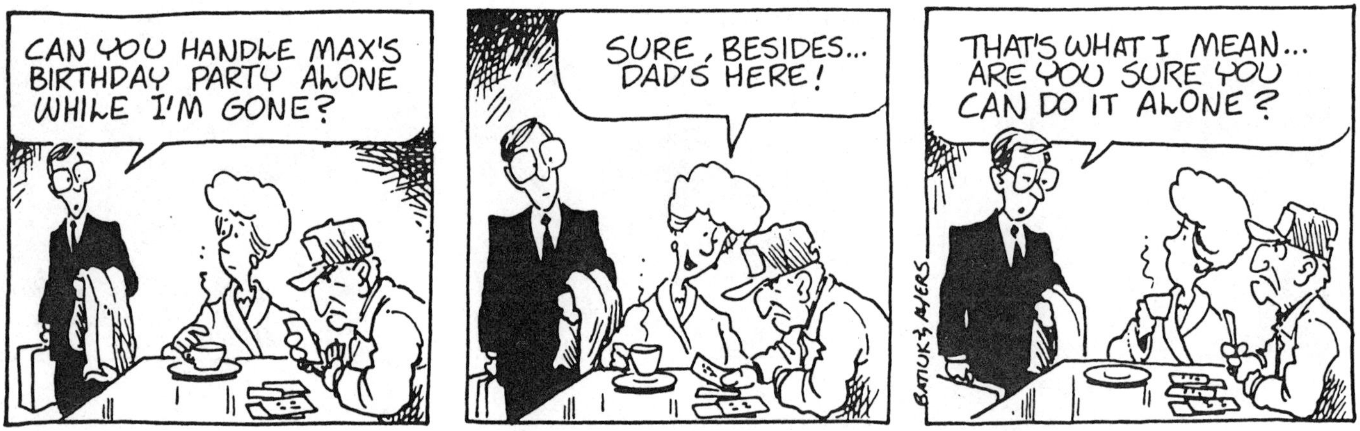
CAN YOU HANDLE MAX'S BIRTHDAY PARTY ALONE WHILE I'M GONE?
SURE, BESIDES... DAD'S HERE!
THAT'S WHAT I MEAN... ARE YOU SURE YOU CAN DO IT ALONE?
BATIUK & AYERS

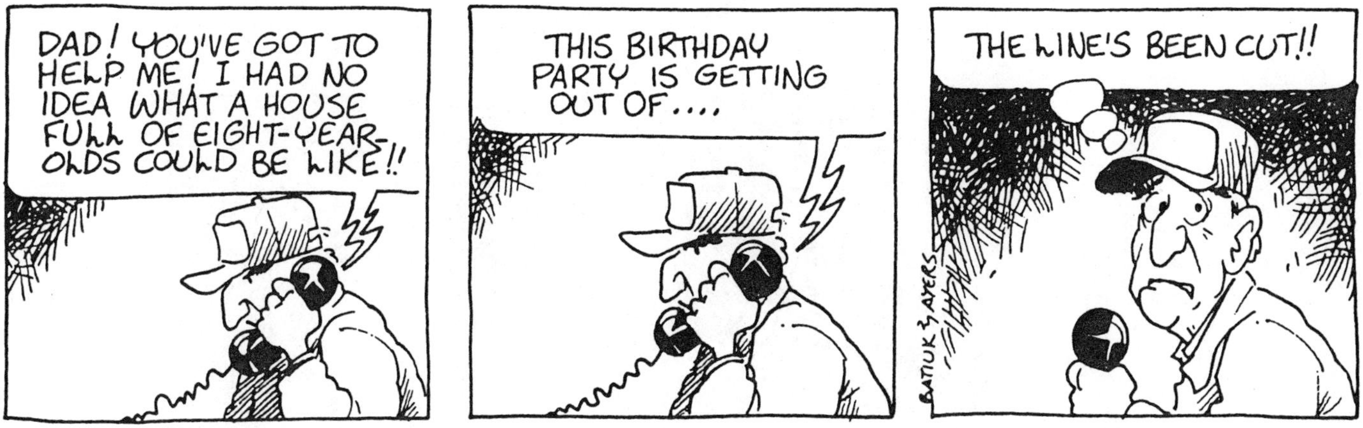
DAD! YOU'VE GOT TO HELP ME! I HAD NO IDEA WHAT A HOUSE FULL OF EIGHT-YEAR-OLDS COULD BE LIKE!!
THIS BIRTHDAY PARTY IS GETTING OUT OF....
THE LINE'S BEEN CUT!!
BATIUK & AYERS

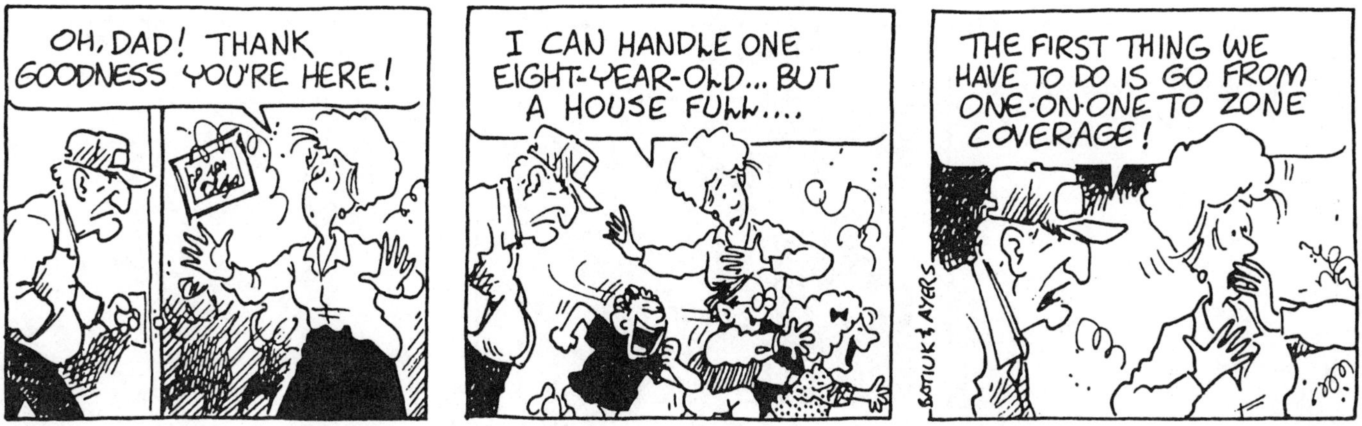
OH, DAD! THANK GOODNESS YOU'RE HERE!
I CAN HANDLE ONE EIGHT-YEAR-OLD... BUT A HOUSE FULL....
THE FIRST THING WE HAVE TO DO IS GO FROM ONE-ON-ONE TO ZONE COVERAGE!
BATIUK & AYERS

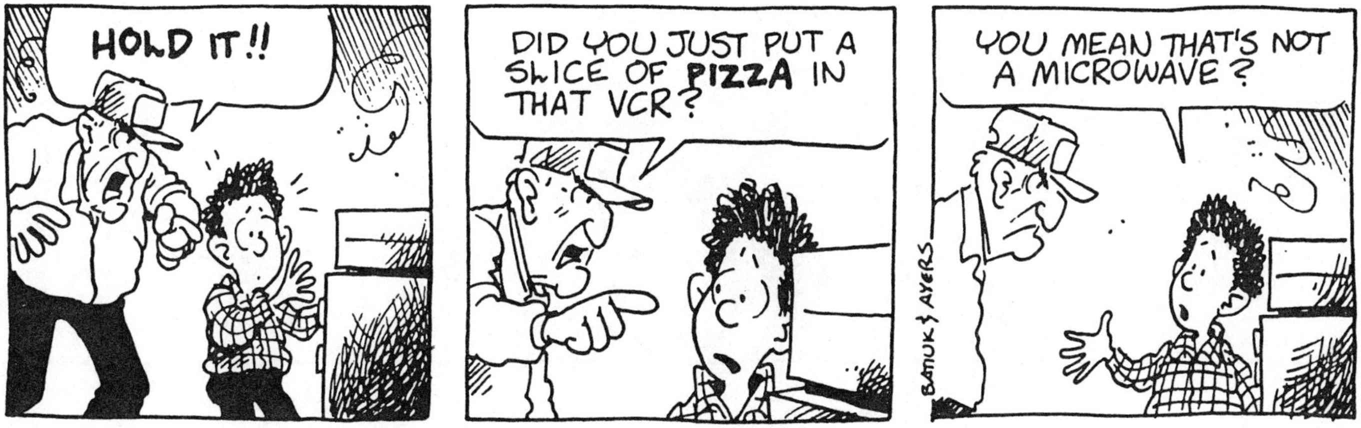
HOLD IT!!
DID YOU JUST PUT A SLICE OF PIZZA IN THAT VCR?
YOU MEAN THAT'S NOT A MICROWAVE?
BATIUK & AYERS

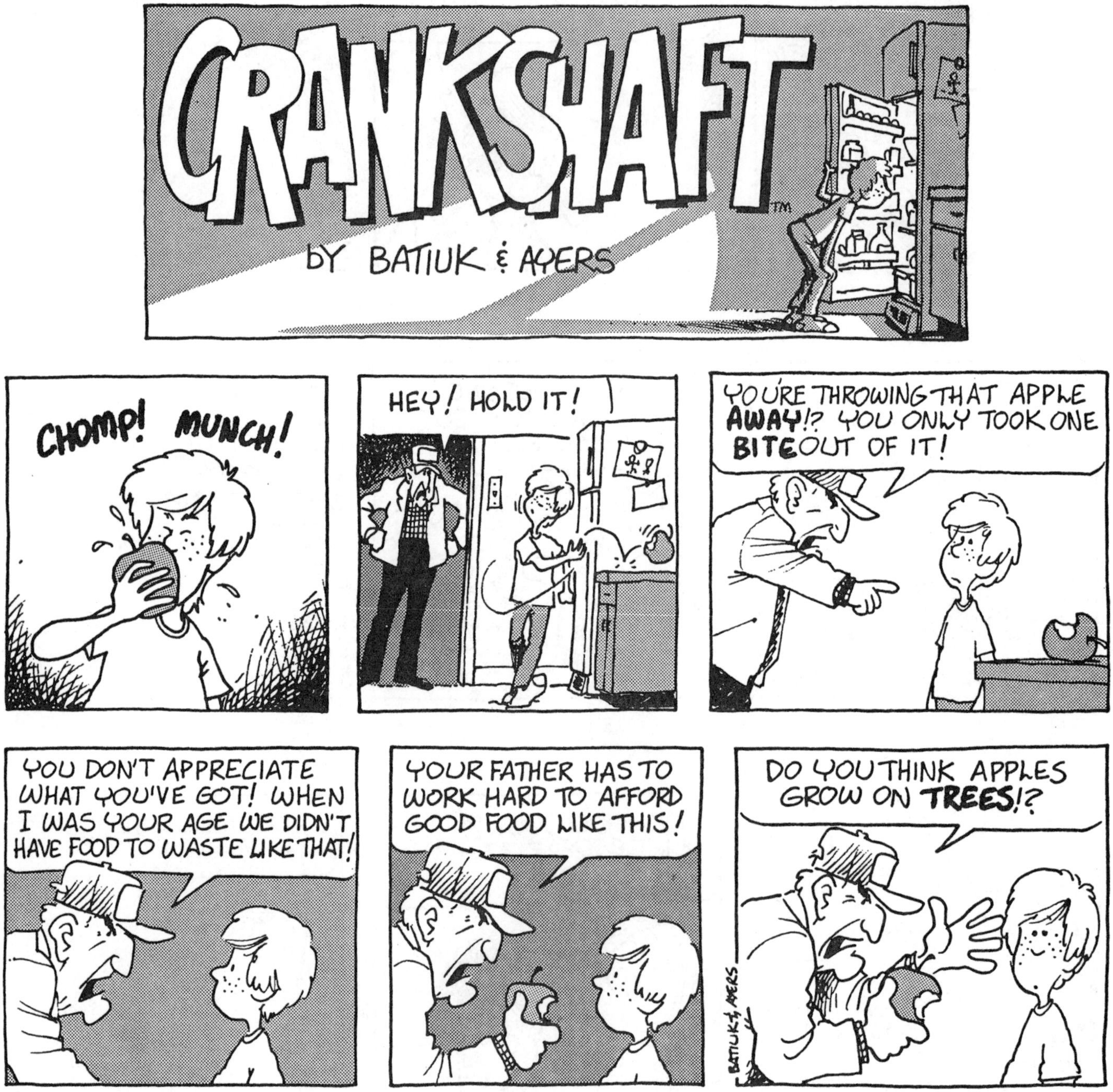

CRANKSHAFT
TM
BY BATIUK & AYERS
CHOMP! MUNCH!
HEY! HOLD IT!
YOU'RE THROWING THAT APPLE AWAY!? YOU ONLY TOOK ONE BITE OUT OF IT!
YOU DON'T APPRECIATE WHAT YOU'VE GOT! WHEN I WAS YOUR AGE WE DIDN'T HAVE FOOD TO WASTE LIKE THAT!
YOUR FATHER HAS TO WORK HARD TO AFFORD GOOD FOOD LIKE THIS!
DO YOU THINK APPLES GROW ON TREES!?
BATIUK & AYERS

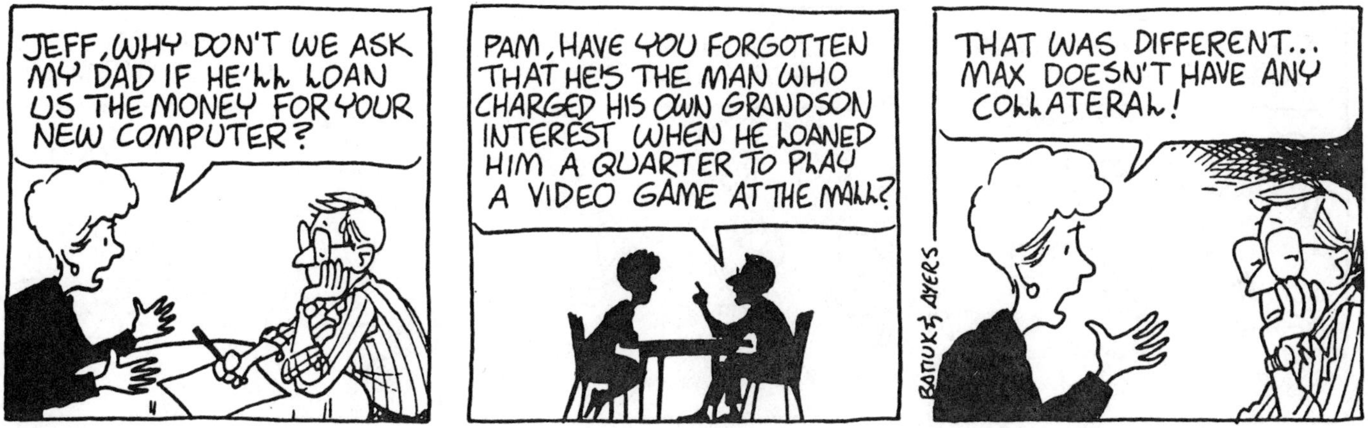
JEFF, WHY DON'T WE ASK MY DAD IF HE'LL LOAN US THE MONEY FOR YOUR NEW COMPUTER?
PAM, HAVE YOU FORGOTTEN THAT HE'S THE MAN WHO CHARGED HIS OWN GRANDSON INTEREST WHEN HE LOANED HIM A QUARTER TO PLAY A VIDEO GAME AT THE MALL?
THAT WAS DIFFERENT... MAX DOESN'T HAVE ANY COLLATERAL!
BATIUK & AYERS

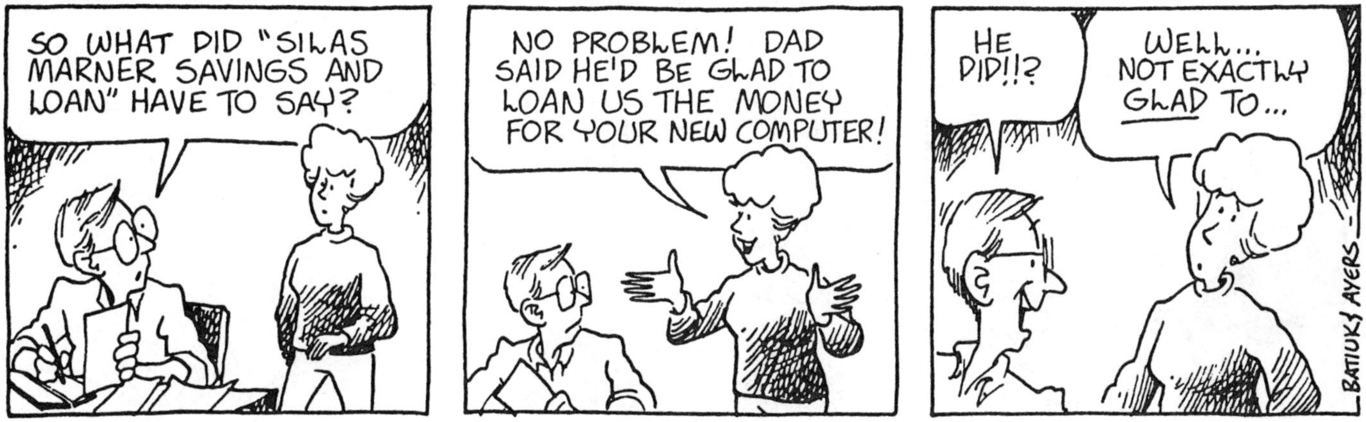
SO WHAT DID "SILAS MARNER SAVINGS AND LOAN" HAVE TO SAY?
NO PROBLEM! DAD SAID HE'D BE GLAD TO LOAN US THE MONEY FOR YOUR NEW COMPUTER!
HE DID!!?
WELL... NOT EXACTLY GLAD TO...
BATIUK & AYERS

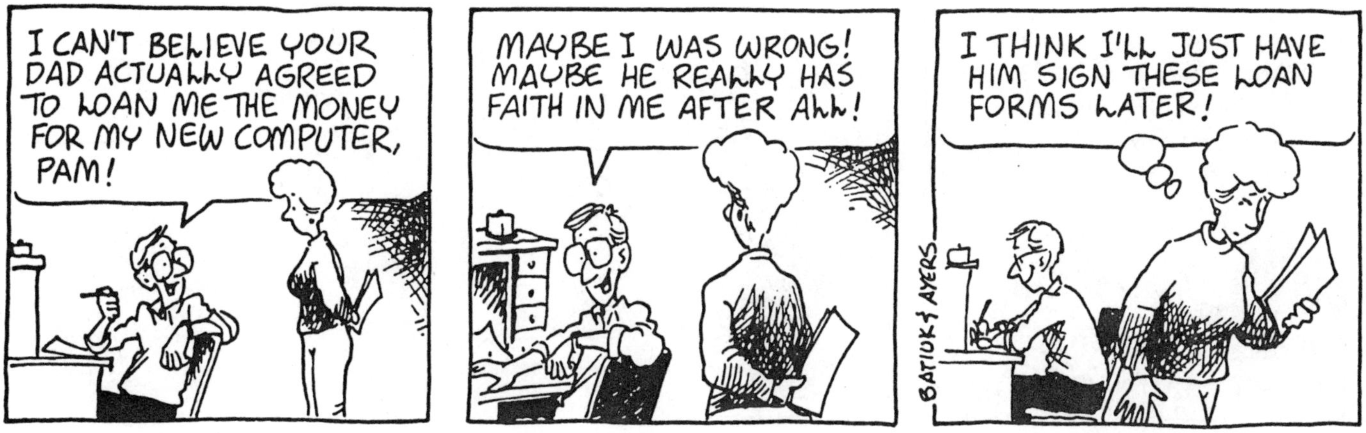
I CAN'T BELIEVE YOUR DAD ACTUALLY AGREED TO LOAN ME THE MONEY FOR MY NEW COMPUTER, PAM!
MAYBE I WAS WRONG! MAYBE HE REALLY HAS FAITH IN ME AFTER ALL!
I THINK I'LL JUST HAVE HIM SIGN THESE LOAN FORMS LATER!
BATIUK & AYERS

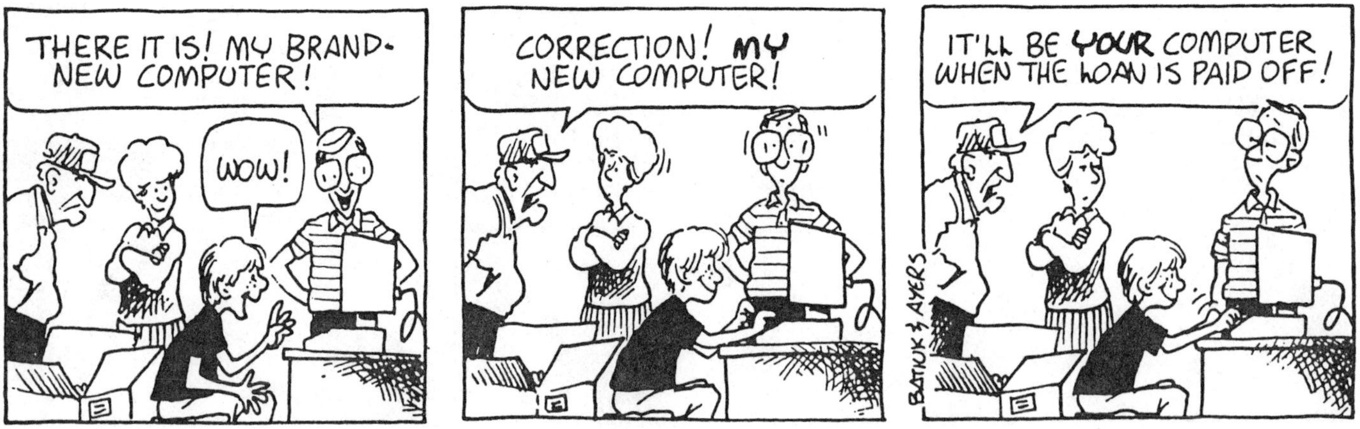
THERE IT IS! MY BRAND-NEW COMPUTER!
WOW!
CORRECTION! **MY** NEW COMPUTER!
IT'LL BE **YOUR** COMPUTER WHEN THE LOAN IS PAID OFF!
BATIUK & AYERS

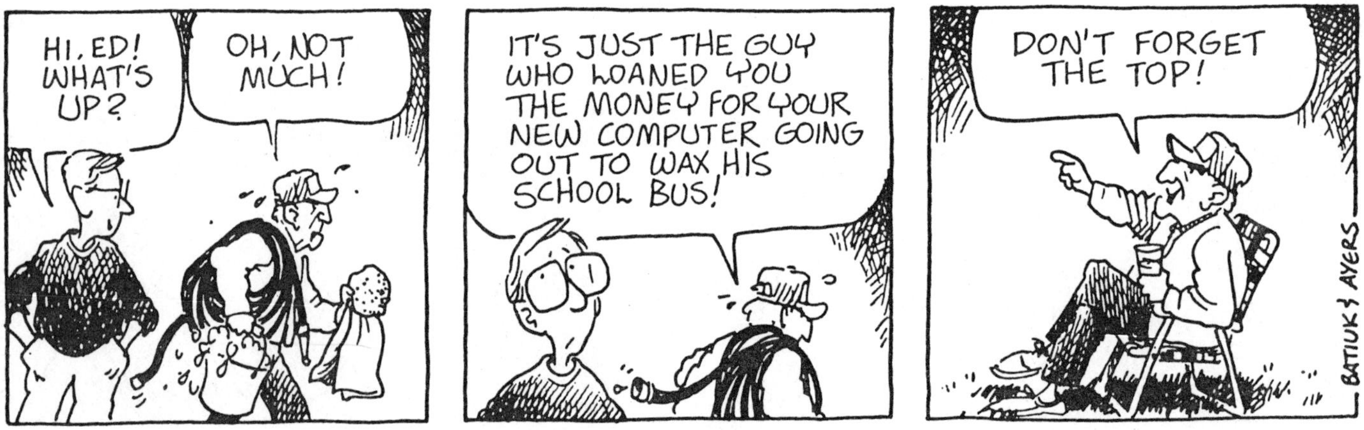
HI, ED! WHAT'S UP?
OH, NOT MUCH!
IT'S JUST THE GUY WHO LOANED YOU THE MONEY FOR YOUR NEW COMPUTER GOING OUT TO WAX HIS SCHOOL BUS!
DON'T FORGET THE TOP!
BATIUK & AYERS

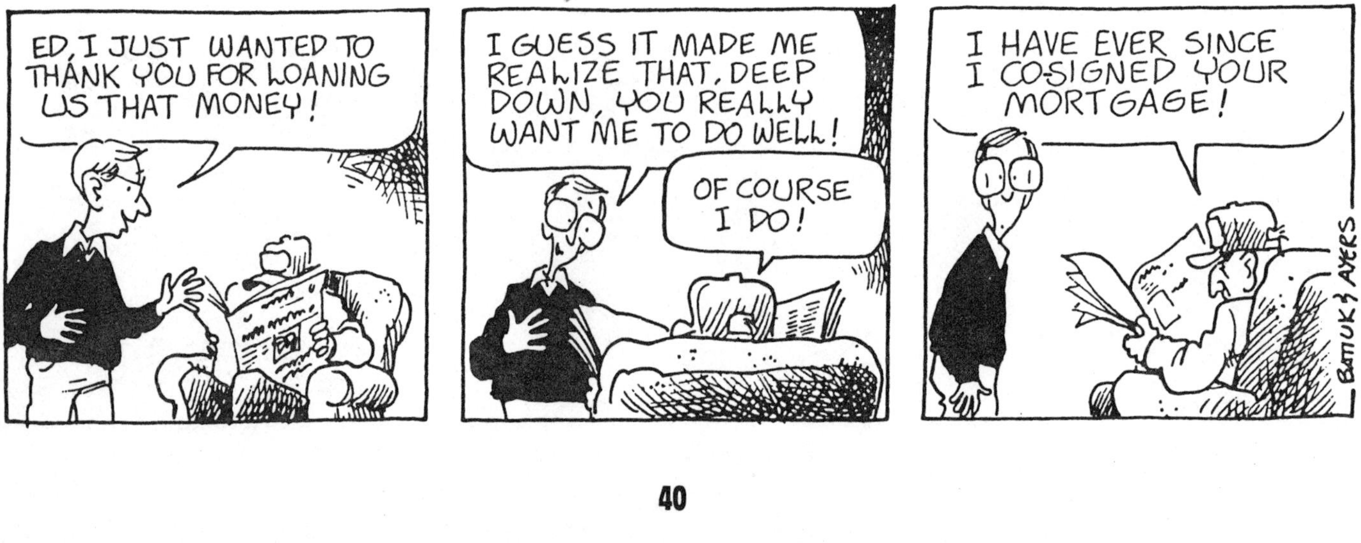
ED, I JUST WANTED TO THANK YOU FOR LOANING US THAT MONEY!
I GUESS IT MADE ME REALIZE THAT, DEEP DOWN, YOU REALLY WANT ME TO DO WELL!
OF COURSE I DO!
I HAVE EVER SINCE I CO-SIGNED YOUR MORTGAGE!
BATIUK & AYERS

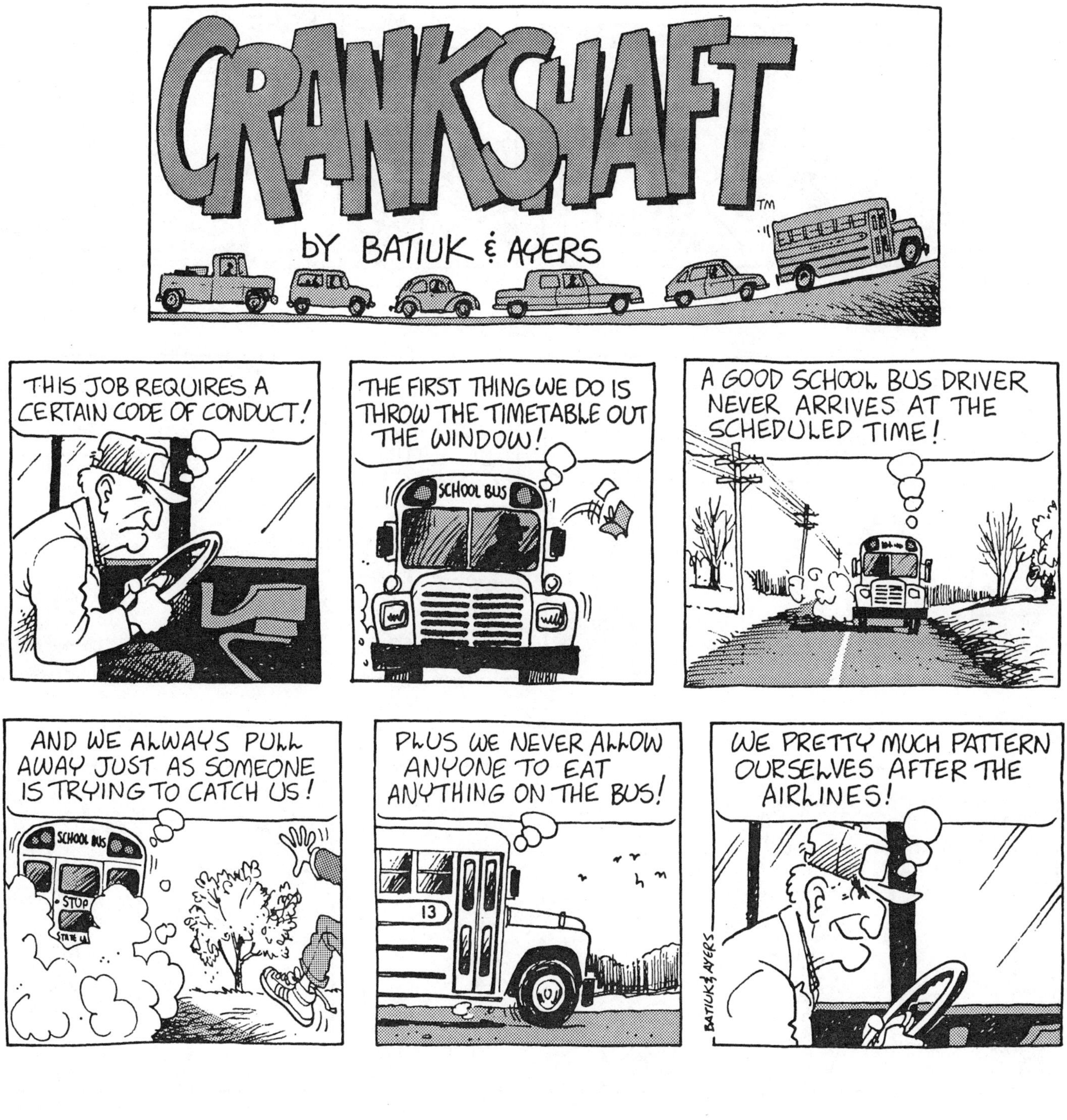
CRANKSHAFT™
BY BATIUK & AYERS
THIS JOB REQUIRES A CERTAIN CODE OF CONDUCT!
THE FIRST THING WE DO IS THROW THE TIMETABLE OUT THE WINDOW!
SCHOOL BUS
A GOOD SCHOOL BUS DRIVER NEVER ARRIVES AT THE SCHEDULED TIME!
AND WE ALWAYS PULL AWAY JUST AS SOMEONE IS TRYING TO CATCH US!
SCHOOL BUS
STOP
PLUS WE NEVER ALLOW ANYONE TO EAT ANYTHING ON THE BUS!
13
WE PRETTY MUCH PATTERN OURSELVES AFTER THE AIRLINES!
BATIUK & AYERS

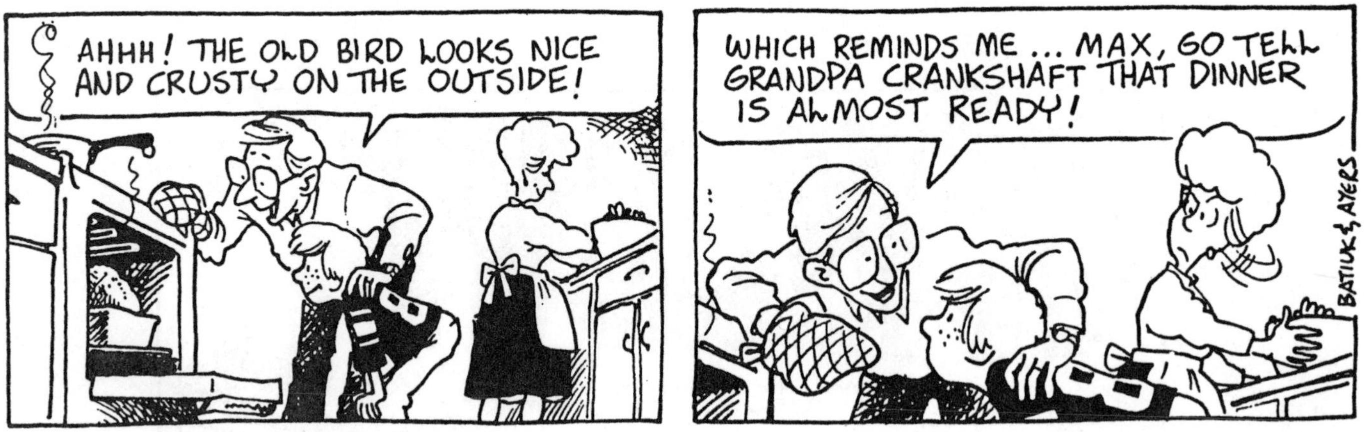
AHHH! THE OLD BIRD LOOKS NICE AND CRUSTY ON THE OUTSIDE!
WHICH REMINDS ME ... MAX, GO TELL GRANDPA CRANKSHAFT THAT DINNER IS ALMOST READY!
BATIUK & AYERS

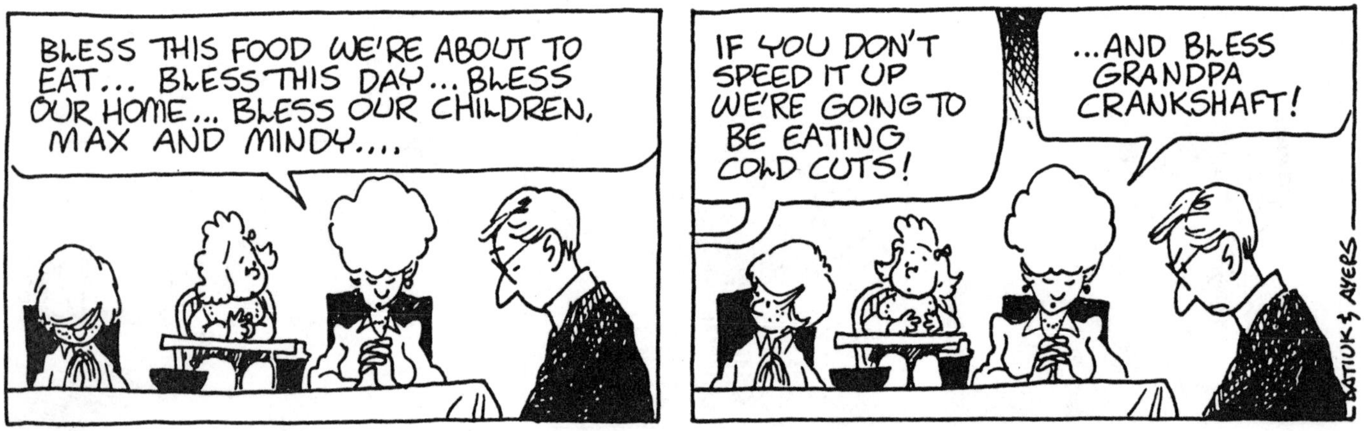
BLESS THIS FOOD WE'RE ABOUT TO EAT... BLESS THIS DAY... BLESS OUR HOME... BLESS OUR CHILDREN, MAX AND MINDY....
IF YOU DON'T SPEED IT UP WE'RE GOING TO BE EATING COLD CUTS!
...AND BLESS GRANDPA CRANKSHAFT!
BATIUK & AYERS

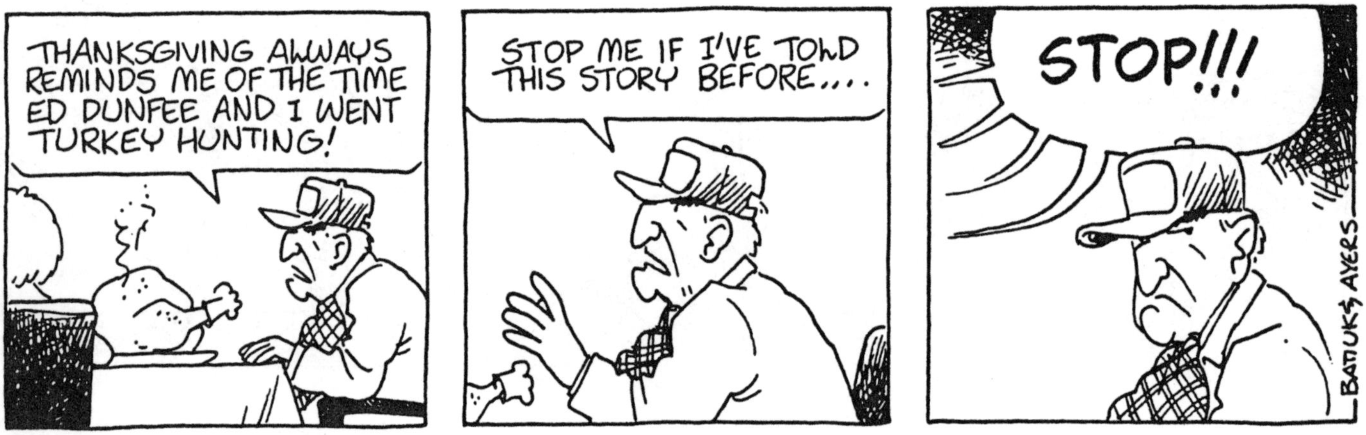
THANKSGIVING ALWAYS REMINDS ME OF THE TIME ED DUNFEE AND I WENT TURKEY HUNTING!
STOP ME IF I'VE TOLD THIS STORY BEFORE....
STOP!!!
BATIUK & AYERS

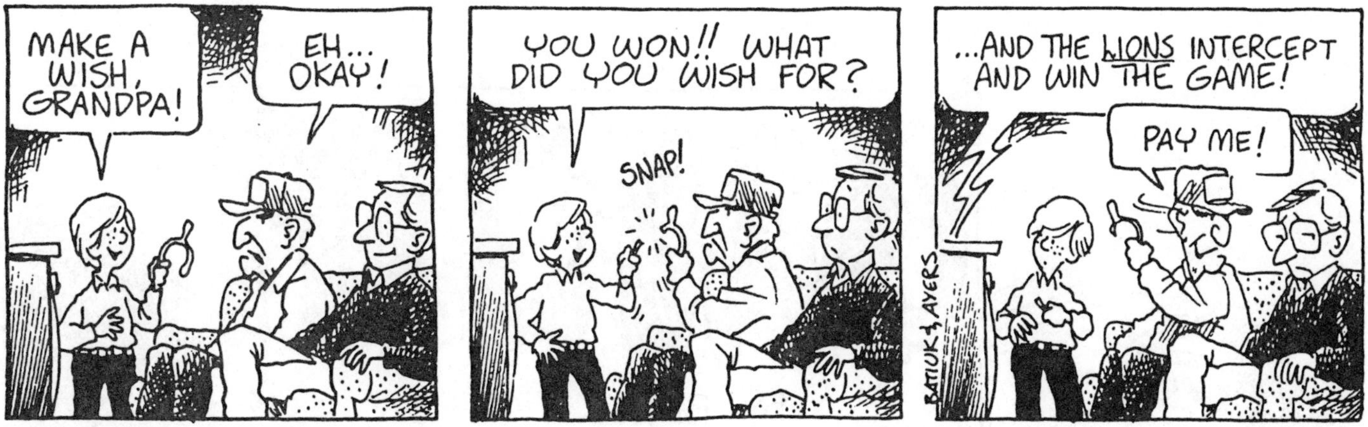
MAKE A WISH, GRANDPA!
EH... OKAY!
YOU WON!! WHAT DID YOU WISH FOR?
SNAP!
...AND THE LIONS INTERCEPT AND WIN THE GAME!
PAY ME!
BATIUK & AYERS

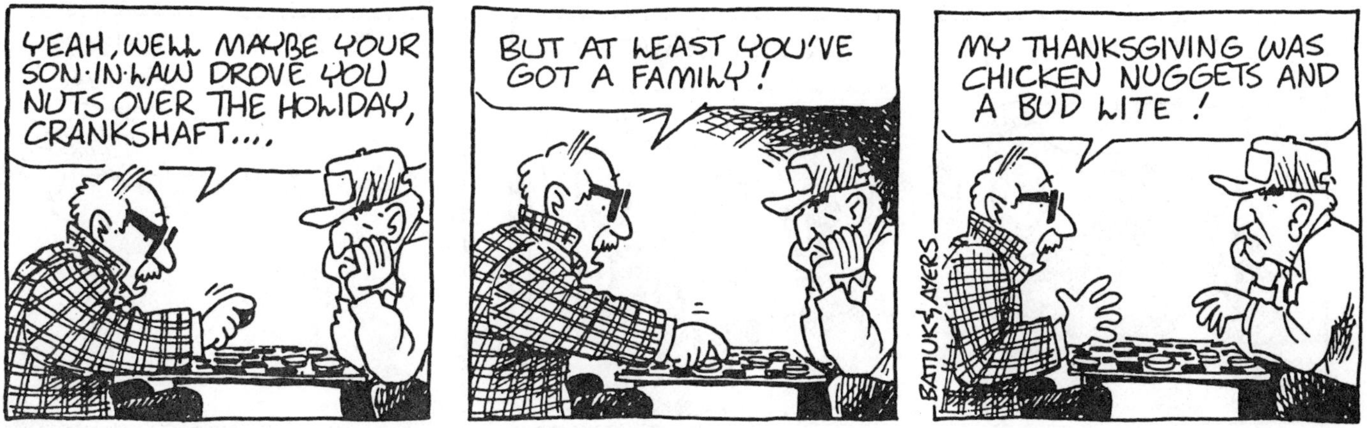
YEAH, WELL MAYBE YOUR SON-IN-LAW DROVE YOU NUTS OVER THE HOLIDAY, CRANKSHAFT....
BUT AT LEAST YOU'VE GOT A FAMILY!
MY THANKSGIVING WAS CHICKEN NUGGETS AND A BUD LITE!
BATIUK & AYERS

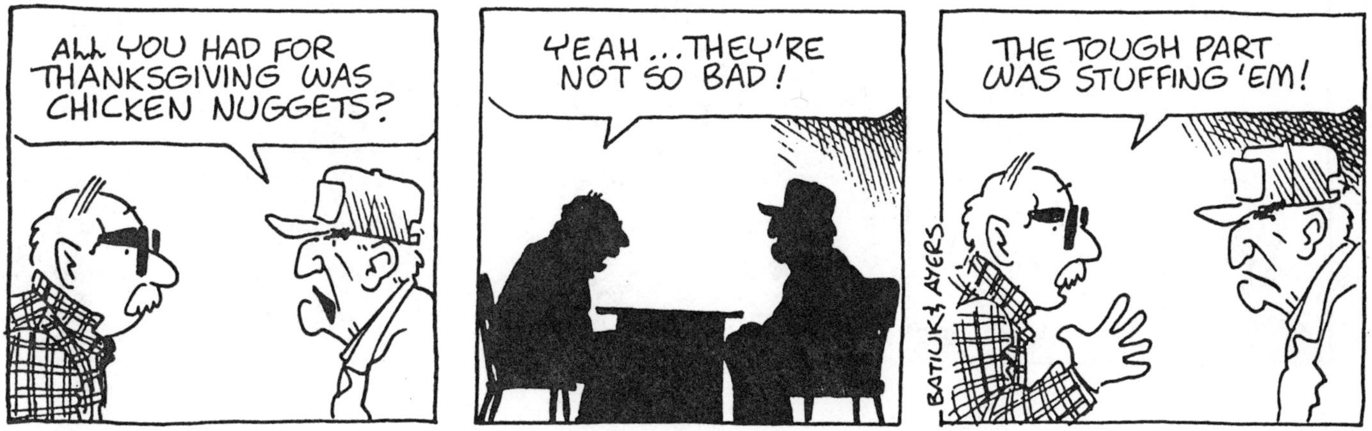
ALL YOU HAD FOR THANKSGIVING WAS CHICKEN NUGGETS?
YEAH...THEY'RE NOT SO BAD!
THE TOUGH PART WAS STUFFING 'EM!
BATIUK & AYERS

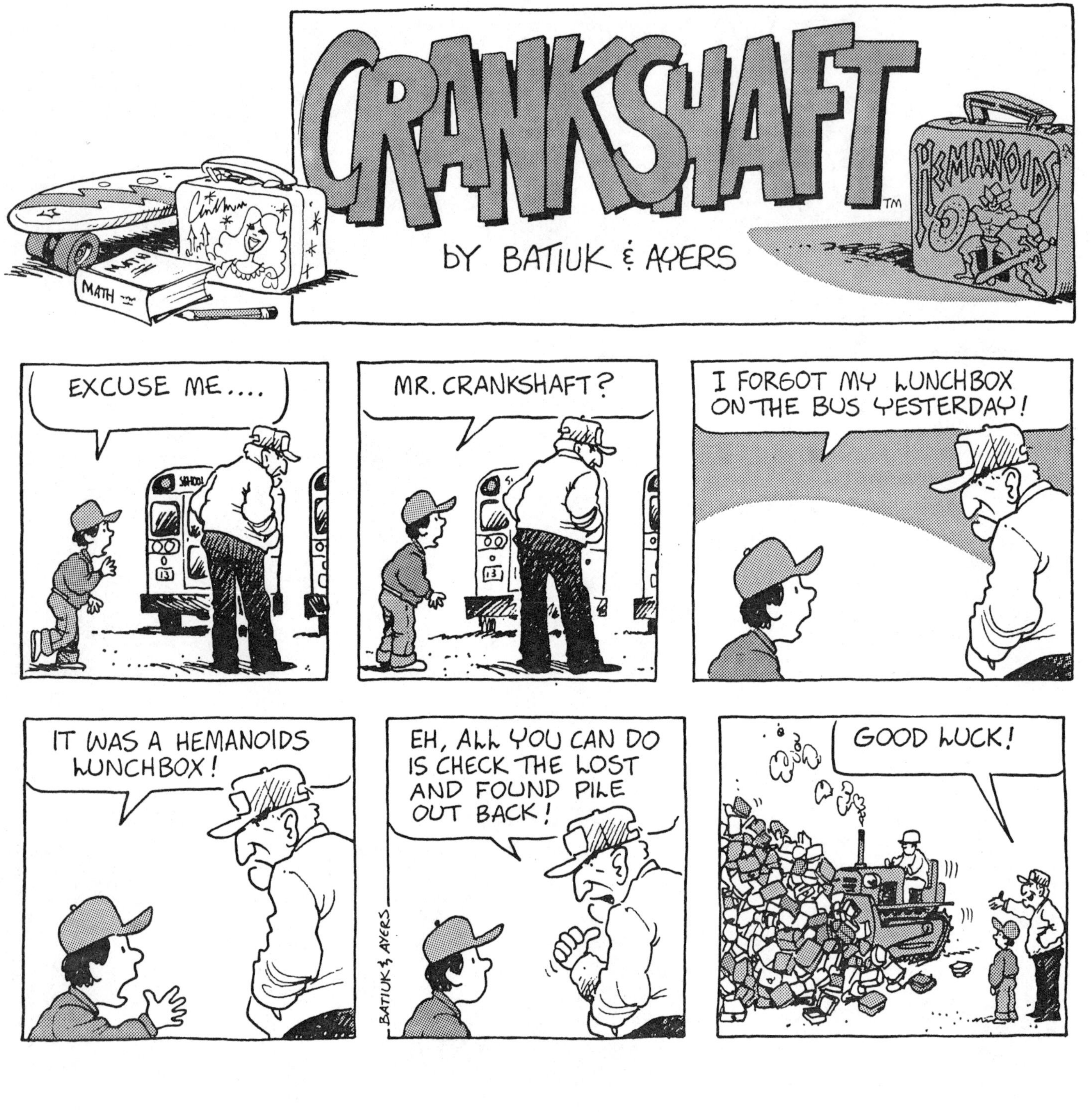
CRANKSHAFT
TM
BY BATIUK & AYERS
HEMANOIDS
MATH
MATH
EXCUSE ME....
MR. CRANKSHAFT?
I FORGOT MY LUNCHBOX ON THE BUS YESTERDAY!
IT WAS A HEMANOIDS LUNCHBOX!
EH, ALL YOU CAN DO IS CHECK THE LOST AND FOUND PILE OUT BACK!
BATIUK & AYERS
GOOD LUCK!

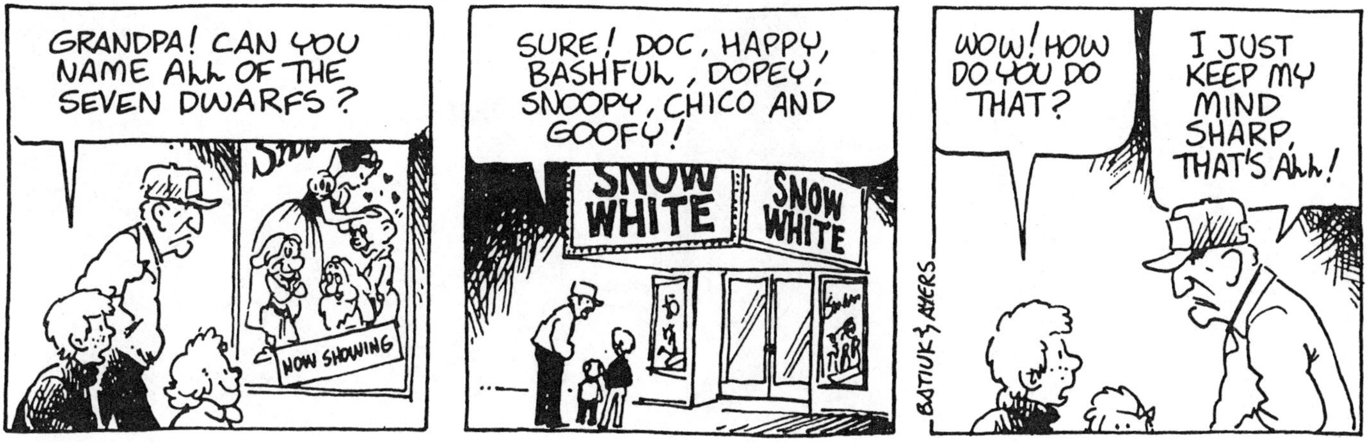
GRANDPA! CAN YOU NAME ALL OF THE SEVEN DWARFS?
NOW SHOWING
SURE! DOC, HAPPY, BASHFUL, DOPEY, SNOOPY, CHICO AND GOOFY!
SNOW WHITE
SNOW WHITE
BATIUK & AYERS
WOW! HOW DO YOU DO THAT?
I JUST KEEP MY MIND SHARP, THAT'S ALL!

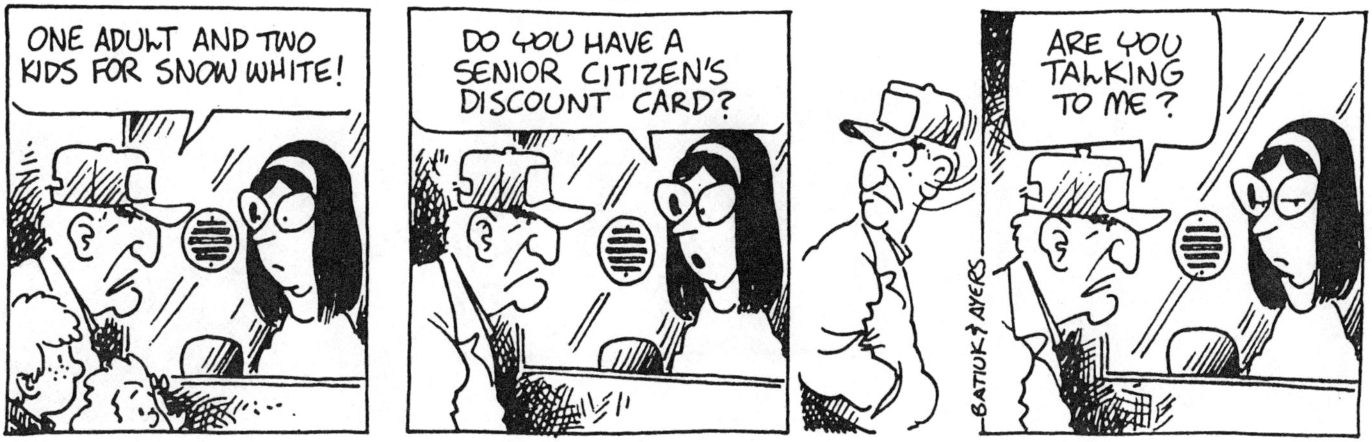
ONE ADULT AND TWO KIDS FOR SNOW WHITE!
DO YOU HAVE A SENIOR CITIZEN'S DISCOUNT CARD?
BATIUK & AYERS
ARE YOU TALKING TO ME?

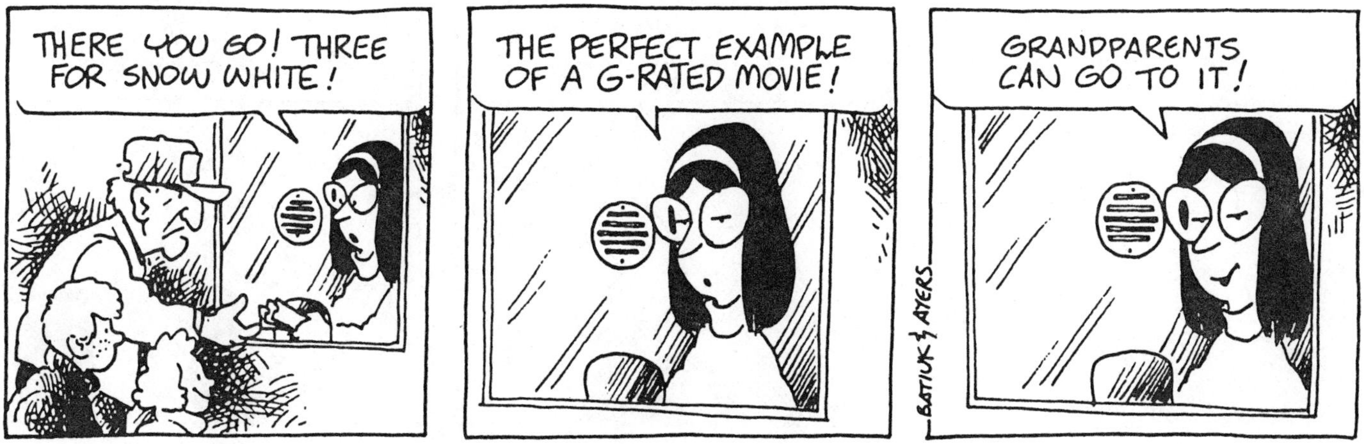
THERE YOU GO! THREE FOR SNOW WHITE!
THE PERFECT EXAMPLE OF A G-RATED MOVIE!
BATIUK & AYERS
GRANDPARENTS CAN GO TO IT!

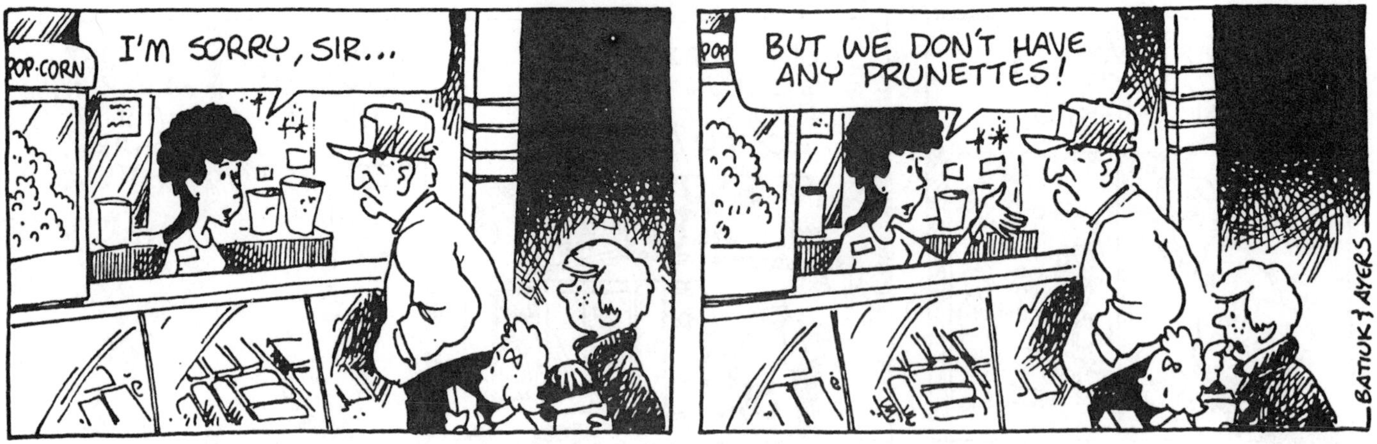
POP·CORN
I'M SORRY, SIR...
BUT WE DON'T HAVE ANY PRUNETTES!
BATIUK & AYERS

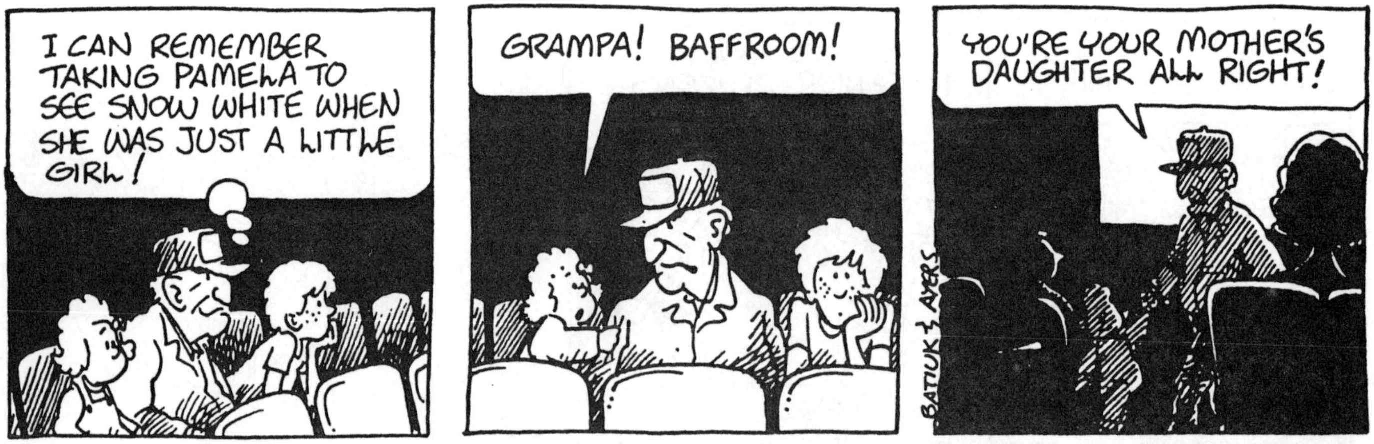
I CAN REMEMBER TAKING PAMELA TO SEE SNOW WHITE WHEN SHE WAS JUST A LITTLE GIRL!
GRAMPA! BAFFROOM!
BATIUK & AYERS
YOU'RE YOUR MOTHER'S DAUGHTER ALL RIGHT!

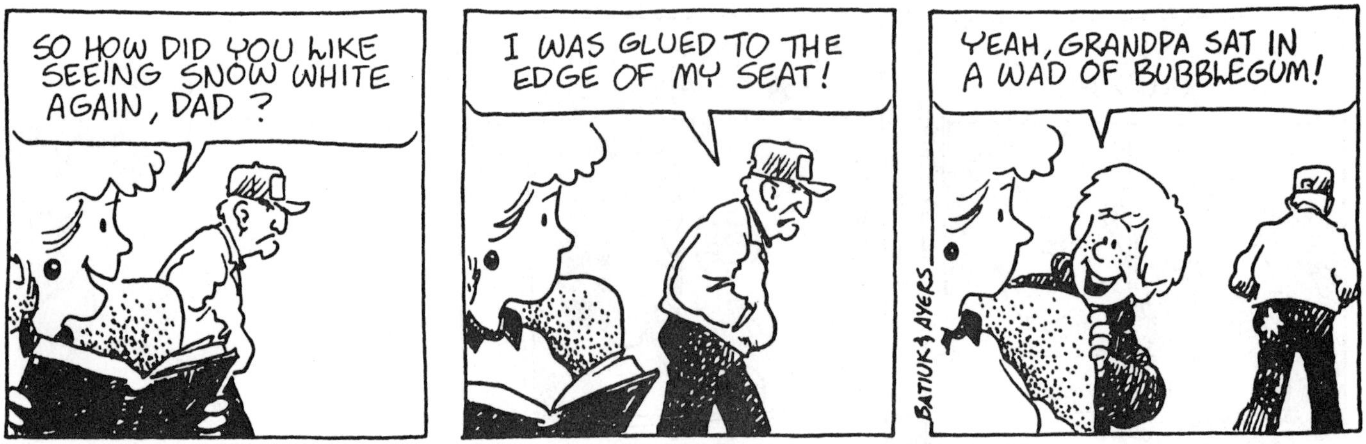
SO HOW DID YOU LIKE SEEING SNOW WHITE AGAIN, DAD?
I WAS GLUED TO THE EDGE OF MY SEAT!
BATIUK & AYERS
YEAH, GRANDPA SAT IN A WAD OF BUBBLEGUM!

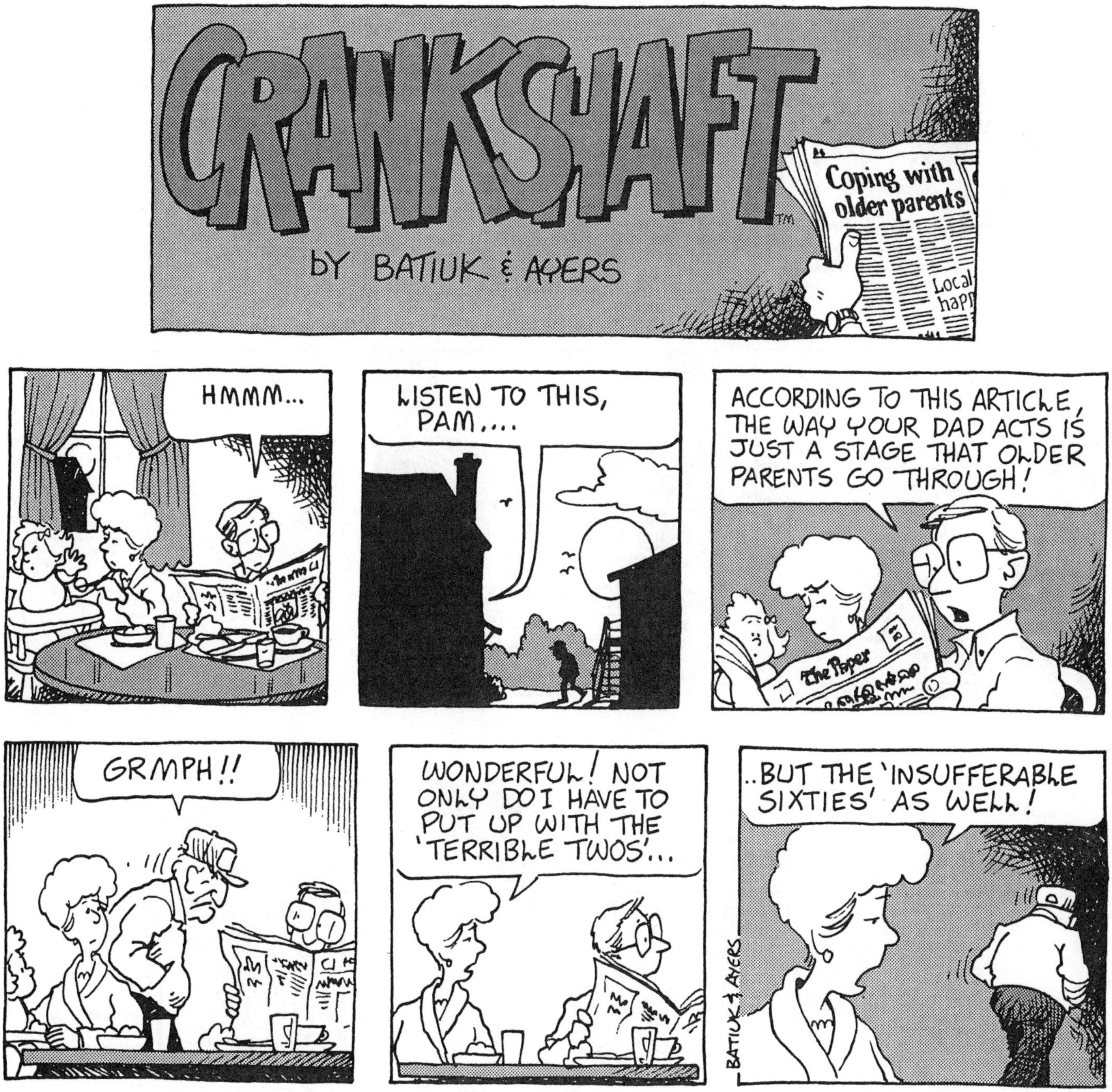
CRANKSHAFT™
BY BATIUK & AYERS
Coping with older parents
HMMM...
LISTEN TO THIS, PAM....
ACCORDING TO THIS ARTICLE, THE WAY YOUR DAD ACTS IS JUST A STAGE THAT OLDER PARENTS GO THROUGH!
The Paper
GRMPH!!
WONDERFUL! NOT ONLY DO I HAVE TO PUT UP WITH THE 'TERRIBLE TWOS'...
..BUT THE 'INSUFFERABLE SIXTIES' AS WELL!
BATIUK & AYERS

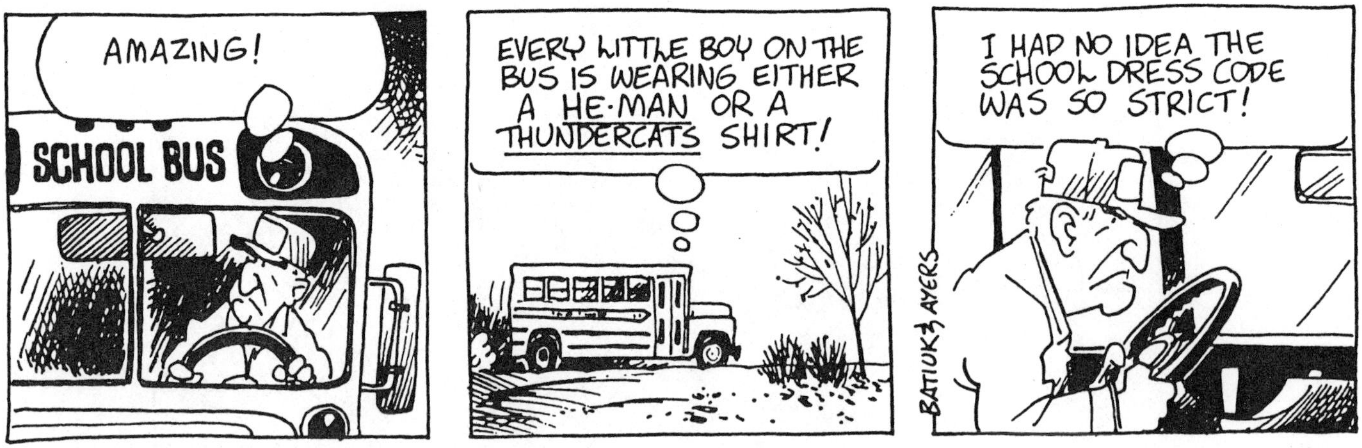
AMAZING!
SCHOOL BUS
EVERY LITTLE BOY ON THE BUS IS WEARING EITHER A HE-MAN OR A THUNDERCATS SHIRT!
BATIUK & AYERS
I HAD NO IDEA THE SCHOOL DRESS CODE WAS SO STRICT!

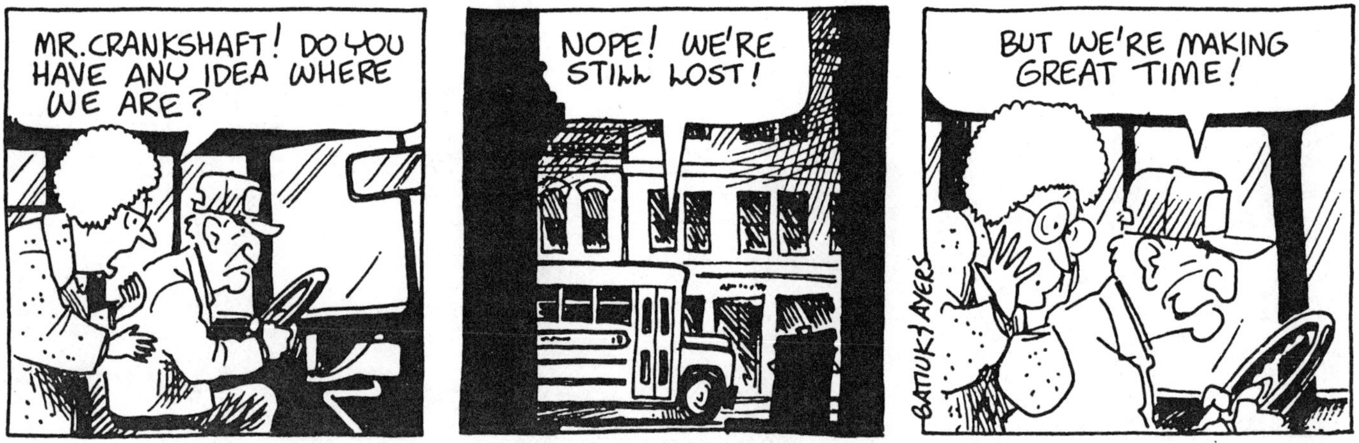
MR. CRANKSHAFT! DO YOU HAVE ANY IDEA WHERE WE ARE?
NOPE! WE'RE STILL LOST!
BATIUK & AYERS
BUT WE'RE MAKING GREAT TIME!

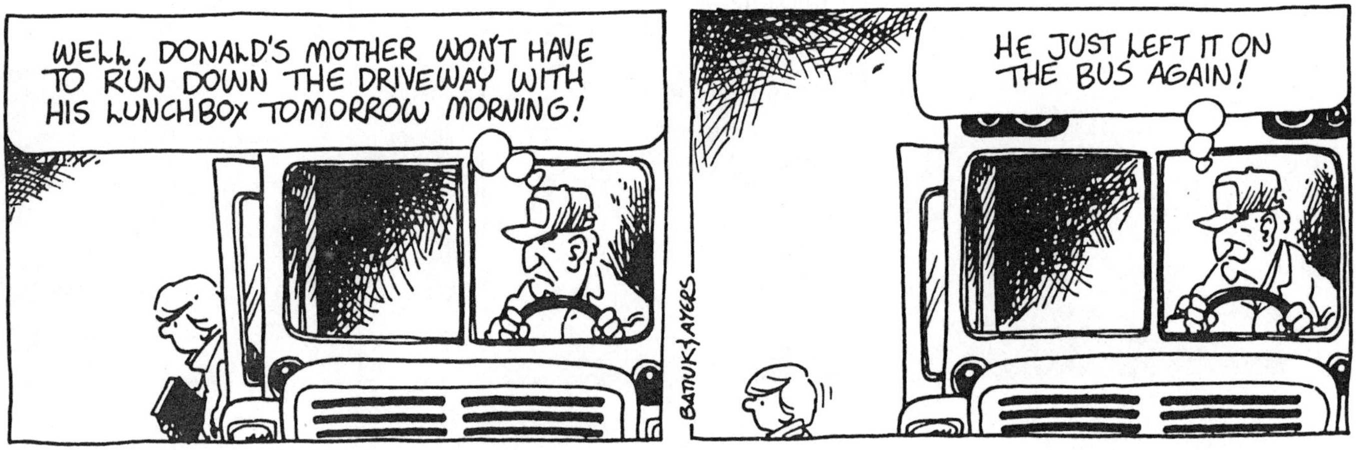
WELL, DONALD'S MOTHER WON'T HAVE TO RUN DOWN THE DRIVEWAY WITH HIS LUNCHBOX TOMORROW MORNING!
BATIUK & AYERS
HE JUST LEFT IT ON THE BUS AGAIN!

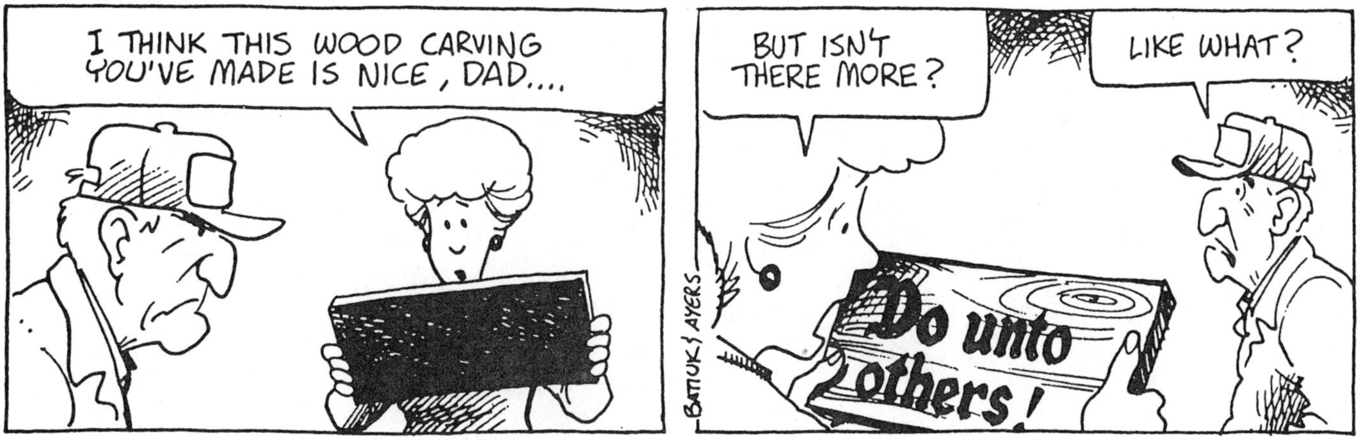
I THINK THIS WOOD CARVING YOU'VE MADE IS NICE, DAD....
BUT ISN'T THERE MORE?
LIKE WHAT?
Do unto others!
BATIUK & AYERS

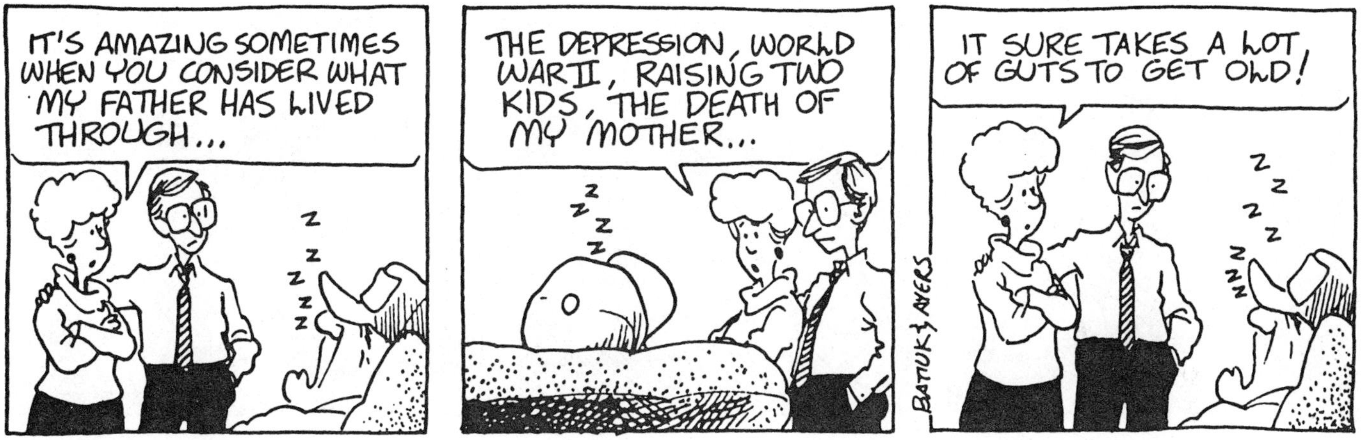
IT'S AMAZING SOMETIMES WHEN YOU CONSIDER WHAT MY FATHER HAS LIVED THROUGH...
THE DEPRESSION, WORLD WAR II, RAISING TWO KIDS, THE DEATH OF MY MOTHER...
IT SURE TAKES A LOT OF GUTS TO GET OLD!
BATIUK & AYERS

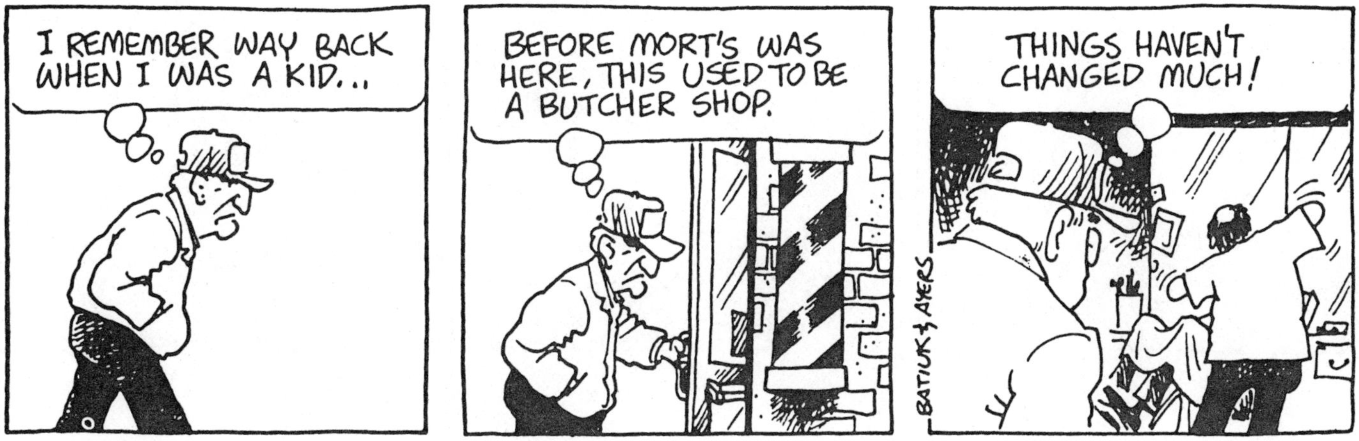
I REMEMBER WAY BACK WHEN I WAS A KID...
BEFORE MORT'S WAS HERE, THIS USED TO BE A BUTCHER SHOP.
THINGS HAVEN'T CHANGED MUCH!
BATIUK & AYERS

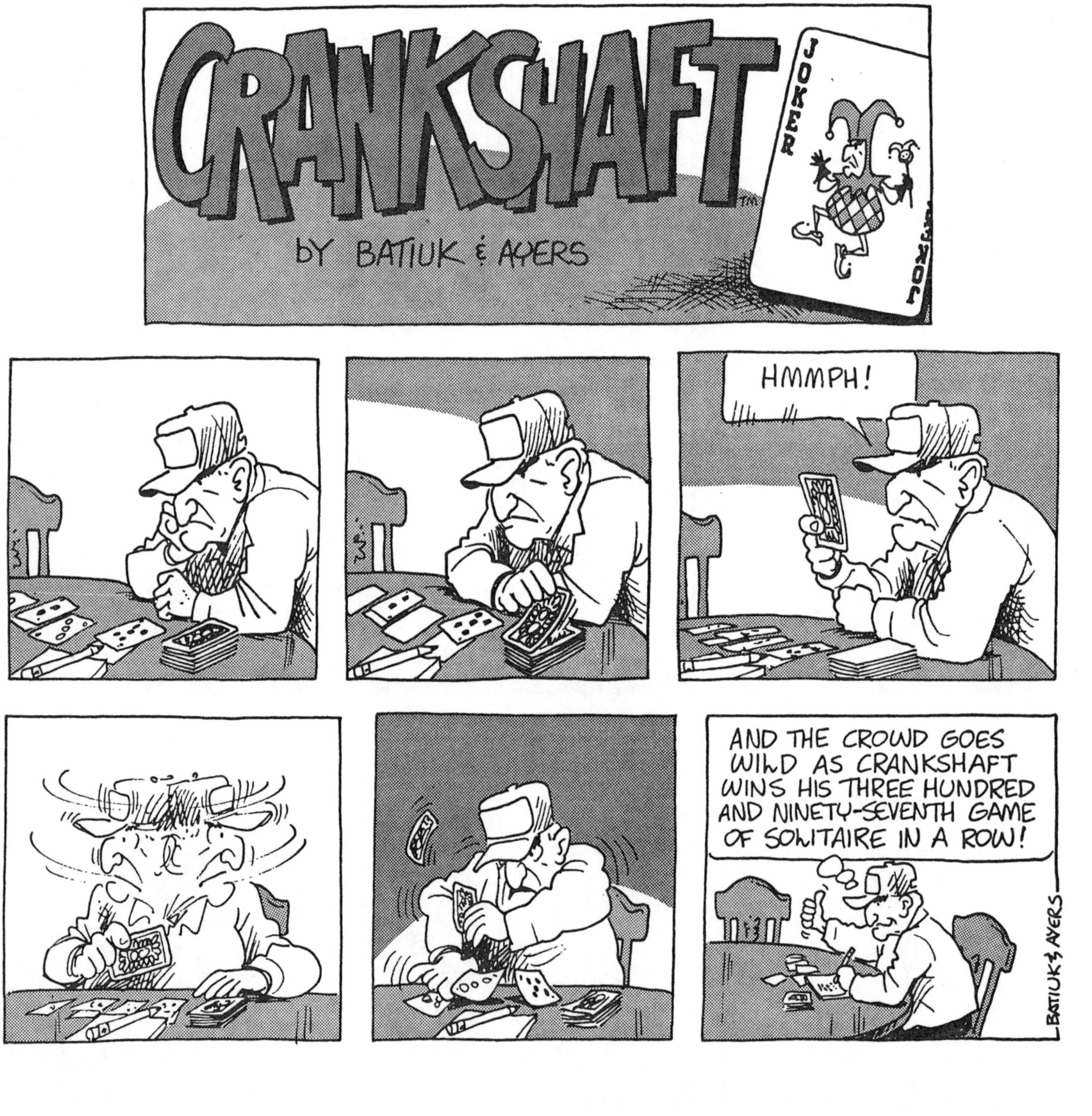
CRANKSHAFT
BY BATIUK & AYERS
JOKER
HMMPH!
AND THE CROWD GOES WILD AS CRANKSHAFT WINS HIS THREE HUNDRED AND NINETY-SEVENTH GAME OF SOLITAIRE IN A ROW!
BATIUK & AYERS

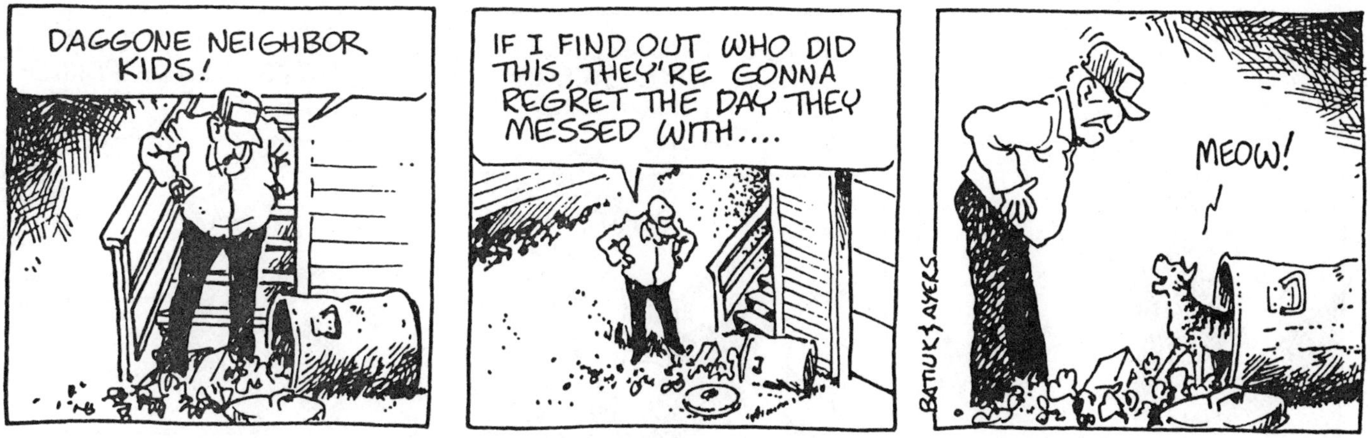
DAGGONE NEIGHBOR KIDS!
IF I FIND OUT WHO DID THIS, THEY'RE GONNA REGRET THE DAY THEY MESSED WITH....
MEOW!
BATIUK & AYERS

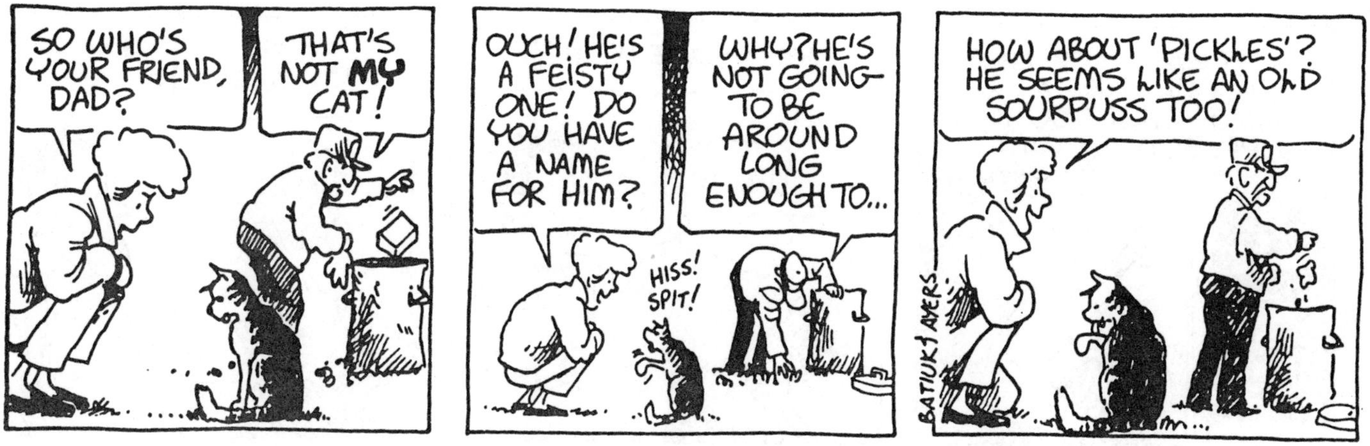
SO WHO'S YOUR FRIEND, DAD?
THAT'S NOT **MY** CAT!
OUCH! HE'S A FEISTY ONE! DO YOU HAVE A NAME FOR HIM?
HISS! SPIT!
WHY? HE'S NOT GOING TO BE AROUND LONG ENOUGH TO...
HOW ABOUT 'PICKLES'? HE SEEMS LIKE AN OLD SOURPUSS TOO!
BATIUK & AYERS

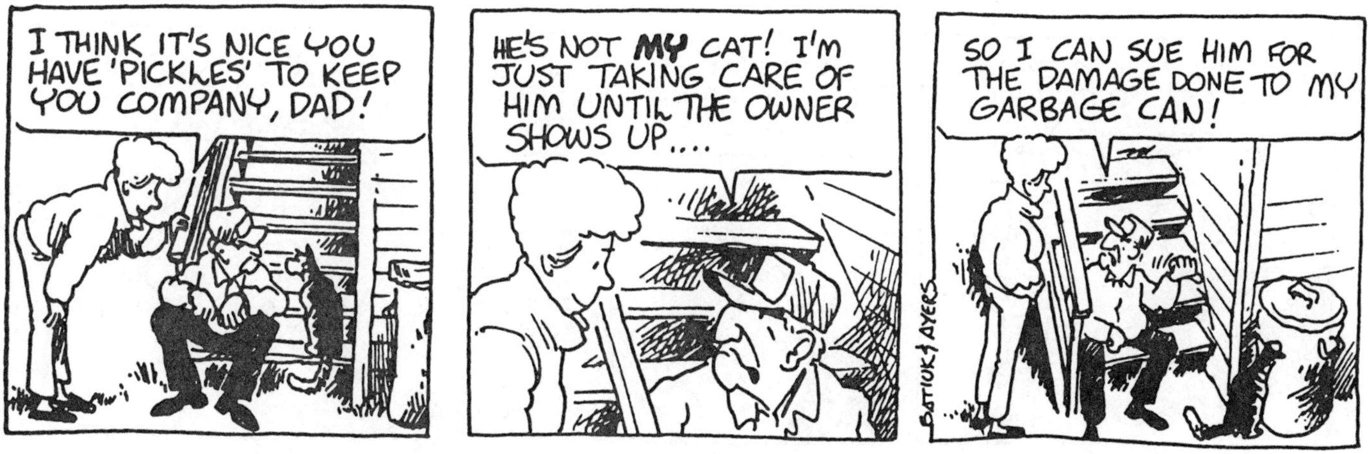
I THINK IT'S NICE YOU HAVE 'PICKLES' TO KEEP YOU COMPANY, DAD!
HE'S NOT **MY** CAT! I'M JUST TAKING CARE OF HIM UNTIL THE OWNER SHOWS UP....
SO I CAN SUE HIM FOR THE DAMAGE DONE TO MY GARBAGE CAN!
BATIUK & AYERS

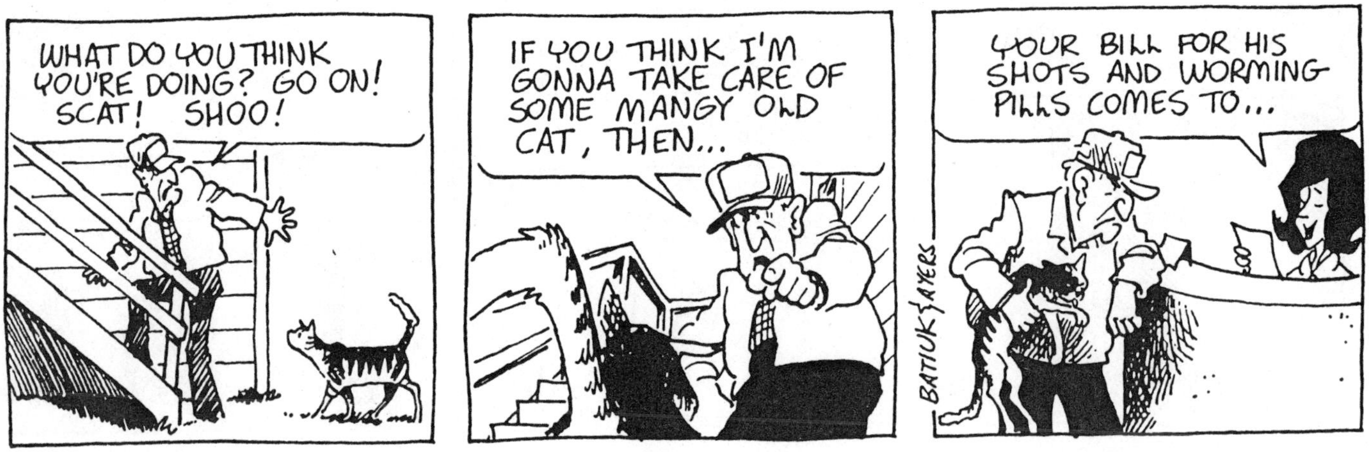
WHAT DO YOU THINK YOU'RE DOING? GO ON! SCAT! SHOO!
IF YOU THINK I'M GONNA TAKE CARE OF SOME MANGY OLD CAT, THEN...
YOUR BILL FOR HIS SHOTS AND WORMING PILLS COMES TO...
BATIUK & AYERS

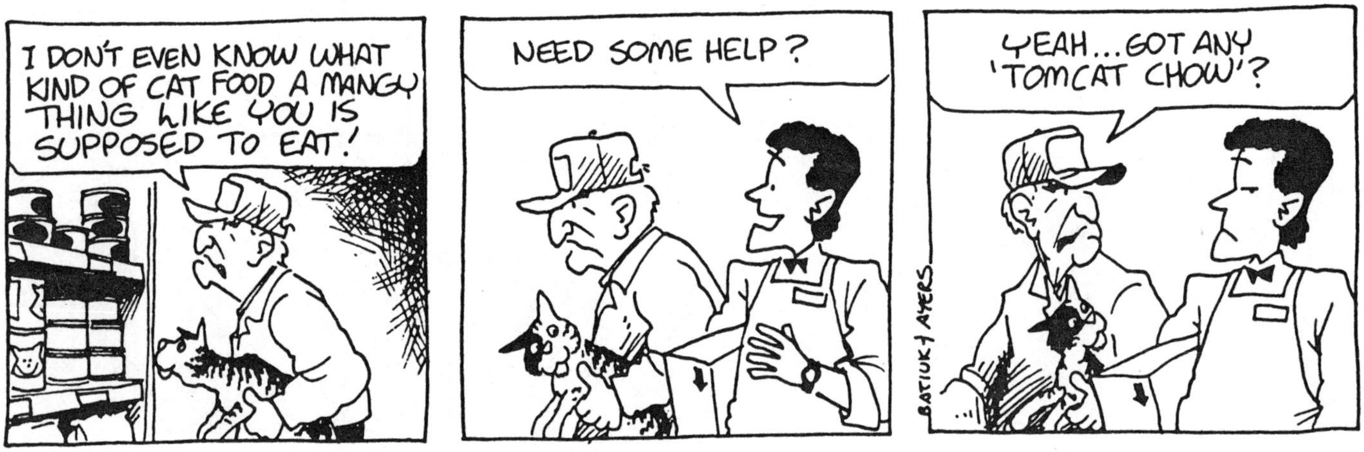
I DON'T EVEN KNOW WHAT KIND OF CAT FOOD A MANGY THING LIKE YOU IS SUPPOSED TO EAT!
NEED SOME HELP?
YEAH... GOT ANY 'TOMCAT CHOW'?
BATIUK & AYERS

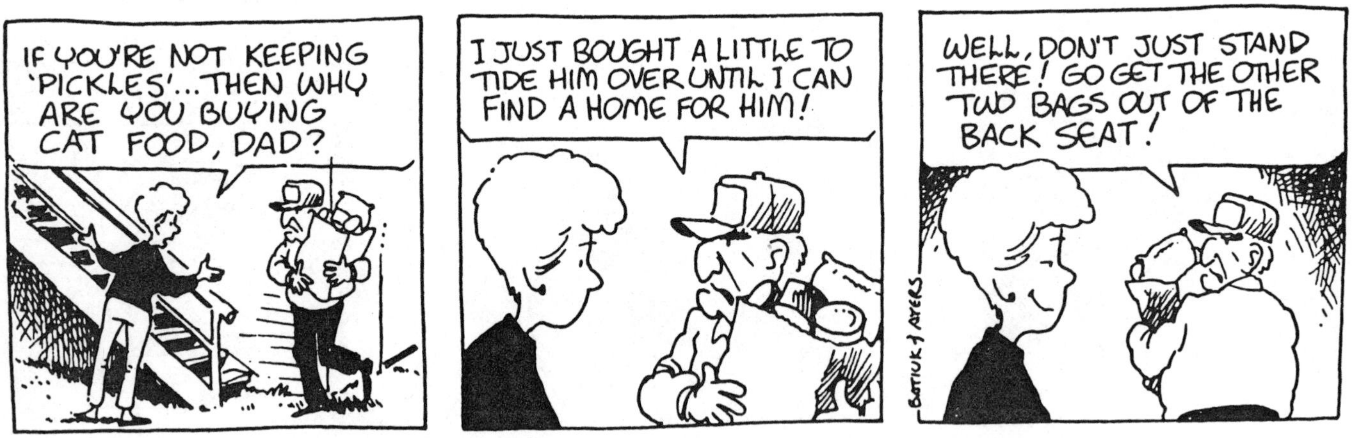
IF YOU'RE NOT KEEPING 'PICKLES'... THEN WHY ARE YOU BUYING CAT FOOD, DAD?
I JUST BOUGHT A LITTLE TO TIDE HIM OVER UNTIL I CAN FIND A HOME FOR HIM!
WELL, DON'T JUST STAND THERE! GO GET THE OTHER TWO BAGS OUT OF THE BACK SEAT!
BATIUK & AYERS

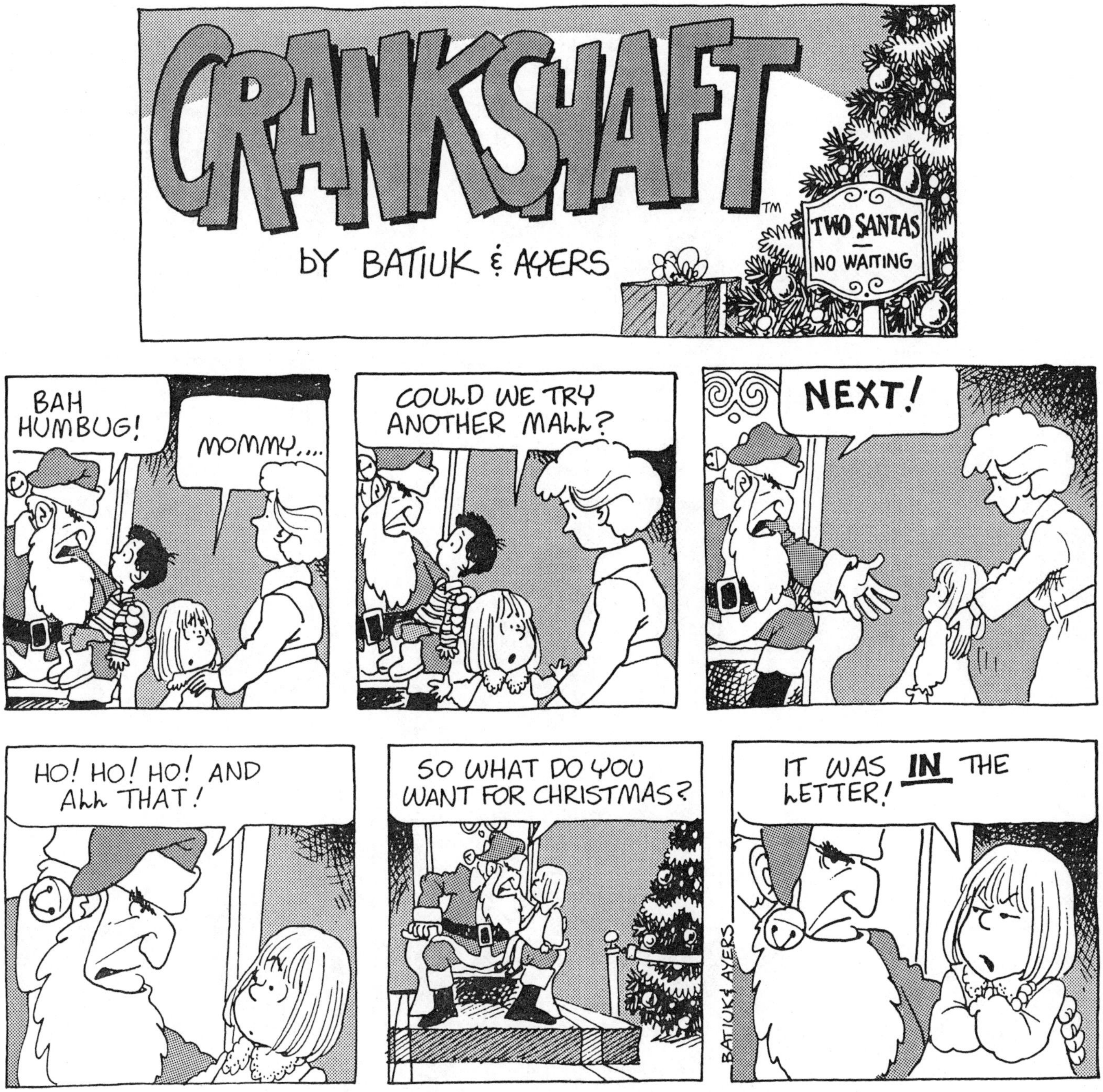
CRANKSHAFT
BY BATIUK & AYERS
TWO SANTAS — NO WAITING
BAH HUMBUG!
MOMMY,...
COULD WE TRY ANOTHER MALL?
NEXT!
HO! HO! HO! AND ALL THAT!
SO WHAT DO YOU WANT FOR CHRISTMAS?
BATIUK & AYERS
IT WAS **IN** THE LETTER!

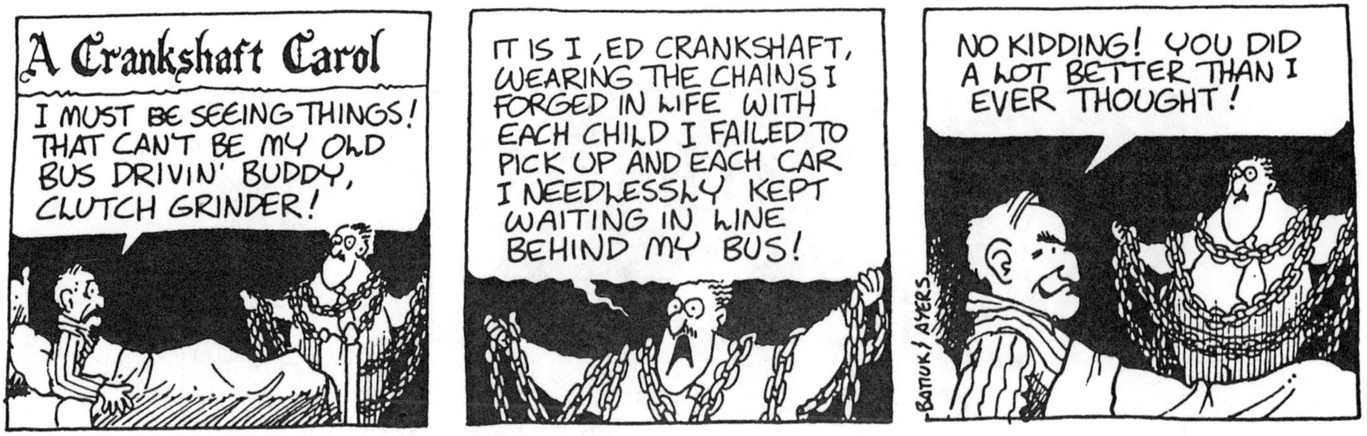
A Crankshaft Carol
I MUST BE SEEING THINGS! THAT CAN'T BE MY OLD BUS DRIVIN' BUDDY, CLUTCH GRINDER!
IT IS I, ED CRANKSHAFT, WEARING THE CHAINS I FORGED IN LIFE WITH EACH CHILD I FAILED TO PICK UP AND EACH CAR I NEEDLESSLY KEPT WAITING IN LINE BEHIND MY BUS!
NO KIDDING! YOU DID A LOT BETTER THAN I EVER THOUGHT!
BATIUK / AYERS

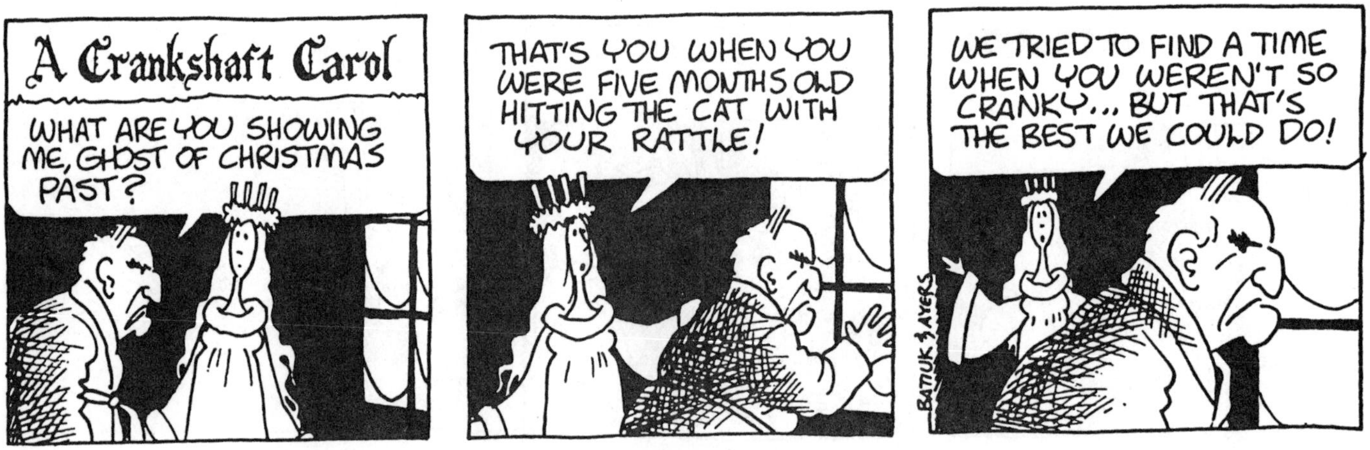
A Crankshaft Carol
WHAT ARE YOU SHOWING ME, GHOST OF CHRISTMAS PAST?
THAT'S YOU WHEN YOU WERE FIVE MONTHS OLD HITTING THE CAT WITH YOUR RATTLE!
WE TRIED TO FIND A TIME WHEN YOU WEREN'T SO CRANKY... BUT THAT'S THE BEST WE COULD DO!
BATIUK & AYERS

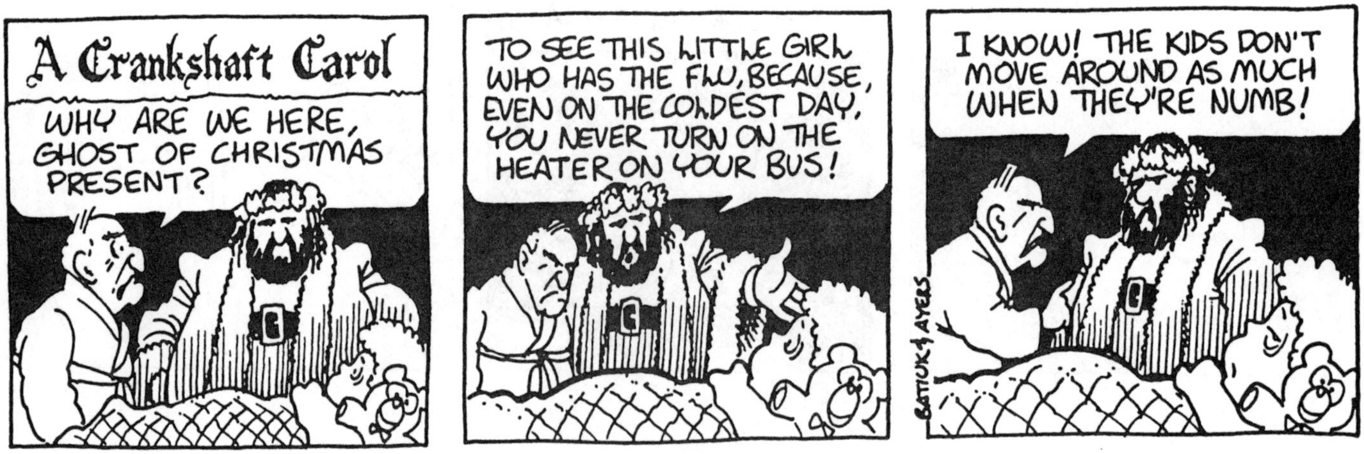
A Crankshaft Carol
WHY ARE WE HERE, GHOST OF CHRISTMAS PRESENT?
TO SEE THIS LITTLE GIRL WHO HAS THE FLU, BECAUSE, EVEN ON THE COLDEST DAY, YOU NEVER TURN ON THE HEATER ON YOUR BUS!
I KNOW! THE KIDS DON'T MOVE AROUND AS MUCH WHEN THEY'RE NUMB!
BATIUK & AYERS

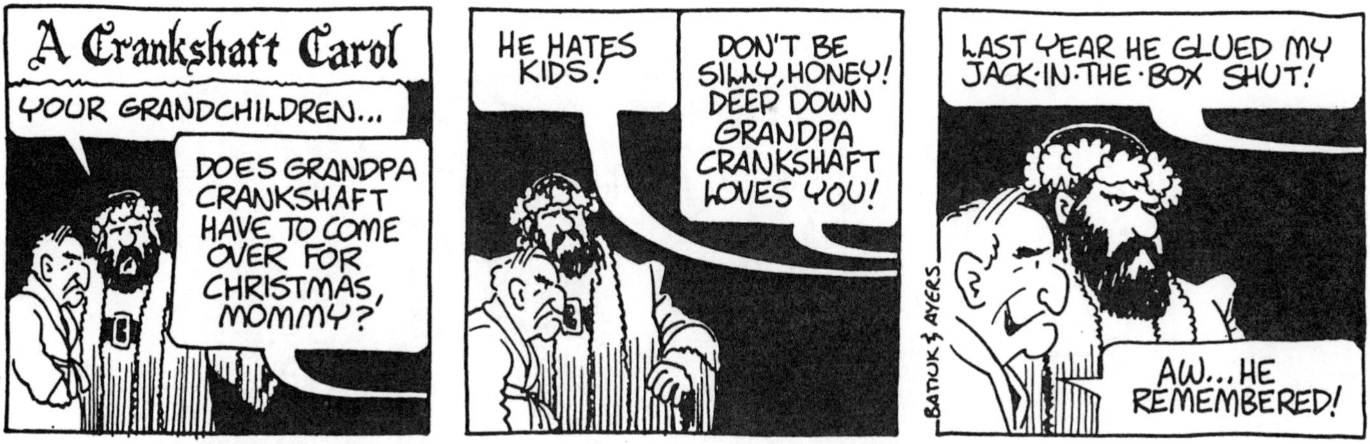
A Crankshaft Carol
YOUR GRANDCHILDREN...
DOES GRANDPA CRANKSHAFT HAVE TO COME OVER FOR CHRISTMAS, MOMMY?
HE HATES KIDS!
DON'T BE SILLY, HONEY! DEEP DOWN GRANDPA CRANKSHAFT LOVES YOU!
LAST YEAR HE GLUED MY JACK-IN-THE-BOX SHUT!
AW... HE REMEMBERED!
BATIUK & AYERS

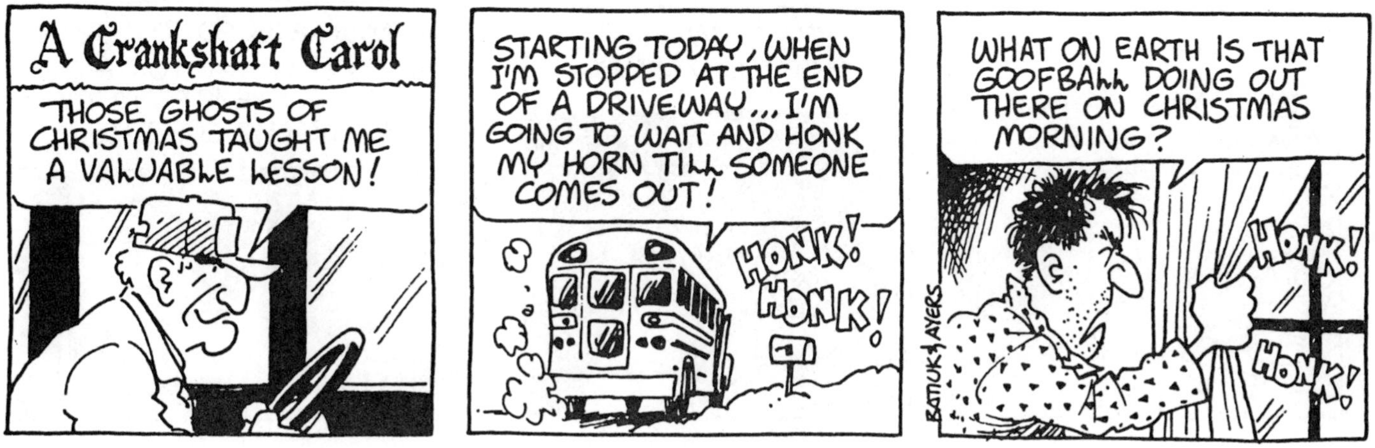
A Crankshaft Carol
THOSE GHOSTS OF CHRISTMAS TAUGHT ME A VALUABLE LESSON!
STARTING TODAY, WHEN I'M STOPPED AT THE END OF A DRIVEWAY... I'M GOING TO WAIT AND HONK MY HORN TILL SOMEONE COMES OUT!
HONK! HONK!
BATIUK & AYERS
WHAT ON EARTH IS THAT GOOFBALL DOING OUT THERE ON CHRISTMAS MORNING?
HONK!
HONK!

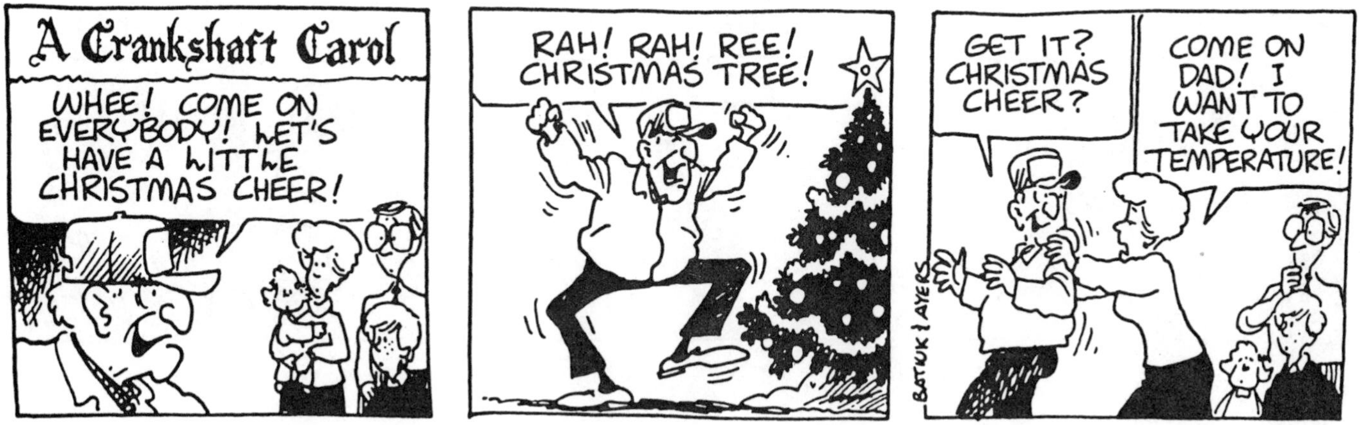
A Crankshaft Carol
WHEE! COME ON EVERYBODY! LET'S HAVE A LITTLE CHRISTMAS CHEER!
RAH! RAH! REE! CHRISTMAS TREE!
GET IT? CHRISTMAS CHEER?
COME ON DAD! I WANT TO TAKE YOUR TEMPERATURE!
BATIUK & AYERS

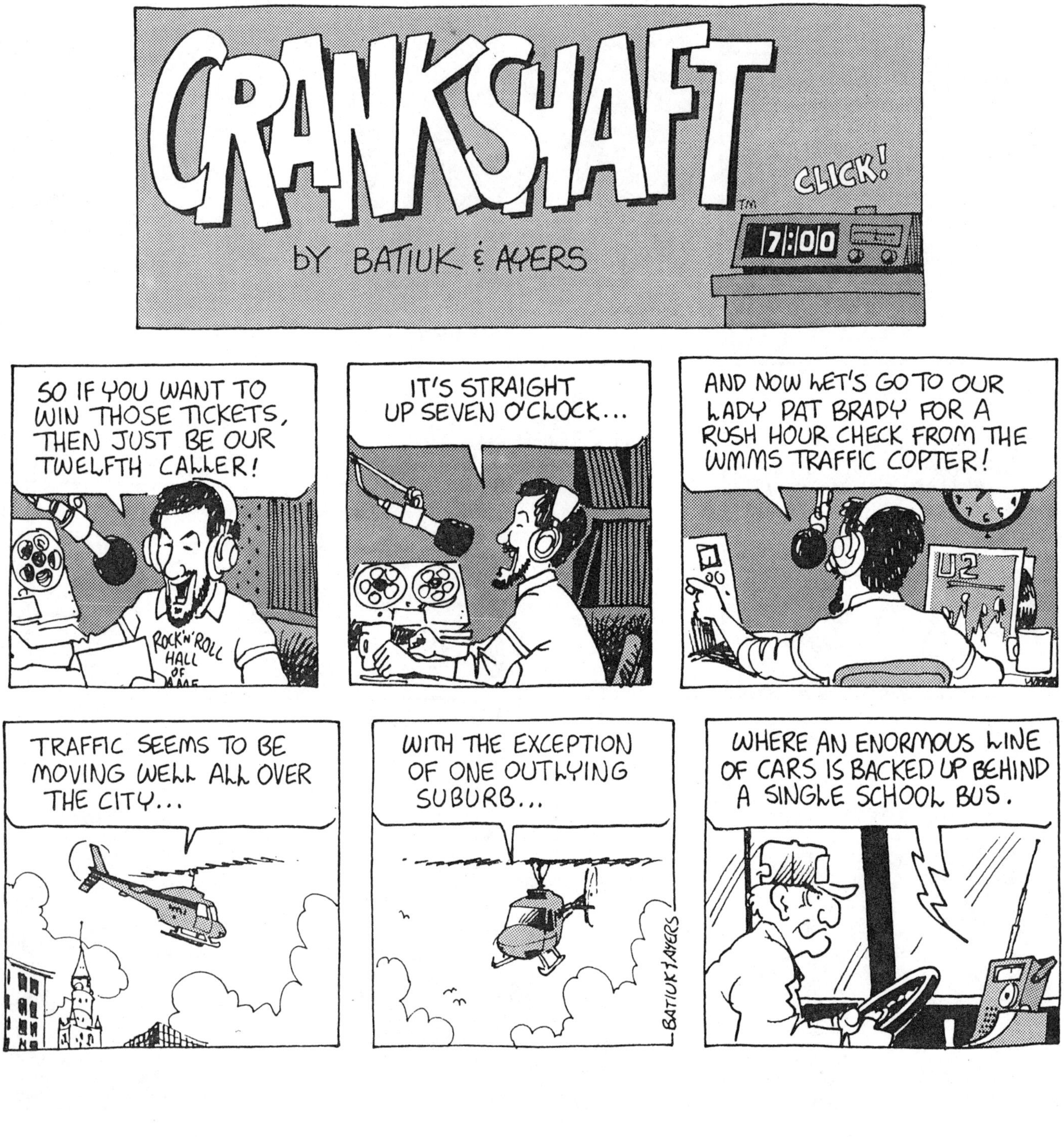
CRANKSHAFT
TM
BY BATIUK & AYERS
CLICK!
7:00
SO IF YOU WANT TO WIN THOSE TICKETS, THEN JUST BE OUR TWELFTH CALLER!
ROCK'N'ROLL HALL OF
IT'S STRAIGHT UP SEVEN O'CLOCK...
AND NOW LET'S GO TO OUR LADY PAT BRADY FOR A RUSH HOUR CHECK FROM THE WMMS TRAFFIC COPTER!
U2
TRAFFIC SEEMS TO BE MOVING WELL ALL OVER THE CITY...
WITH THE EXCEPTION OF ONE OUTLYING SUBURB...
BATIUK & AYERS
WHERE AN ENORMOUS LINE OF CARS IS BACKED UP BEHIND A SINGLE SCHOOL BUS.

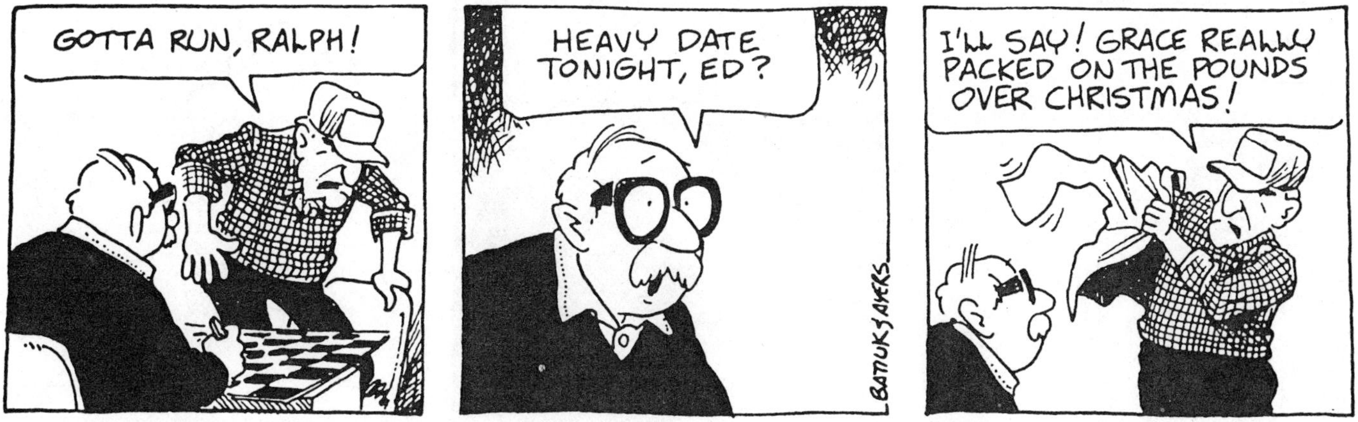
GOTTA RUN, RALPH!
HEAVY DATE TONIGHT, ED?
I'LL SAY! GRACE REALLY PACKED ON THE POUNDS OVER CHRISTMAS!
BATIUK & AYERS

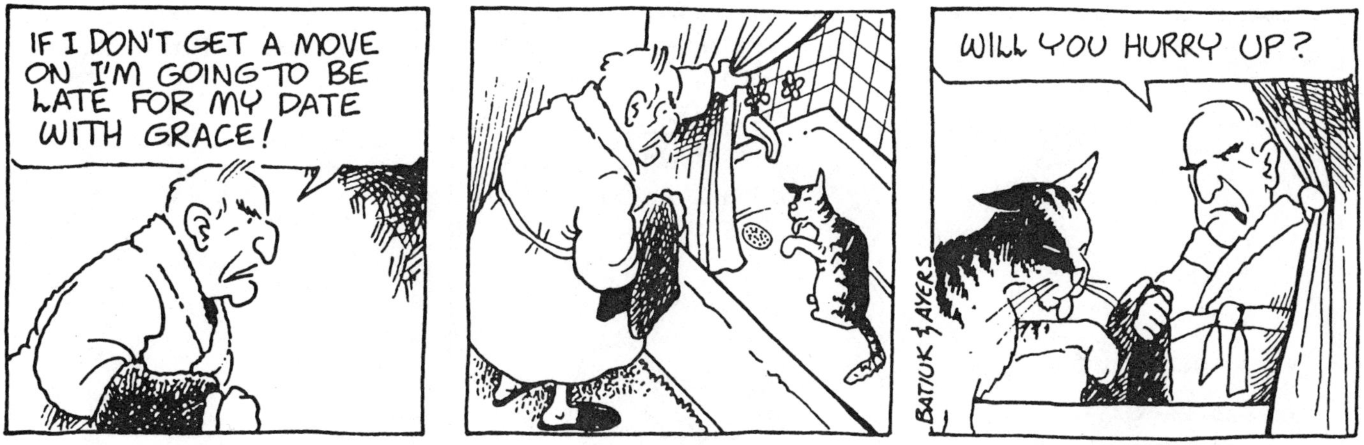
IF I DON'T GET A MOVE ON I'M GOING TO BE LATE FOR MY DATE WITH GRACE!
WILL YOU HURRY UP?
BATIUK & AYERS

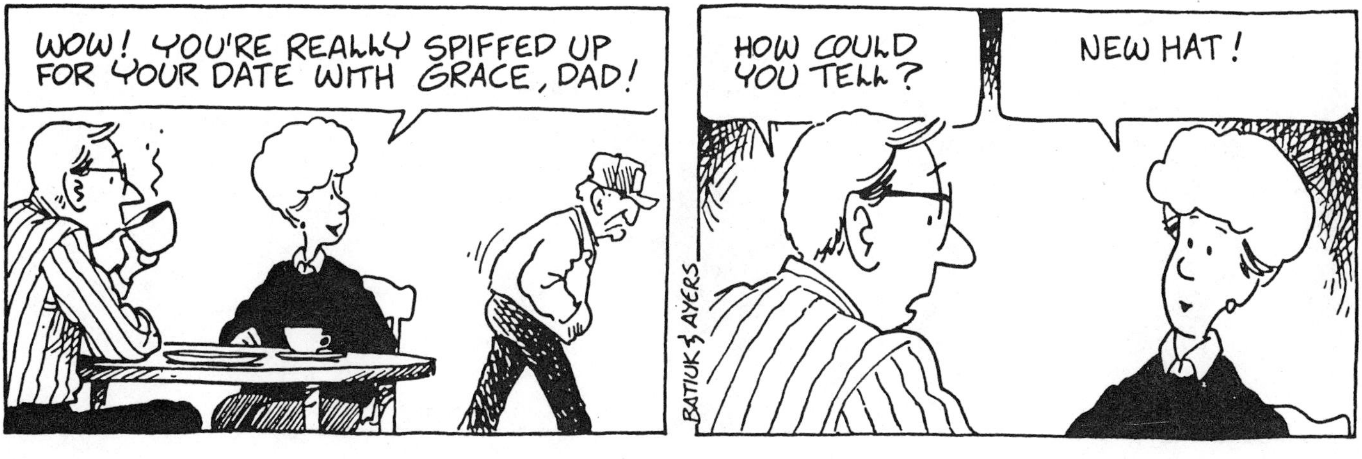
WOW! YOU'RE REALLY SPIFFED UP FOR YOUR DATE WITH GRACE, DAD!
HOW COULD YOU TELL?
NEW HAT!
BATIUK & AYERS

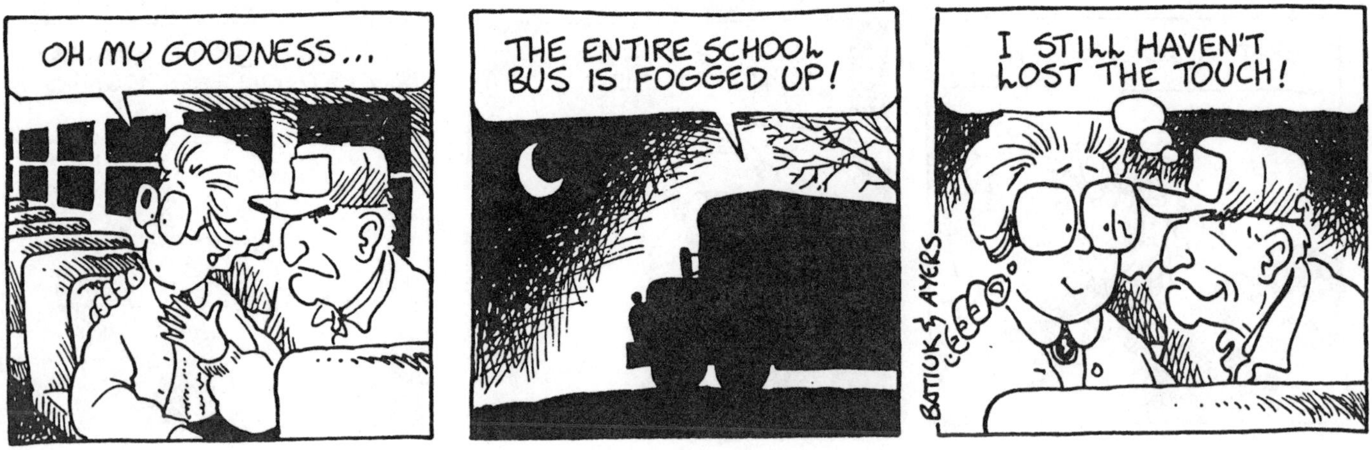
OH MY GOODNESS...
THE ENTIRE SCHOOL BUS IS FOGGED UP!
I STILL HAVEN'T LOST THE TOUCH!
BATIUK & AYERS

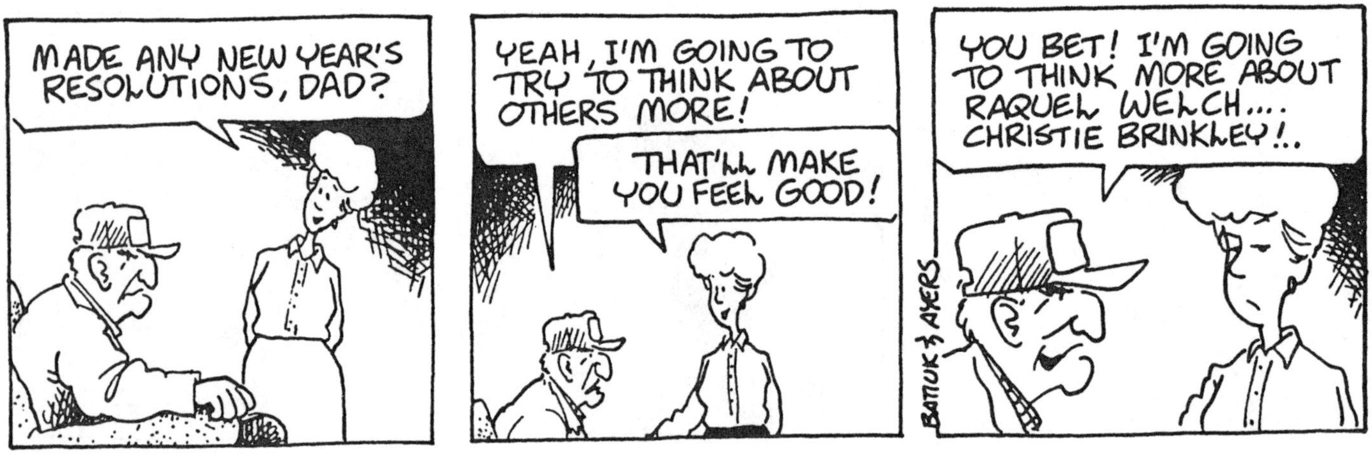
MADE ANY NEW YEAR'S RESOLUTIONS, DAD?
YEAH, I'M GOING TO TRY TO THINK ABOUT OTHERS MORE!
THAT'LL MAKE YOU FEEL GOOD!
YOU BET! I'M GOING TO THINK MORE ABOUT RAQUEL WELCH.... CHRISTIE BRINKLEY!..
BATIUK & AYERS

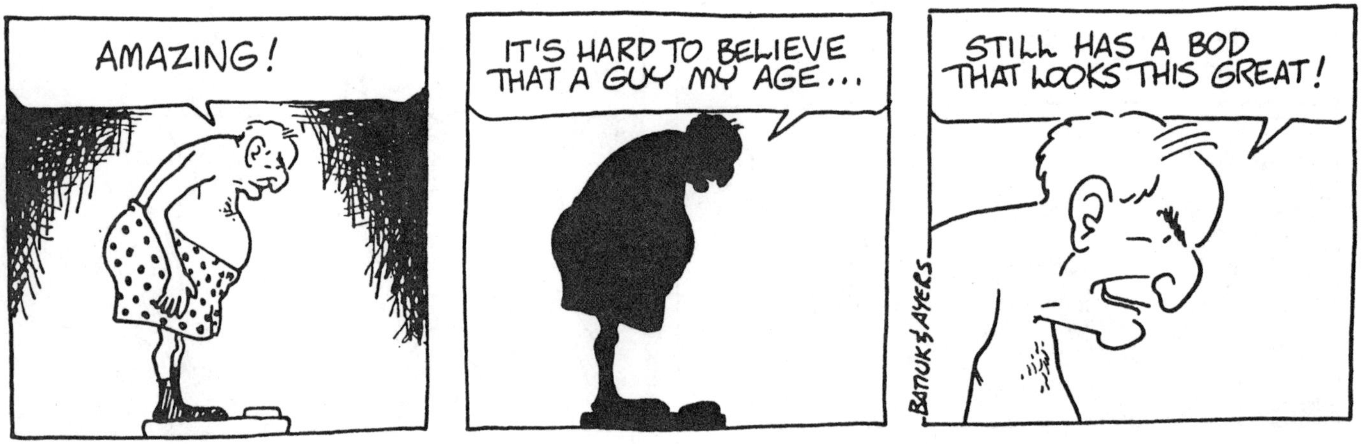
AMAZING!
IT'S HARD TO BELIEVE THAT A GUY MY AGE...
STILL HAS A BOD THAT LOOKS THIS GREAT!
BATIUK & AYERS

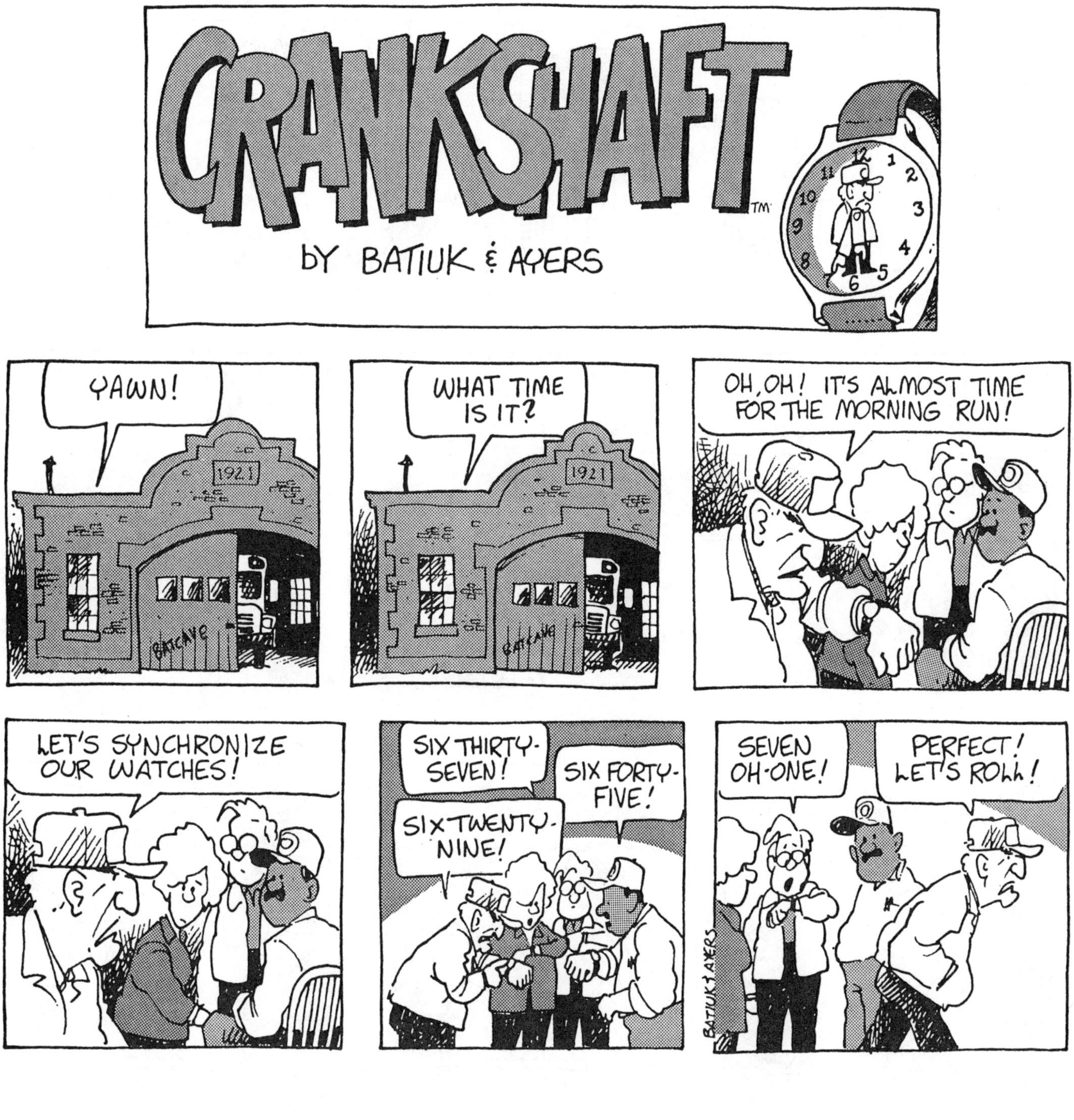

CRANKSHAFT
BY BATIUK & AYERS
1921
BATCAVE
YAWN!
WHAT TIME IS IT?
OH, OH! IT'S ALMOST TIME FOR THE MORNING RUN!
LET'S SYNCHRONIZE OUR WATCHES!
SIX THIRTY-SEVEN!
SIX FORTY-FIVE!
SIX TWENTY-NINE!
SEVEN OH-ONE!
PERFECT! LET'S ROLL!
BATIUK & AYERS

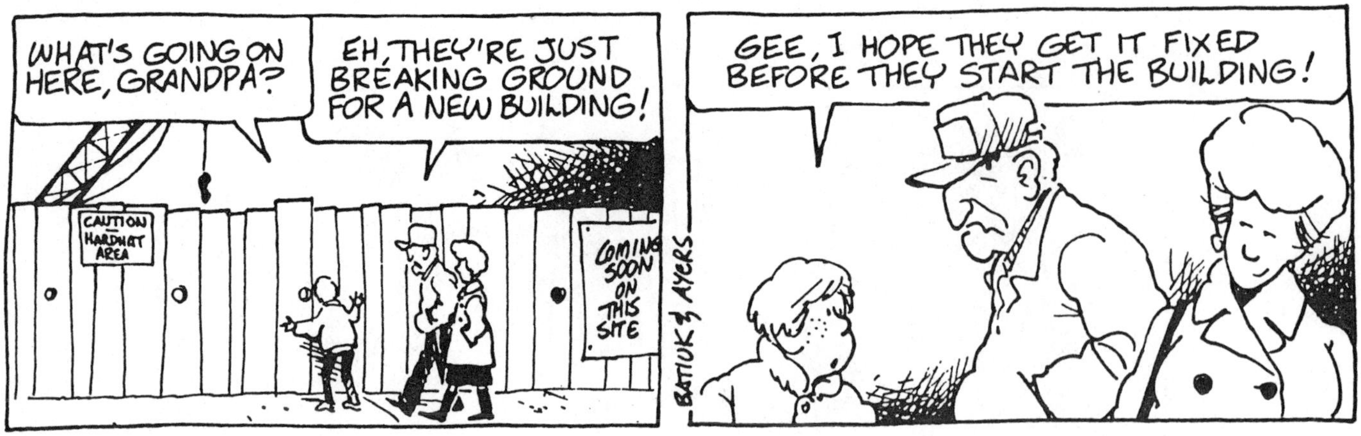
WHAT'S GOING ON HERE, GRANDPA?
EH, THEY'RE JUST BREAKING GROUND FOR A NEW BUILDING!
CAUTION — HARDHAT AREA
COMING SOON ON THIS SITE
BATIUK & AYERS
GEE, I HOPE THEY GET IT FIXED BEFORE THEY START THE BUILDING!

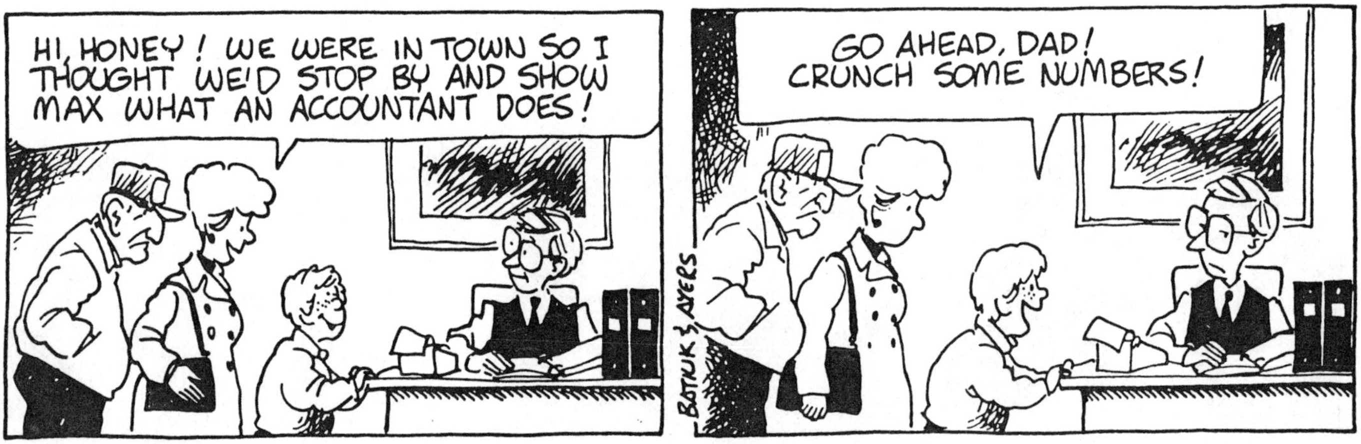
HI, HONEY! WE WERE IN TOWN SO I THOUGHT WE'D STOP BY AND SHOW MAX WHAT AN ACCOUNTANT DOES!
BATIUK & AYERS
GO AHEAD, DAD! CRUNCH SOME NUMBERS!

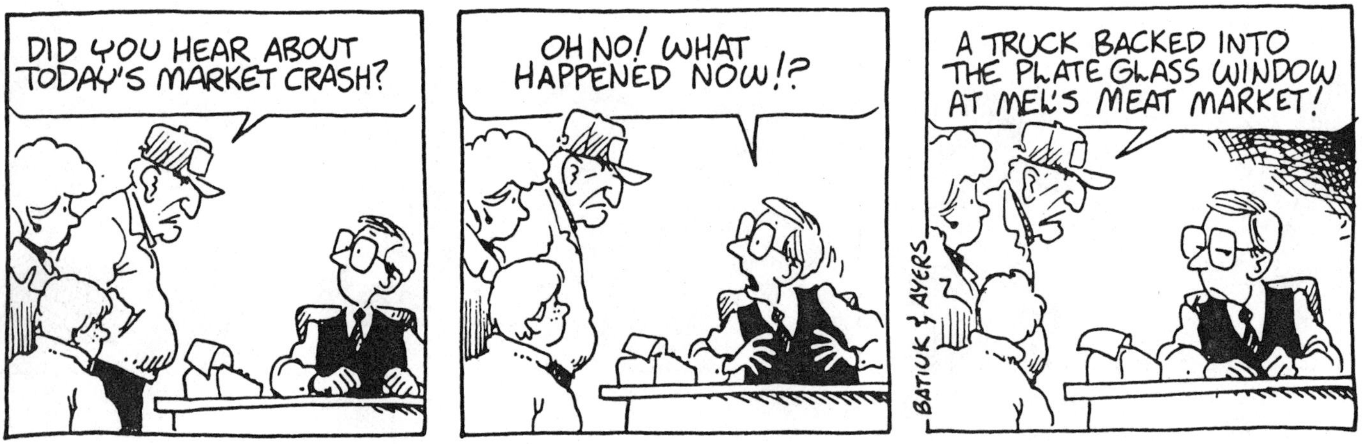
DID YOU HEAR ABOUT TODAY'S MARKET CRASH?
OH NO! WHAT HAPPENED NOW!?
BATIUK & AYERS
A TRUCK BACKED INTO THE PLATE GLASS WINDOW AT MEL'S MEAT MARKET!

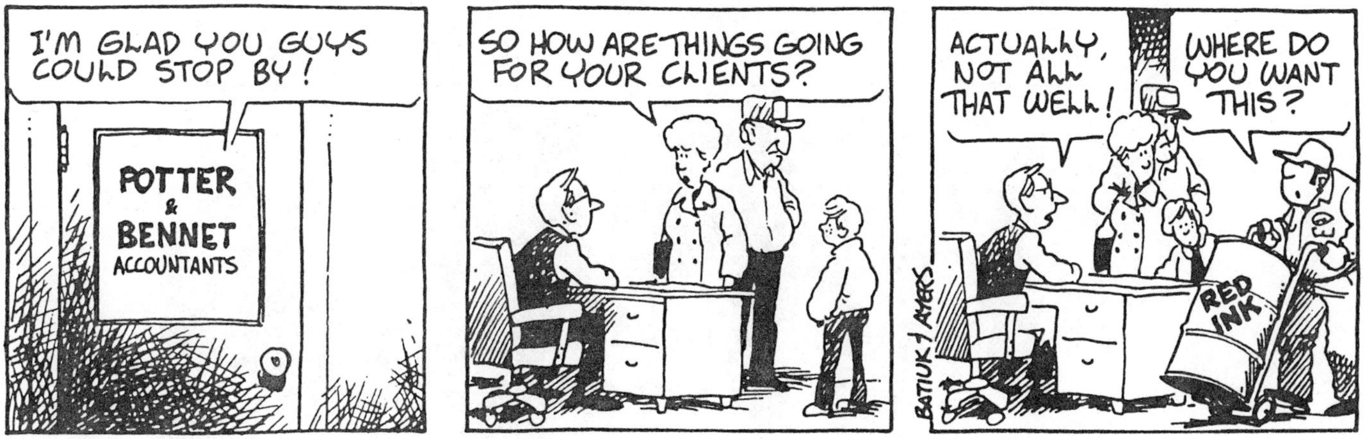
I'M GLAD YOU GUYS COULD STOP BY!
POTTER & BENNET ACCOUNTANTS
SO HOW ARE THINGS GOING FOR YOUR CLIENTS?
ACTUALLY, NOT ALL THAT WELL!
WHERE DO YOU WANT THIS?
RED INK

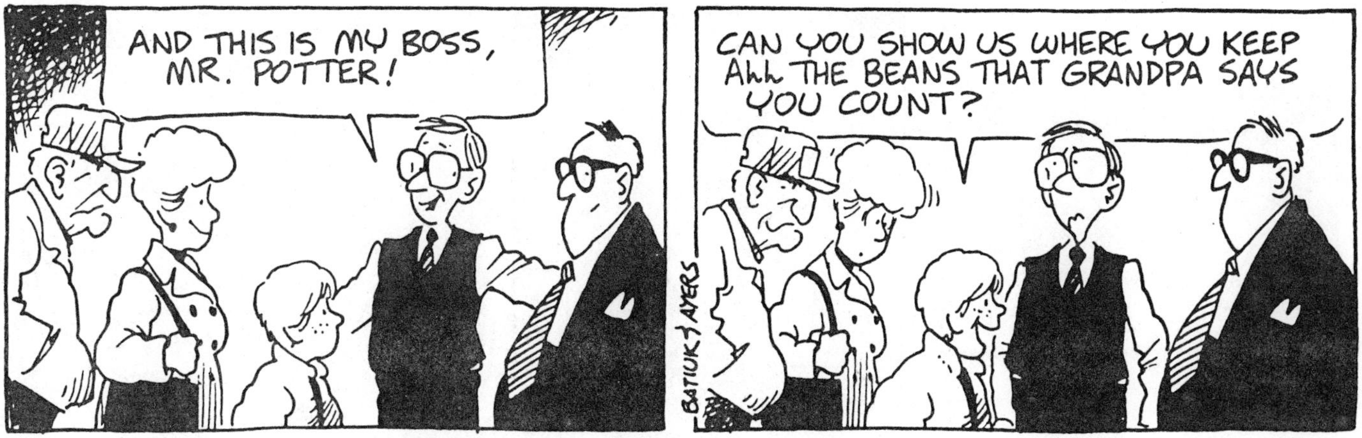
AND THIS IS MY BOSS, MR. POTTER!
CAN YOU SHOW US WHERE YOU KEEP ALL THE BEANS THAT GRANDPA SAYS YOU COUNT?

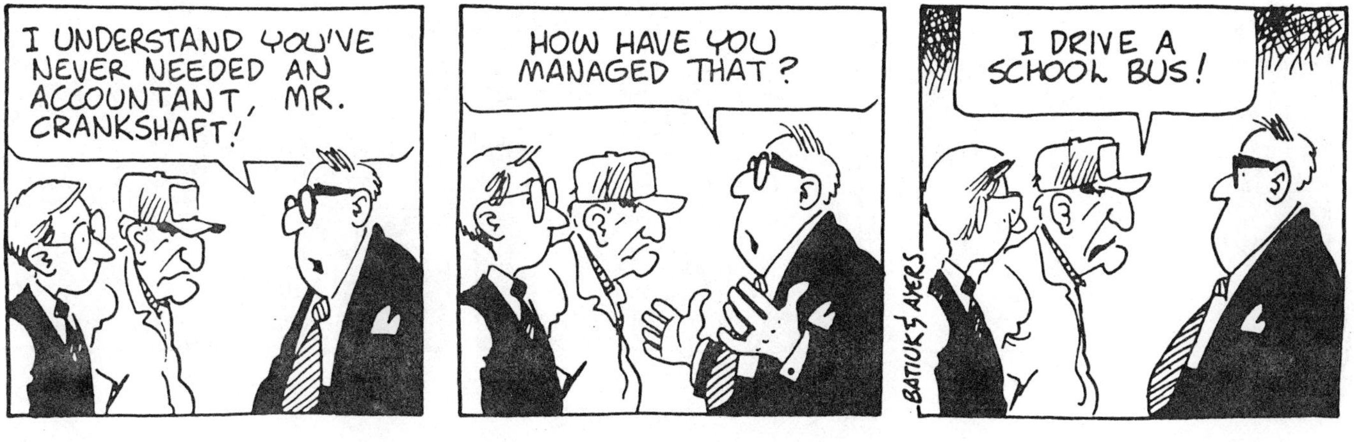
I UNDERSTAND YOU'VE NEVER NEEDED AN ACCOUNTANT, MR. CRANKSHAFT!
HOW HAVE YOU MANAGED THAT?
I DRIVE A SCHOOL BUS!

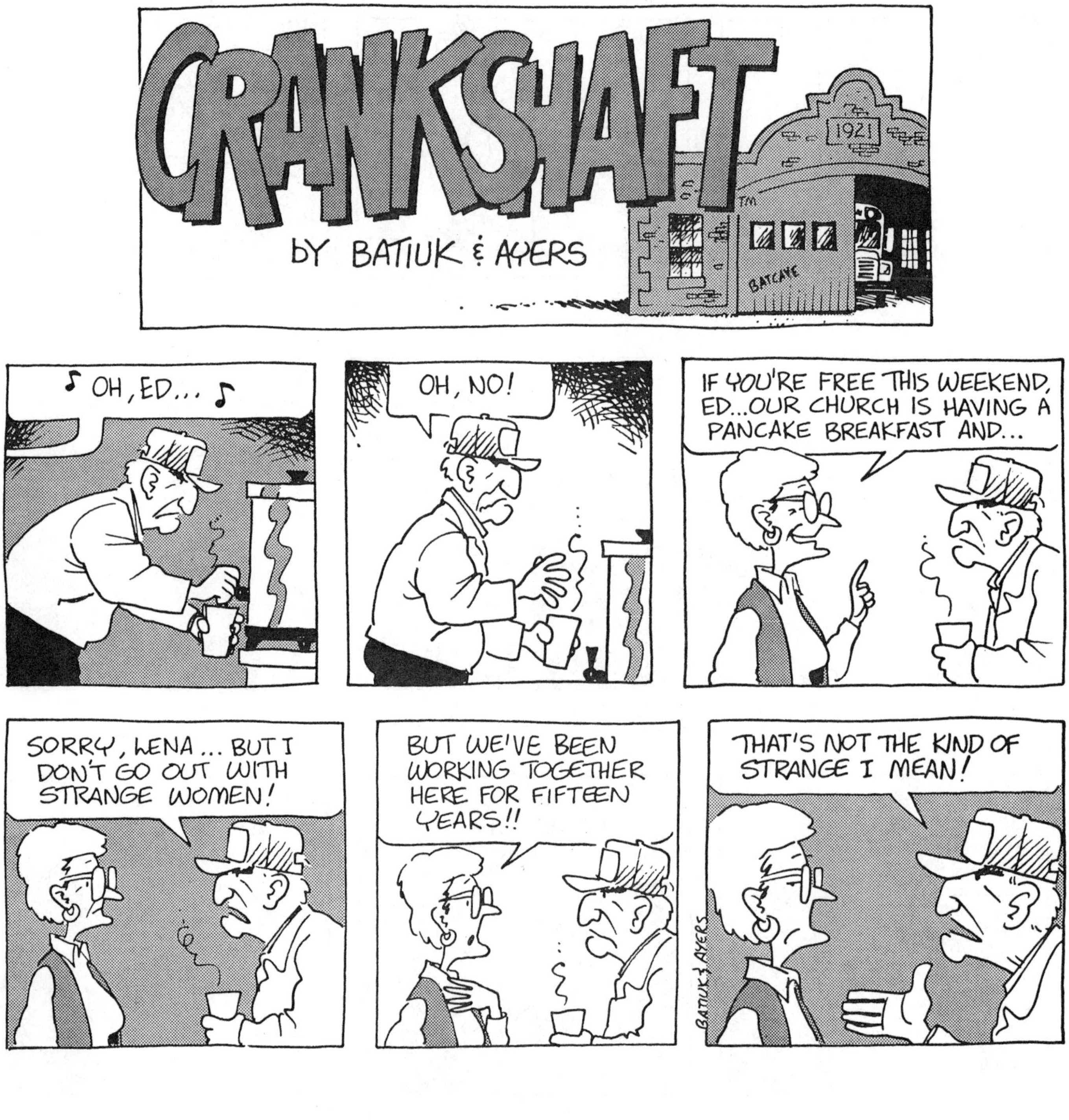
CRANKSHAFT
BY BATIUK & AYERS
1921
BATCAVE
OH, ED...
OH, NO!
IF YOU'RE FREE THIS WEEKEND, ED...OUR CHURCH IS HAVING A PANCAKE BREAKFAST AND...
SORRY, LENA... BUT I DON'T GO OUT WITH STRANGE WOMEN!
BUT WE'VE BEEN WORKING TOGETHER HERE FOR FIFTEEN YEARS!!
BATIUK & AYERS
THAT'S NOT THE KIND OF STRANGE I MEAN!

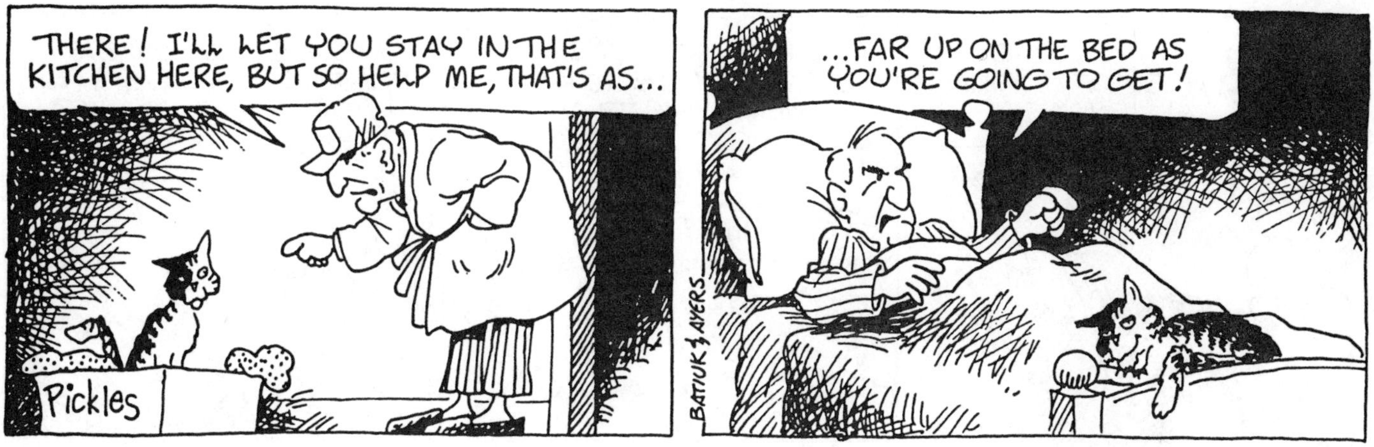
THERE! I'LL LET YOU STAY IN THE KITCHEN HERE, BUT SO HELP ME, THAT'S AS...
Pickles
BATIUK & AYERS
...FAR UP ON THE BED AS YOU'RE GOING TO GET!

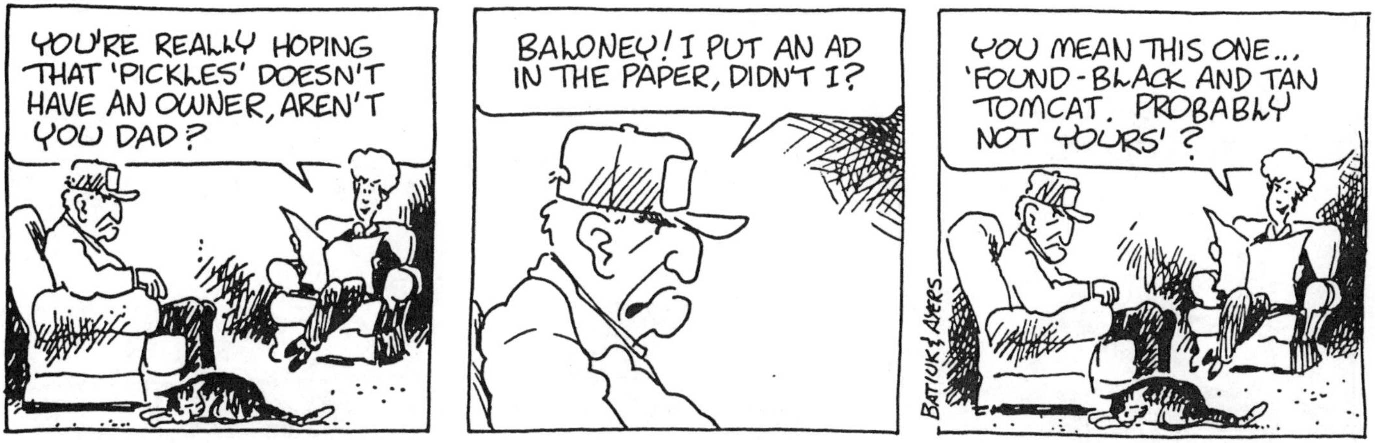
YOU'RE REALLY HOPING THAT 'PICKLES' DOESN'T HAVE AN OWNER, AREN'T YOU DAD?
BALONEY! I PUT AN AD IN THE PAPER, DIDN'T I?
BATIUK & AYERS
YOU MEAN THIS ONE... 'FOUND - BLACK AND TAN TOMCAT. PROBABLY NOT YOURS'?

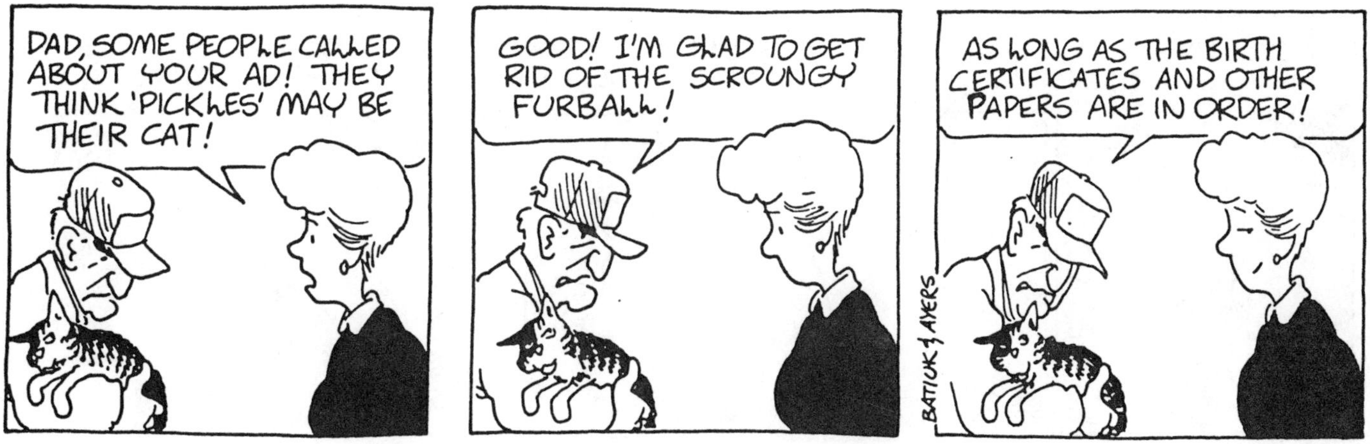
DAD, SOME PEOPLE CALLED ABOUT YOUR AD! THEY THINK 'PICKLES' MAY BE THEIR CAT!
GOOD! I'M GLAD TO GET RID OF THE SCROUNGY FURBALL!
BATIUK & AYERS
AS LONG AS THE BIRTH CERTIFICATES AND OTHER PAPERS ARE IN ORDER!

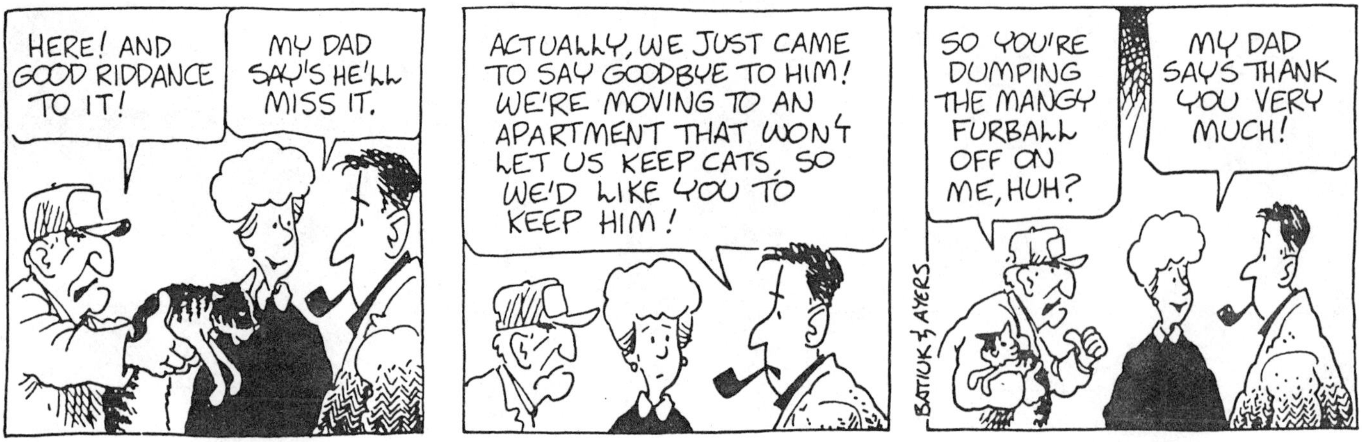
HERE! AND GOOD RIDDANCE TO IT!
MY DAD SAY'S HE'LL MISS IT.
ACTUALLY, WE JUST CAME TO SAY GOODBYE TO HIM! WE'RE MOVING TO AN APARTMENT THAT WON'T LET US KEEP CATS, SO WE'D LIKE YOU TO KEEP HIM!
SO YOU'RE DUMPING THE MANGY FURBALL OFF ON ME, HUH?
MY DAD SAYS THANK YOU VERY MUCH!
BATIUK & AYERS

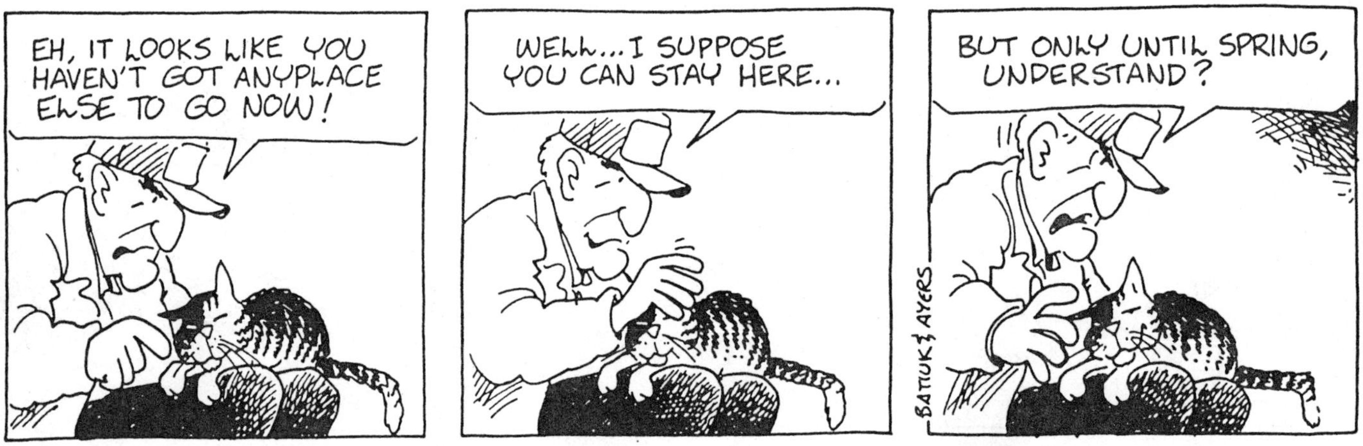
EH, IT LOOKS LIKE YOU HAVEN'T GOT ANYPLACE ELSE TO GO NOW!
WELL... I SUPPOSE YOU CAN STAY HERE...
BUT ONLY UNTIL SPRING, UNDERSTAND?
BATIUK & AYERS

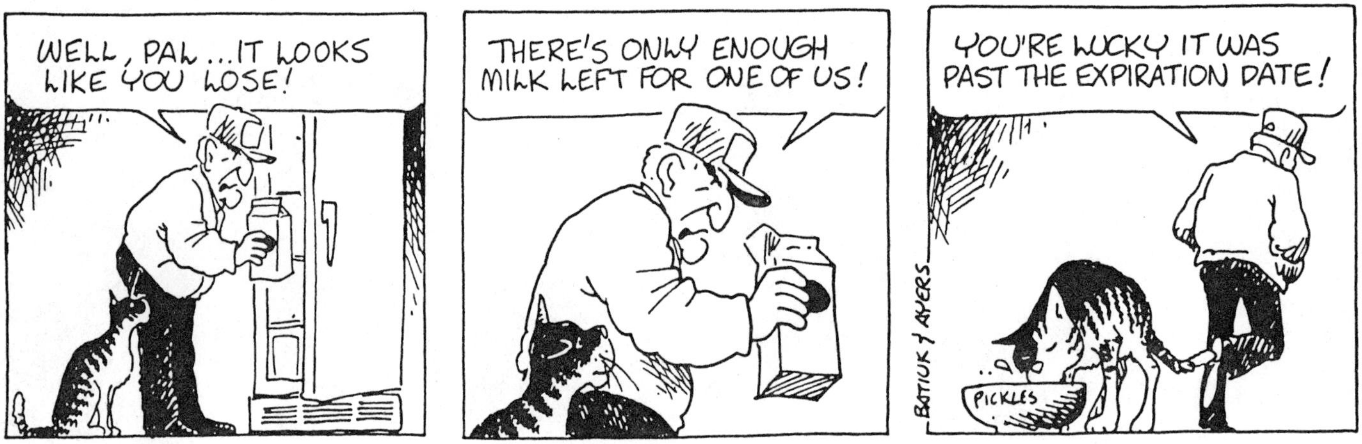
WELL, PAL... IT LOOKS LIKE YOU LOSE!
THERE'S ONLY ENOUGH MILK LEFT FOR ONE OF US!
YOU'RE LUCKY IT WAS PAST THE EXPIRATION DATE!
PICKLES
BATIUK & AYERS

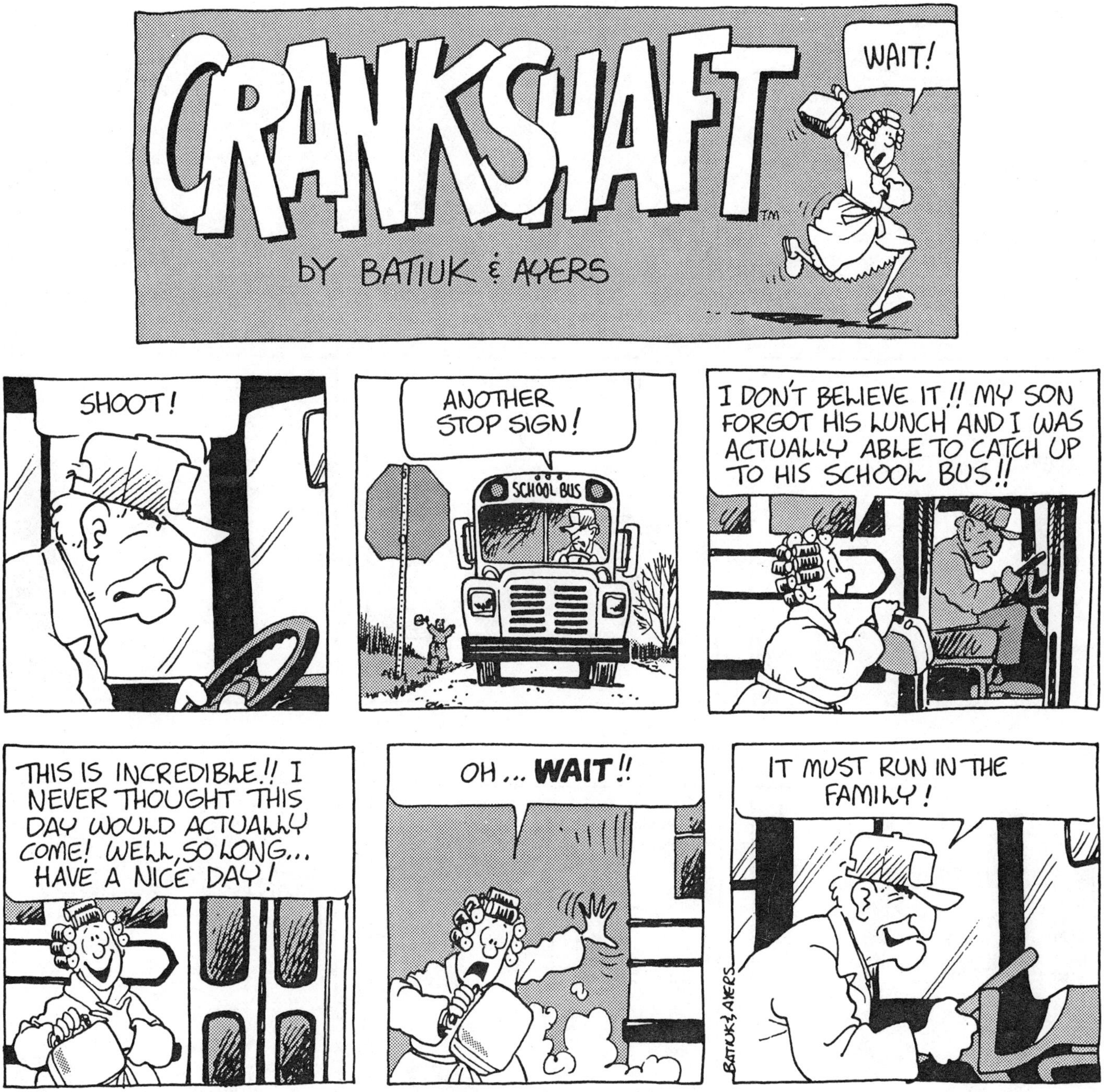
CRANKSHAFT™
BY BATIUK & AYERS
WAIT!
SHOOT!
ANOTHER STOP SIGN!
SCHOOL BUS
I DON'T BELIEVE IT!! MY SON FORGOT HIS LUNCH AND I WAS ACTUALLY ABLE TO CATCH UP TO HIS SCHOOL BUS!!
THIS IS INCREDIBLE!! I NEVER THOUGHT THIS DAY WOULD ACTUALLY COME! WELL, SO LONG... HAVE A NICE DAY!
OH... **WAIT**!!
IT MUST RUN IN THE FAMILY!
BATIUK & AYERS

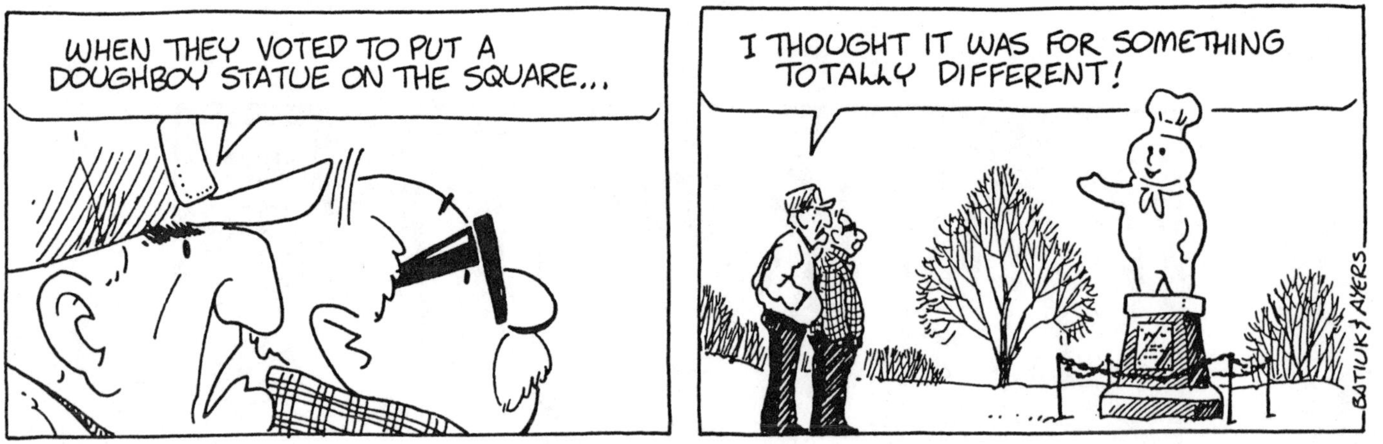
WHEN THEY VOTED TO PUT A DOUGHBOY STATUE ON THE SQUARE...
I THOUGHT IT WAS FOR SOMETHING TOTALLY DIFFERENT!

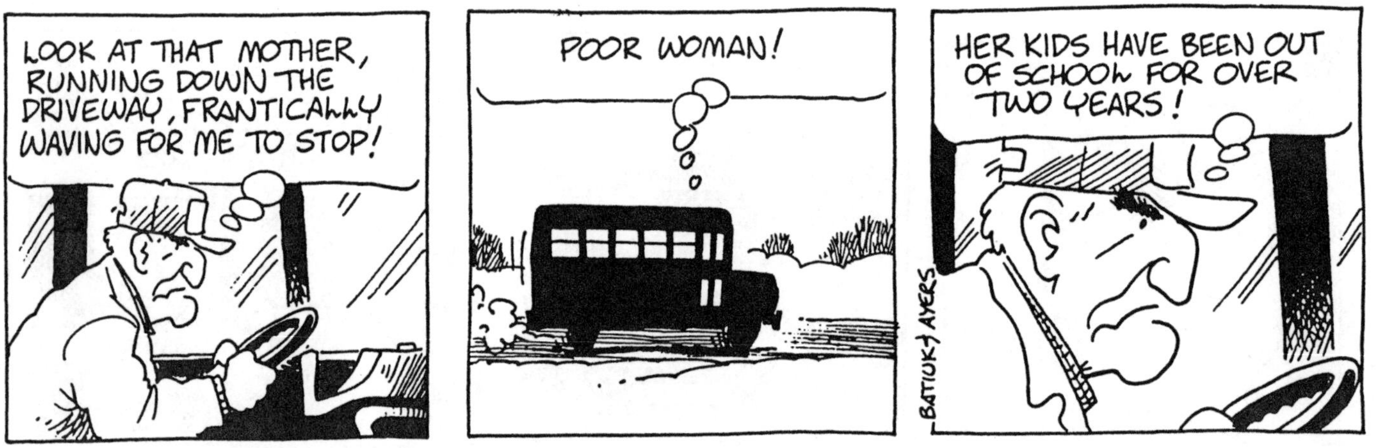
LOOK AT THAT MOTHER, RUNNING DOWN THE DRIVEWAY, FRANTICALLY WAVING FOR ME TO STOP!
POOR WOMAN!
HER KIDS HAVE BEEN OUT OF SCHOOL FOR OVER TWO YEARS!

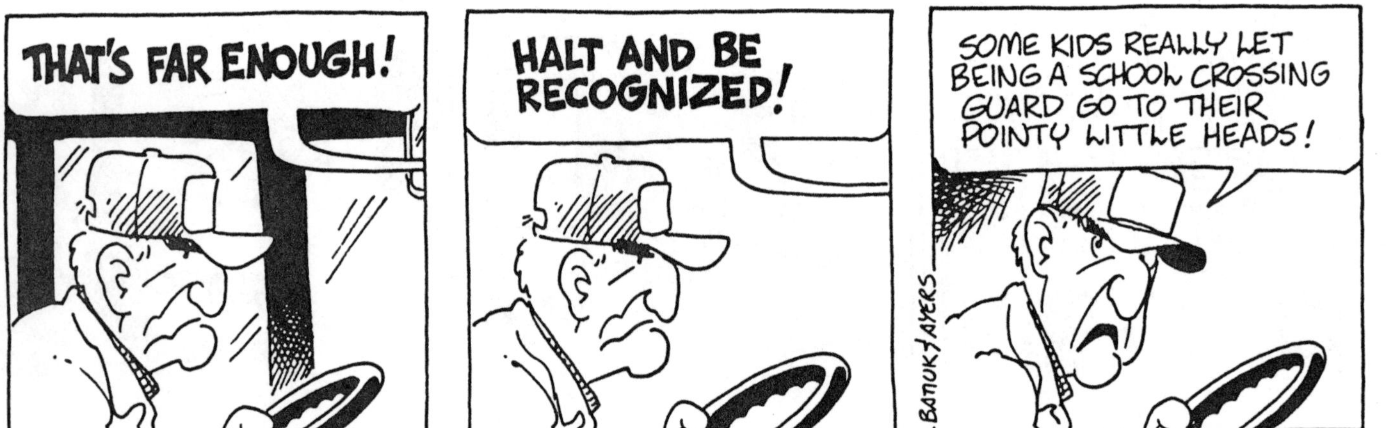
THAT'S FAR ENOUGH!
HALT AND BE RECOGNIZED!
SOME KIDS REALLY LET BEING A SCHOOL CROSSING GUARD GO TO THEIR POINTY LITTLE HEADS!

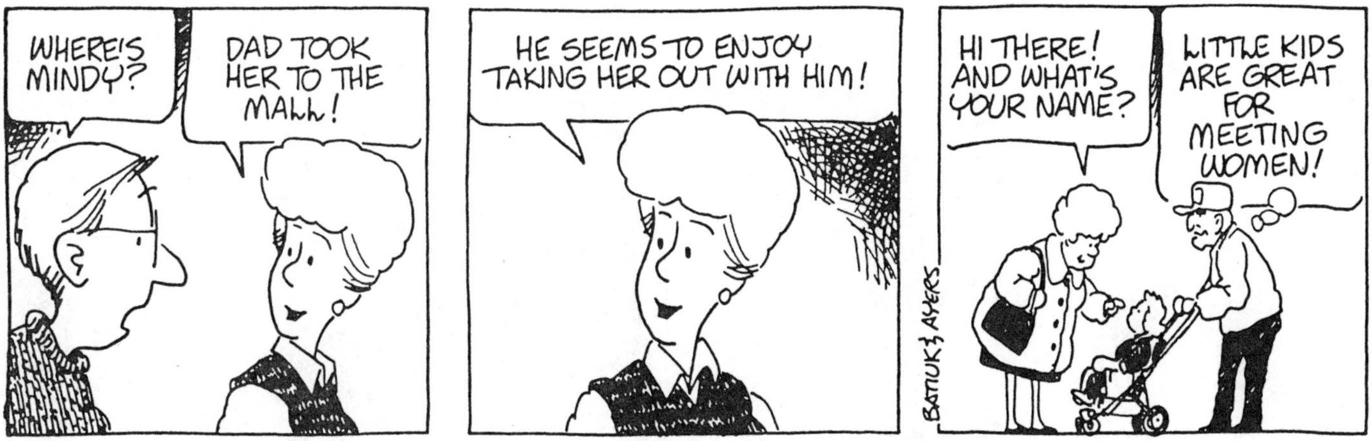
WHERE'S MINDY?
DAD TOOK HER TO THE MALL!
HE SEEMS TO ENJOY TAKING HER OUT WITH HIM!
HI THERE! AND WHAT'S YOUR NAME?
LITTLE KIDS ARE GREAT FOR MEETING WOMEN!
BATIUK & AYERS

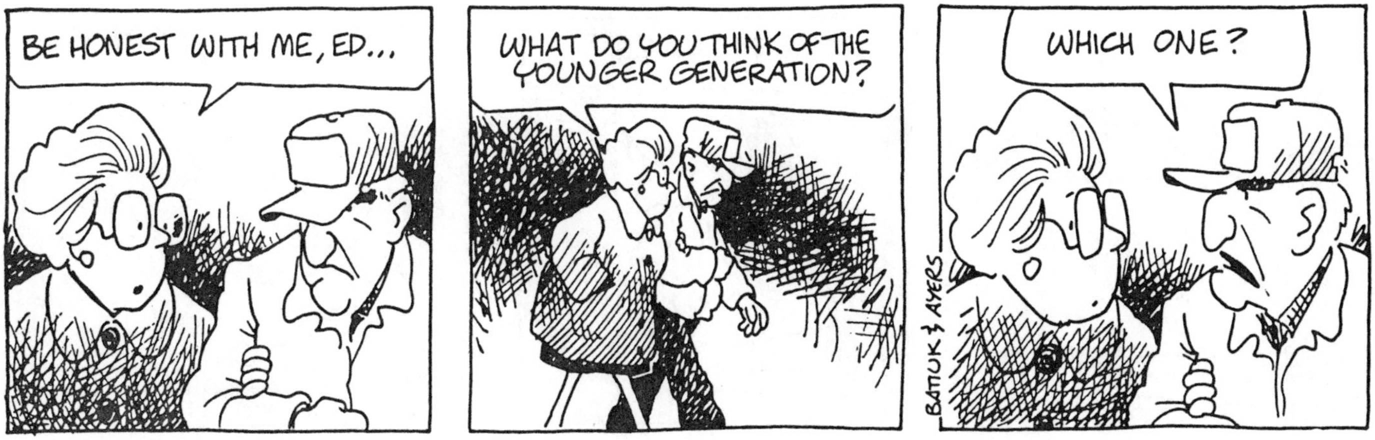
BE HONEST WITH ME, ED...
WHAT DO YOU THINK OF THE YOUNGER GENERATION?
WHICH ONE?
BATIUK & AYERS

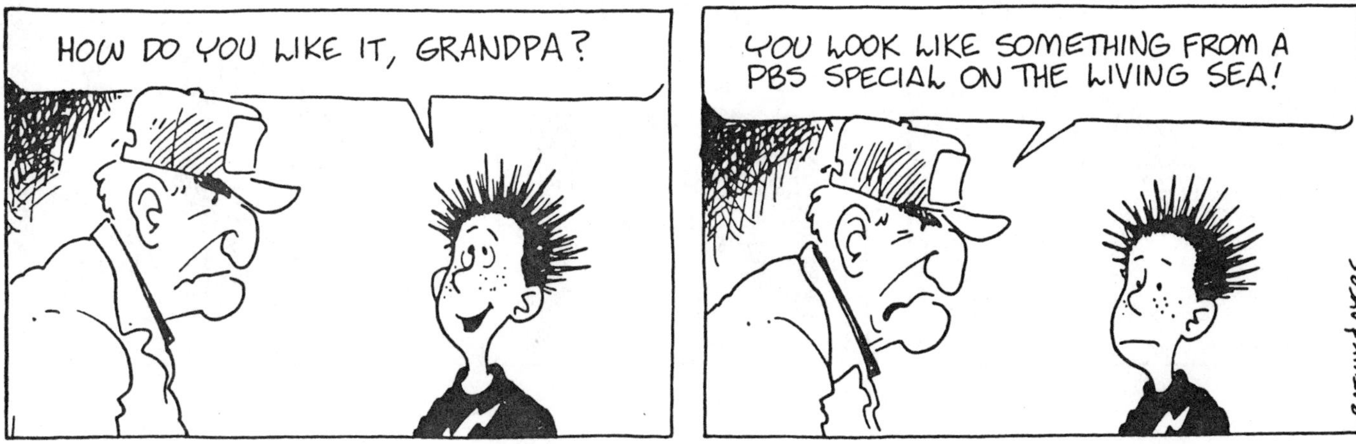
HOW DO YOU LIKE IT, GRANDPA?
YOU LOOK LIKE SOMETHING FROM A PBS SPECIAL ON THE LIVING SEA!
BATIUK & AYERS

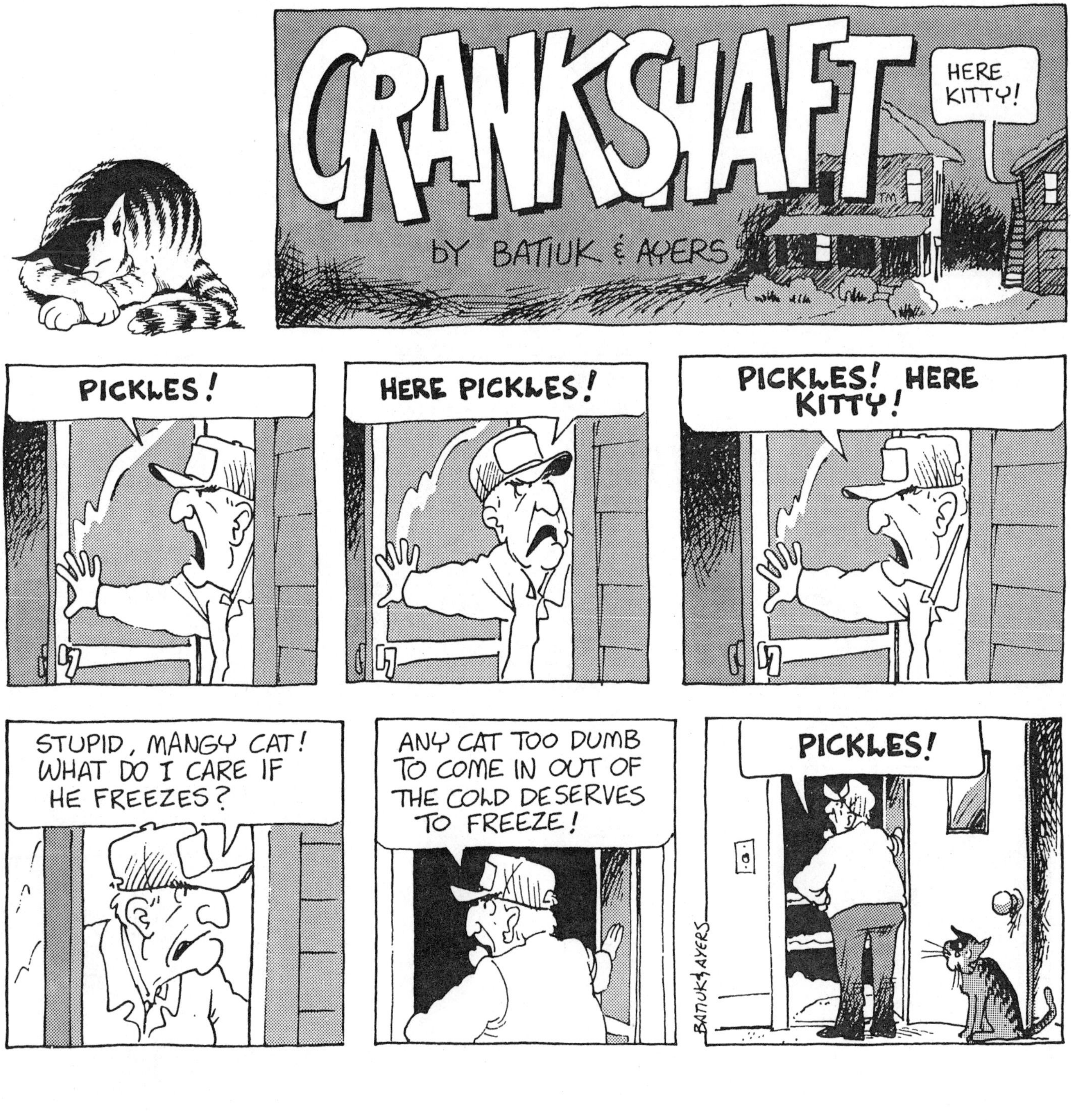
CRANKSHAFT
TM
BY BATIUK & AYERS
HERE KITTY!
PICKLES!
HERE PICKLES!
PICKLES! HERE KITTY!
STUPID, MANGY CAT! WHAT DO I CARE IF HE FREEZES?
ANY CAT TOO DUMB TO COME IN OUT OF THE COLD DESERVES TO FREEZE!
PICKLES!
BATIUK & AYERS

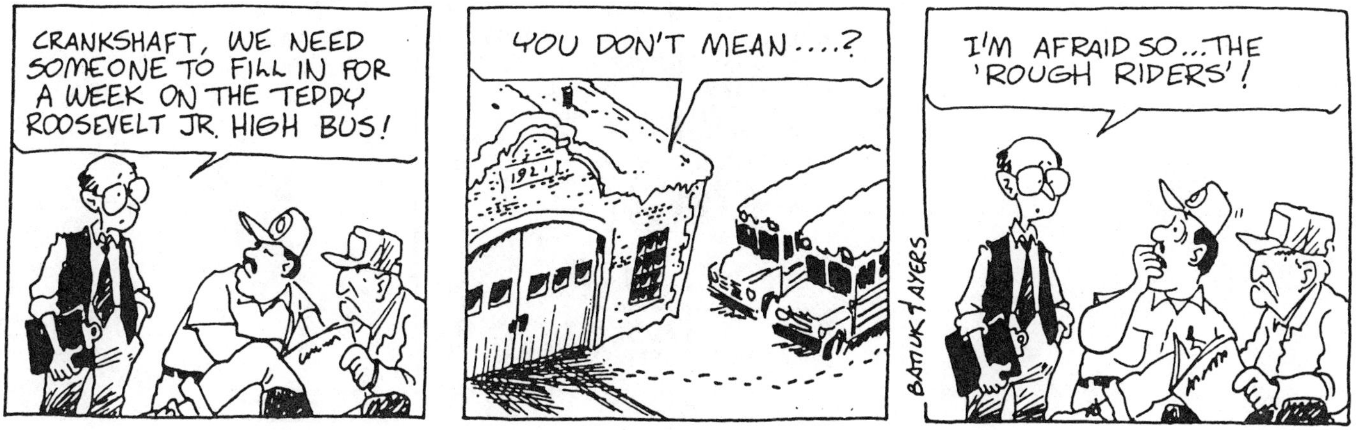
CRANKSHAFT, WE NEED SOMEONE TO FILL IN FOR A WEEK ON THE TEDDY ROOSEVELT JR. HIGH BUS!
1921
YOU DON'T MEAN....?
BATIUK + AYERS
I'M AFRAID SO...THE 'ROUGH RIDERS'!

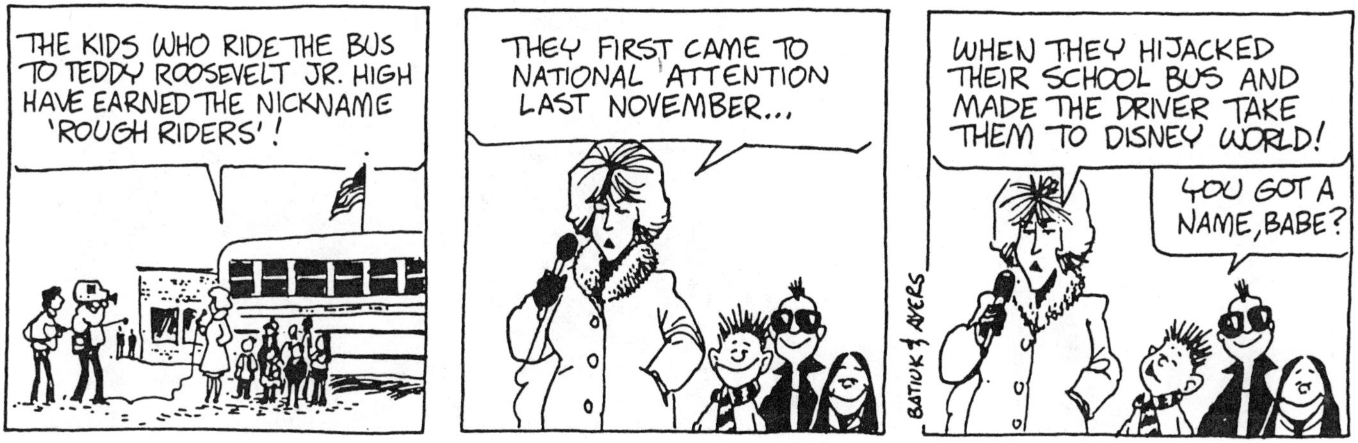
THE KIDS WHO RIDE THE BUS TO TEDDY ROOSEVELT JR. HIGH HAVE EARNED THE NICKNAME 'ROUGH RIDERS'!
THEY FIRST CAME TO NATIONAL ATTENTION LAST NOVEMBER...
BATIUK + AYERS
WHEN THEY HIJACKED THEIR SCHOOL BUS AND MADE THE DRIVER TAKE THEM TO DISNEY WORLD!
YOU GOT A NAME, BABE?

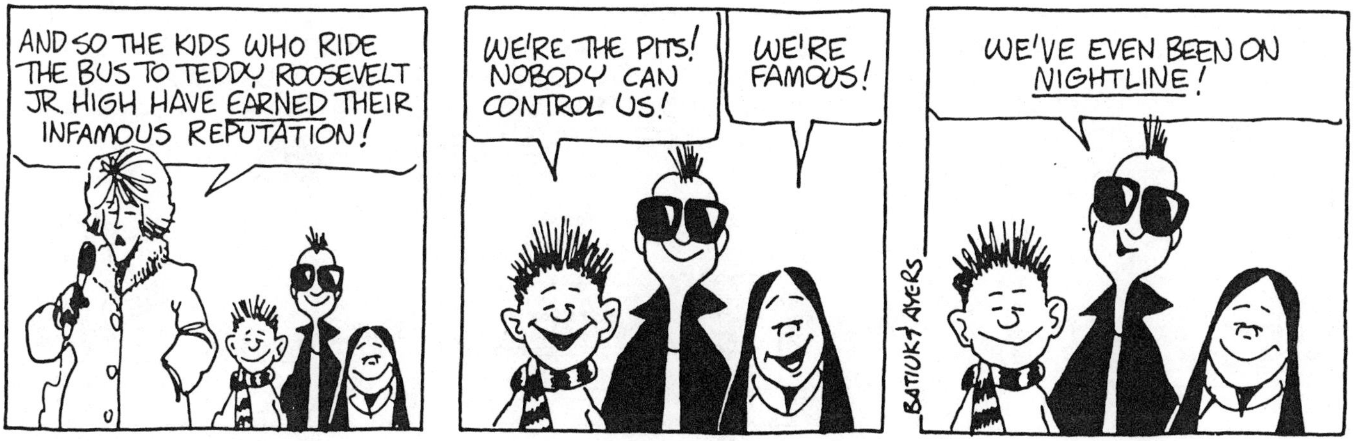
AND SO THE KIDS WHO RIDE THE BUS TO TEDDY ROOSEVELT JR. HIGH HAVE EARNED THEIR INFAMOUS REPUTATION!
WE'RE THE PITS! NOBODY CAN CONTROL US!
WE'RE FAMOUS!
BATIUK + AYERS
WE'VE EVEN BEEN ON NIGHTLINE!

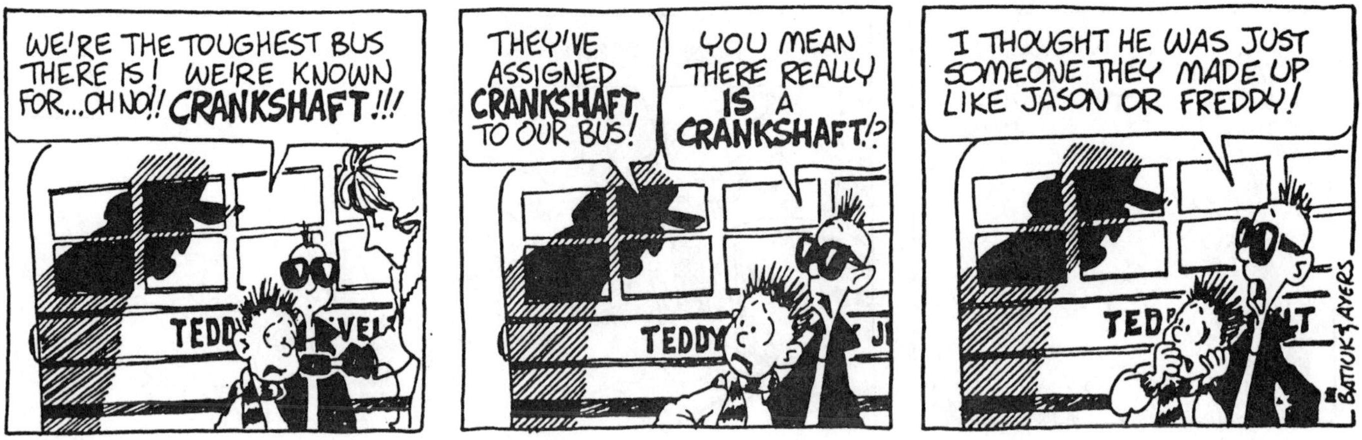

WE'RE THE TOUGHEST BUS THERE IS! WE'RE KNOWN FOR...OH NO!! CRANKSHAFT!!!
THEY'VE ASSIGNED CRANKSHAFT TO OUR BUS!
YOU MEAN THERE REALLY IS A CRANKSHAFT!?
I THOUGHT HE WAS JUST SOMEONE THEY MADE UP LIKE JASON OR FREDDY!
BATIUK & AYERS

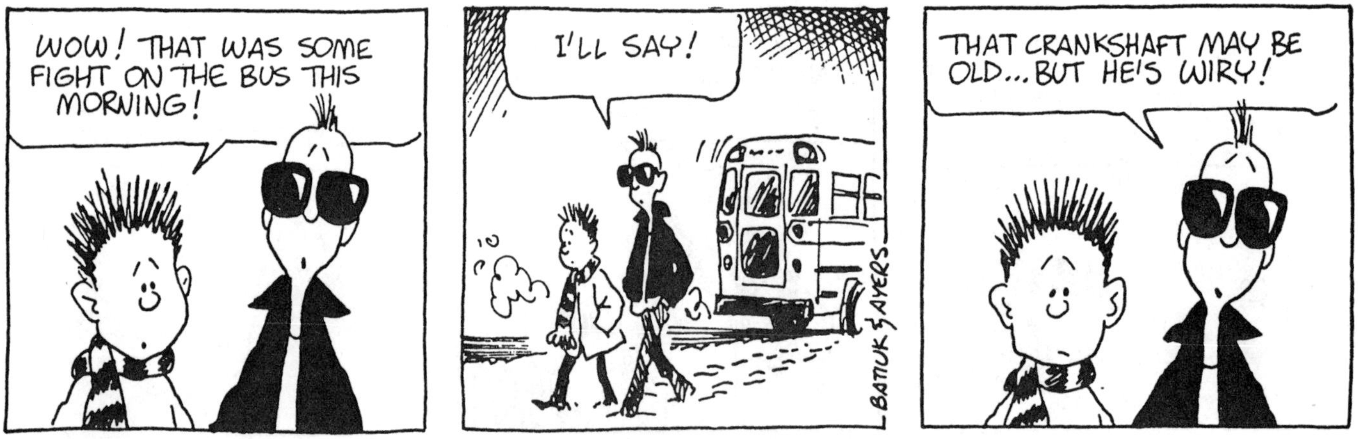

WOW! THAT WAS SOME FIGHT ON THE BUS THIS MORNING!
I'LL SAY!
BATIUK & AYERS
THAT CRANKSHAFT MAY BE OLD... BUT HE'S WIRY!

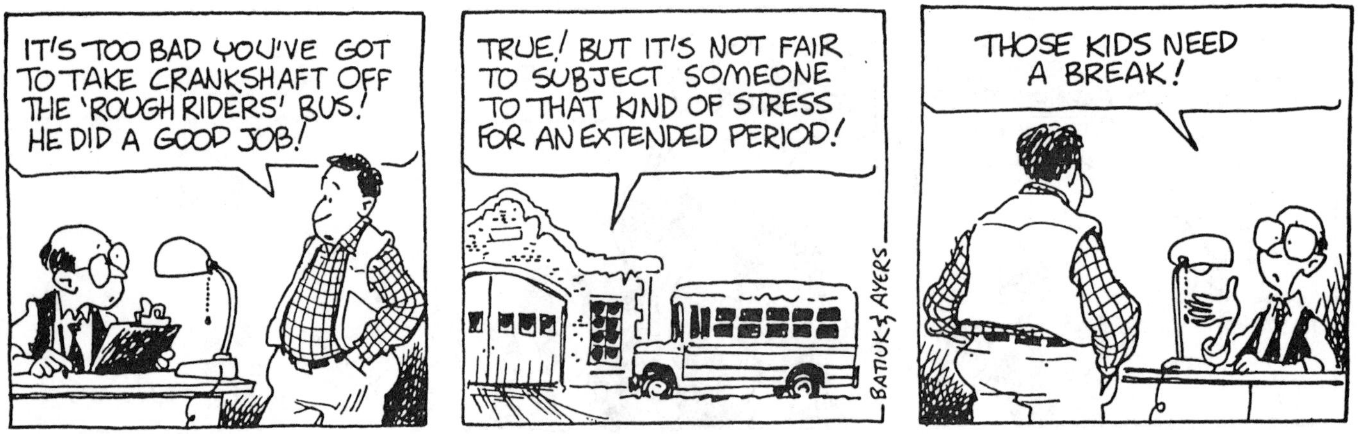

IT'S TOO BAD YOU'VE GOT TO TAKE CRANKSHAFT OFF THE 'ROUGH RIDERS' BUS! HE DID A GOOD JOB!
TRUE! BUT IT'S NOT FAIR TO SUBJECT SOMEONE TO THAT KIND OF STRESS FOR AN EXTENDED PERIOD!
BATIUK & AYERS
THOSE KIDS NEED A BREAK!

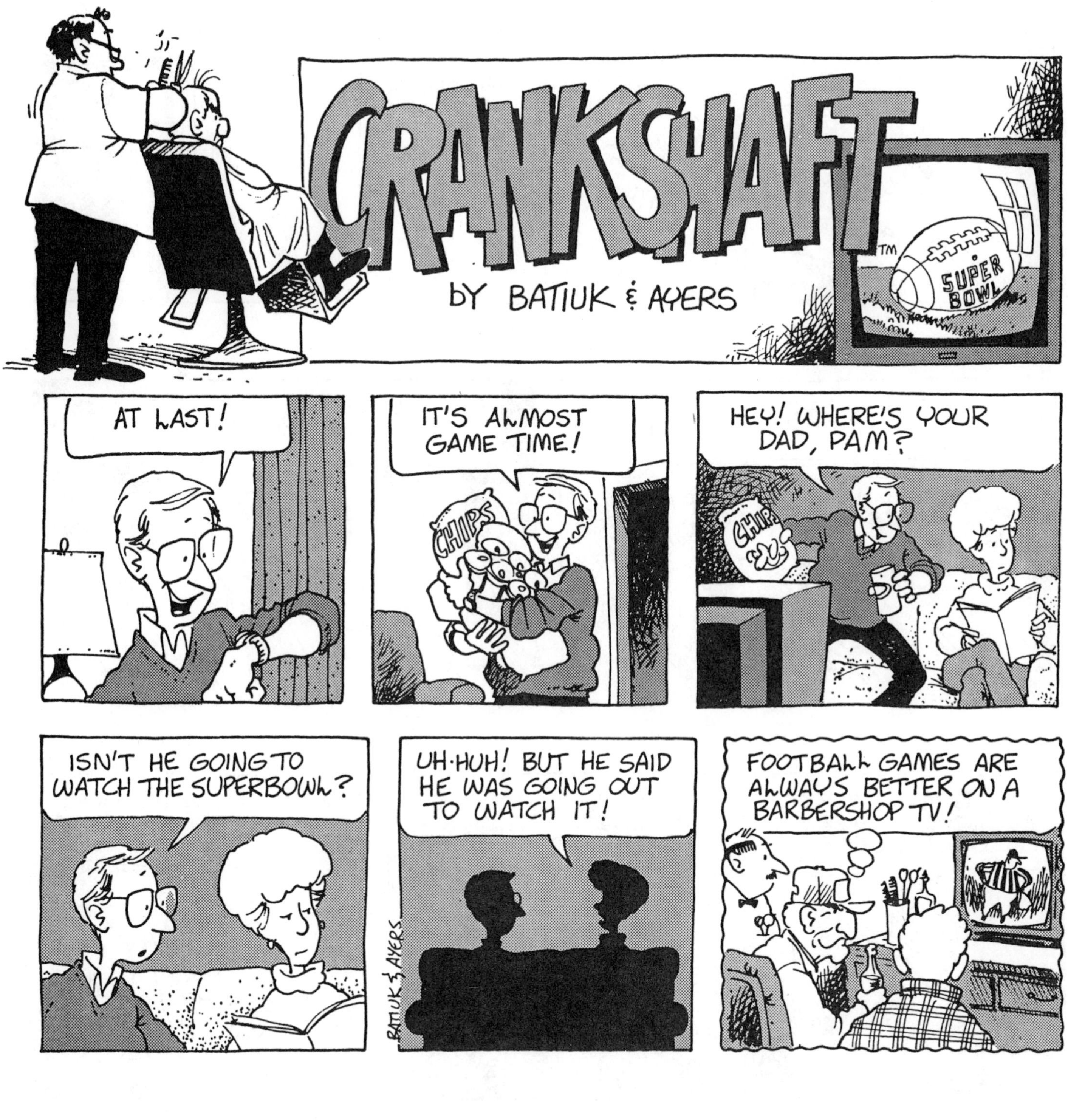
CRANKSHAFT
TM
BY BATIUK & AYERS
SUPER BOWL
AT LAST!
IT'S ALMOST GAME TIME!
CHIPS
HEY! WHERE'S YOUR DAD, PAM?
ISN'T HE GOING TO WATCH THE SUPERBOWL?
UH-HUH! BUT HE SAID HE WAS GOING OUT TO WATCH IT!
BATIUK & AYERS
FOOTBALL GAMES ARE ALWAYS BETTER ON A BARBERSHOP TV!

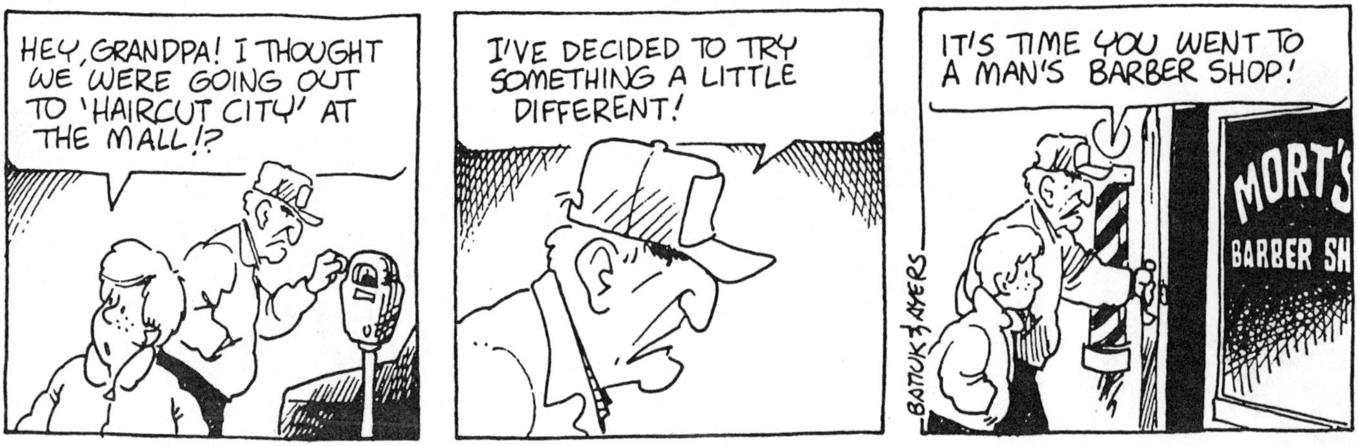
HEY, GRANDPA! I THOUGHT WE WERE GOING OUT TO 'HAIRCUT CITY' AT THE MALL!?
I'VE DECIDED TO TRY SOMETHING A LITTLE DIFFERENT!
IT'S TIME YOU WENT TO A MAN'S BARBER SHOP!
MORT'S
BARBER SH
BATIUK & AYERS

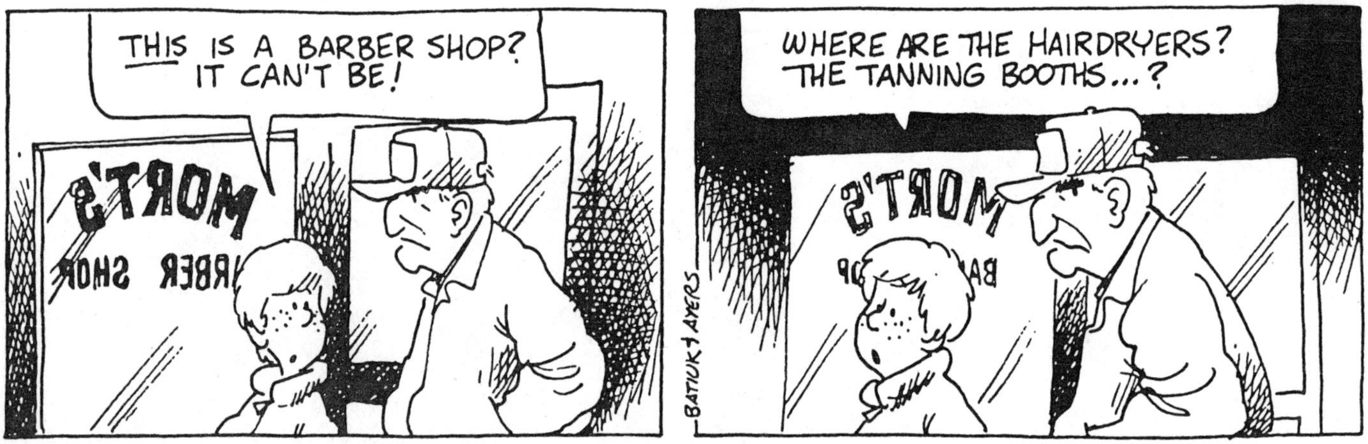
THIS IS A BARBER SHOP? IT CAN'T BE!
BATIUK & AYERS
WHERE ARE THE HAIRDRYERS? THE TANNING BOOTHS...?

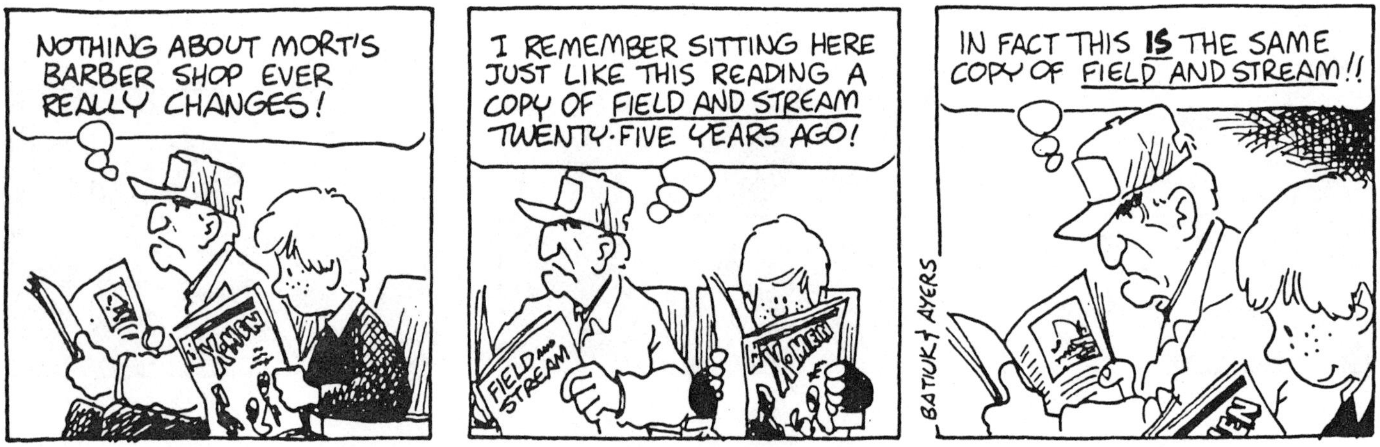
NOTHING ABOUT MORT'S BARBER SHOP EVER REALLY CHANGES!
I REMEMBER SITTING HERE JUST LIKE THIS READING A COPY OF FIELD AND STREAM TWENTY-FIVE YEARS AGO!
FIELD AND STREAM
X-MEN
BATIUK & AYERS
IN FACT THIS **IS** THE SAME COPY OF FIELD AND STREAM!!

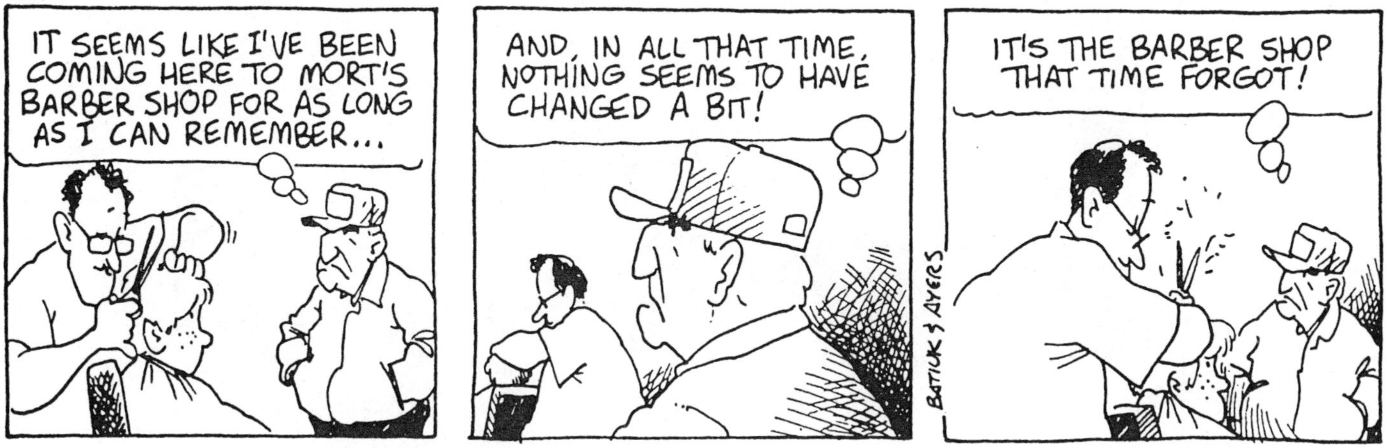
IT SEEMS LIKE I'VE BEEN COMING HERE TO MORT'S BARBER SHOP FOR AS LONG AS I CAN REMEMBER...
AND, IN ALL THAT TIME, NOTHING SEEMS TO HAVE CHANGED A BIT!
BATIUK & AYERS
IT'S THE BARBER SHOP THAT TIME FORGOT!

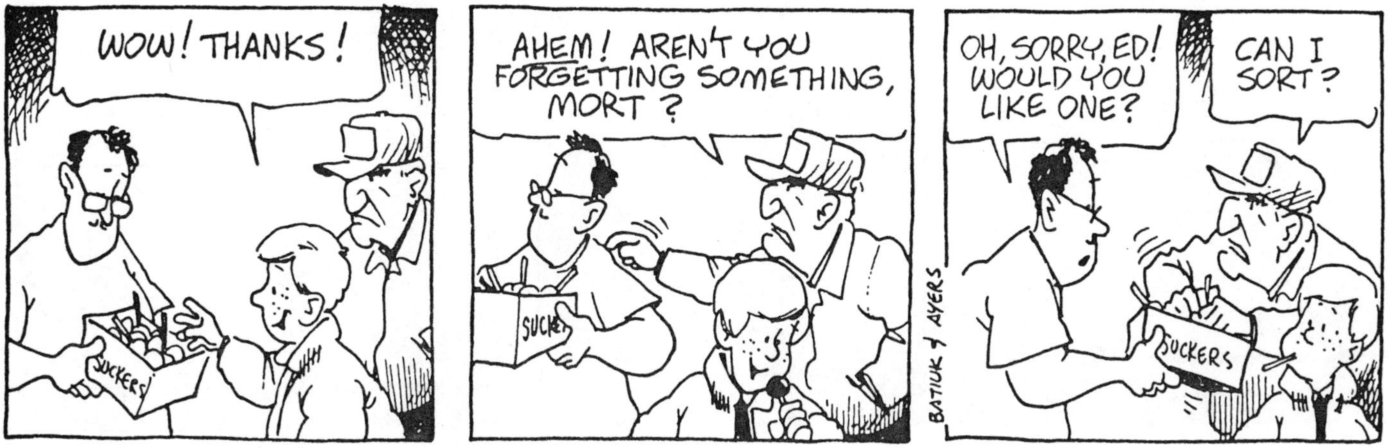
WOW! THANKS!
SUCKERS
AHEM! AREN'T YOU FORGETTING SOMETHING, MORT?
BATIUK & AYERS
OH, SORRY, ED! WOULD YOU LIKE ONE?
CAN I SORT?
SUCKERS

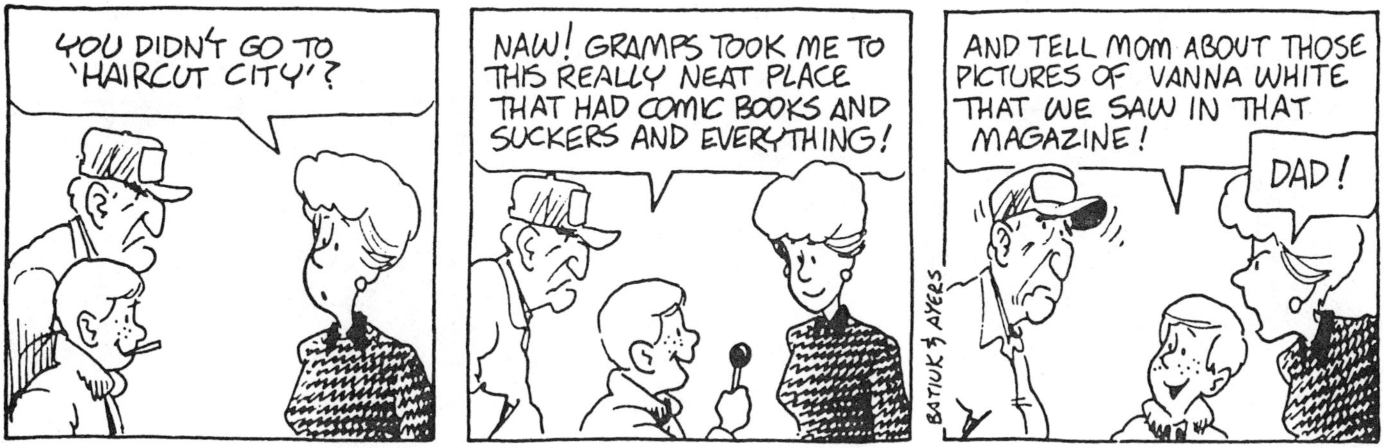
YOU DIDN'T GO TO 'HAIRCUT CITY'?
NAW! GRAMPS TOOK ME TO THIS REALLY NEAT PLACE THAT HAD COMIC BOOKS AND SUCKERS AND EVERYTHING!
BATIUK & AYERS
AND TELL MOM ABOUT THOSE PICTURES OF VANNA WHITE THAT WE SAW IN THAT MAGAZINE!
DAD!

CRANKSHAFT by BATIUK & AYERS — October 1929

WITH THE STOCK MARKET AS GOOFY AS IT'S BEEN...

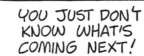

YOU JUST DON'T KNOW WHAT'S COMING NEXT!

WITH THE WAY THINGS ARE GOING, IT MAKES YOU WONDER IF WE'RE HEADING INTO ANOTHER DEPRESSION!

WHAT WAS IT LIKE FOR YOUR FAMILY DURING THE LAST DEPRESSION, DAD? WERE YOU REAL POOR?

NAW, WE WEREN'T POOR...

WE JUST DIDN'T HAVE ANY MONEY, THAT'S AHH!

BATIUK/AYERS

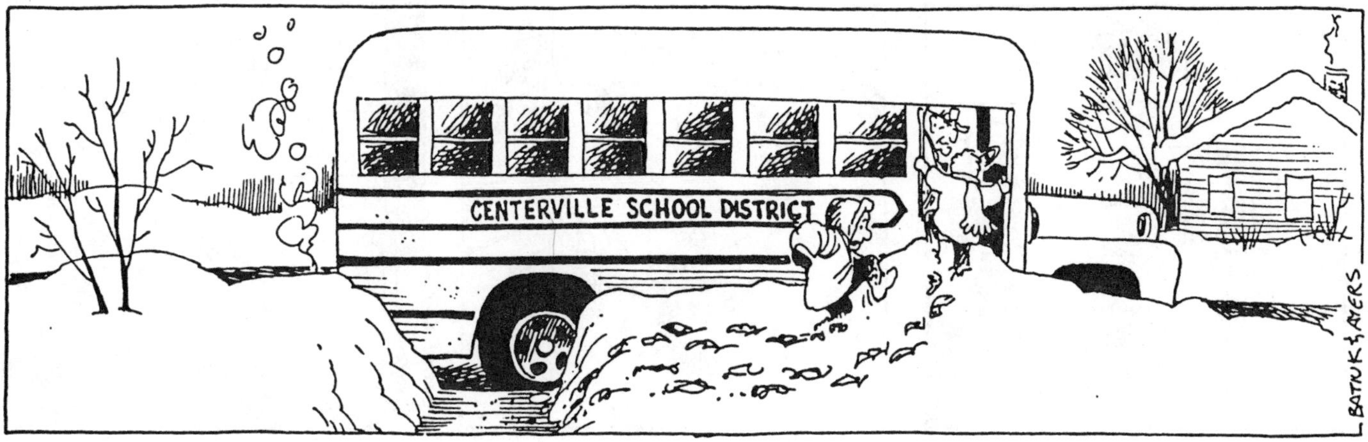
CENTERVILLE SCHOOL DISTRICT
BATIUK & AYERS

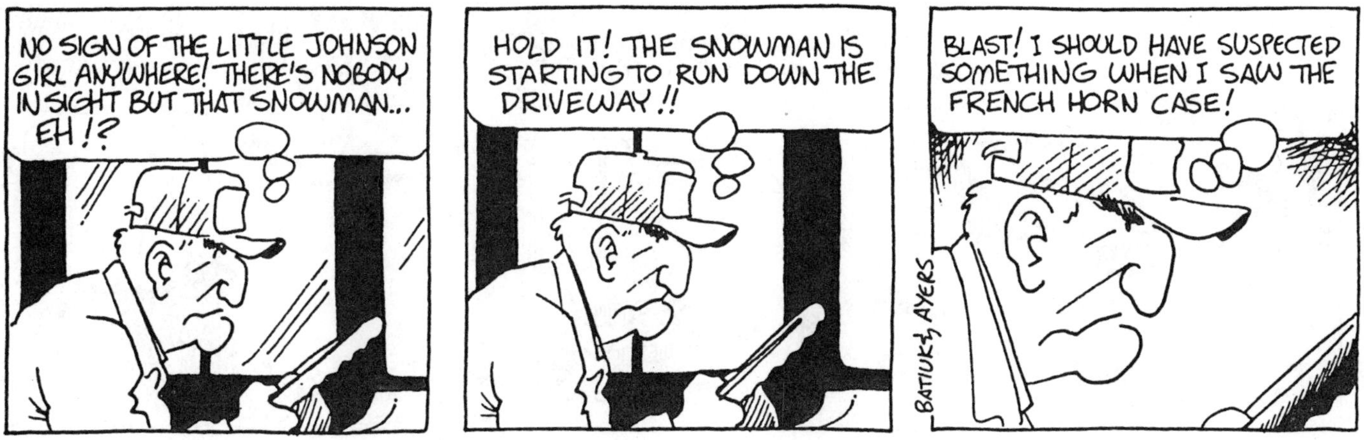
NO SIGN OF THE LITTLE JOHNSON GIRL ANYWHERE! THERE'S NOBODY IN SIGHT BUT THAT SNOWMAN... EH!?
HOLD IT! THE SNOWMAN IS STARTING TO RUN DOWN THE DRIVEWAY!!
BLAST! I SHOULD HAVE SUSPECTED SOMETHING WHEN I SAW THE FRENCH HORN CASE!
BATIUK & AYERS

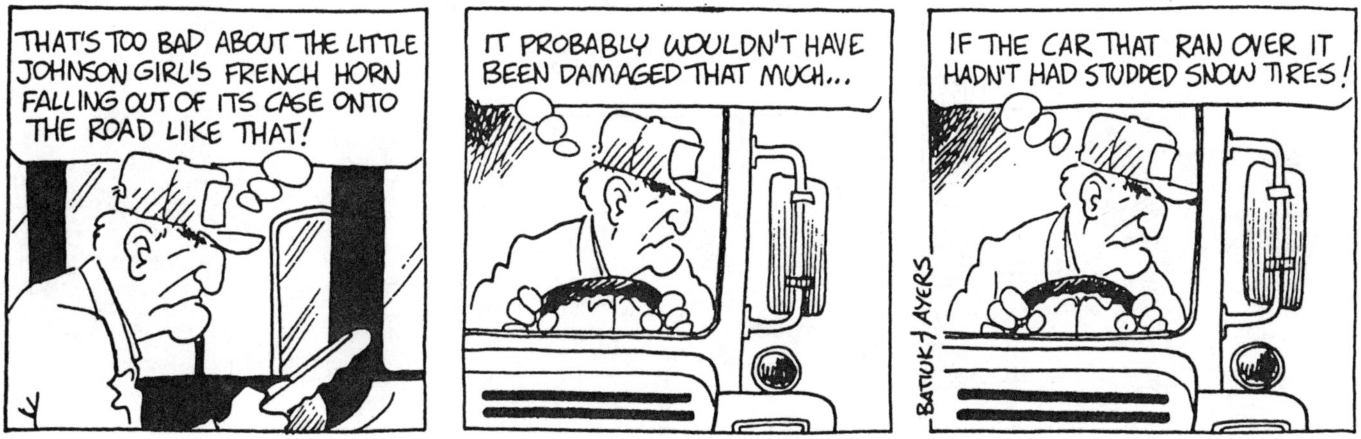
THAT'S TOO BAD ABOUT THE LITTLE JOHNSON GIRL'S FRENCH HORN FALLING OUT OF ITS CASE ONTO THE ROAD LIKE THAT!
IT PROBABLY WOULDN'T HAVE BEEN DAMAGED THAT MUCH...
IF THE CAR THAT RAN OVER IT HADN'T HAD STUDDED SNOW TIRES!
BATIUK & AYERS

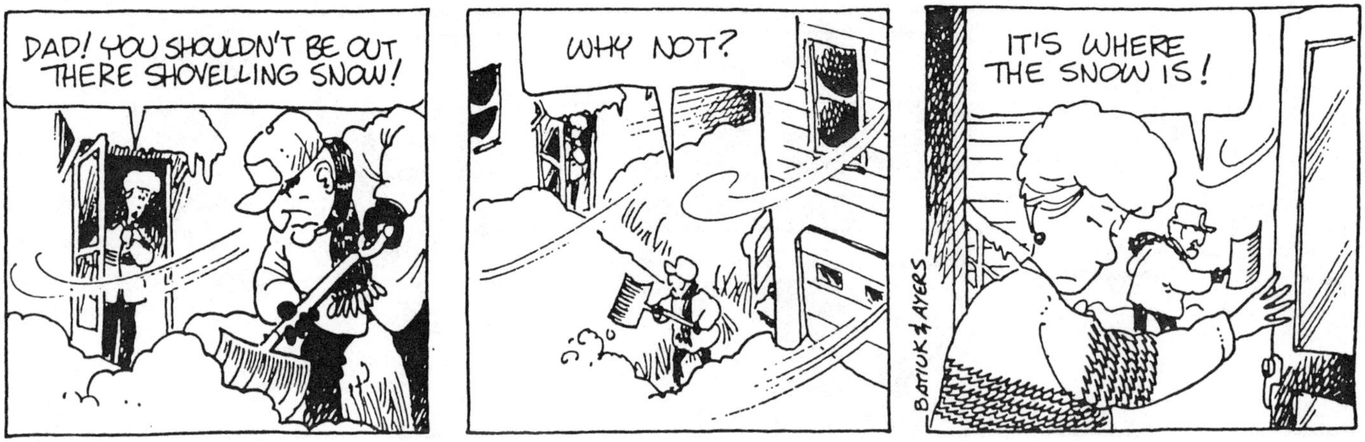
DAD! YOU SHOULDN'T BE OUT THERE SHOVELLING SNOW!
WHY NOT?
IT'S WHERE THE SNOW IS!
BATIUK & AYERS

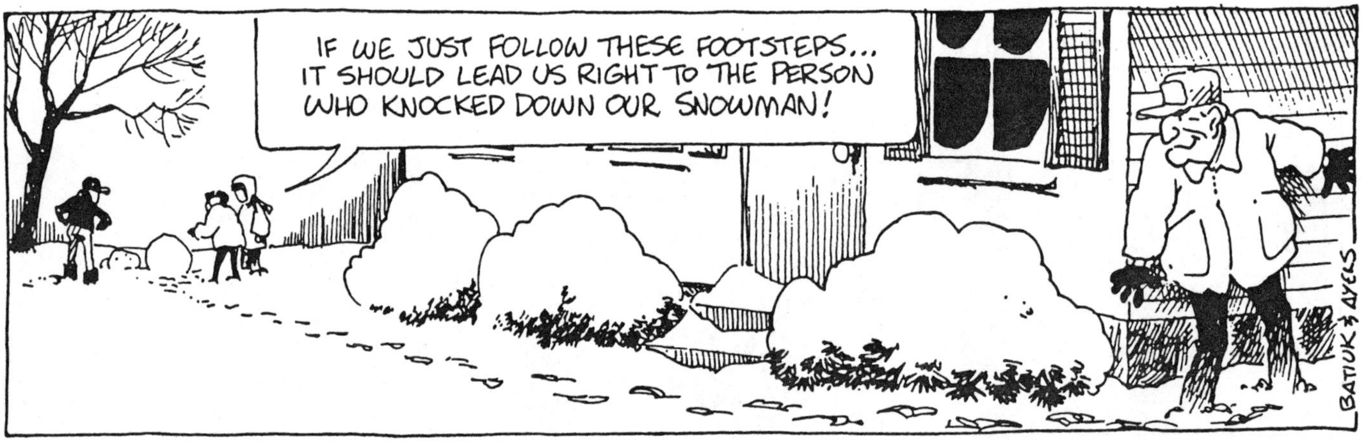
IF WE JUST FOLLOW THESE FOOTSTEPS... IT SHOULD LEAD US RIGHT TO THE PERSON WHO KNOCKED DOWN OUR SNOWMAN!
BATIUK & AYERS

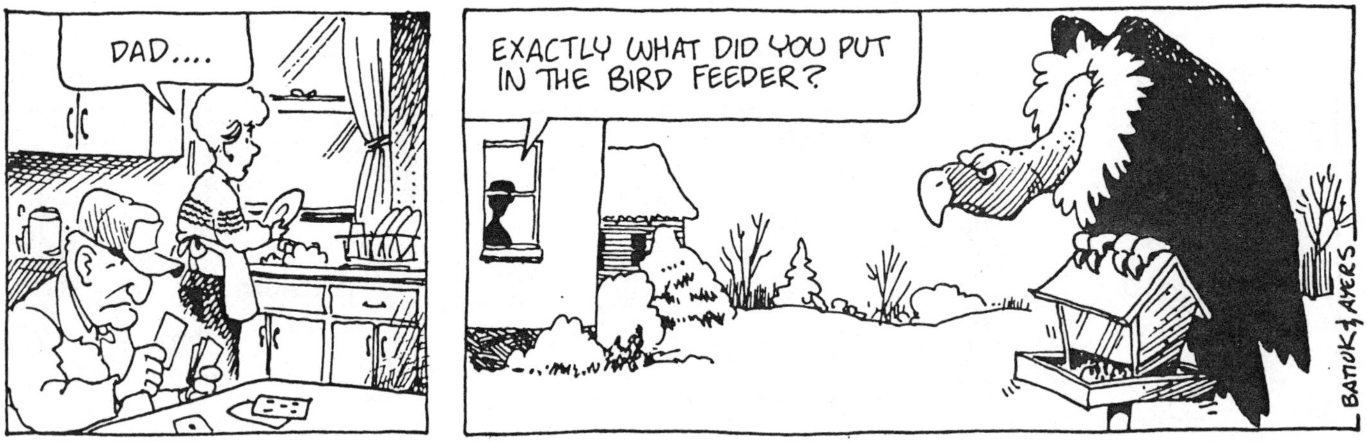
DAD....
EXACTLY WHAT DID YOU PUT IN THE BIRD FEEDER?
BATIUK & AYERS

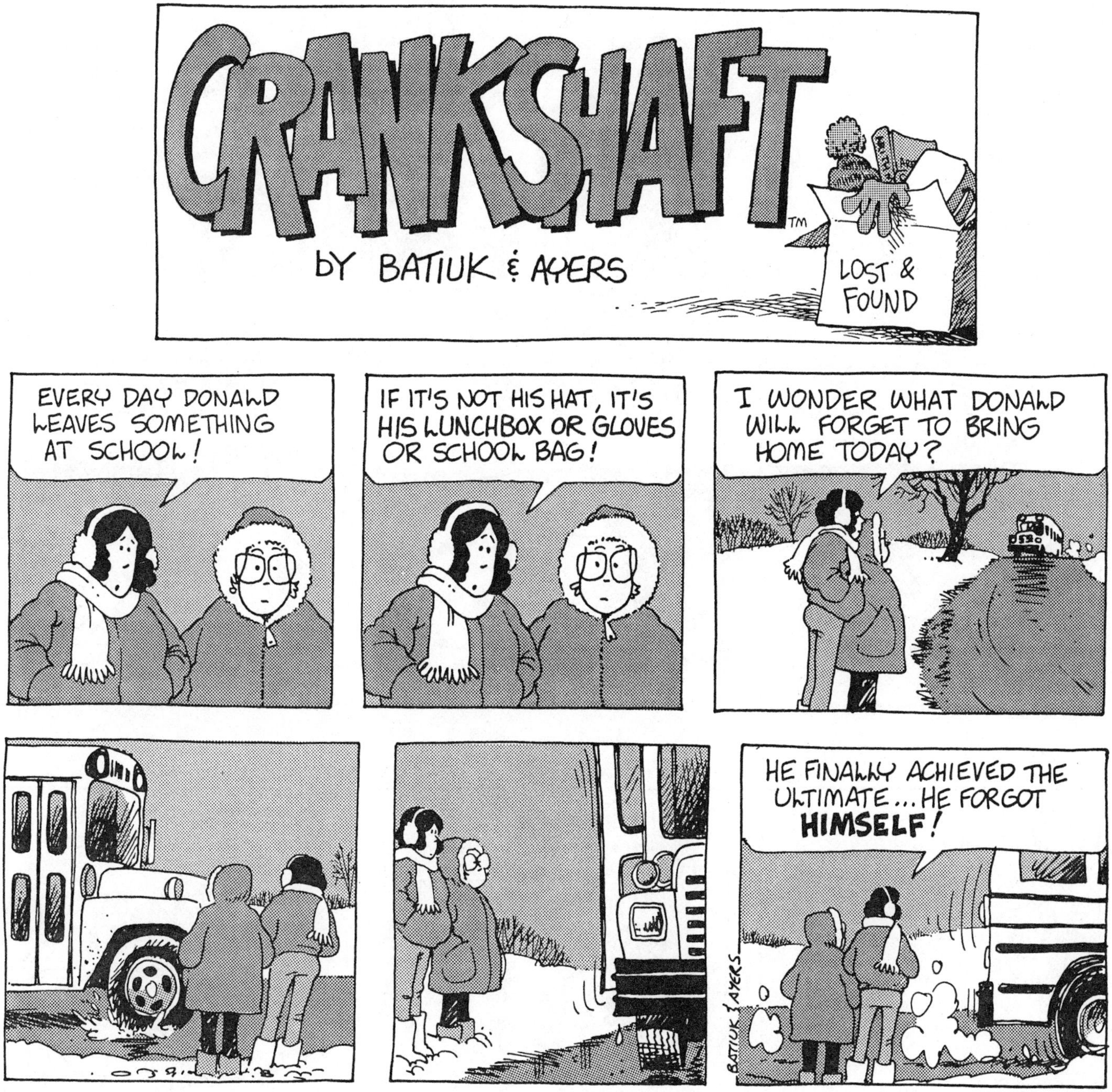
CRANKSHAFT
BY BATIUK & AYERS
LOST & FOUND
EVERY DAY DONALD LEAVES SOMETHING AT SCHOOL!
IF IT'S NOT HIS HAT, IT'S HIS LUNCHBOX OR GLOVES OR SCHOOL BAG!
I WONDER WHAT DONALD WILL FORGET TO BRING HOME TODAY?
HE FINALLY ACHIEVED THE ULTIMATE... HE FORGOT HIMSELF!
BATIUK & AYERS

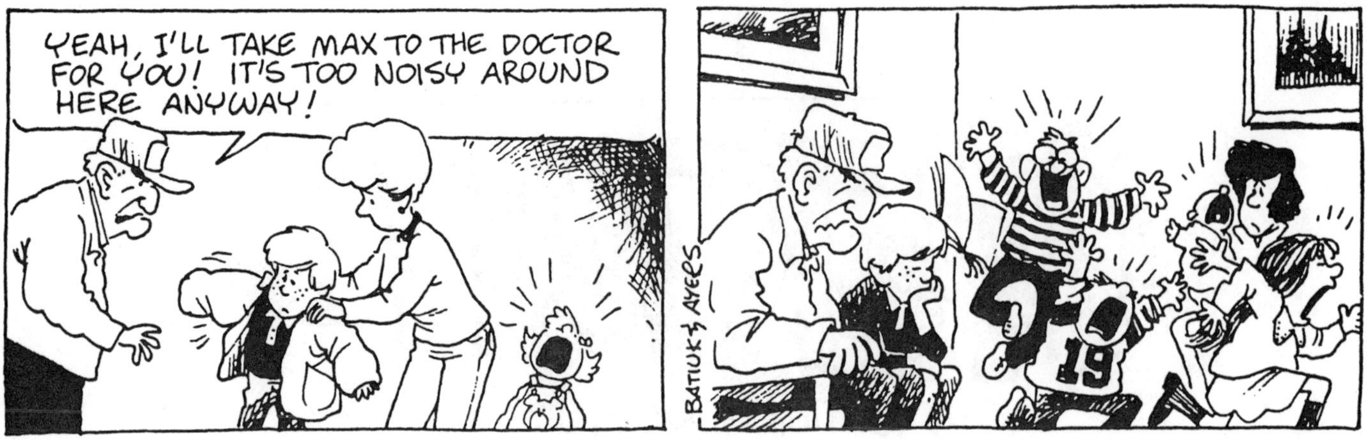
YEAH, I'LL TAKE MAX TO THE DOCTOR FOR YOU! IT'S TOO NOISY AROUND HERE ANYWAY!
BATIUK & AYERS
19

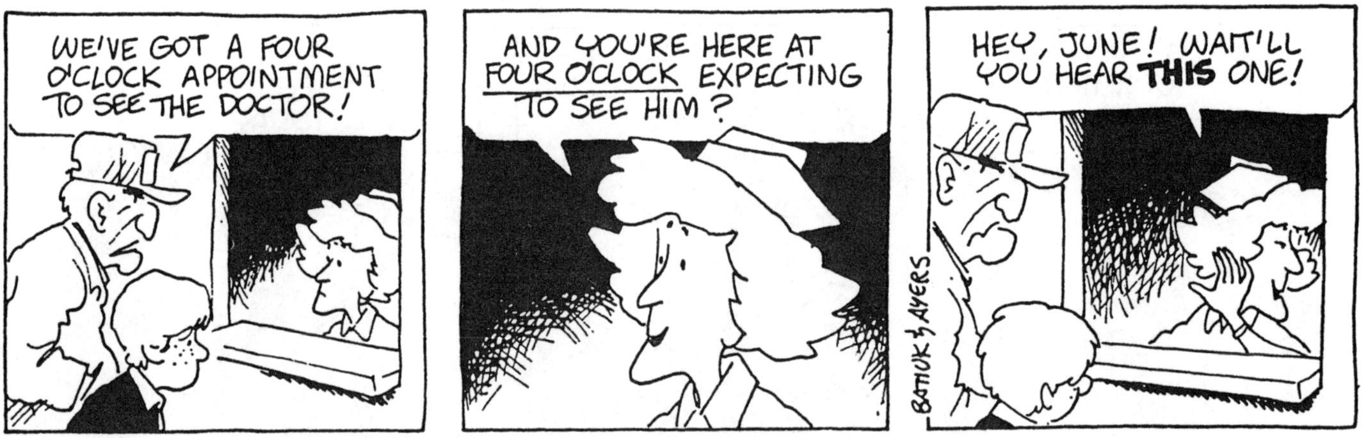
WE'VE GOT A FOUR O'CLOCK APPOINTMENT TO SEE THE DOCTOR!
AND YOU'RE HERE AT FOUR O'CLOCK EXPECTING TO SEE HIM?
HEY, JUNE! WAIT'LL YOU HEAR **THIS** ONE!
BATIUK & AYERS

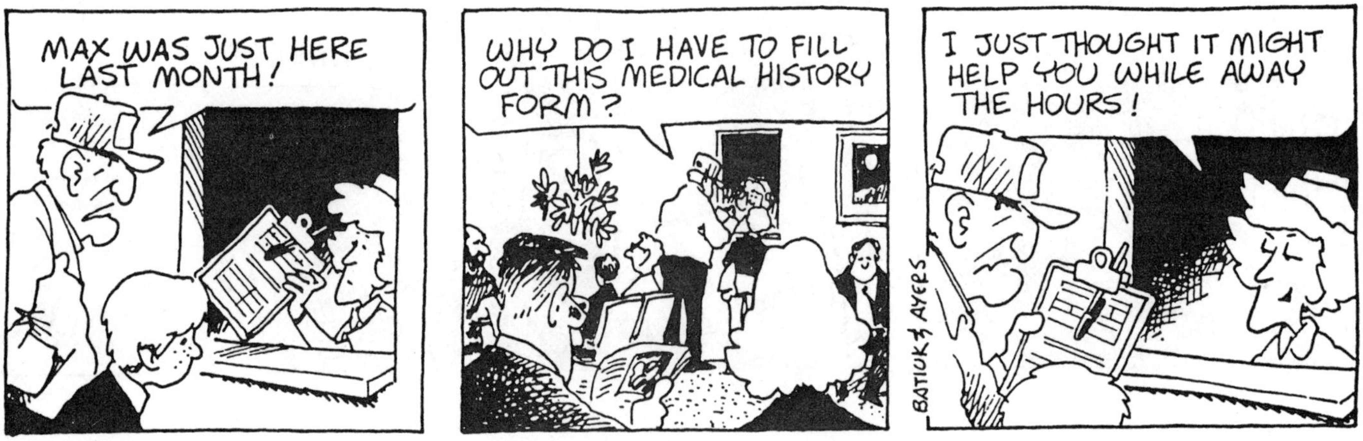
MAX WAS JUST HERE LAST MONTH!
WHY DO I HAVE TO FILL OUT THIS MEDICAL HISTORY FORM?
I JUST THOUGHT IT MIGHT HELP YOU WHILE AWAY THE HOURS!
BATIUK & AYERS

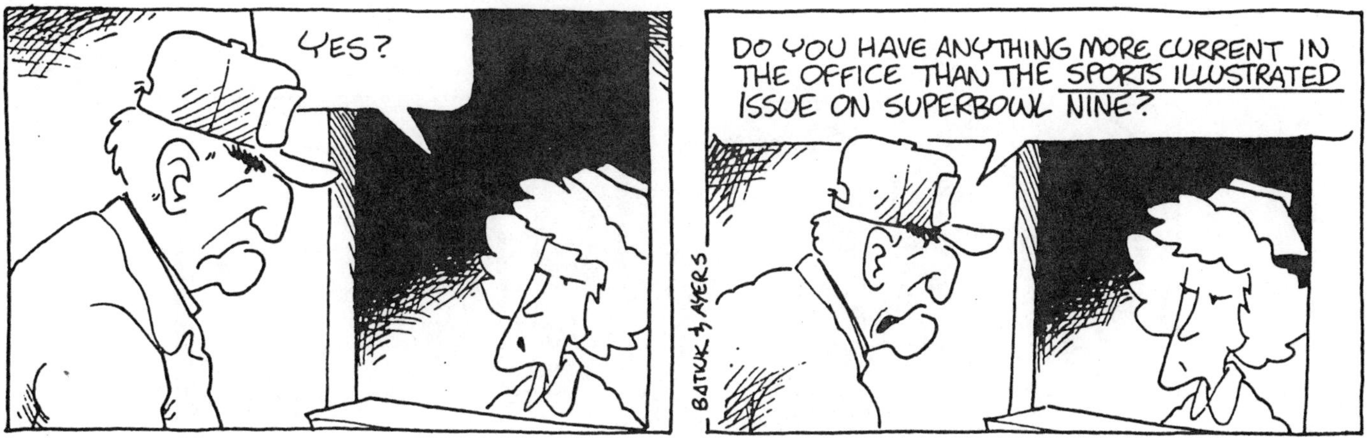
YES?
DO YOU HAVE ANYTHING MORE CURRENT IN THE OFFICE THAN THE SPORTS ILLUSTRATED ISSUE ON SUPERBOWL NINE?
BATIUK & AYERS

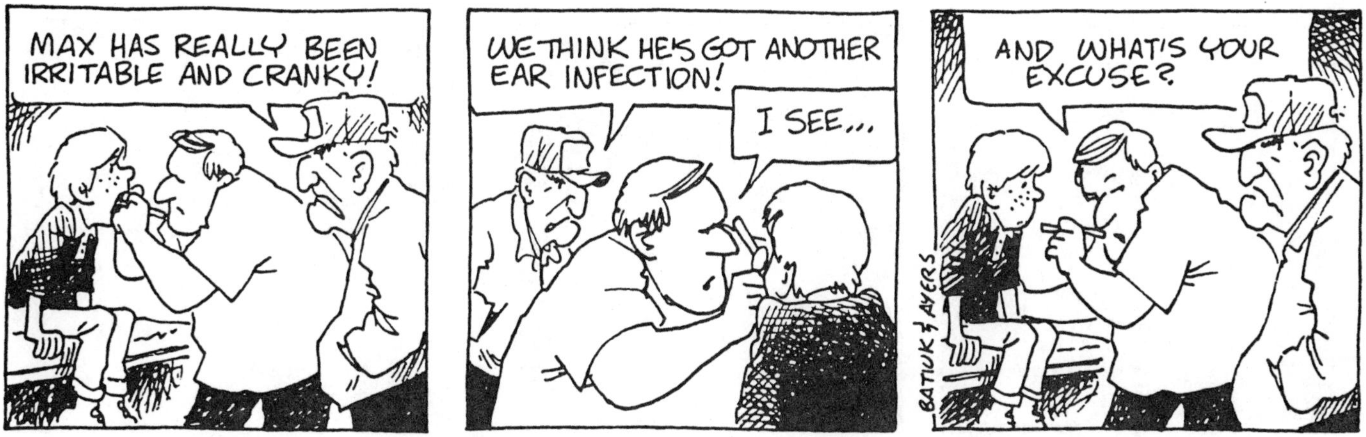
MAX HAS REALLY BEEN IRRITABLE AND CRANKY!
WE THINK HE'S GOT ANOTHER EAR INFECTION!
I SEE...
AND WHAT'S YOUR EXCUSE?
BATIUK & AYERS

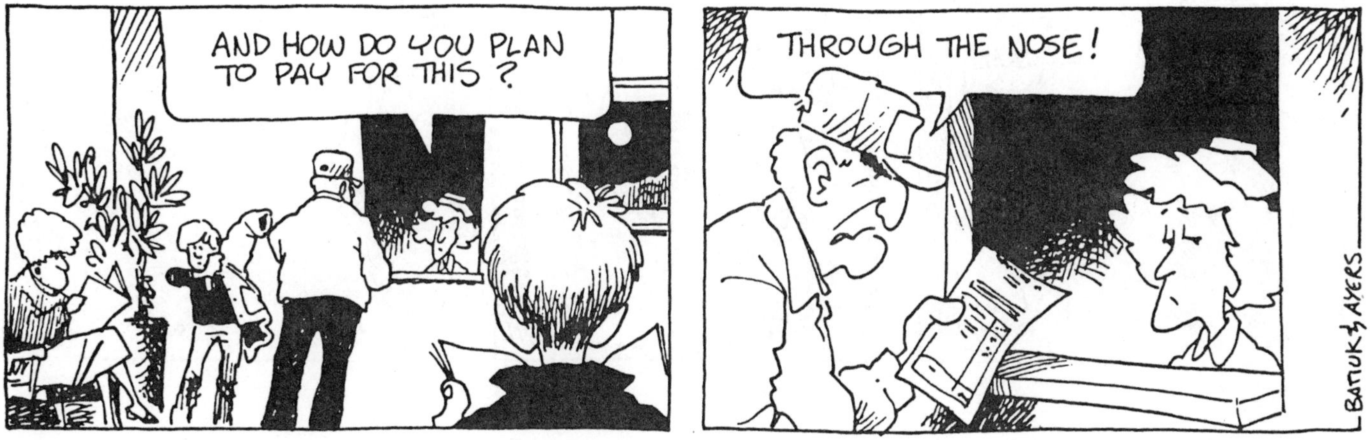
AND HOW DO YOU PLAN TO PAY FOR THIS?
THROUGH THE NOSE!
BATIUK & AYERS

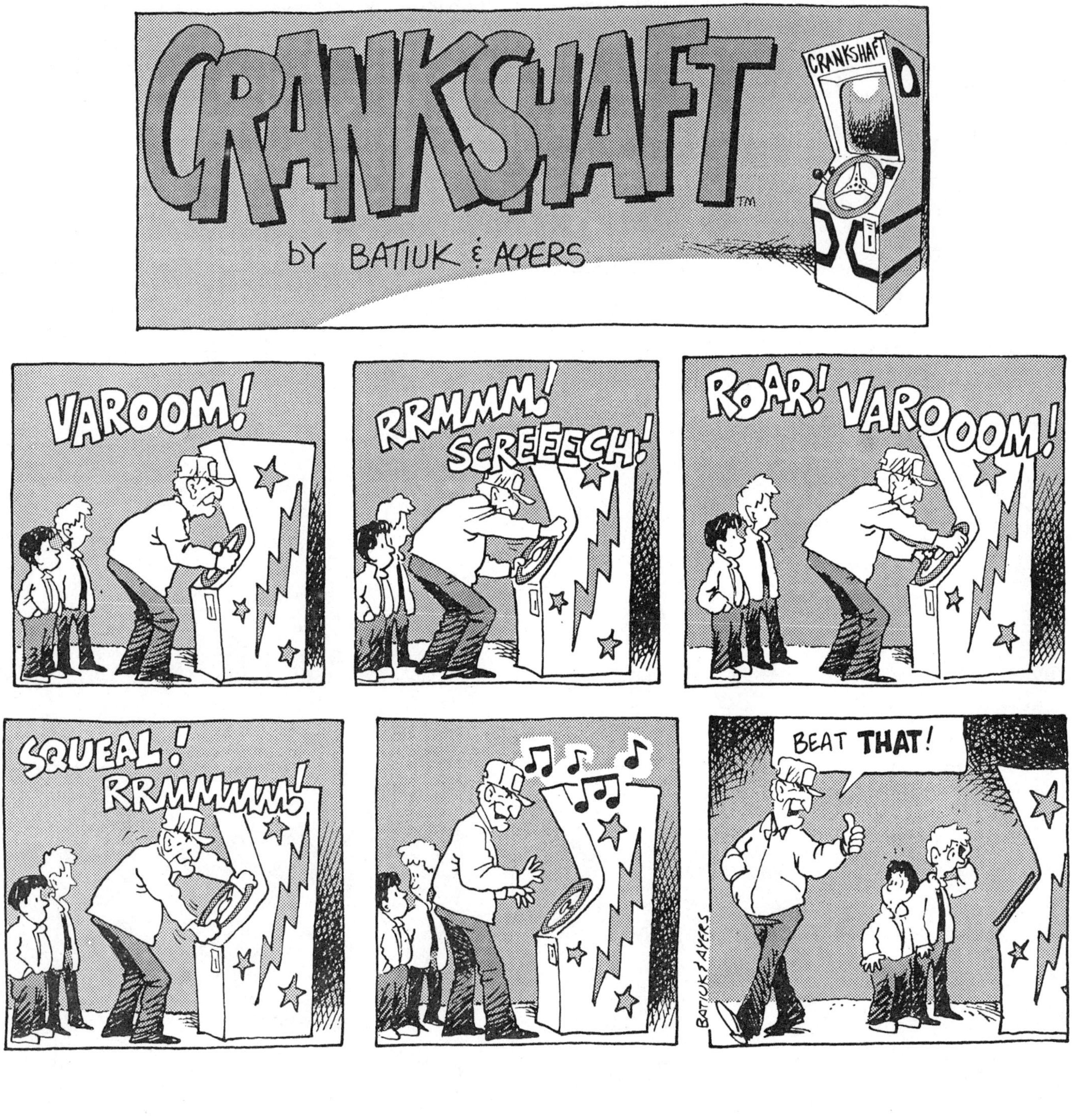
CRANKSHAFT™
BY BATIUK & AYERS
CRANKSHAFT
VAROOM!
RRMMM! SCREEECH!
ROAR! VAROOOM!
SQUEAL! RRMMMM!
BEAT THAT!
BATIUK & AYERS

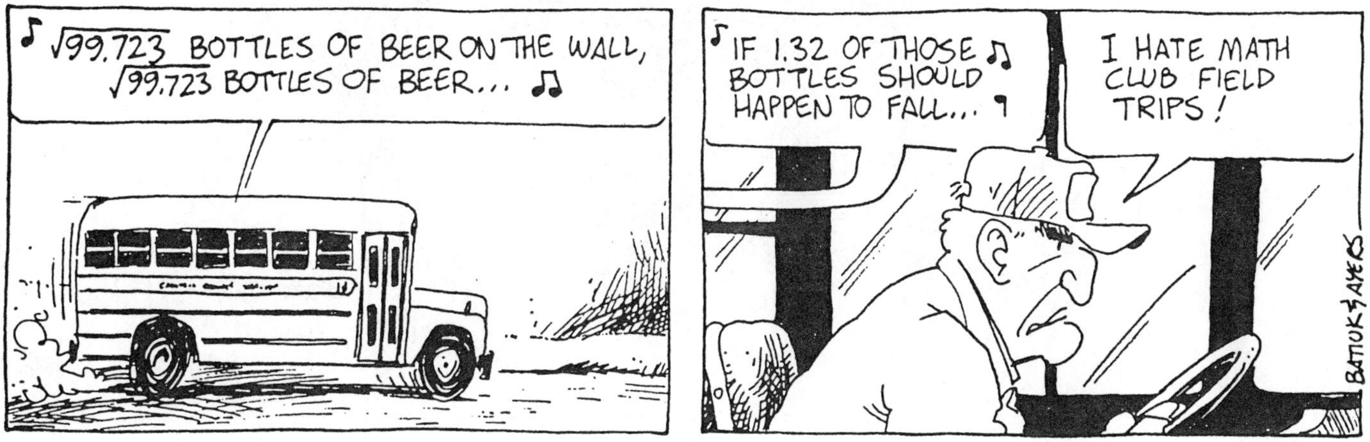
♪ $\sqrt{99.723}$ BOTTLES OF BEER ON THE WALL, $\sqrt{99.723}$ BOTTLES OF BEER... ♫
♪ IF 1.32 OF THOSE ♫ BOTTLES SHOULD HAPPEN TO FALL... ♪
I HATE MATH CLUB FIELD TRIPS!
BATIUK & AYERS

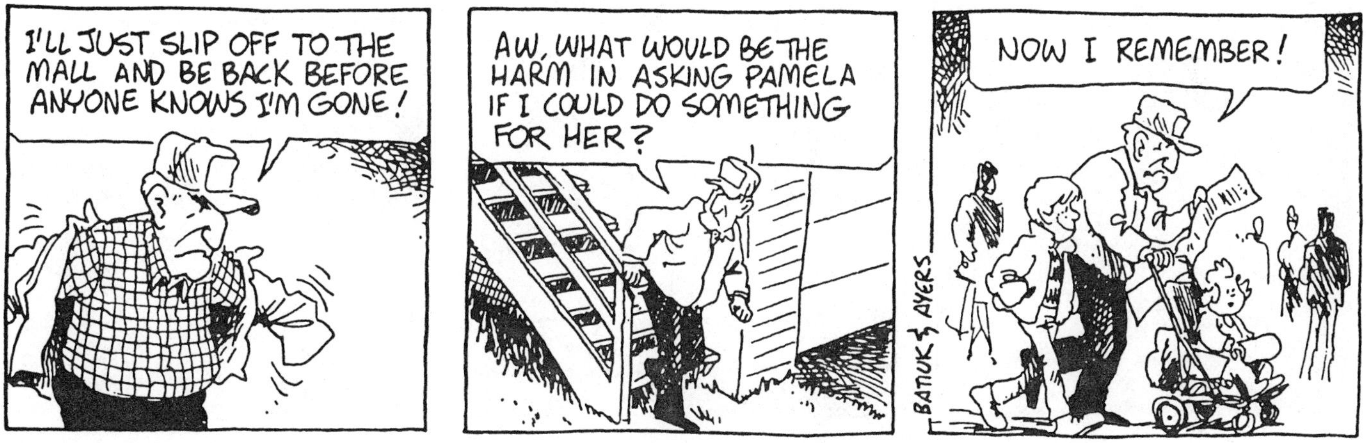
I'LL JUST SLIP OFF TO THE MALL AND BE BACK BEFORE ANYONE KNOWS I'M GONE!
AW, WHAT WOULD BE THE HARM IN ASKING PAMELA IF I COULD DO SOMETHING FOR HER?
NOW I REMEMBER!
BATIUK & AYERS

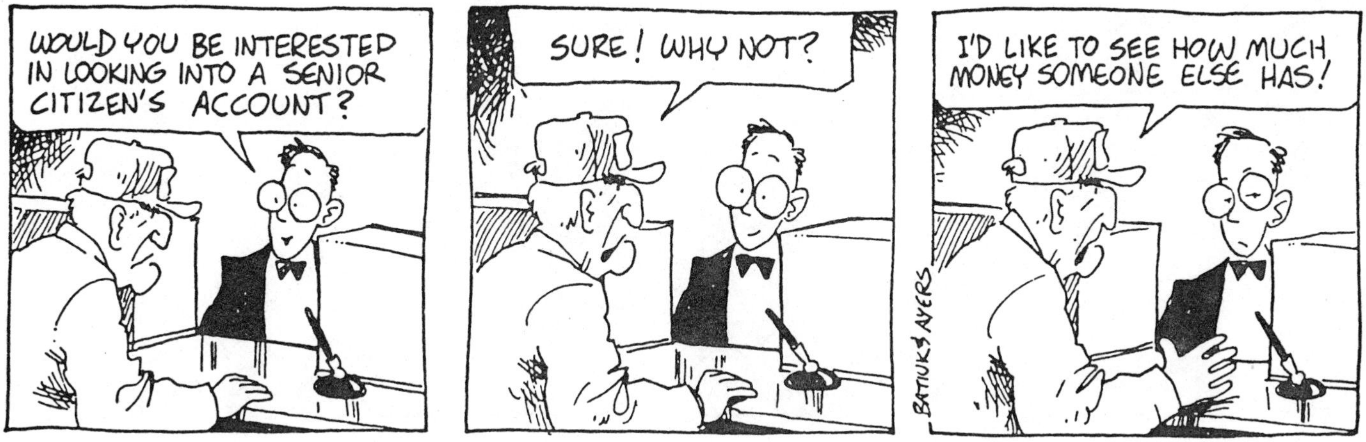
WOULD YOU BE INTERESTED IN LOOKING INTO A SENIOR CITIZEN'S ACCOUNT?
SURE! WHY NOT?
I'D LIKE TO SEE HOW MUCH MONEY SOMEONE ELSE HAS!
BATIUK & AYERS

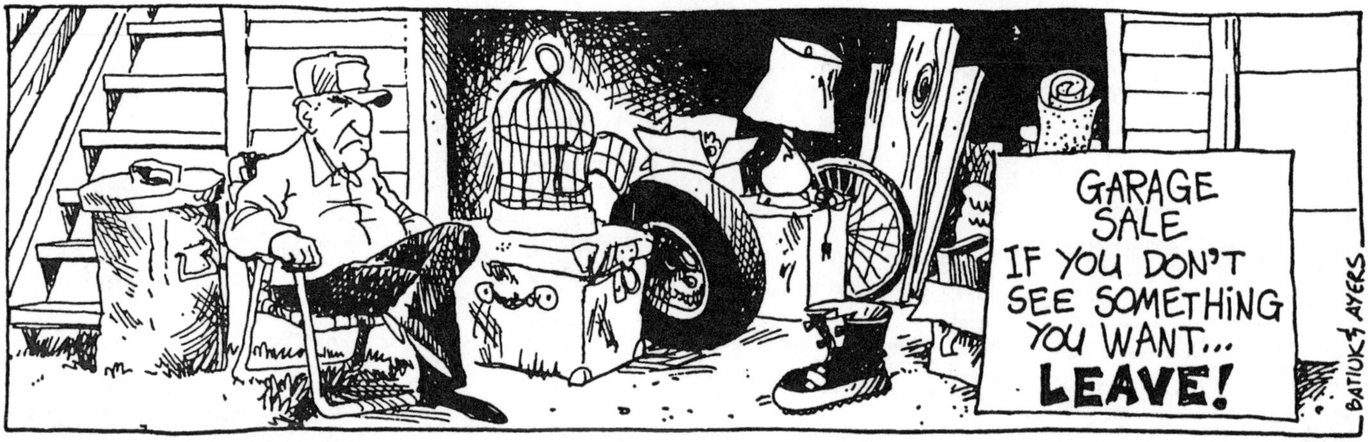
GARAGE SALE IF YOU DON'T SEE SOMETHING YOU WANT... LEAVE!
BATIUK & AYERS

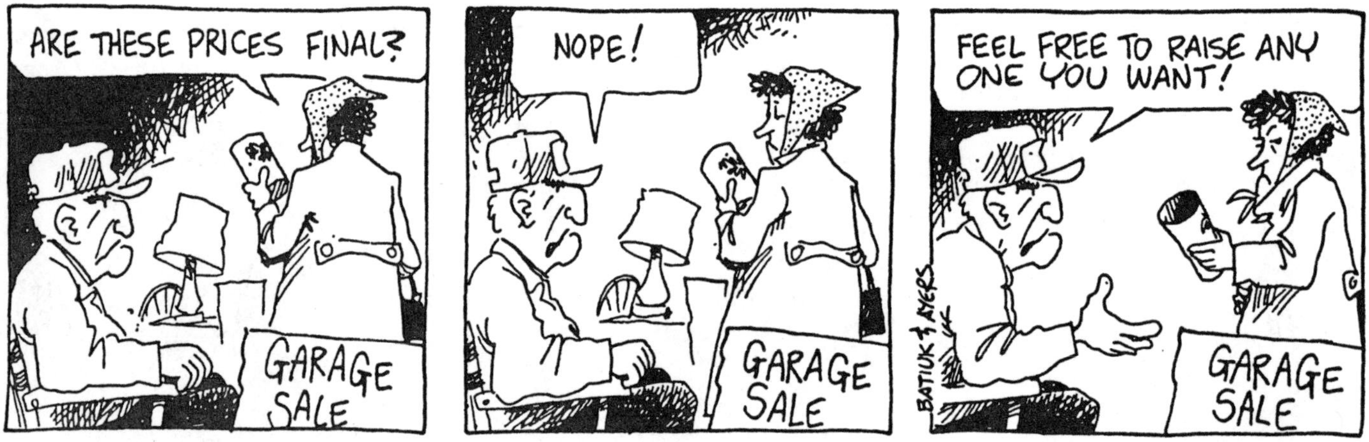
ARE THESE PRICES FINAL?
GARAGE SALE
NOPE!
GARAGE SALE
FEEL FREE TO RAISE ANY ONE YOU WANT!
BATIUK & AYERS
GARAGE SALE

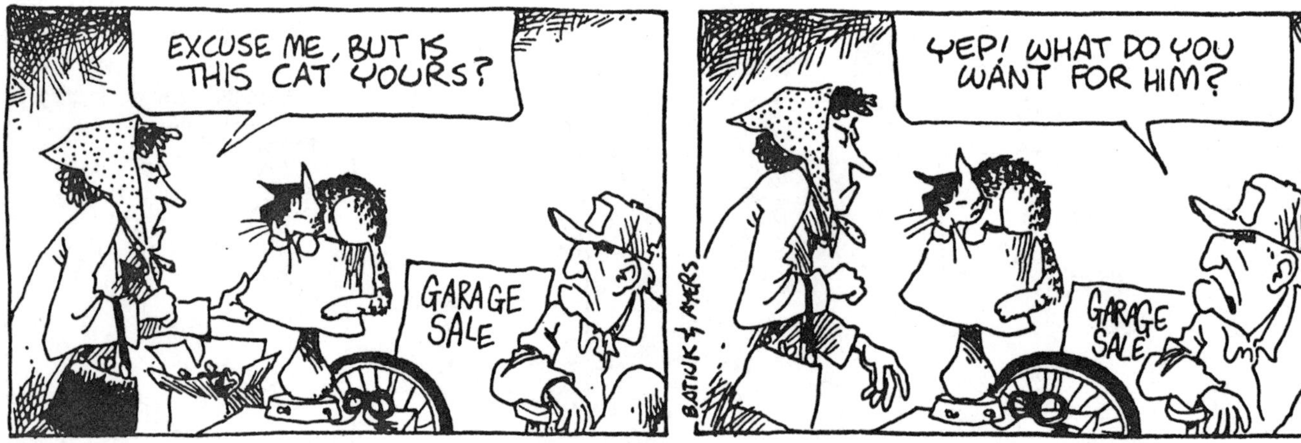
EXCUSE ME, BUT IS THIS CAT YOURS?
GARAGE SALE
BATIUK & AYERS
YEP! WHAT DO YOU WANT FOR HIM?
GARAGE SALE

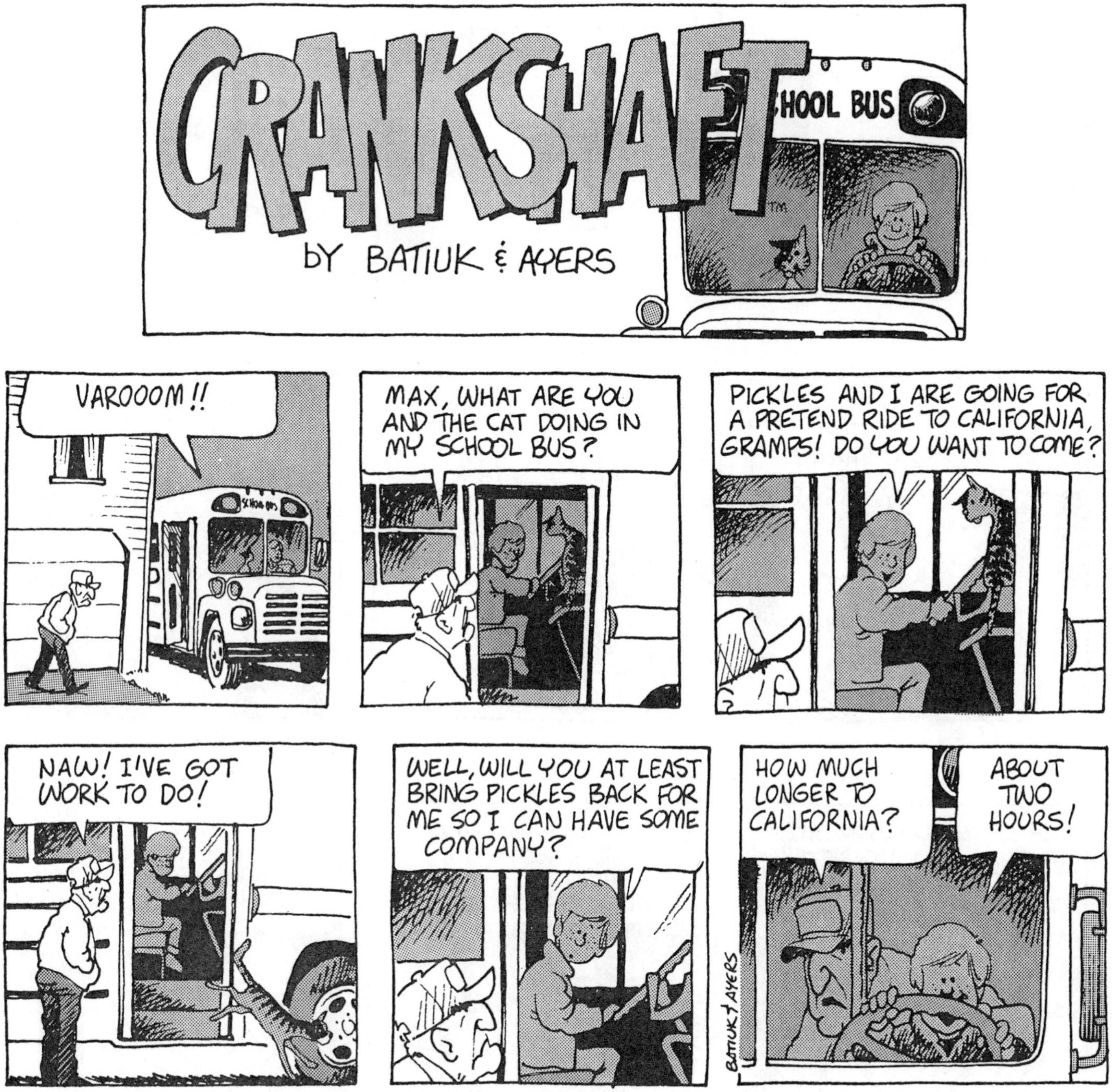
CRANKSHAFT
by BATIUK & AYERS
VAROOOM!!
MAX, WHAT ARE YOU AND THE CAT DOING IN MY SCHOOL BUS?
PICKLES AND I ARE GOING FOR A PRETEND RIDE TO CALIFORNIA, GRAMPS! DO YOU WANT TO COME?
NAW! I'VE GOT WORK TO DO!
WELL, WILL YOU AT LEAST BRING PICKLES BACK FOR ME SO I CAN HAVE SOME COMPANY?
HOW MUCH LONGER TO CALIFORNIA?
ABOUT TWO HOURS!
BATIUK + AYERS

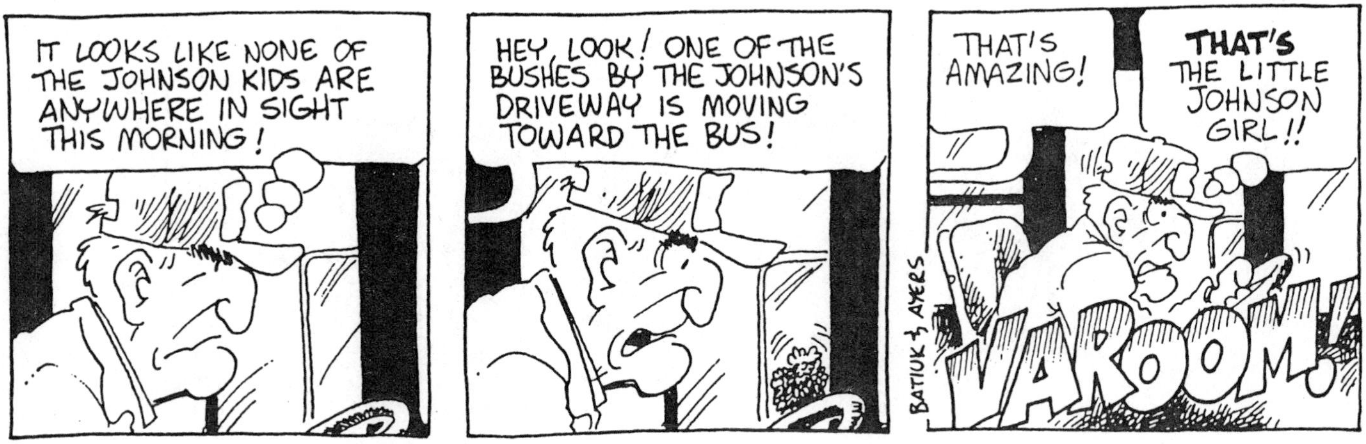
IT LOOKS LIKE NONE OF THE JOHNSON KIDS ARE ANYWHERE IN SIGHT THIS MORNING!
HEY, LOOK! ONE OF THE BUSHES BY THE JOHNSON'S DRIVEWAY IS MOVING TOWARD THE BUS!
THAT'S AMAZING!
THAT'S THE LITTLE JOHNSON GIRL!!
VAROOM!
BATIUK & AYERS

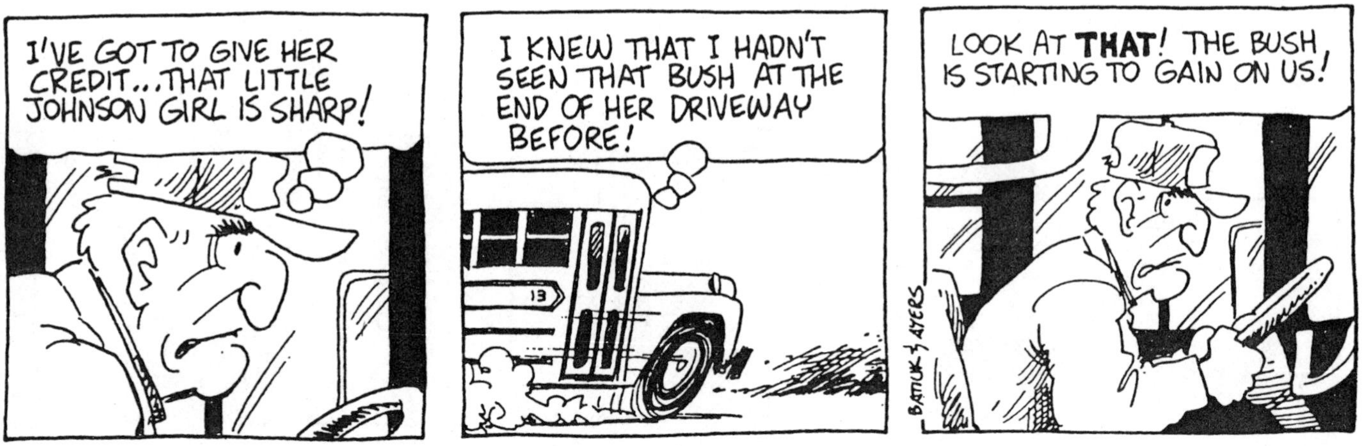
I'VE GOT TO GIVE HER CREDIT... THAT LITTLE JOHNSON GIRL IS SHARP!
I KNEW THAT I HADN'T SEEN THAT BUSH AT THE END OF HER DRIVEWAY BEFORE!
13
LOOK AT **THAT**! THE BUSH IS STARTING TO GAIN ON US!
BATIUK & AYERS

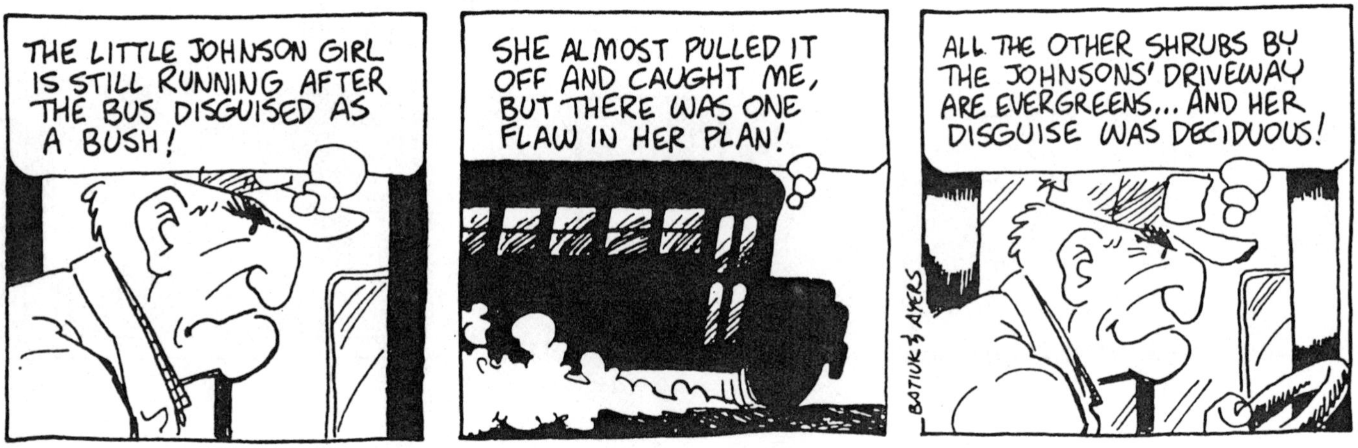
THE LITTLE JOHNSON GIRL IS STILL RUNNING AFTER THE BUS DISGUISED AS A BUSH!
SHE ALMOST PULLED IT OFF AND CAUGHT ME, BUT THERE WAS ONE FLAW IN HER PLAN!
ALL THE OTHER SHRUBS BY THE JOHNSONS' DRIVEWAY ARE EVERGREENS... AND HER DISGUISE WAS DECIDUOUS!
BATIUK & AYERS

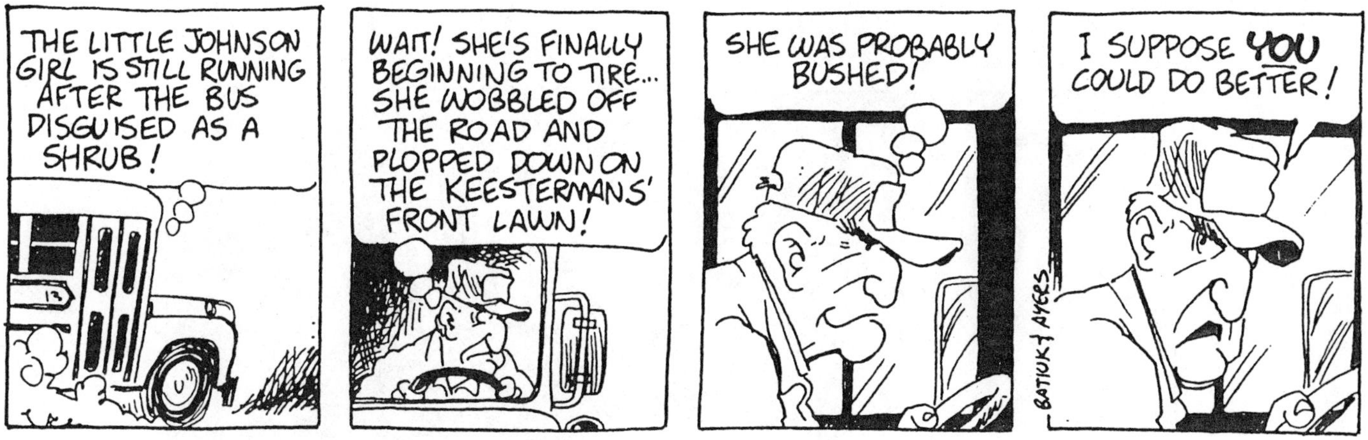
THE LITTLE JOHNSON GIRL IS STILL RUNNING AFTER THE BUS DISGUISED AS A SHRUB!
13
WAIT! SHE'S FINALLY BEGINNING TO TIRE... SHE WOBBLED OFF THE ROAD AND PLOPPED DOWN ON THE KEESTERMANS' FRONT LAWN!
SHE WAS PROBABLY BUSHED!
BATIUK & AYERS
I SUPPOSE YOU COULD DO BETTER!

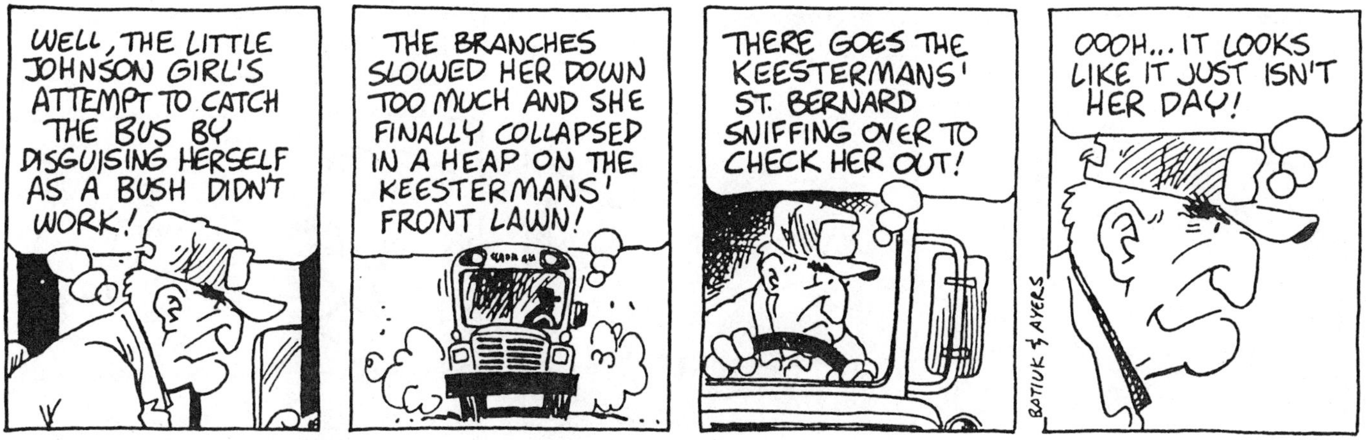
WELL, THE LITTLE JOHNSON GIRL'S ATTEMPT TO CATCH THE BUS BY DISGUISING HERSELF AS A BUSH DIDN'T WORK!
THE BRANCHES SLOWED HER DOWN TOO MUCH AND SHE FINALLY COLLAPSED IN A HEAP ON THE KEESTERMANS' FRONT LAWN!
THERE GOES THE KEESTERMANS' ST. BERNARD SNIFFING OVER TO CHECK HER OUT!
BATIUK & AYERS
OOOH... IT LOOKS LIKE IT JUST ISN'T HER DAY!

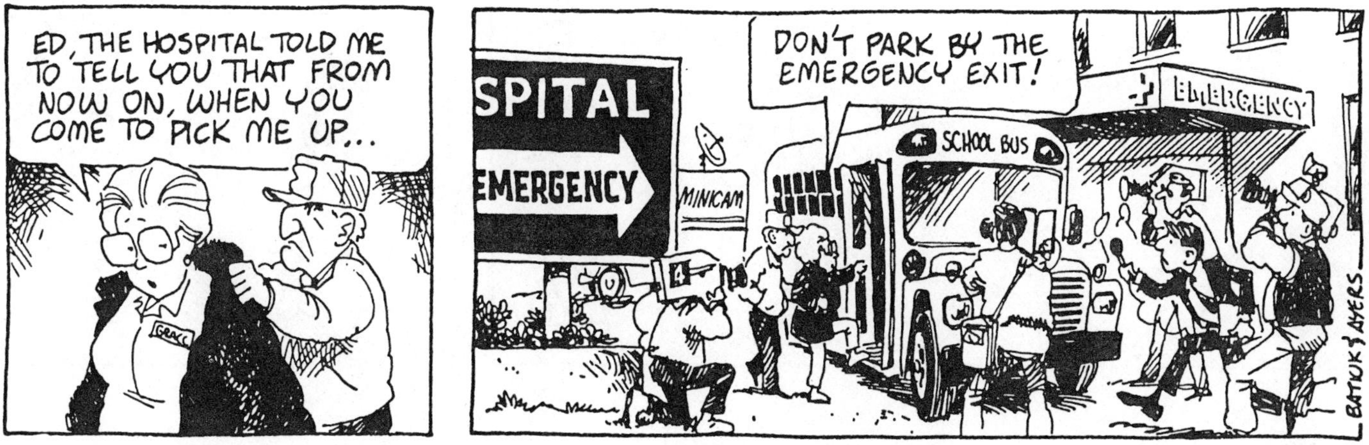
ED, THE HOSPITAL TOLD ME TO TELL YOU THAT FROM NOW ON, WHEN YOU COME TO PICK ME UP...
GRACE
SPITAL
EMERGENCY
MINICAM
DON'T PARK BY THE EMERGENCY EXIT!
SCHOOL BUS
EMERGENCY
4
BATIUK & AYERS

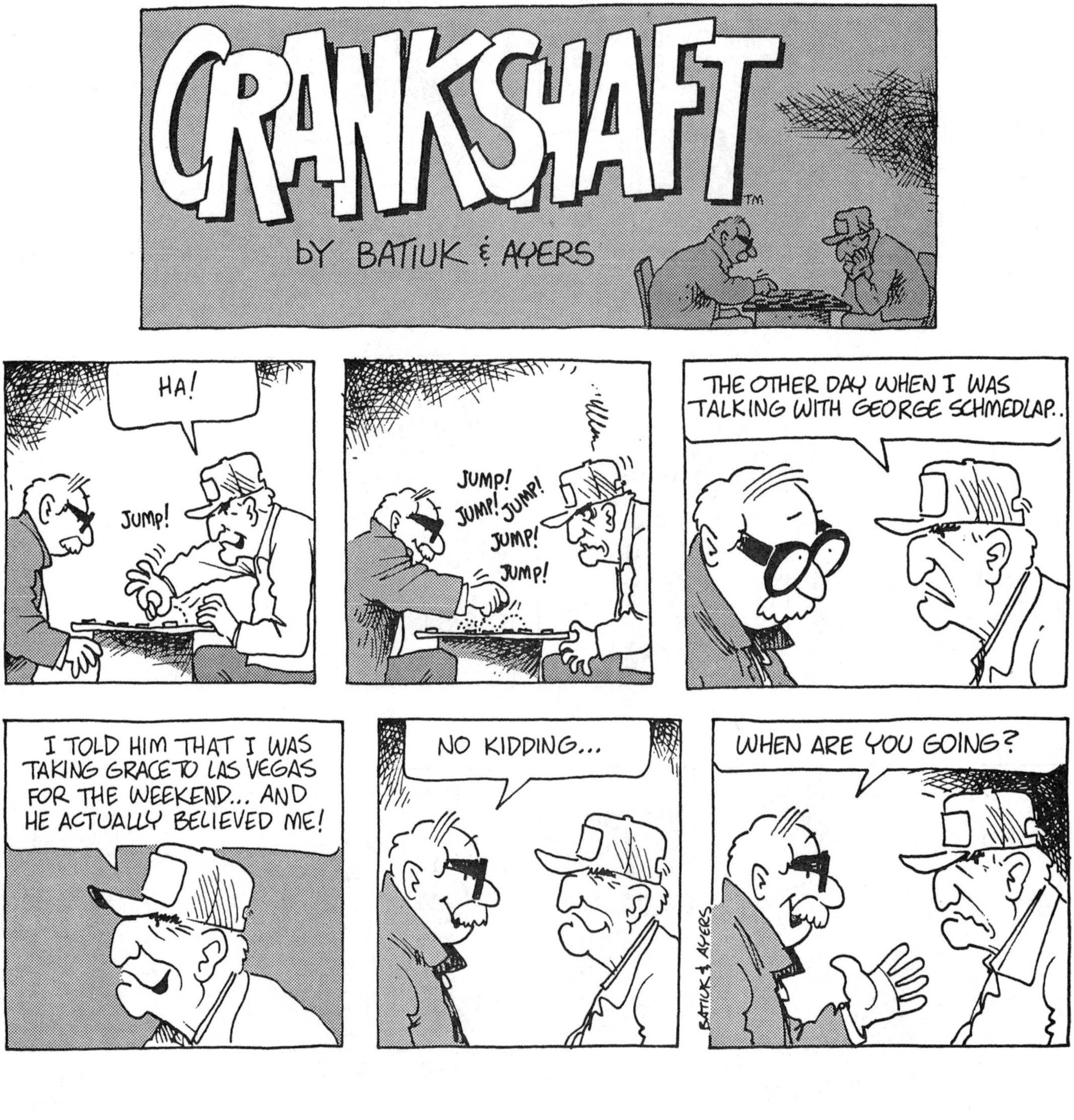
CRANKSHAFT™
BY BATIUK & AYERS
HA!
JUMP!
JUMP!
JUMP!
JUMP!
JUMP!
JUMP!
THE OTHER DAY WHEN I WAS TALKING WITH GEORGE SCHMEDLAP..
I TOLD HIM THAT I WAS TAKING GRACE TO LAS VEGAS FOR THE WEEKEND... AND HE ACTUALLY BELIEVED ME!
NO KIDDING...
BATIUK & AYERS
WHEN ARE YOU GOING?

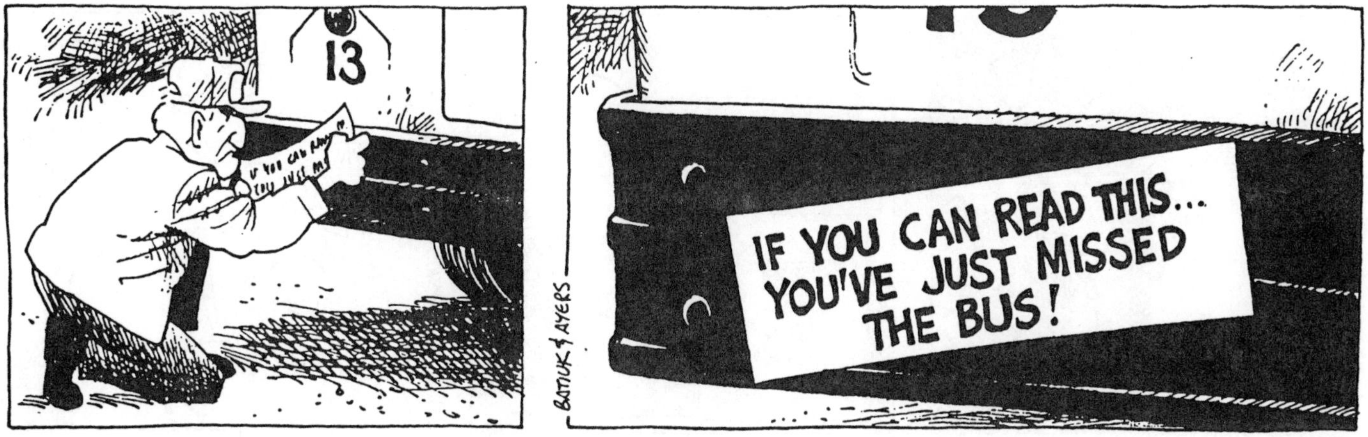
13
IF YOU CAN READ THIS... YOU'VE JUST MISSED THE BUS!
BATIUK & AYERS

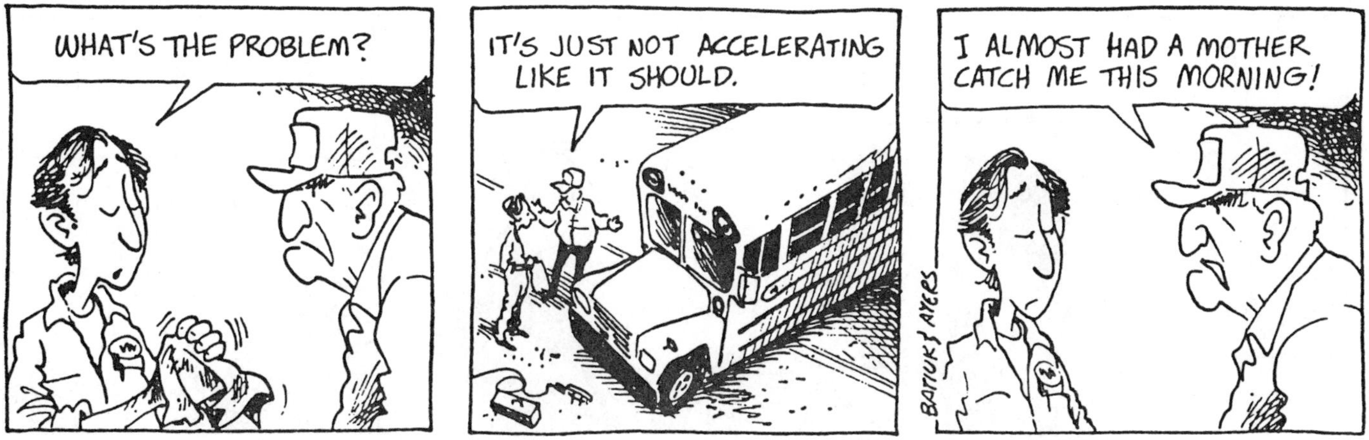
WHAT'S THE PROBLEM?
IT'S JUST NOT ACCELERATING LIKE IT SHOULD.
I ALMOST HAD A MOTHER CATCH ME THIS MORNING!
BATIUK & AYERS

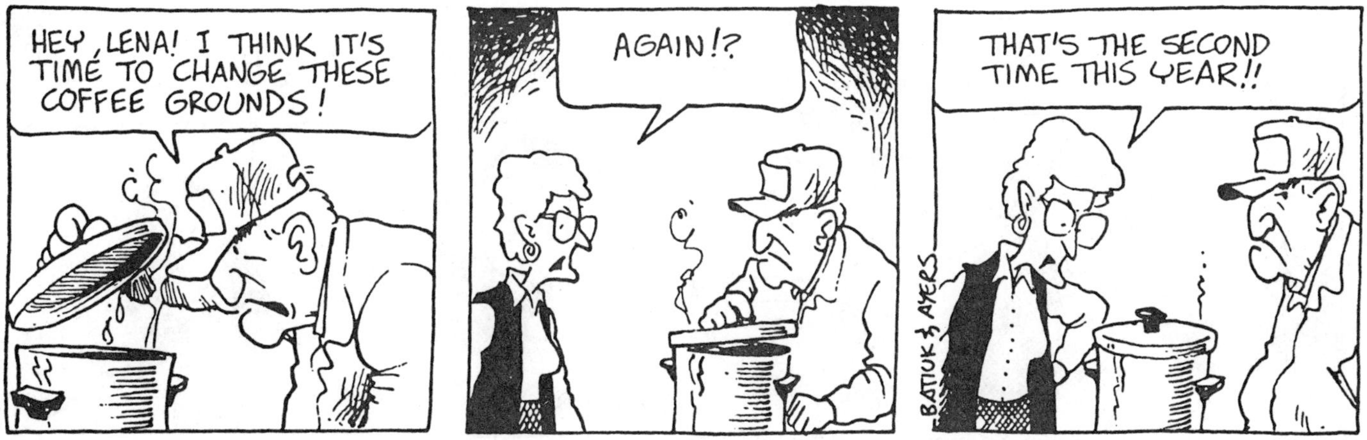
HEY, LENA! I THINK IT'S TIME TO CHANGE THESE COFFEE GROUNDS!
AGAIN!?
THAT'S THE SECOND TIME THIS YEAR!!
BATIUK & AYERS

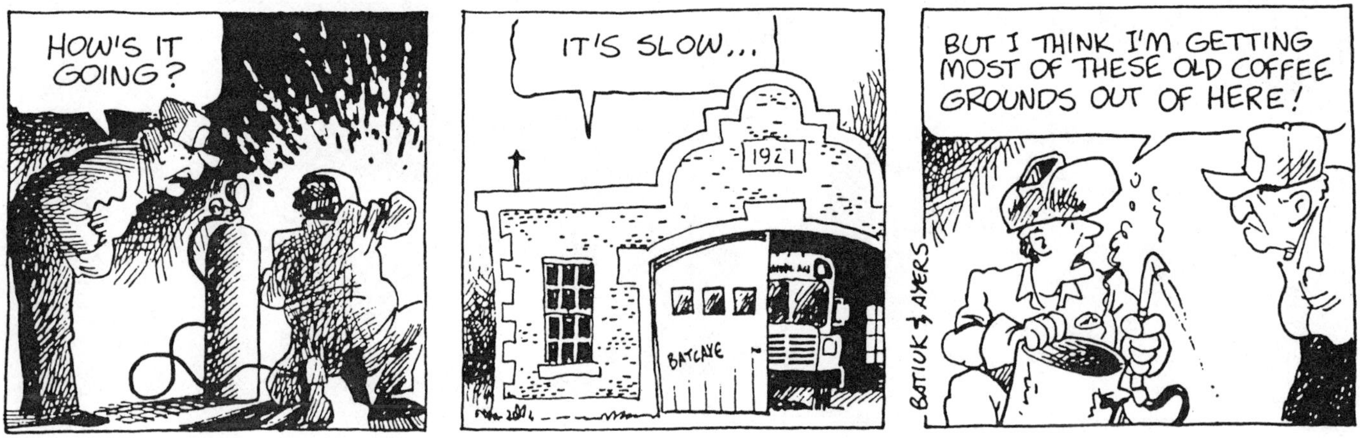
HOW'S IT GOING?
IT'S SLOW...
1921
BATCAVE
BUT I THINK I'M GETTING MOST OF THESE OLD COFFEE GROUNDS OUT OF HERE!
BATIUK & AYERS

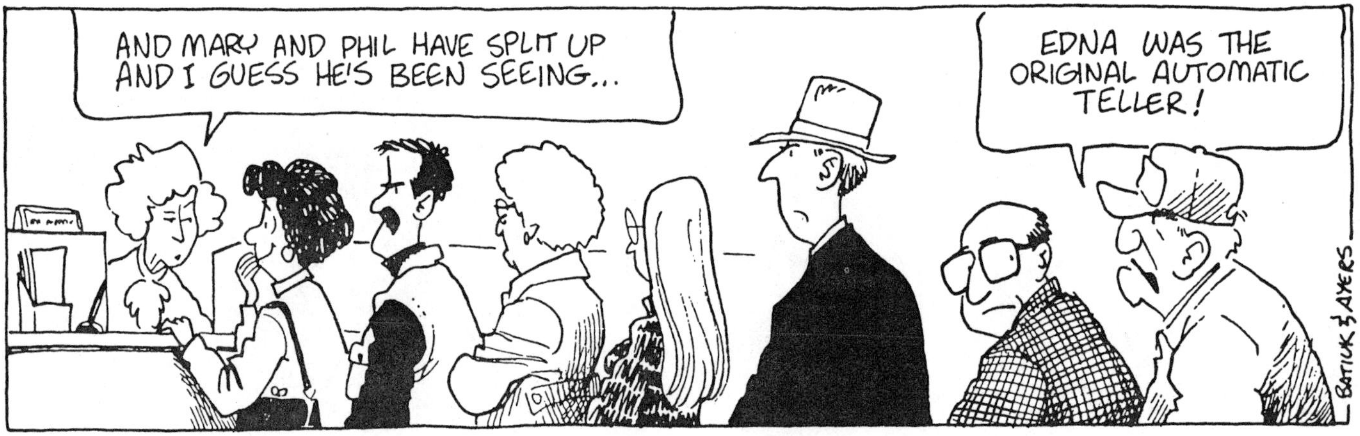
AND MARY AND PHIL HAVE SPLIT UP AND I GUESS HE'S BEEN SEEING...
EDNA WAS THE ORIGINAL AUTOMATIC TELLER!
BATIUK & AYERS

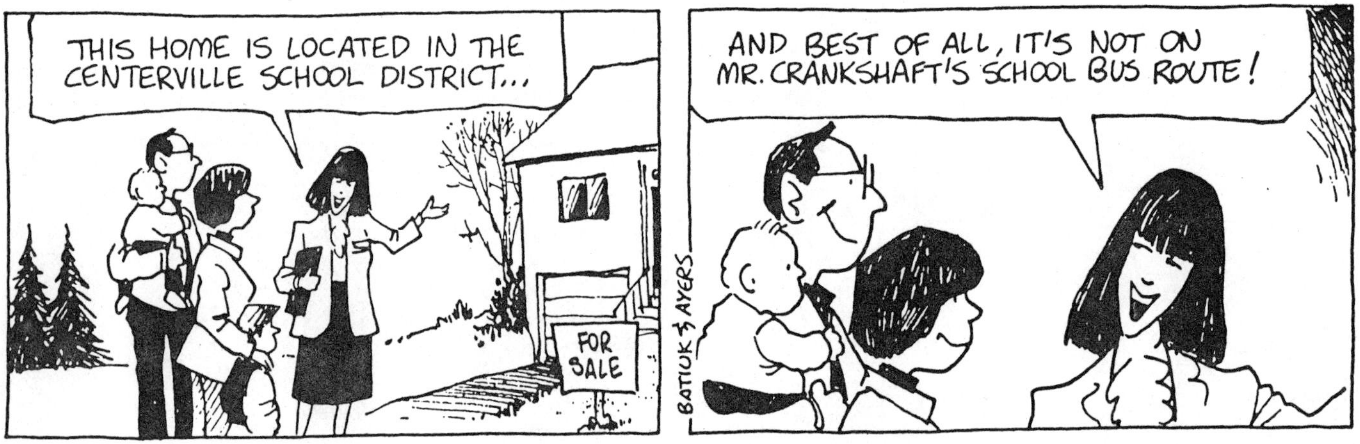
THIS HOME IS LOCATED IN THE CENTERVILLE SCHOOL DISTRICT...
FOR SALE
BATIUK & AYERS
AND BEST OF ALL, IT'S NOT ON MR. CRANKSHAFT'S SCHOOL BUS ROUTE!

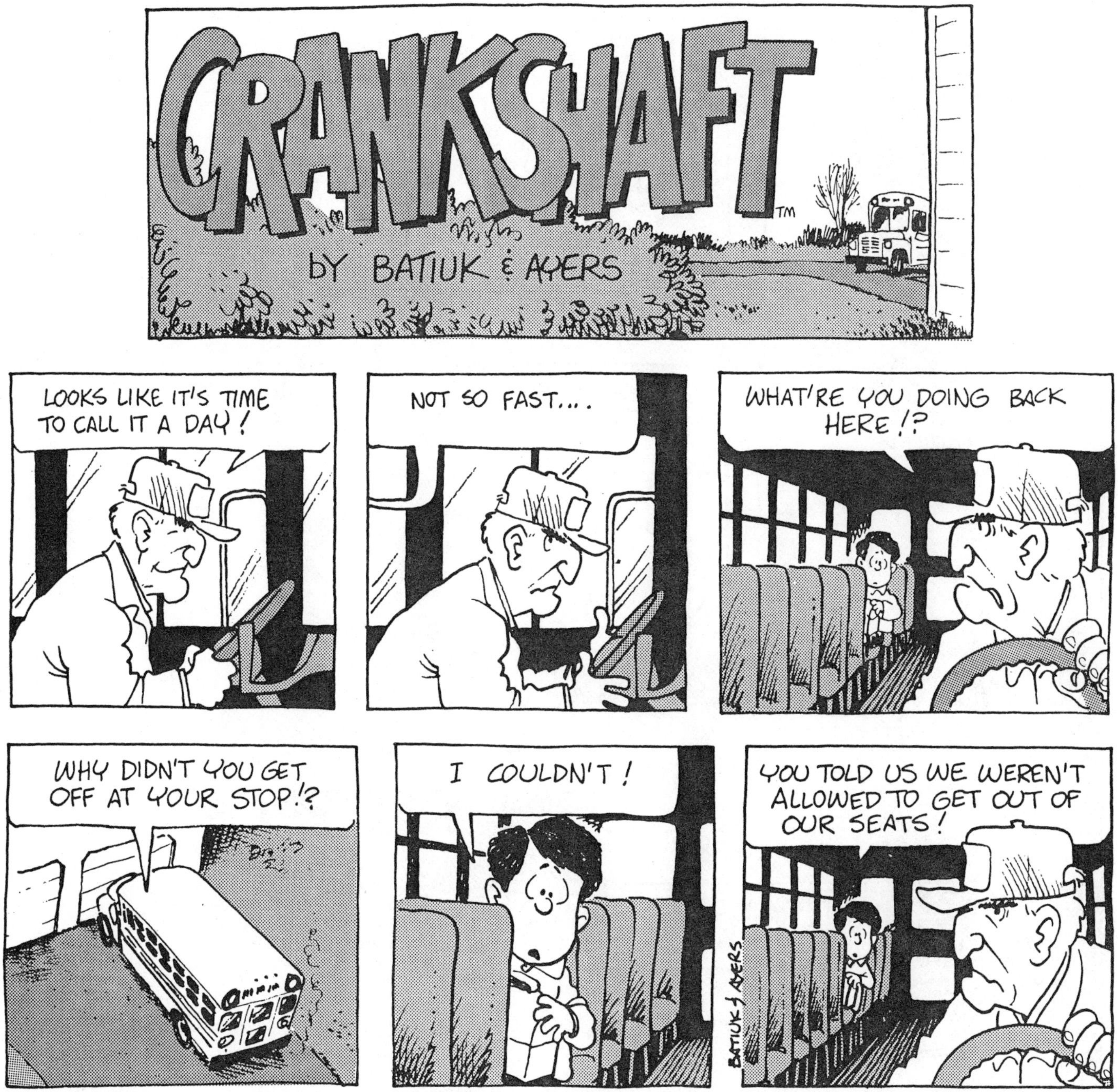
CRANKSHAFT
TM
BY BATIUK & AYERS
LOOKS LIKE IT'S TIME TO CALL IT A DAY!
NOT SO FAST....
WHAT'RE YOU DOING BACK HERE!?
WHY DIDN'T YOU GET OFF AT YOUR STOP!?
I COULDN'T!
YOU TOLD US WE WEREN'T ALLOWED TO GET OUT OF OUR SEATS!
BATIUK & AYERS

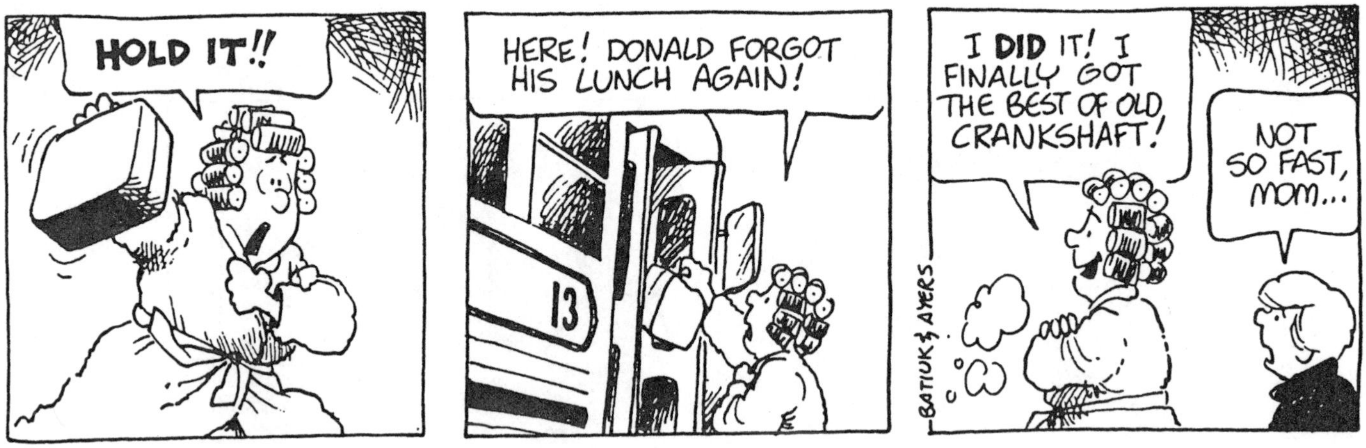
HOLD IT!!
HERE! DONALD FORGOT HIS LUNCH AGAIN!
13
I DID IT! I FINALLY GOT THE BEST OF OLD CRANKSHAFT!
NOT SO FAST, MOM...
BATIUK & AYERS

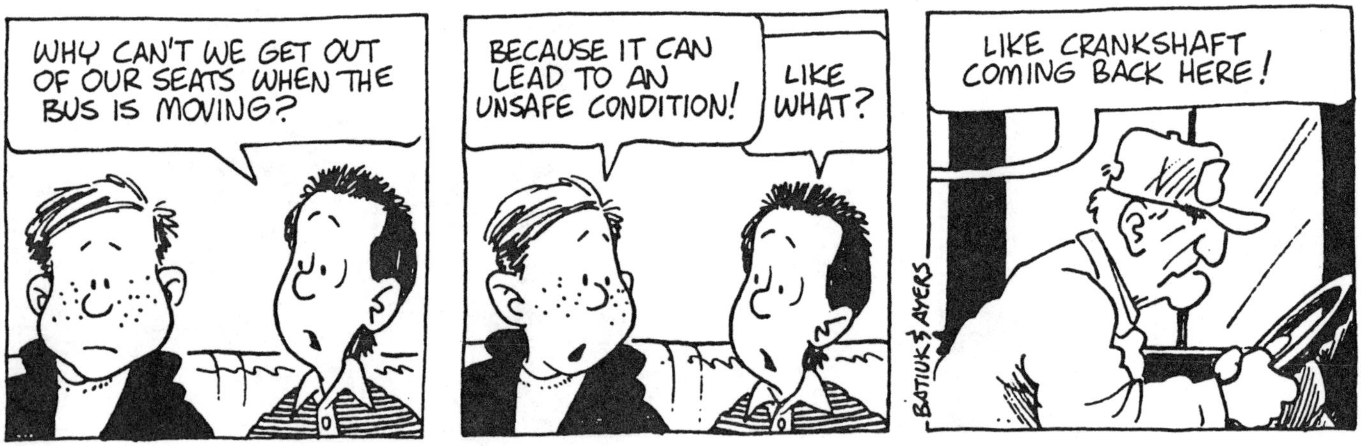
WHY CAN'T WE GET OUT OF OUR SEATS WHEN THE BUS IS MOVING?
BECAUSE IT CAN LEAD TO AN UNSAFE CONDITION!
LIKE WHAT?
LIKE CRANKSHAFT COMING BACK HERE!
BATIUK & AYERS

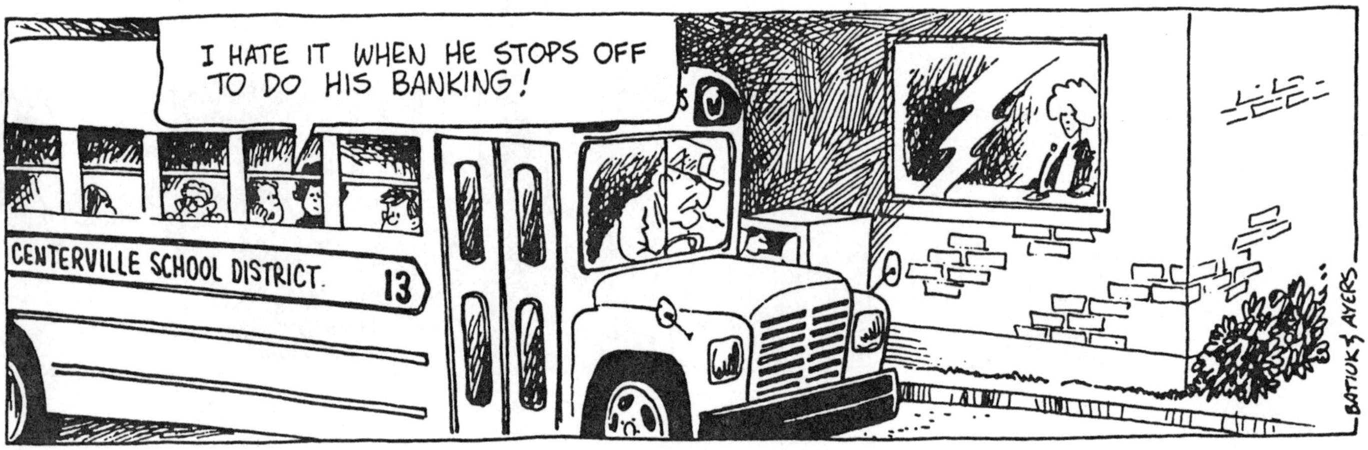
I HATE IT WHEN HE STOPS OFF TO DO HIS BANKING!
CENTERVILLE SCHOOL DISTRICT
13
BATIUK & AYERS

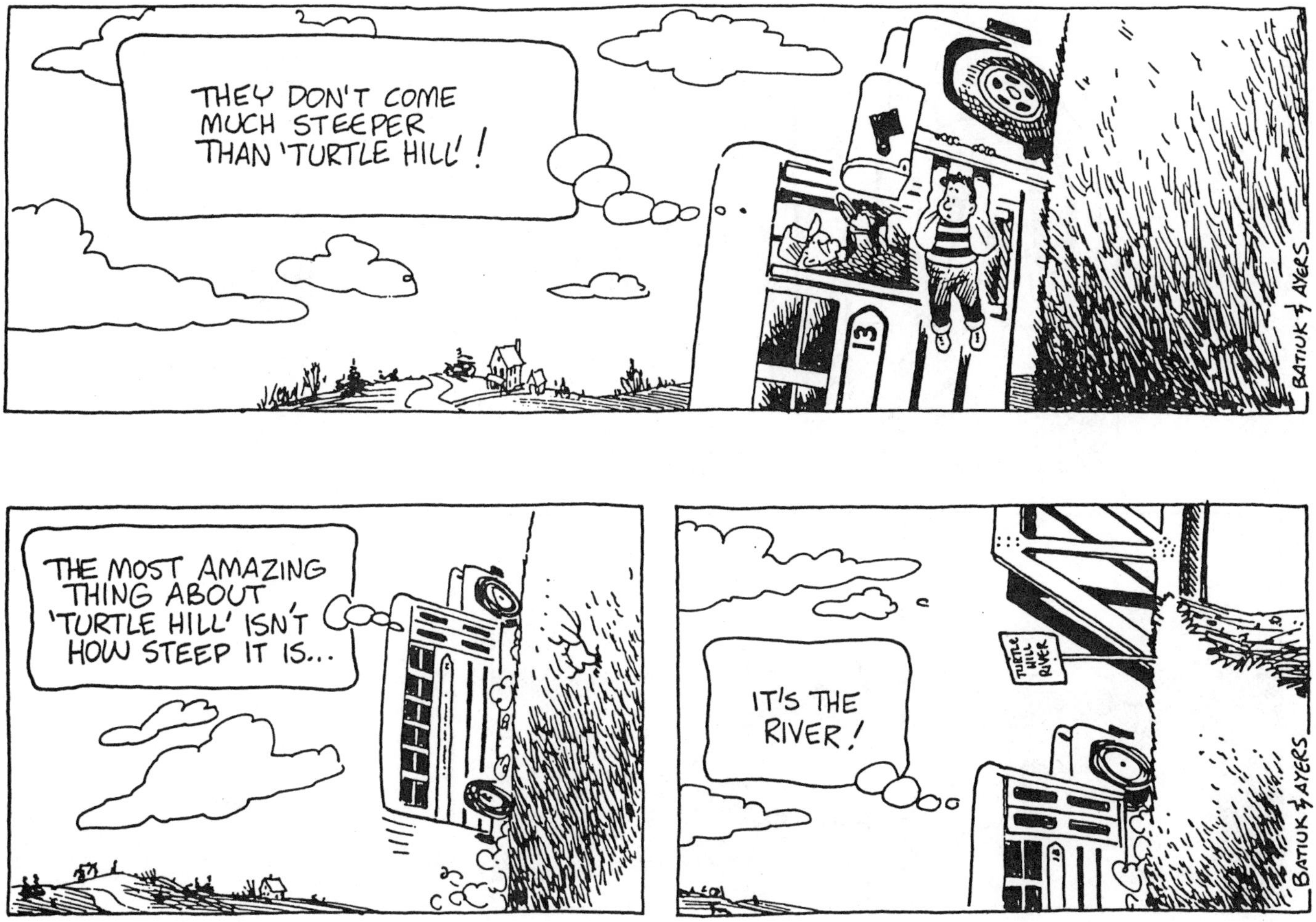
THEY DON'T COME MUCH STEEPER THAN 'TURTLE HILL'!
13
BATIUK & AYERS
THE MOST AMAZING THING ABOUT 'TURTLE HILL' ISN'T HOW STEEP IT IS...
IT'S THE RIVER!
TURTLE HILL RIVER
BATIUK & AYERS

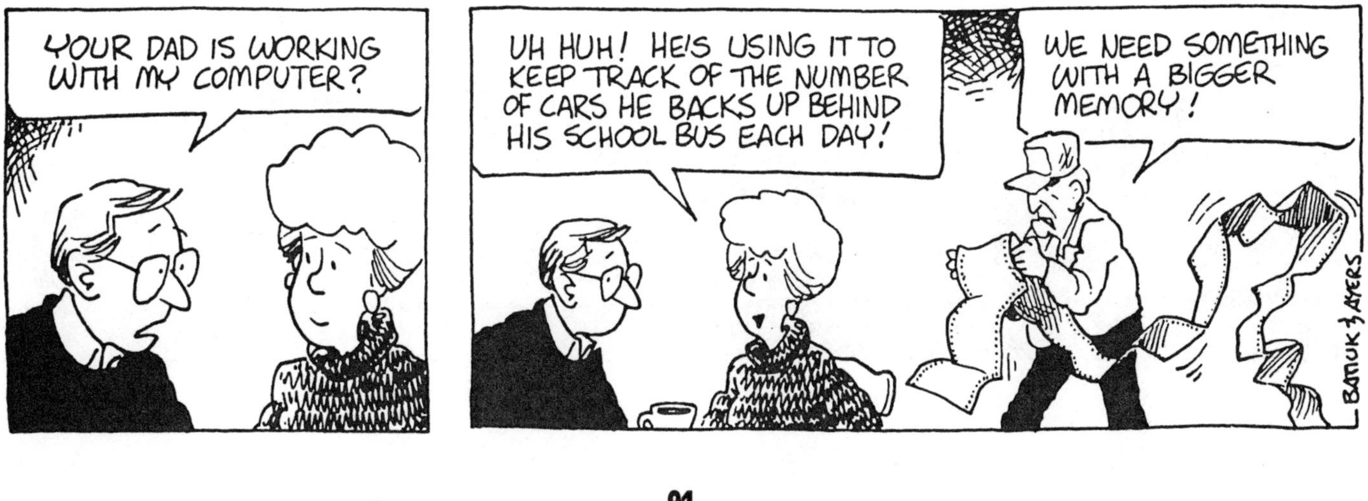
YOUR DAD IS WORKING WITH MY COMPUTER?
UH HUH! HE'S USING IT TO KEEP TRACK OF THE NUMBER OF CARS HE BACKS UP BEHIND HIS SCHOOL BUS EACH DAY!
WE NEED SOMETHING WITH A BIGGER MEMORY!
BATIUK & AYERS

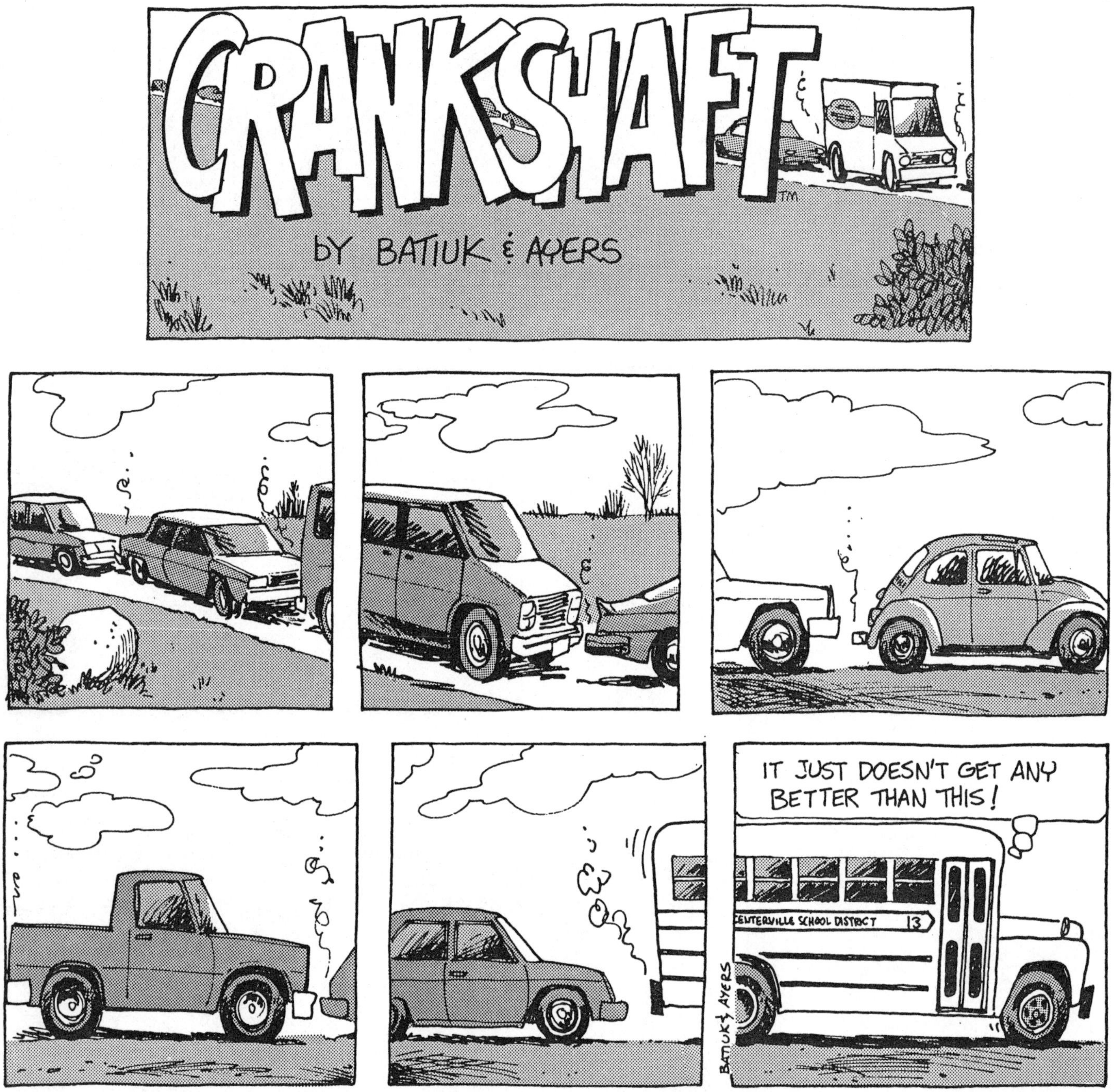
CRANKSHAFT
TM
BY BATIUK & AYERS
CENTERVILLE SCHOOL DISTRICT 13
IT JUST DOESN'T GET ANY BETTER THAN THIS!
BATIUK & AYERS

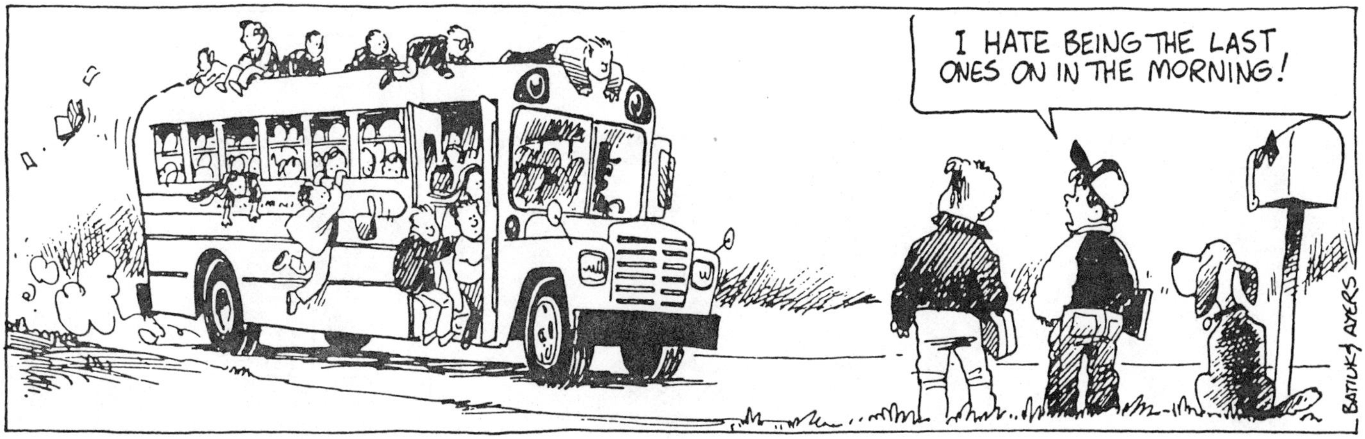
I HATE BEING THE LAST ONES ON IN THE MORNING!
BATIUK & AYERS

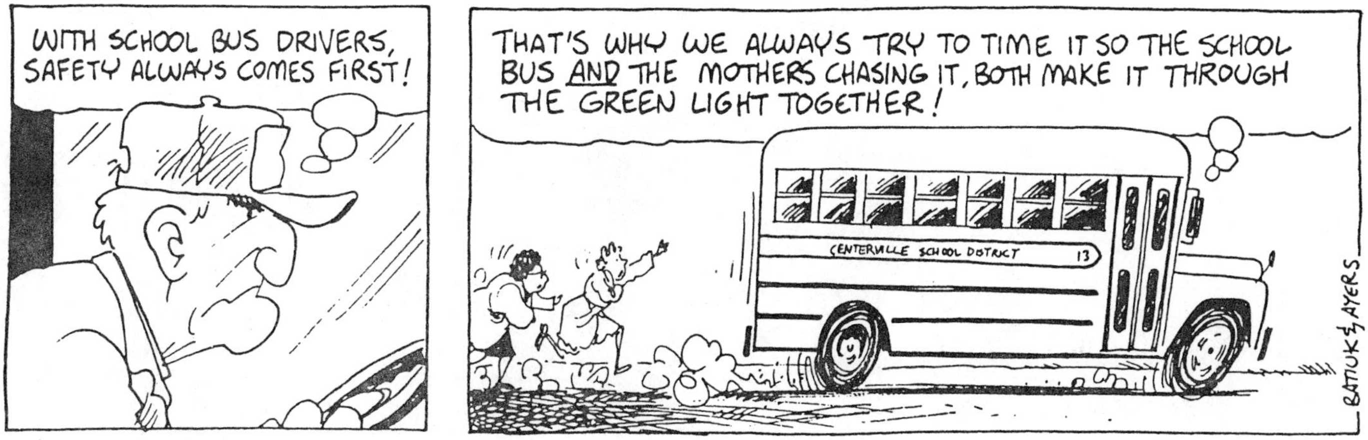
WITH SCHOOL BUS DRIVERS, SAFETY ALWAYS COMES FIRST!
THAT'S WHY WE ALWAYS TRY TO TIME IT SO THE SCHOOL BUS AND THE MOTHERS CHASING IT, BOTH MAKE IT THROUGH THE GREEN LIGHT TOGETHER!
CENTERVILLE SCHOOL DISTRICT
13
BATIUK & AYERS

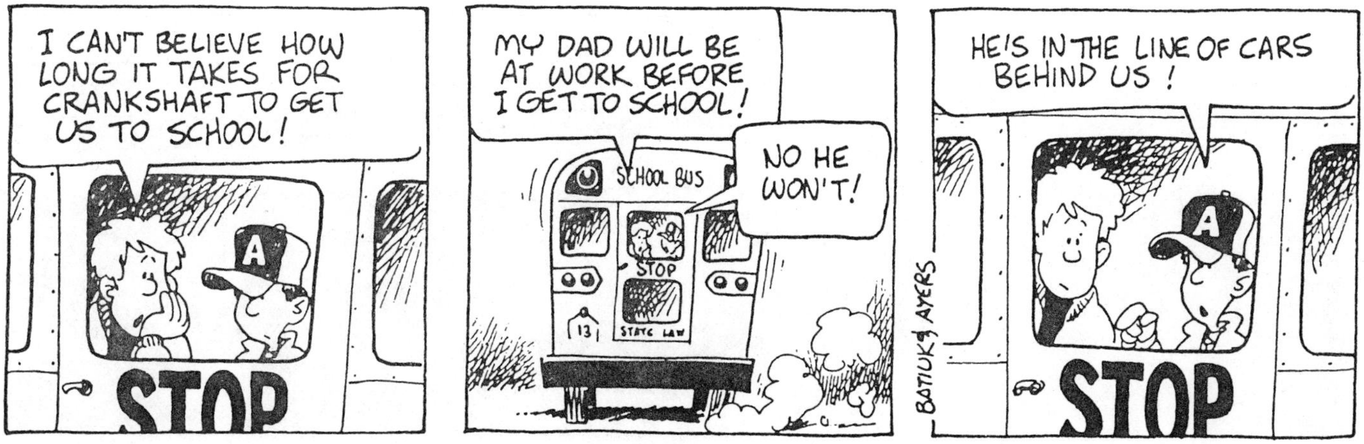
I CAN'T BELIEVE HOW LONG IT TAKES FOR CRANKSHAFT TO GET US TO SCHOOL!
STOP
MY DAD WILL BE AT WORK BEFORE I GET TO SCHOOL!
NO HE WON'T!
SCHOOL BUS
STOP
13
STATE LAW
BATIUK & AYERS
HE'S IN THE LINE OF CARS BEHIND US!
STOP

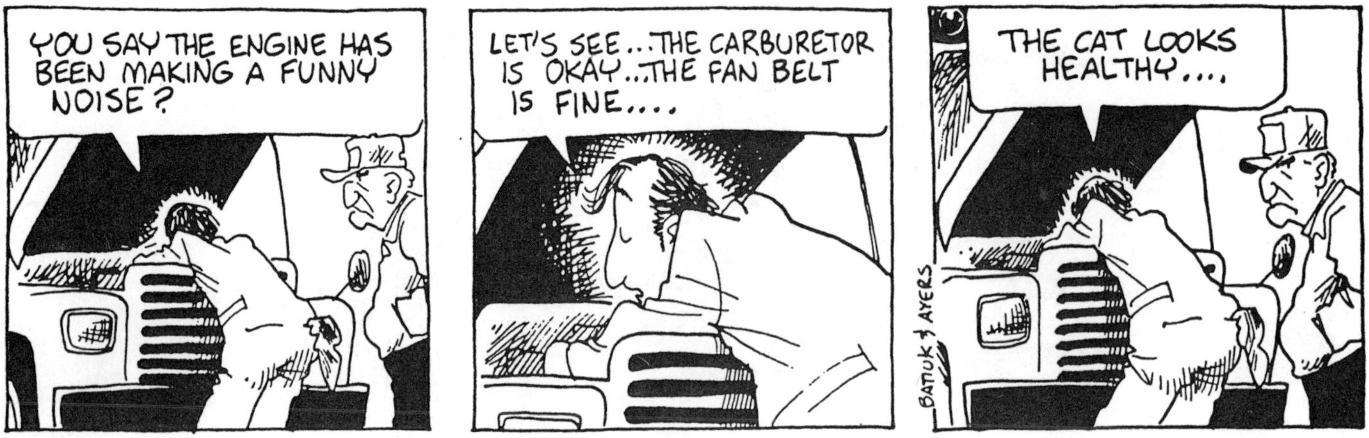
YOU SAY THE ENGINE HAS BEEN MAKING A FUNNY NOISE?
LET'S SEE... THE CARBURETOR IS OKAY... THE FAN BELT IS FINE....
THE CAT LOOKS HEALTHY....
BATIUK & AYERS

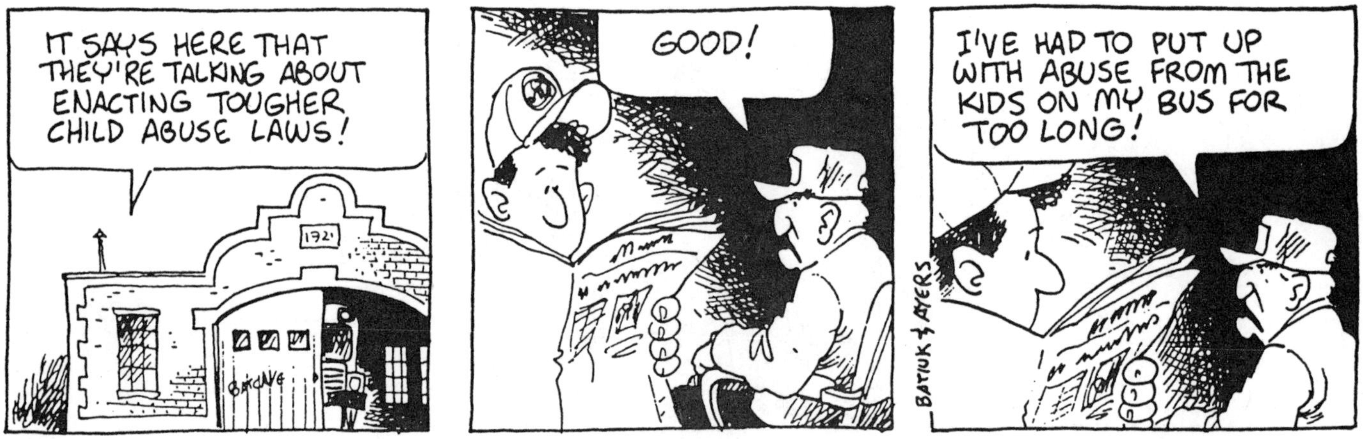
IT SAYS HERE THAT THEY'RE TALKING ABOUT ENACTING TOUGHER CHILD ABUSE LAWS!
GOOD!
I'VE HAD TO PUT UP WITH ABUSE FROM THE KIDS ON MY BUS FOR TOO LONG!
BATIUK & AYERS

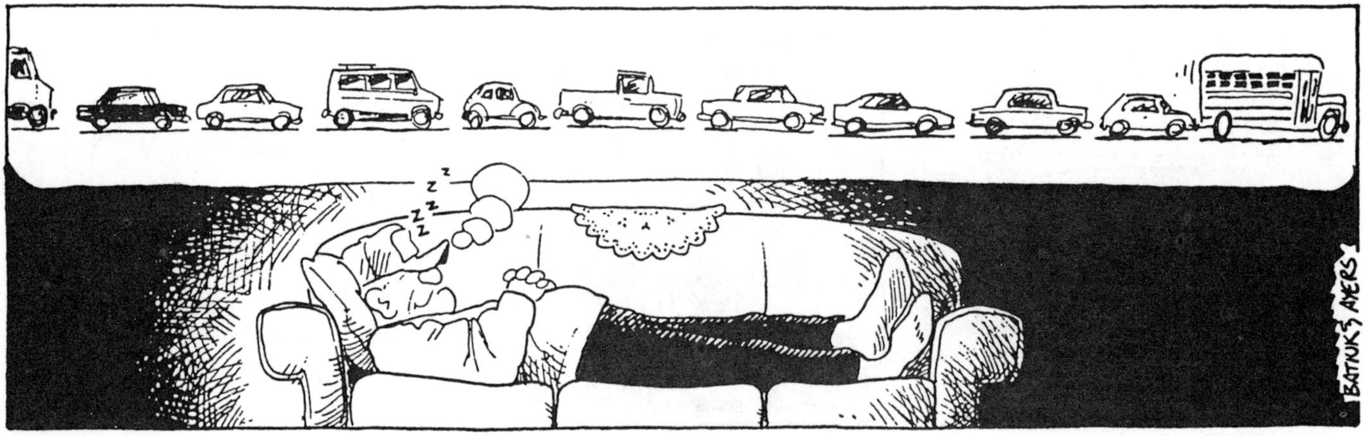
BATIUK & AYERS

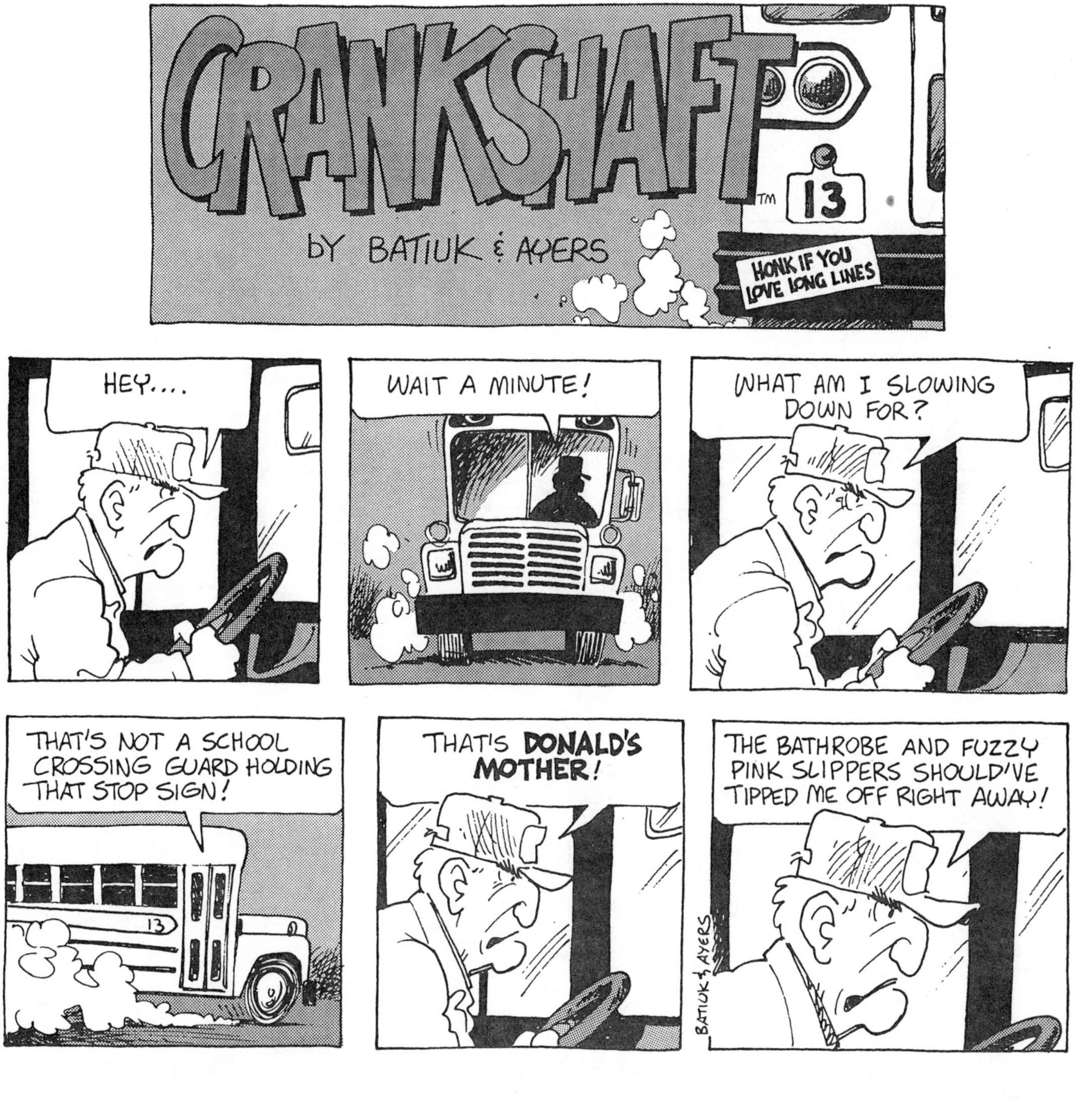
CRANKSHAFT
TM
13
BY BATIUK & AYERS
HONK IF YOU LOVE LONG LINES
HEY....
WAIT A MINUTE!
WHAT AM I SLOWING DOWN FOR?
THAT'S NOT A SCHOOL CROSSING GUARD HOLDING THAT STOP SIGN!
13
THAT'S **DONALD'S MOTHER**!
BATIUK & AYERS
THE BATHROBE AND FUZZY PINK SLIPPERS SHOULD'VE TIPPED ME OFF RIGHT AWAY!

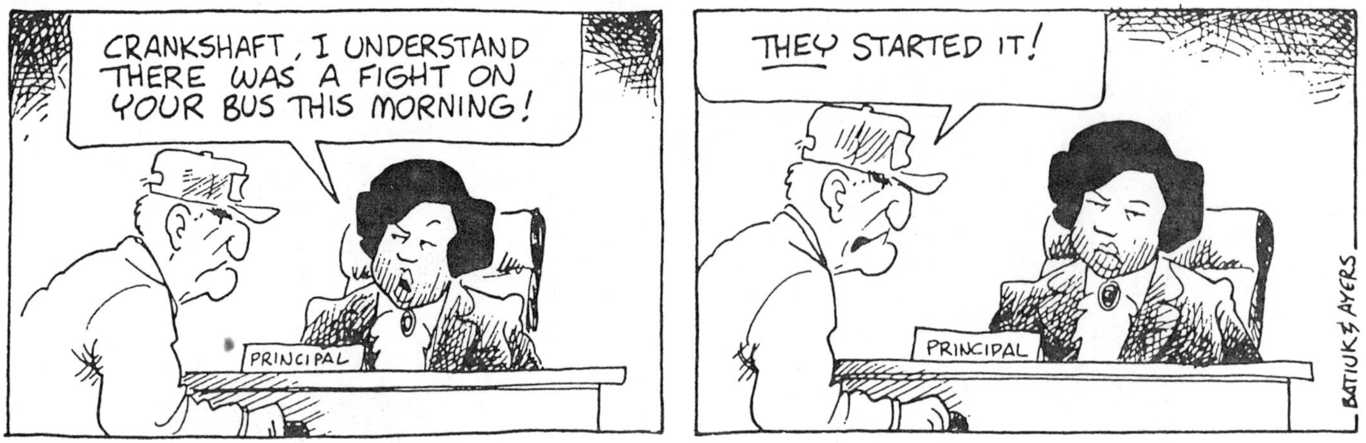
CRANKSHAFT, I UNDERSTAND THERE WAS A FIGHT ON YOUR BUS THIS MORNING!
PRINCIPAL
THEY STARTED IT!
PRINCIPAL
BATIUK & AYERS

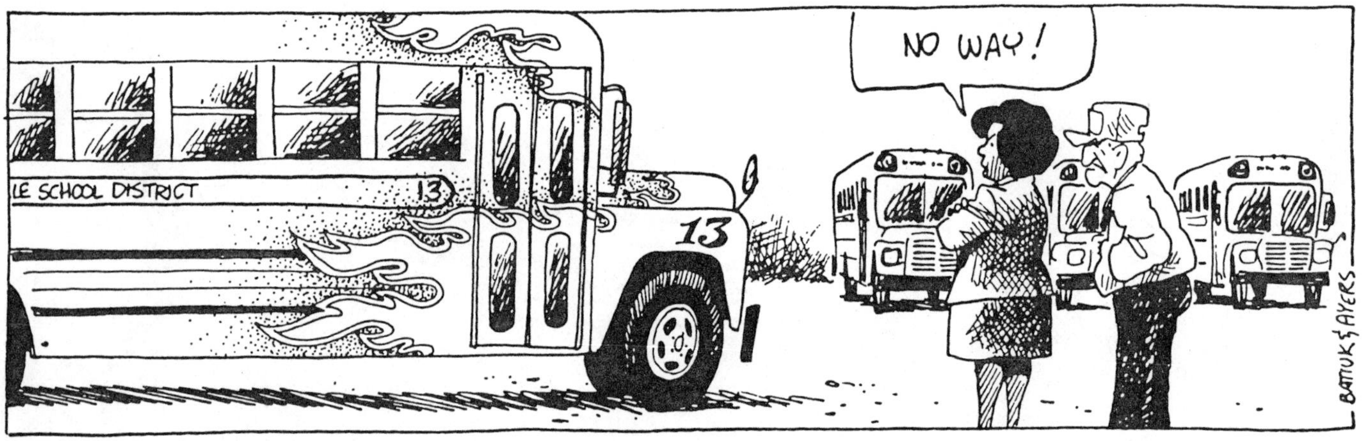
LE SCHOOL DISTRICT
13
13
NO WAY!
BATIUK & AYERS

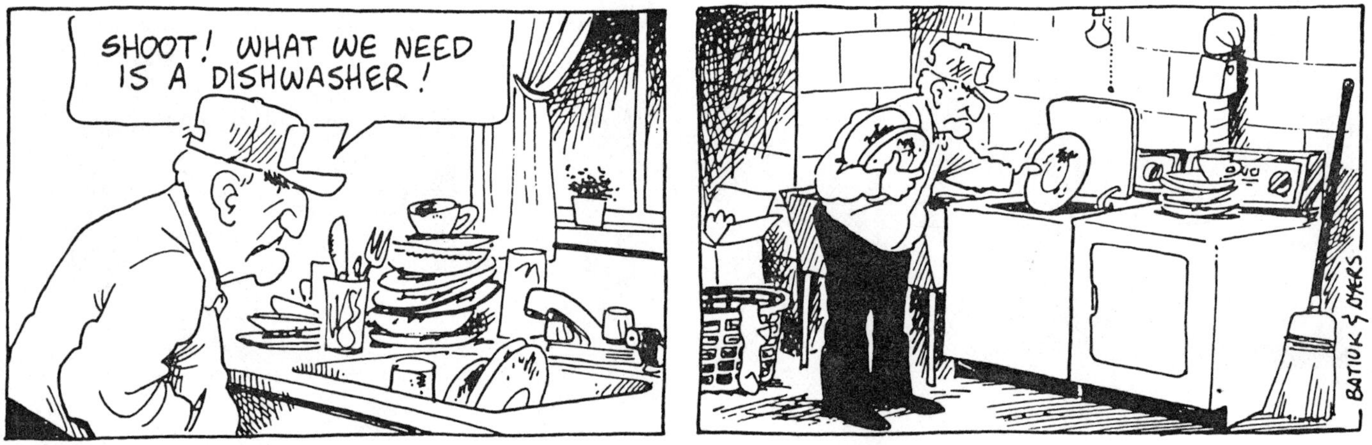
SHOOT! WHAT WE NEED IS A DISHWASHER!
BATIUK & AYERS

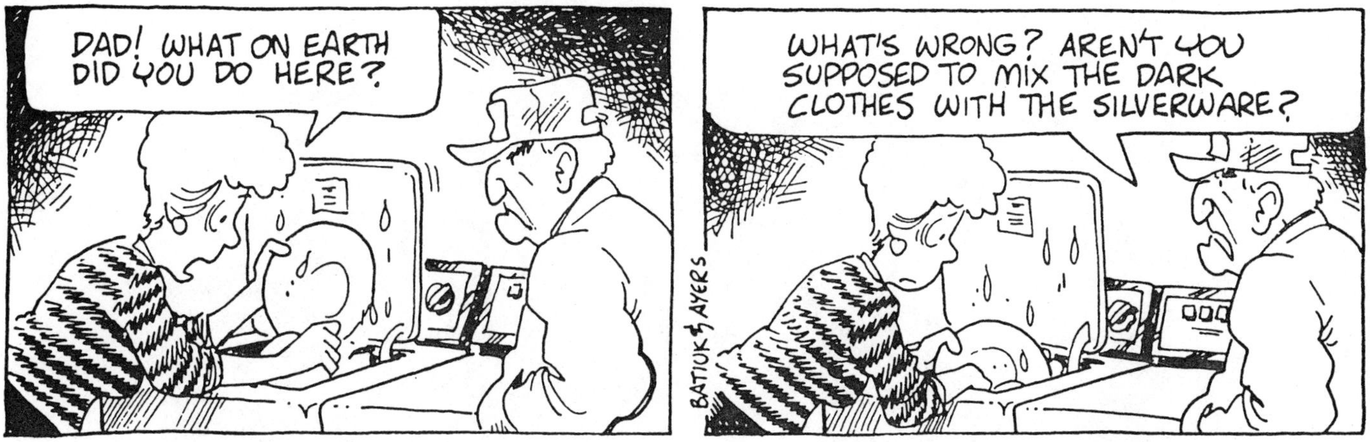
DAD! WHAT ON EARTH DID YOU DO HERE?
BATIUK & AYERS
WHAT'S WRONG? AREN'T YOU SUPPOSED TO MIX THE DARK CLOTHES WITH THE SILVERWARE?

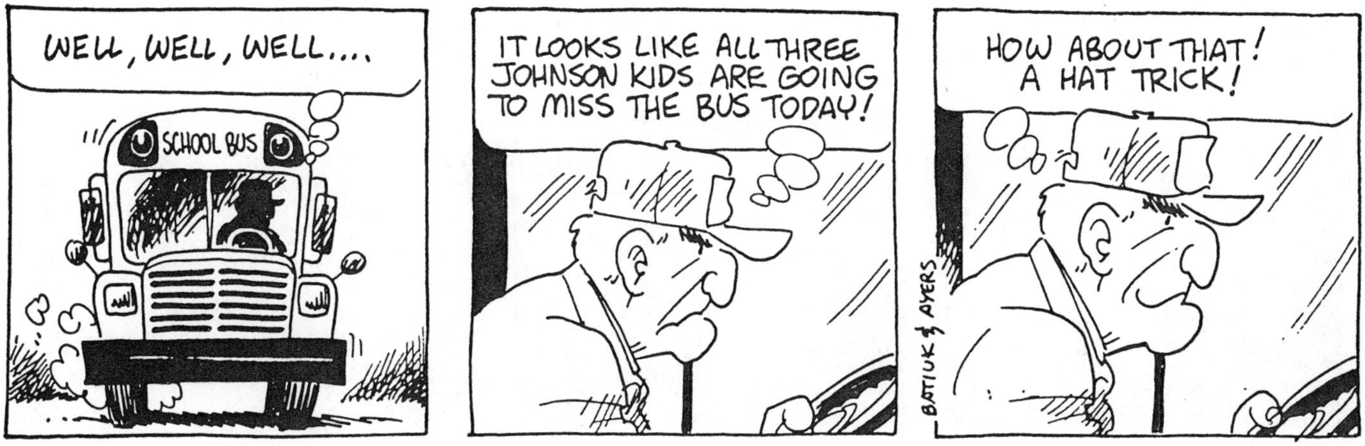
WELL, WELL, WELL....
SCHOOL BUS
IT LOOKS LIKE ALL THREE JOHNSON KIDS ARE GOING TO MISS THE BUS TODAY!
BATIUK & AYERS
HOW ABOUT THAT! A HAT TRICK!

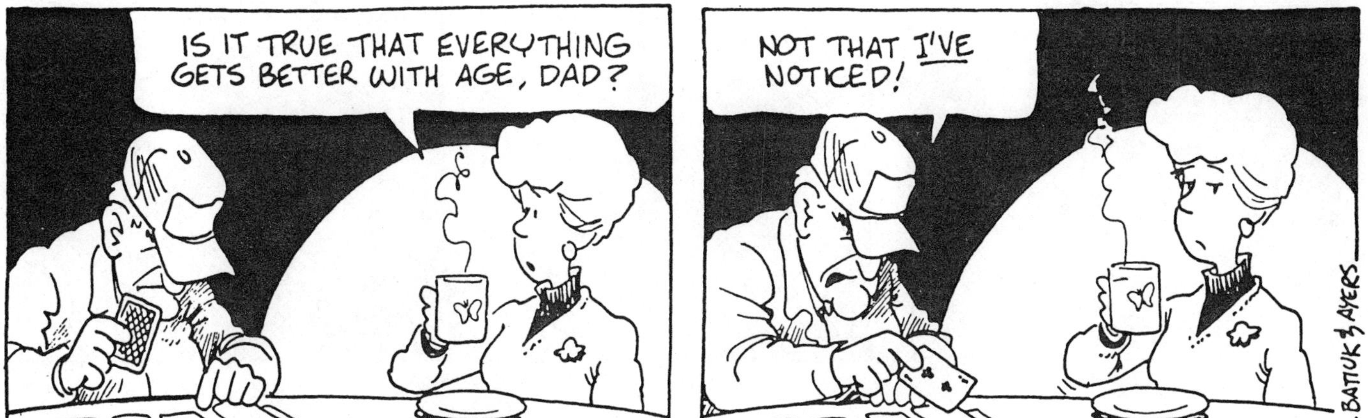
IS IT TRUE THAT EVERYTHING GETS BETTER WITH AGE, DAD?
NOT THAT I'VE NOTICED!
BATIUK & AYERS

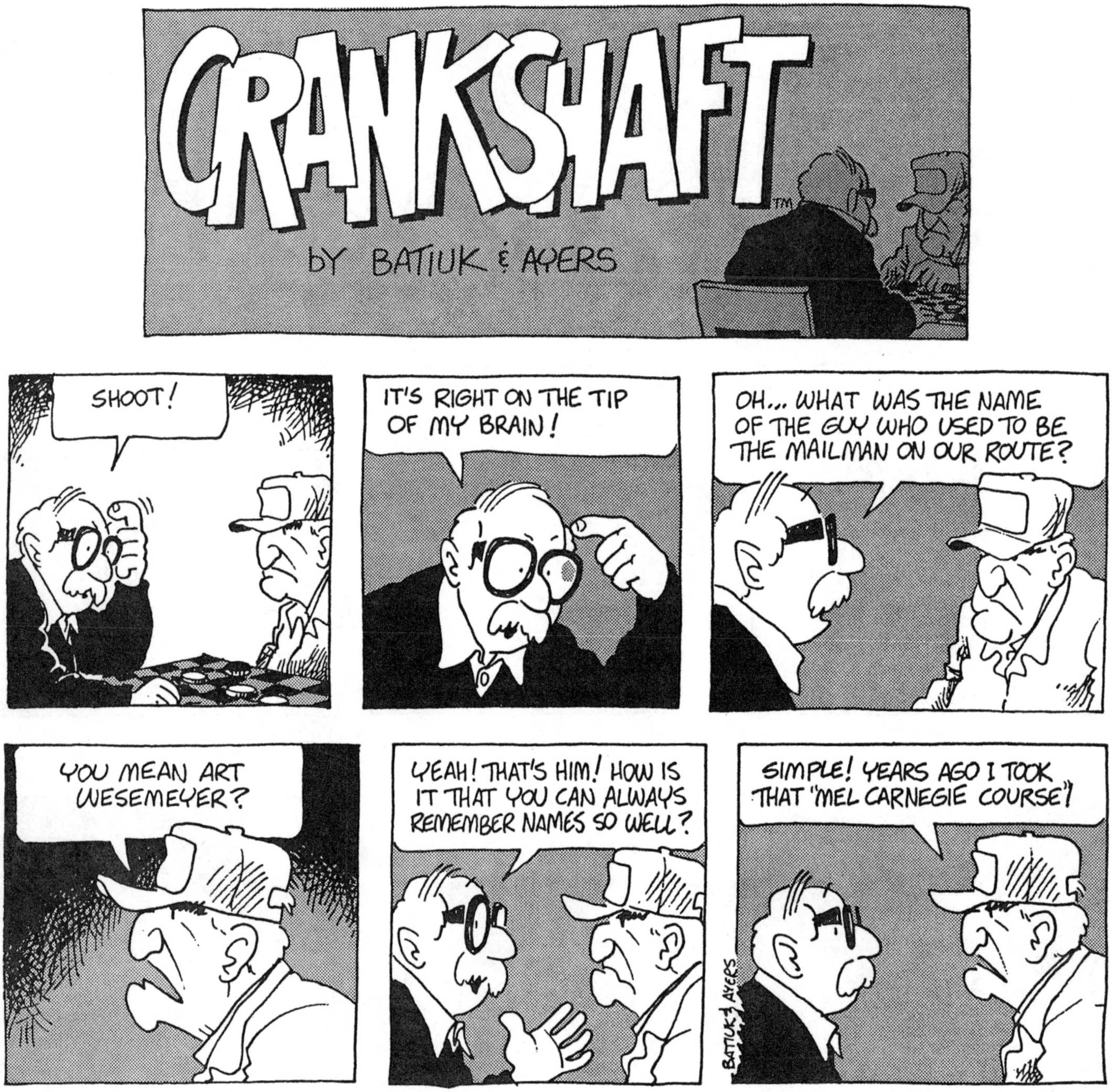
CRANKSHAFT
TM
BY BATIUK & AYERS
SHOOT!
IT'S RIGHT ON THE TIP OF MY BRAIN!
OH... WHAT WAS THE NAME OF THE GUY WHO USED TO BE THE MAILMAN ON OUR ROUTE?
YOU MEAN ART WESEMEYER?
YEAH! THAT'S HIM! HOW IS IT THAT YOU CAN ALWAYS REMEMBER NAMES SO WELL?
SIMPLE! YEARS AGO I TOOK THAT "MEL CARNEGIE COURSE"!
BATIUK & AYERS

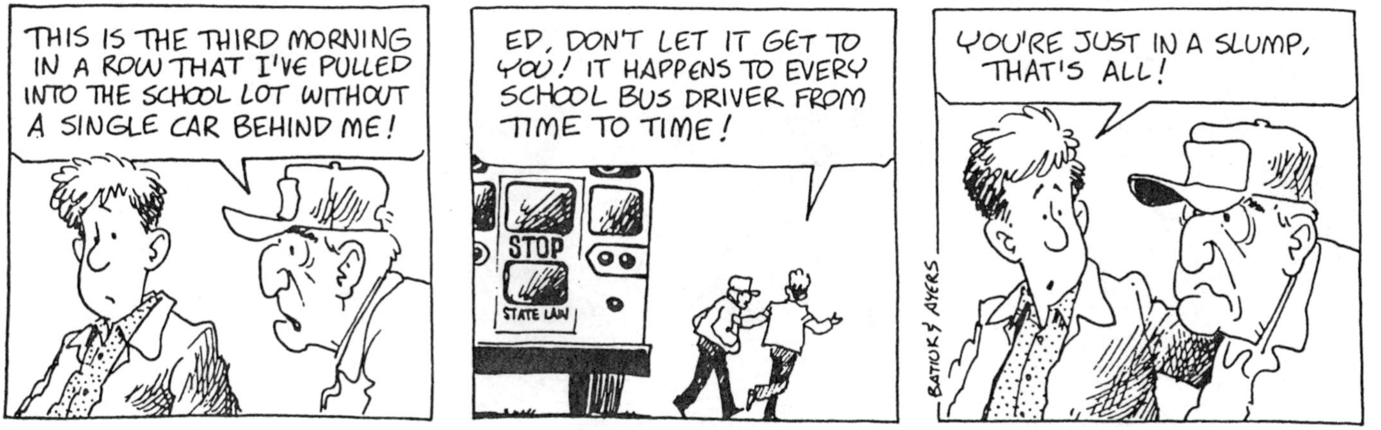

THIS IS THE THIRD MORNING IN A ROW THAT I'VE PULLED INTO THE SCHOOL LOT WITHOUT A SINGLE CAR BEHIND ME!
ED, DON'T LET IT GET TO YOU! IT HAPPENS TO EVERY SCHOOL BUS DRIVER FROM TIME TO TIME!
STOP
STATE LAW
YOU'RE JUST IN A SLUMP, THAT'S ALL!
BATIUK & AYERS

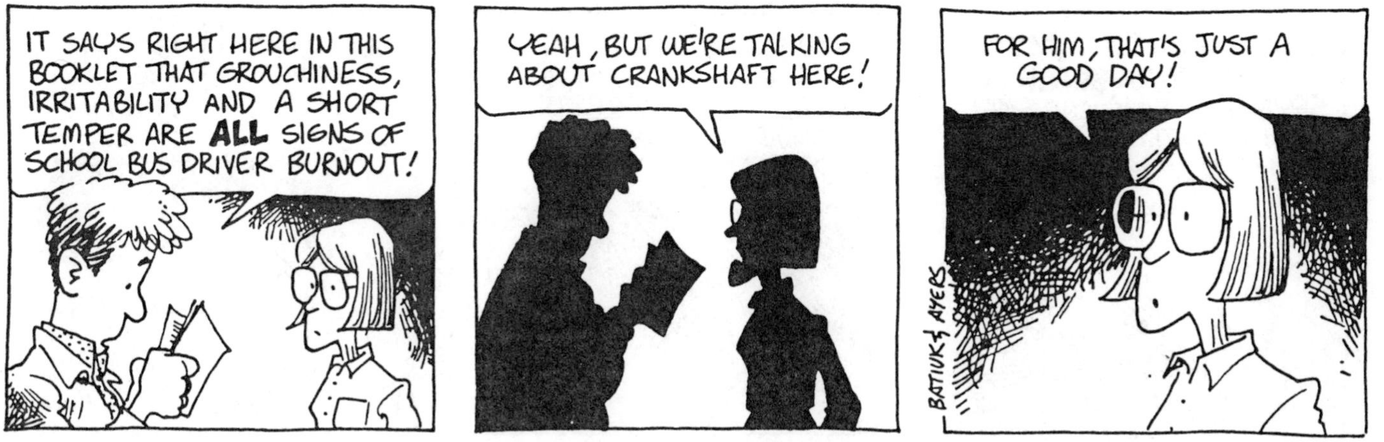

IT SAYS RIGHT HERE IN THIS BOOKLET THAT GROUCHINESS, IRRITABILITY AND A SHORT TEMPER ARE **ALL** SIGNS OF SCHOOL BUS DRIVER BURNOUT!
YEAH, BUT WE'RE TALKING ABOUT CRANKSHAFT HERE!
FOR HIM, THAT'S JUST A GOOD DAY!
BATIUK & AYERS

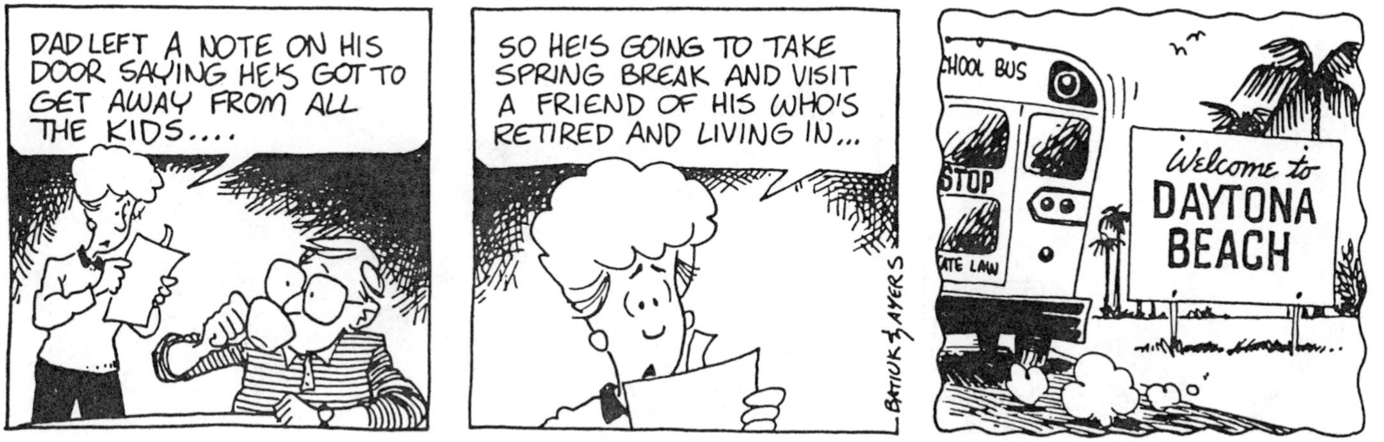

DAD LEFT A NOTE ON HIS DOOR SAYING HE'S GOT TO GET AWAY FROM ALL THE KIDS....
SO HE'S GOING TO TAKE SPRING BREAK AND VISIT A FRIEND OF HIS WHO'S RETIRED AND LIVING IN...
BATIUK & AYERS
STOP
Welcome to
DAYTONA BEACH

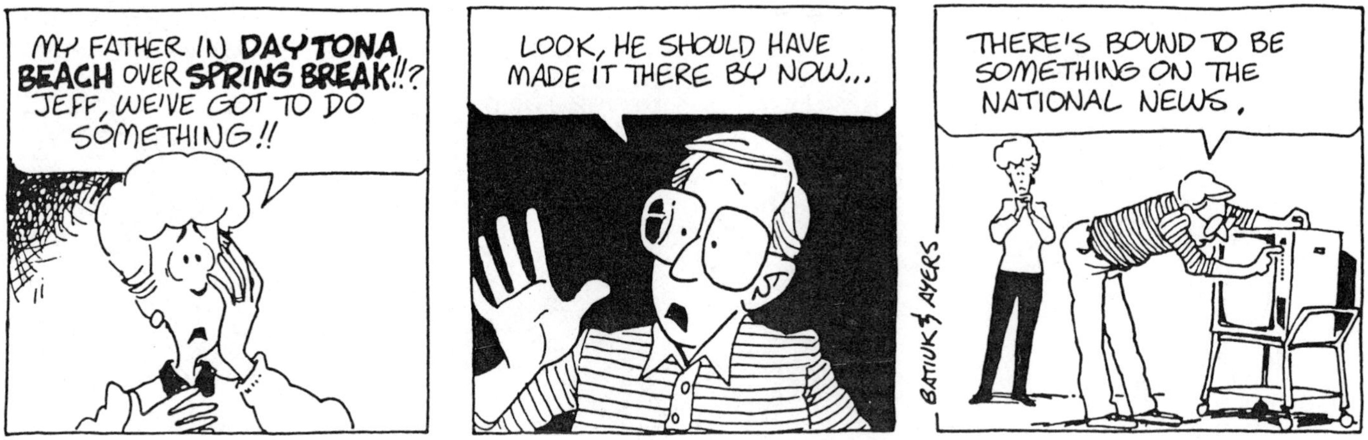
MY FATHER IN DAYTONA BEACH OVER SPRING BREAK!!? JEFF, WE'VE GOT TO DO SOMETHING!!
LOOK, HE SHOULD HAVE MADE IT THERE BY NOW...
THERE'S BOUND TO BE SOMETHING ON THE NATIONAL NEWS.
BATIUK & AYERS

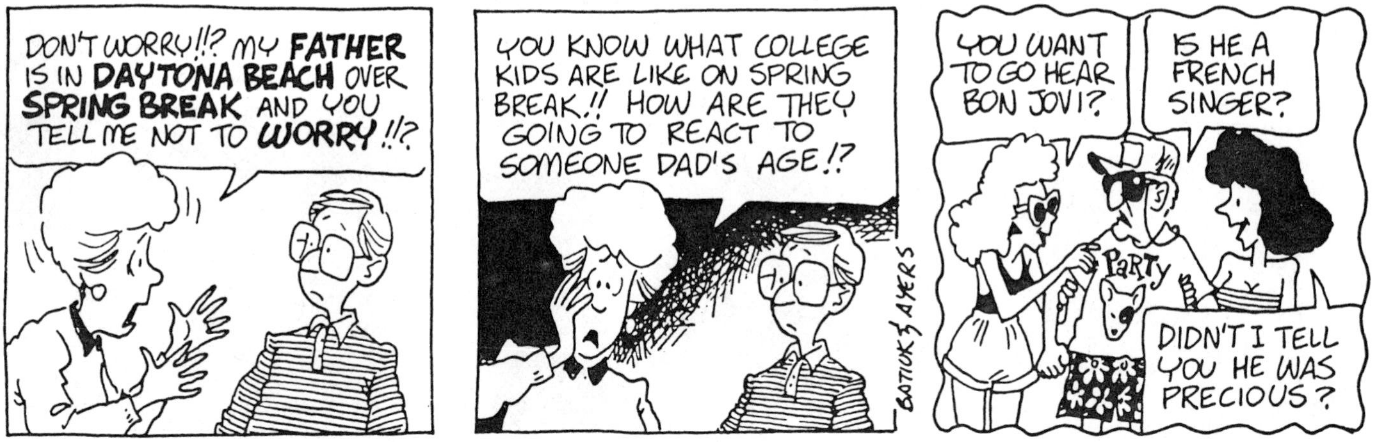
DON'T WORRY!!? MY FATHER IS IN DAYTONA BEACH OVER SPRING BREAK AND YOU TELL ME NOT TO WORRY!!?
YOU KNOW WHAT COLLEGE KIDS ARE LIKE ON SPRING BREAK!! HOW ARE THEY GOING TO REACT TO SOMEONE DAD'S AGE!?
BATIUK & AYERS
YOU WANT TO GO HEAR BON JOVI?
IS HE A FRENCH SINGER?
PARTY
DIDN'T I TELL YOU HE WAS PRECIOUS?

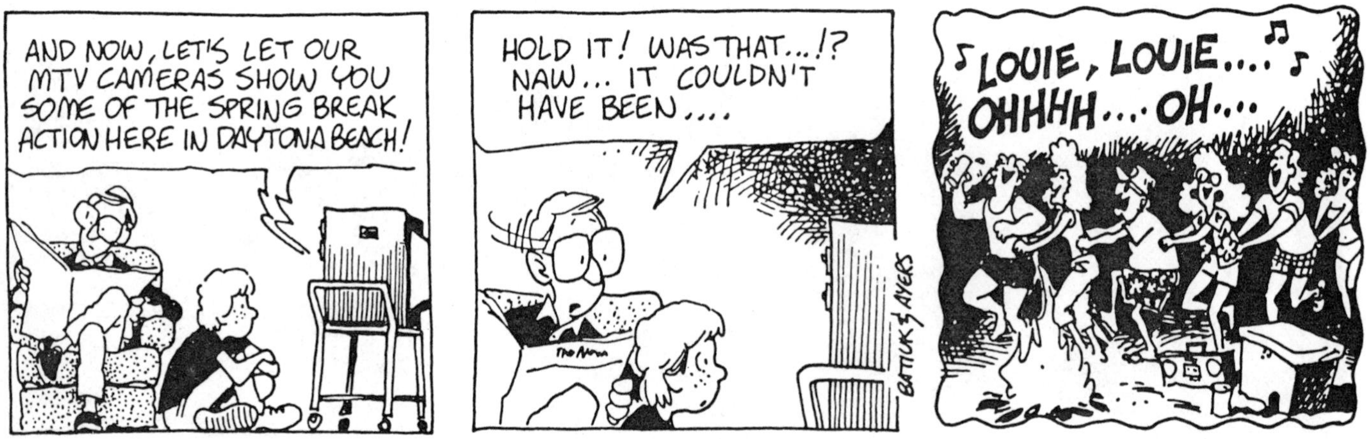
AND NOW, LET'S LET OUR MTV CAMERAS SHOW YOU SOME OF THE SPRING BREAK ACTION HERE IN DAYTONA BEACH!
HOLD IT! WAS THAT...!? NAW... IT COULDN'T HAVE BEEN....
BATIUK & AYERS
LOUIE, LOUIE.... OHHHH.... OH....

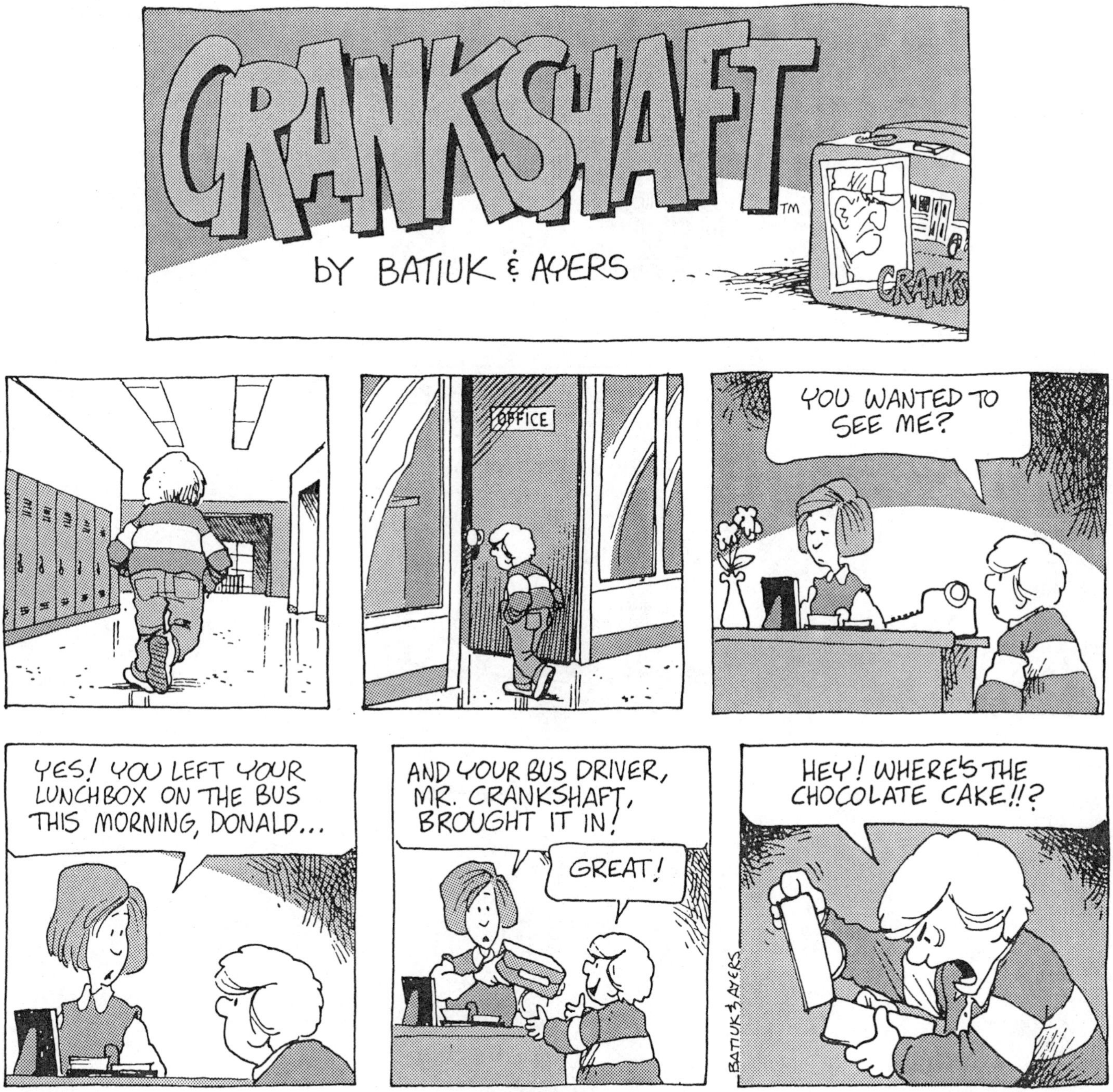
CRANKSHAFT
TM
BY BATIUK & AYERS
CRANKS
OFFICE
YOU WANTED TO SEE ME?
YES! YOU LEFT YOUR LUNCHBOX ON THE BUS THIS MORNING, DONALD...
AND YOUR BUS DRIVER, MR. CRANKSHAFT, BROUGHT IT IN!
GREAT!
BATIUK & AYERS
HEY! WHERE'S THE CHOCOLATE CAKE!!?

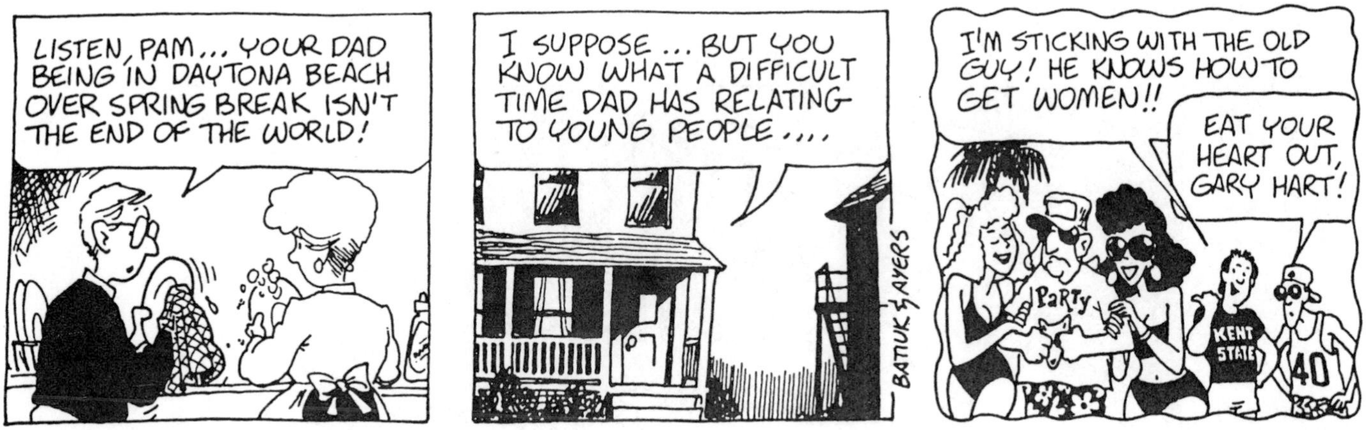
LISTEN, PAM... YOUR DAD BEING IN DAYTONA BEACH OVER SPRING BREAK ISN'T THE END OF THE WORLD!
I SUPPOSE ... BUT YOU KNOW WHAT A DIFFICULT TIME DAD HAS RELATING TO YOUNG PEOPLE....
BATIUK & AYERS
I'M STICKING WITH THE OLD GUY! HE KNOWS HOW TO GET WOMEN!!
EAT YOUR HEART OUT, GARY HART!
PARTY
KENT STATE
40

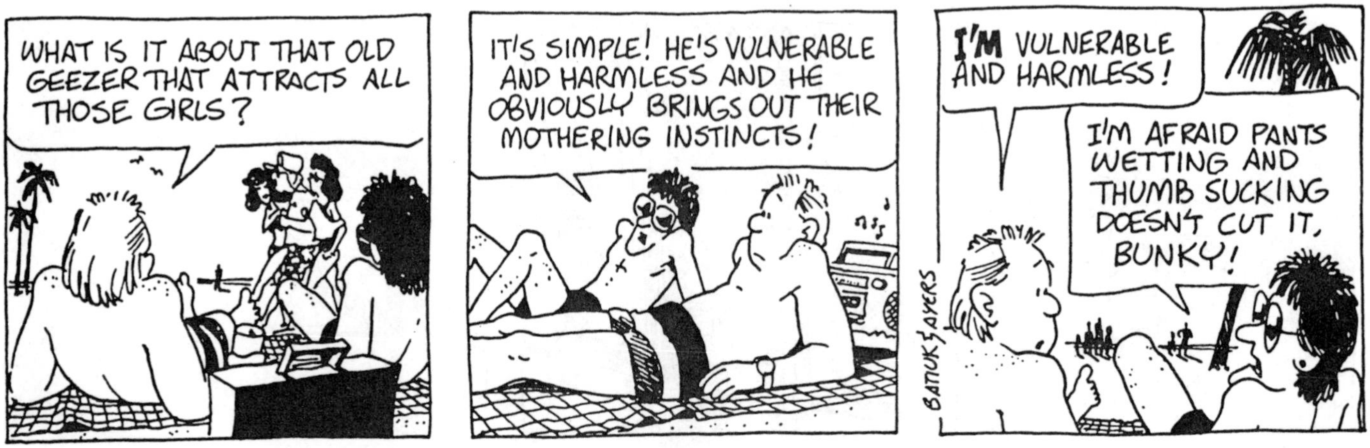
WHAT IS IT ABOUT THAT OLD GEEZER THAT ATTRACTS ALL THOSE GIRLS?
IT'S SIMPLE! HE'S VULNERABLE AND HARMLESS AND HE OBVIOUSLY BRINGS OUT THEIR MOTHERING INSTINCTS!
BATIUK & AYERS
I'M VULNERABLE AND HARMLESS!
I'M AFRAID PANTS WETTING AND THUMB SUCKING DOESN'T CUT IT, BUNKY!

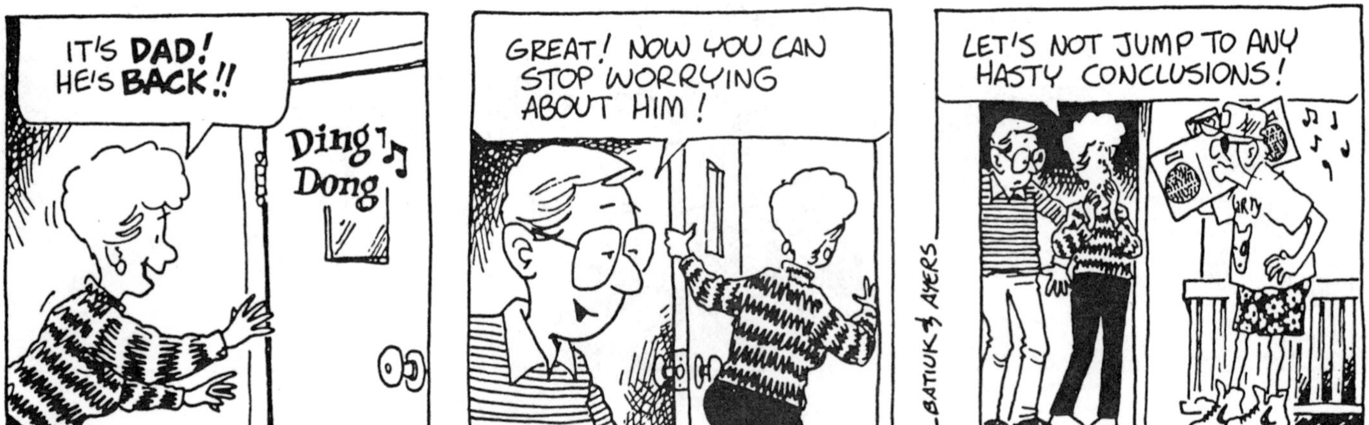
IT'S DAD! HE'S BACK!!
Ding Dong
GREAT! NOW YOU CAN STOP WORRYING ABOUT HIM!
BATIUK & AYERS
LET'S NOT JUMP TO ANY HASTY CONCLUSIONS!

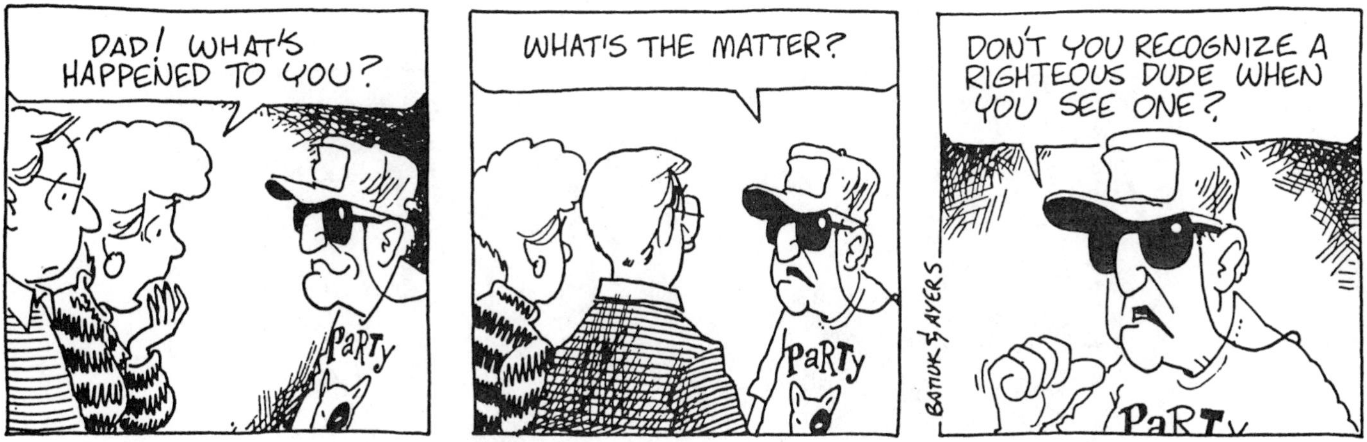
DAD! WHAT'S HAPPENED TO YOU?
WHAT'S THE MATTER?
DON'T YOU RECOGNIZE A RIGHTEOUS DUDE WHEN YOU SEE ONE?
PaRTy
BATIUK & AYERS

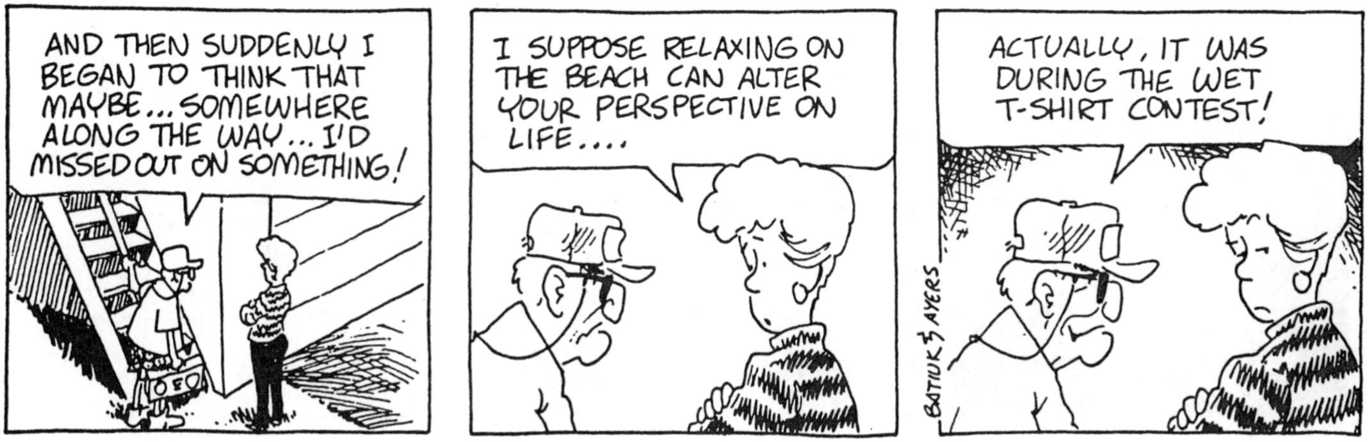
AND THEN SUDDENLY I BEGAN TO THINK THAT MAYBE... SOMEWHERE ALONG THE WAY... I'D MISSED OUT ON SOMETHING!
I SUPPOSE RELAXING ON THE BEACH CAN ALTER YOUR PERSPECTIVE ON LIFE....
ACTUALLY, IT WAS DURING THE WET T-SHIRT CONTEST!
BATIUK & AYERS

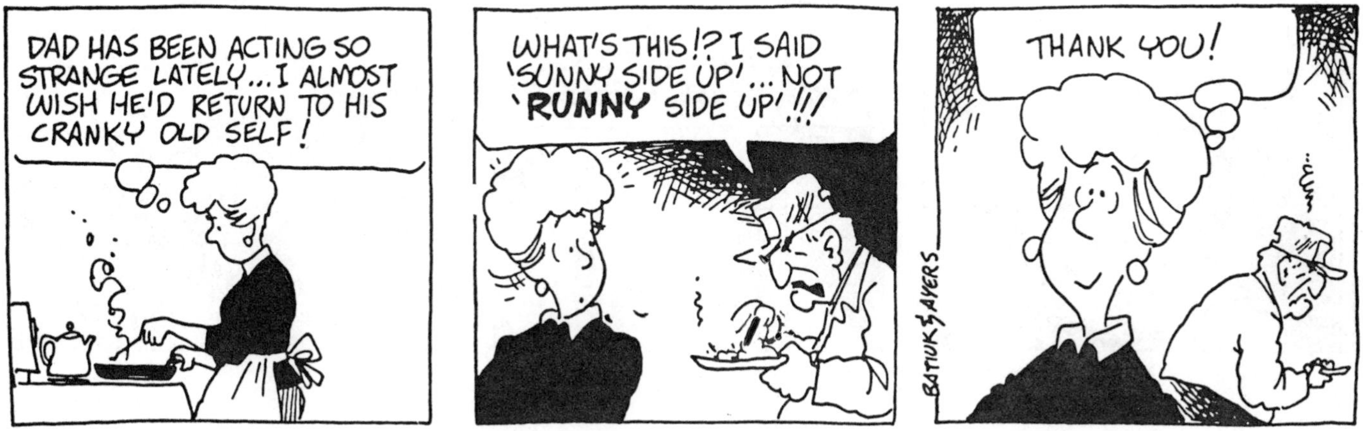
DAD HAS BEEN ACTING SO STRANGE LATELY... I ALMOST WISH HE'D RETURN TO HIS CRANKY OLD SELF!
WHAT'S THIS!? I SAID 'SUNNY SIDE UP'... NOT '**RUNNY** SIDE UP'!!!
THANK YOU!
BATIUK & AYERS

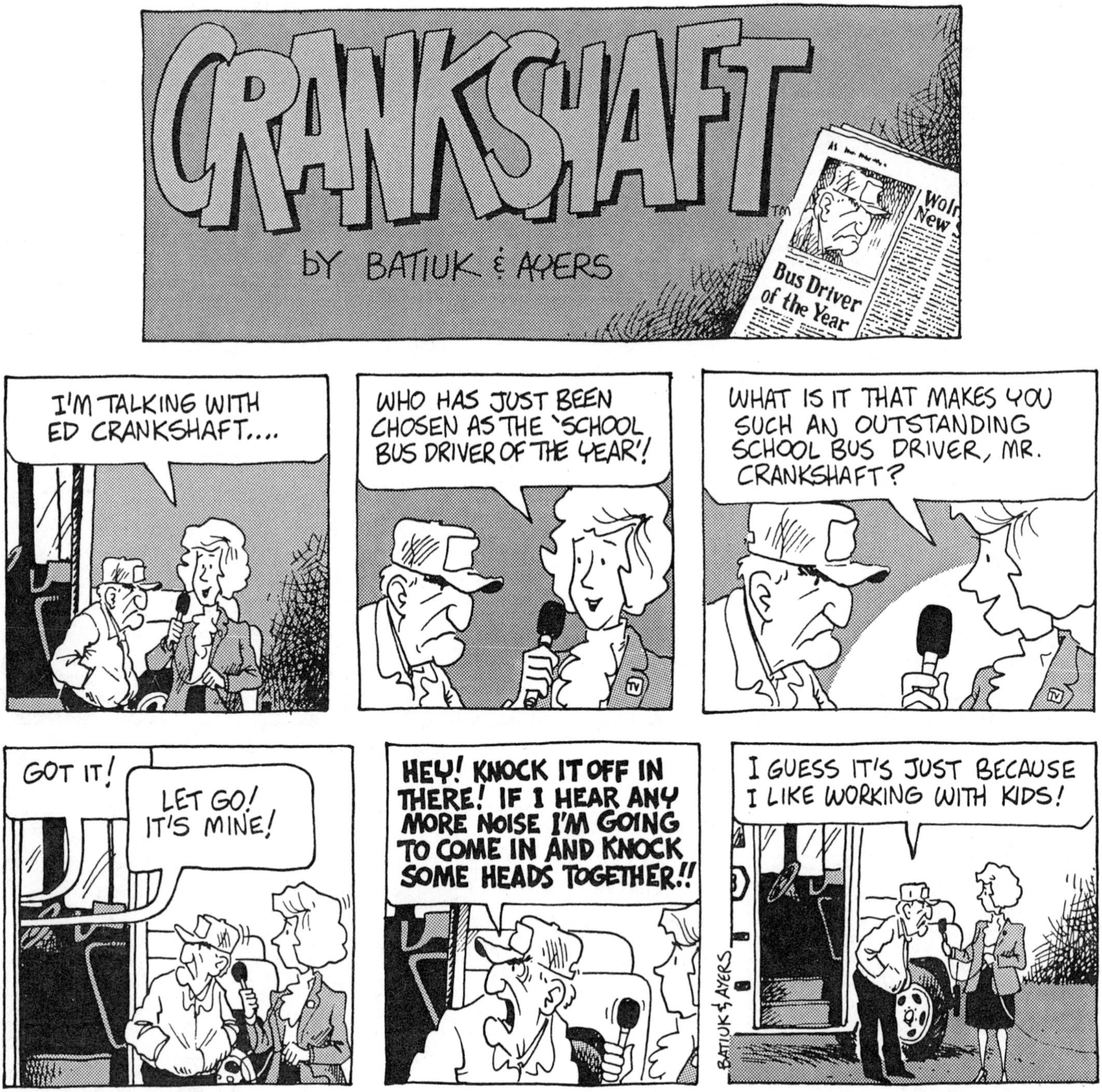
CRANKSHAFT
BY BATIUK & AYERS
Bus Driver of the Year
I'M TALKING WITH ED CRANKSHAFT....
WHO HAS JUST BEEN CHOSEN AS THE 'SCHOOL BUS DRIVER OF THE YEAR'!
WHAT IS IT THAT MAKES YOU SUCH AN OUTSTANDING SCHOOL BUS DRIVER, MR. CRANKSHAFT?
TV
GOT IT!
LET GO! IT'S MINE!
HEY! KNOCK IT OFF IN THERE! IF I HEAR ANY MORE NOISE I'M GOING TO COME IN AND KNOCK SOME HEADS TOGETHER!!
BATIUK & AYERS
I GUESS IT'S JUST BECAUSE I LIKE WORKING WITH KIDS!

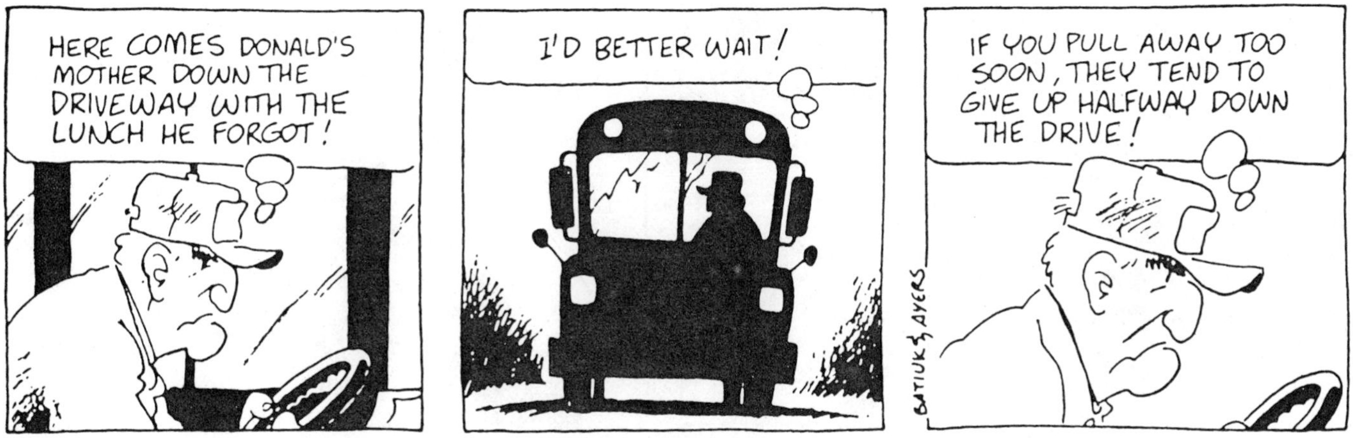
HERE COMES DONALD'S MOTHER DOWN THE DRIVEWAY WITH THE LUNCH HE FORGOT!
I'D BETTER WAIT!
IF YOU PULL AWAY TOO SOON, THEY TEND TO GIVE UP HALFWAY DOWN THE DRIVE!
BATIUK & AYERS

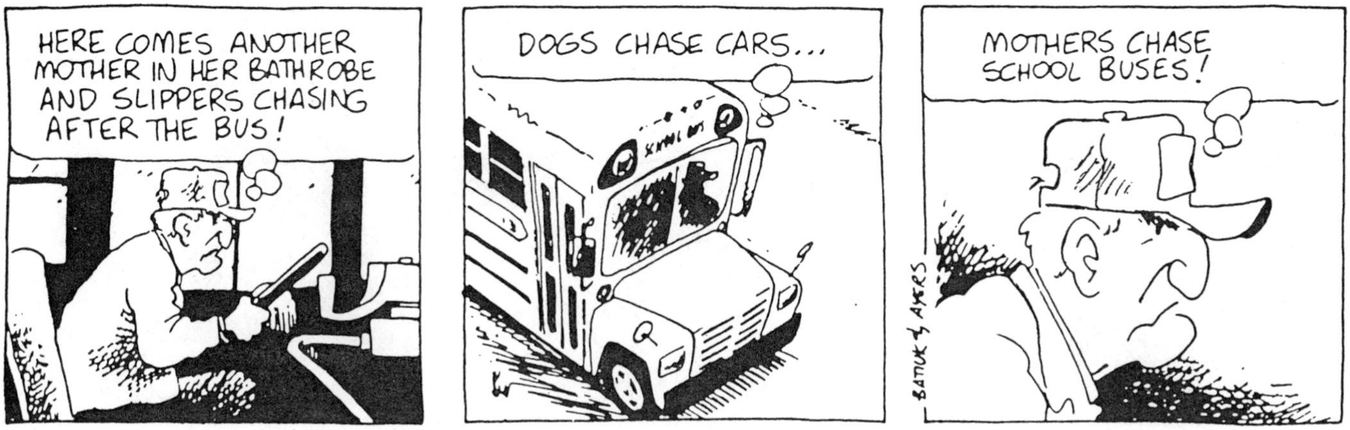
HERE COMES ANOTHER MOTHER IN HER BATHROBE AND SLIPPERS CHASING AFTER THE BUS!
DOGS CHASE CARS...
MOTHERS CHASE SCHOOL BUSES!
BATIUK & AYERS

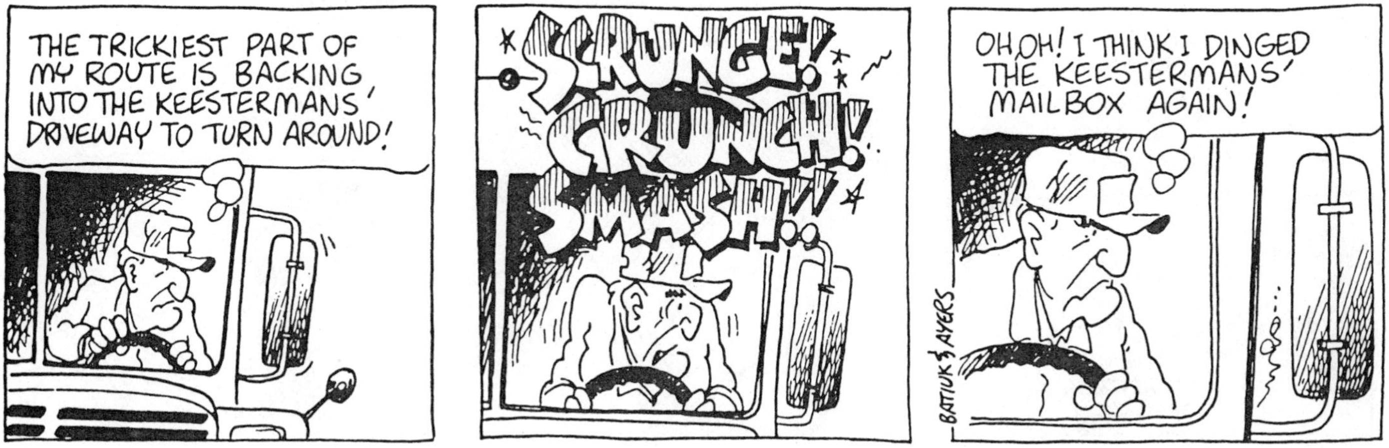
THE TRICKIEST PART OF MY ROUTE IS BACKING INTO THE KEESTERMANS' DRIVEWAY TO TURN AROUND!
SCRUNGE! CRUNCH! SMASH!!
OH,OH! I THINK I DINGED THE KEESTERMANS' MAILBOX AGAIN!
BATIUK & AYERS

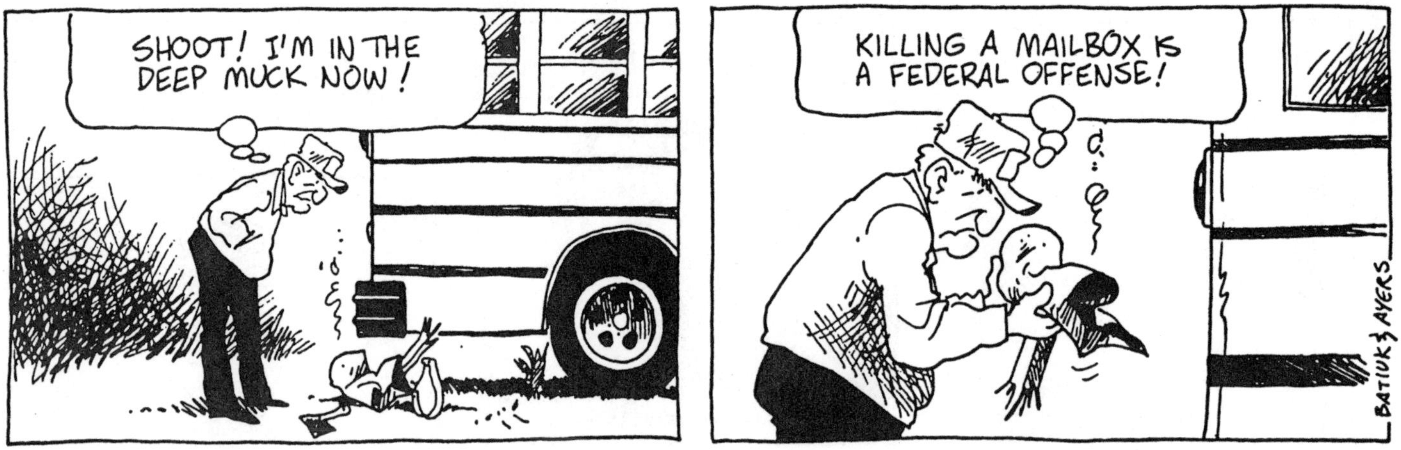
SHOOT! I'M IN THE DEEP MUCK NOW!
KILLING A MAILBOX IS A FEDERAL OFFENSE!
BATIUK & AYERS

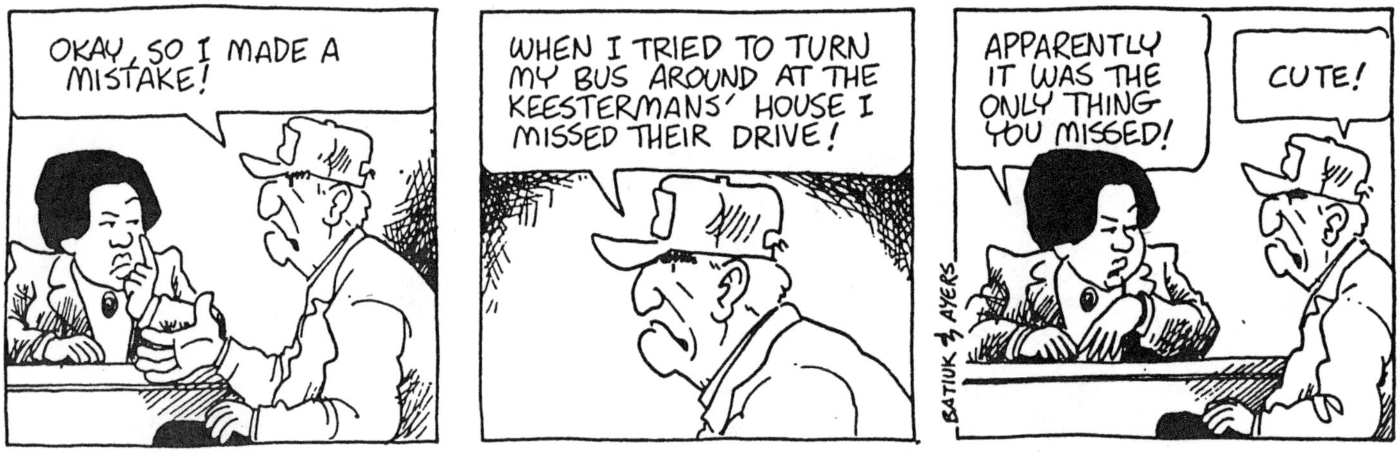
OKAY, SO I MADE A MISTAKE!
WHEN I TRIED TO TURN MY BUS AROUND AT THE KEESTERMANS' HOUSE I MISSED THEIR DRIVE!
BATIUK & AYERS
APPARENTLY IT WAS THE ONLY THING YOU MISSED!
CUTE!

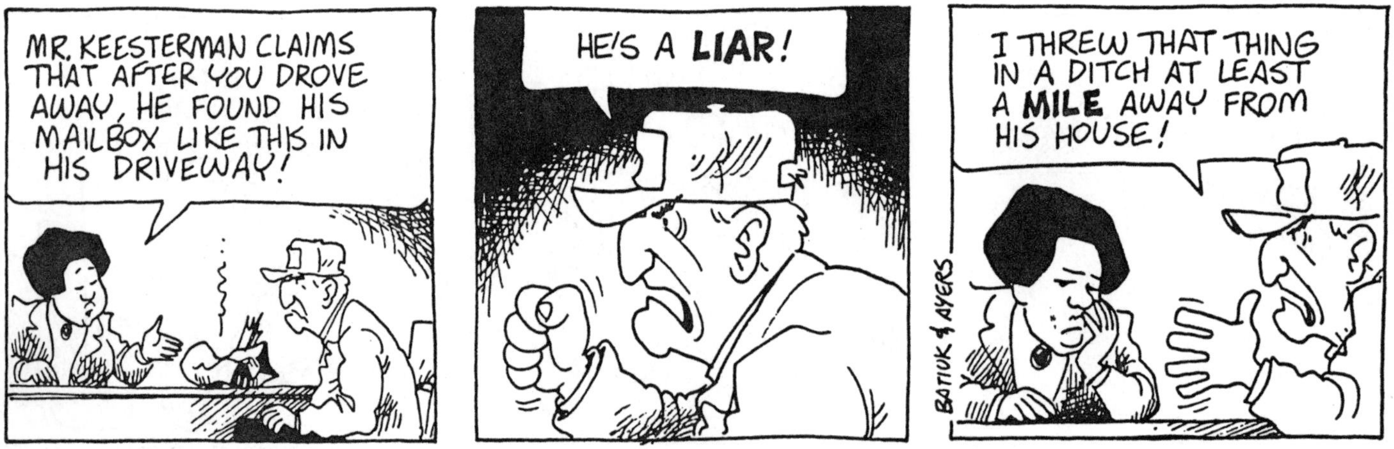
MR. KEESTERMAN CLAIMS THAT AFTER YOU DROVE AWAY, HE FOUND HIS MAILBOX LIKE THIS IN HIS DRIVEWAY!
HE'S A **LIAR**!
BATIUK & AYERS
I THREW THAT THING IN A DITCH AT LEAST A **MILE** AWAY FROM HIS HOUSE!

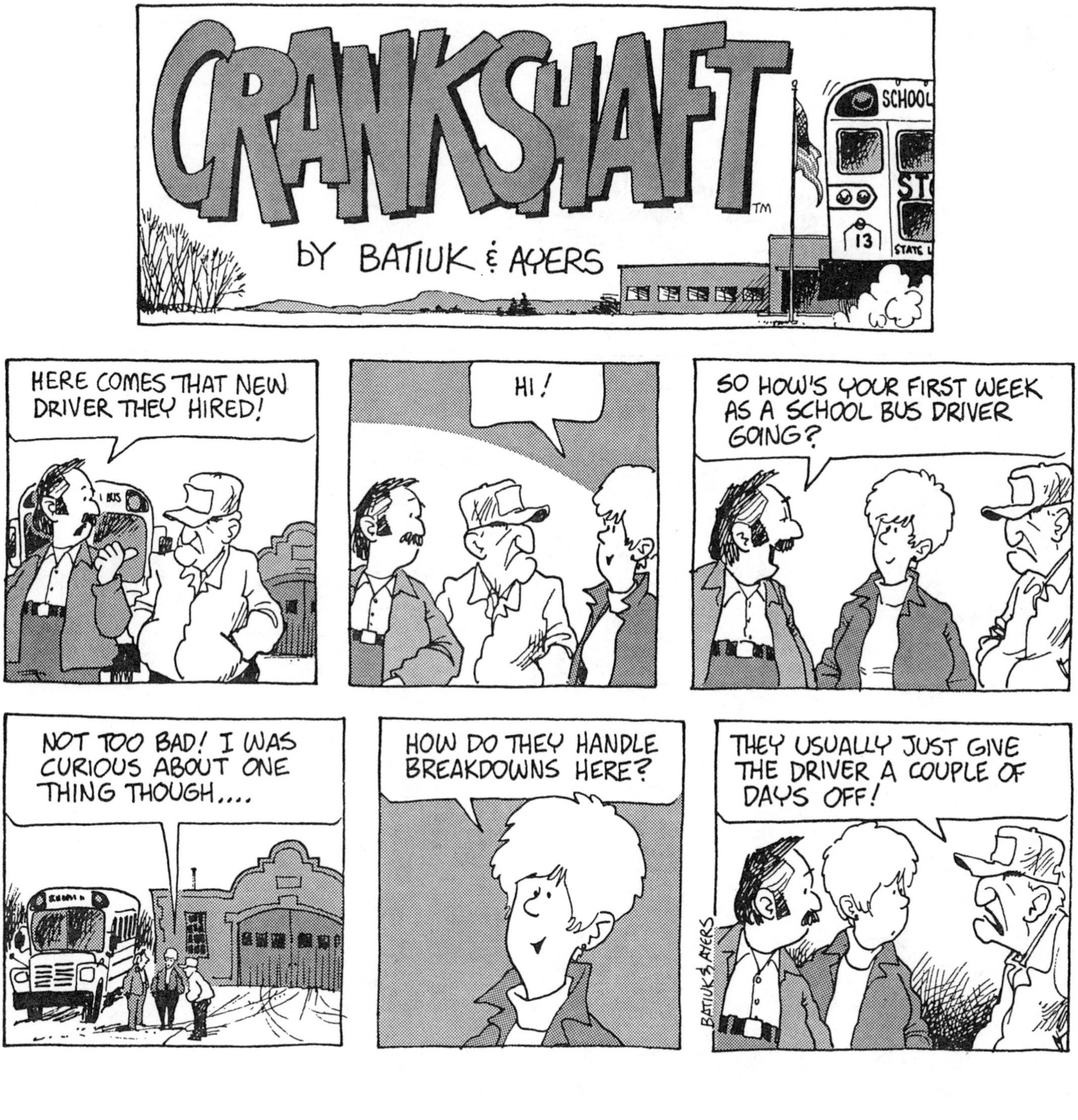
CRANKSHAFT
TM
BY BATIUK & AYERS
SCHOOL
13
HERE COMES THAT NEW DRIVER THEY HIRED!
HI!
SO HOW'S YOUR FIRST WEEK AS A SCHOOL BUS DRIVER GOING?
NOT TOO BAD! I WAS CURIOUS ABOUT ONE THING THOUGH....
HOW DO THEY HANDLE BREAKDOWNS HERE?
THEY USUALLY JUST GIVE THE DRIVER A COUPLE OF DAYS OFF!
BATIUK & AYERS

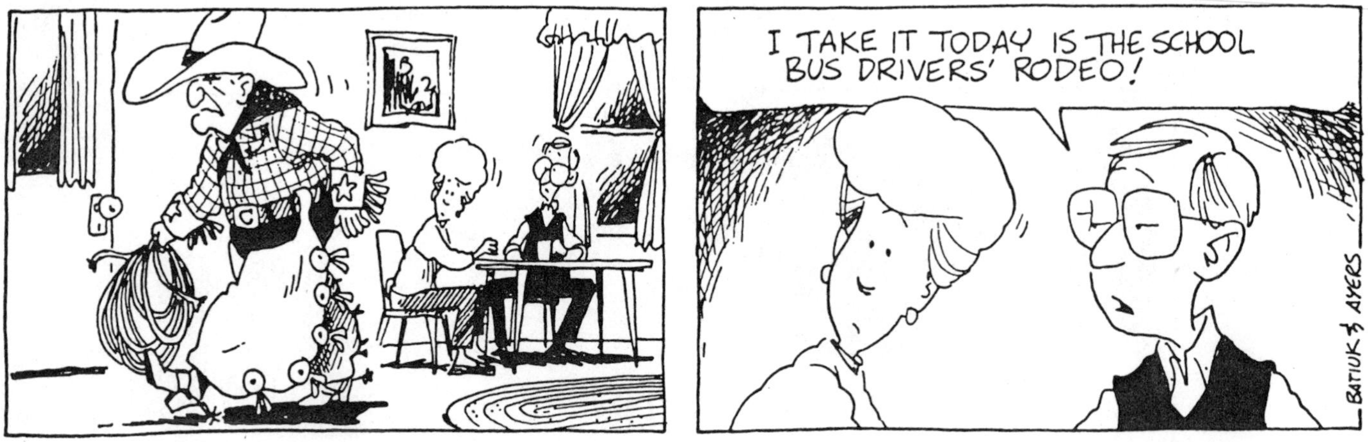
I TAKE IT TODAY IS THE SCHOOL BUS DRIVERS' RODEO!
BATIUK & AYERS

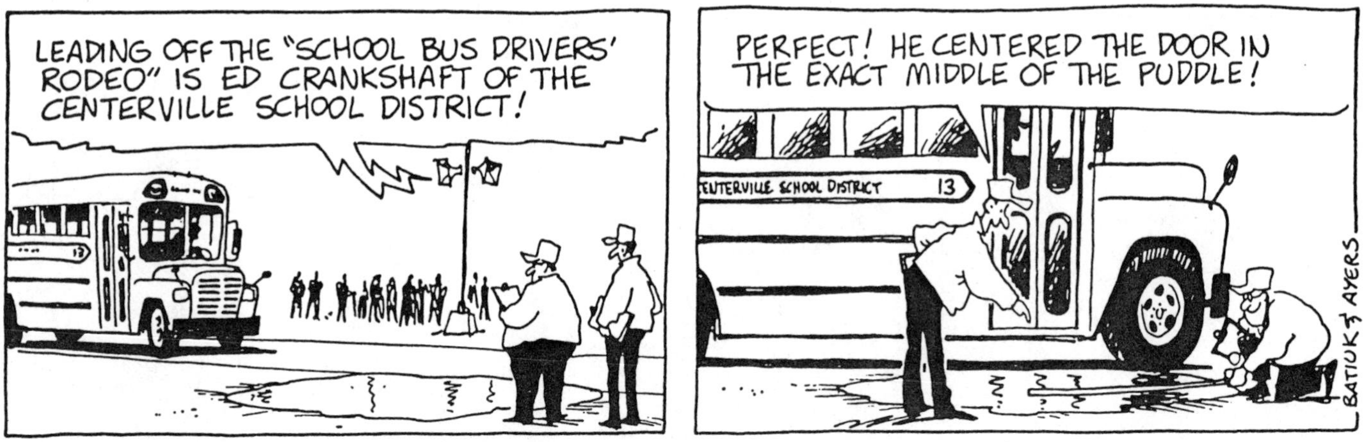
LEADING OFF THE "SCHOOL BUS DRIVERS' RODEO" IS ED CRANKSHAFT OF THE CENTERVILLE SCHOOL DISTRICT!
PERFECT! HE CENTERED THE DOOR IN THE EXACT MIDDLE OF THE PUDDLE!
13
BATIUK & AYERS

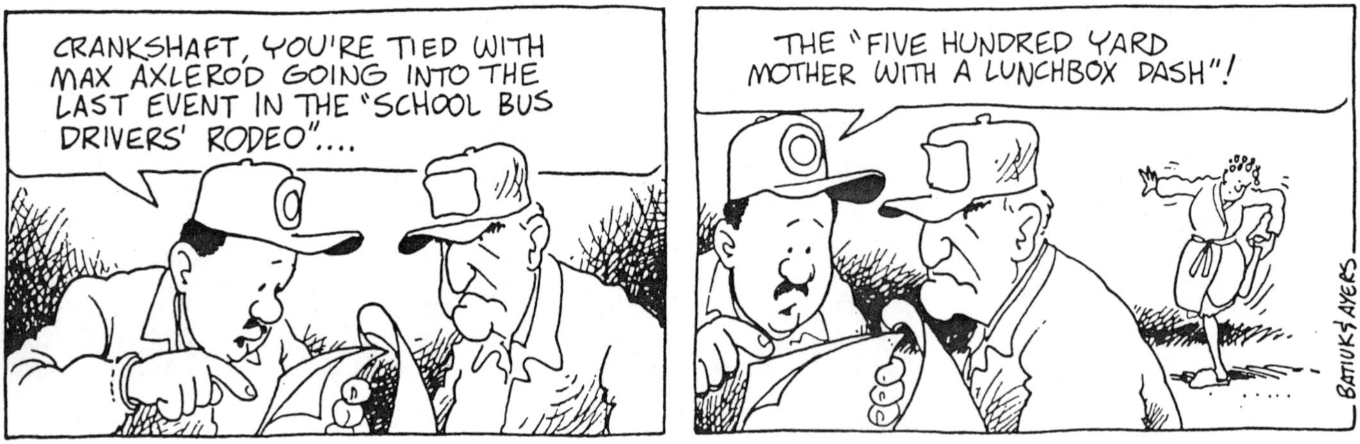
CRANKSHAFT, YOU'RE TIED WITH MAX AXLEROD GOING INTO THE LAST EVENT IN THE "SCHOOL BUS DRIVERS' RODEO"....
THE "FIVE HUNDRED YARD MOTHER WITH A LUNCHBOX DASH"!
BATIUK & AYERS

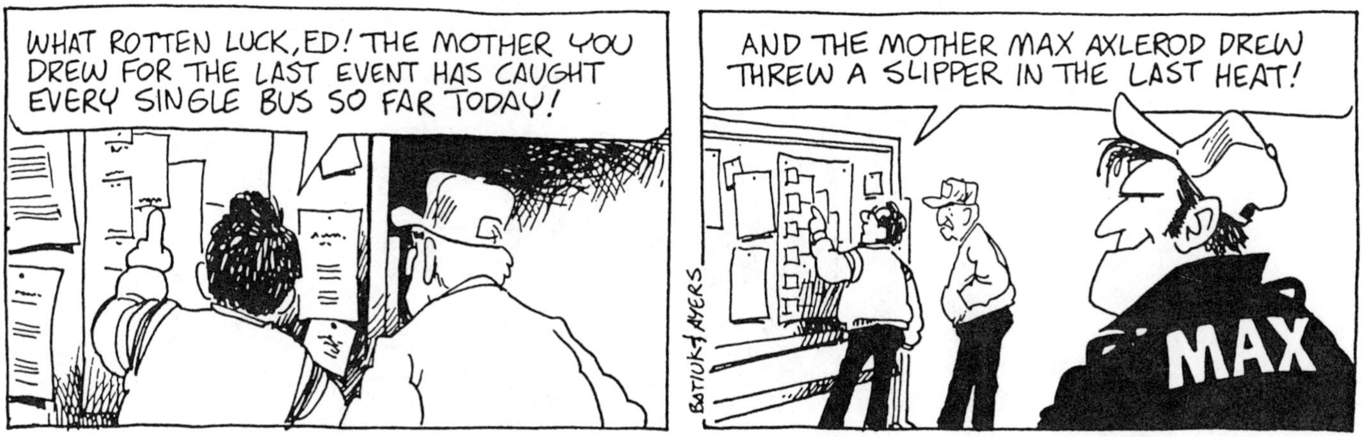
WHAT ROTTEN LUCK, ED! THE MOTHER YOU DREW FOR THE LAST EVENT HAS CAUGHT EVERY SINGLE BUS SO FAR TODAY!
AND THE MOTHER MAX AXLEROD DREW THREW A SLIPPER IN THE LAST HEAT!
BATIUK & AYERS
MAX

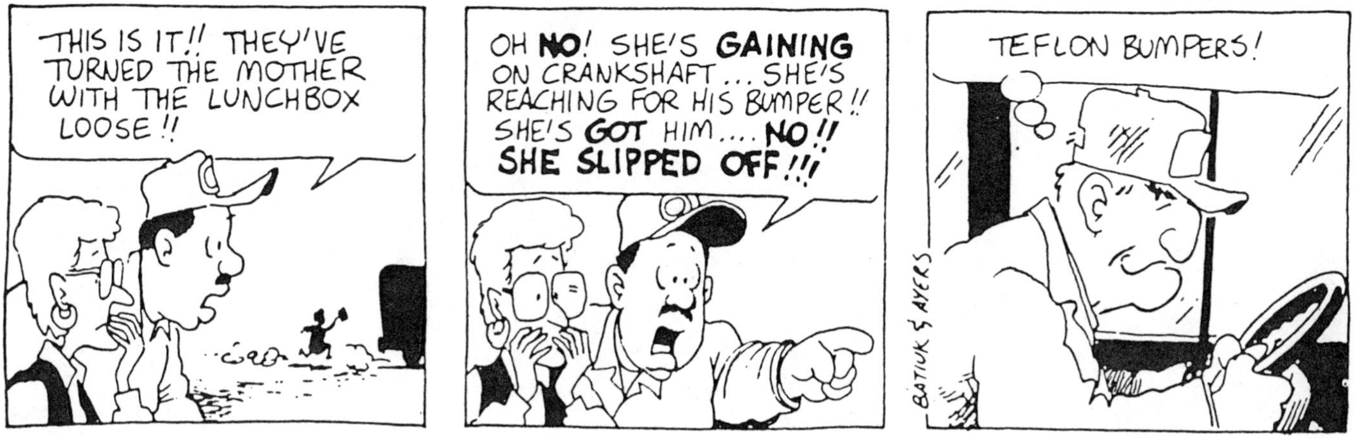
THIS IS IT!! THEY'VE TURNED THE MOTHER WITH THE LUNCHBOX LOOSE!!
OH **NO**! SHE'S **GAINING** ON CRANKSHAFT... SHE'S REACHING FOR HIS BUMPER!! SHE'S **GOT** HIM.... **NO!!** **SHE SLIPPED OFF!!!**
TEFLON BUMPERS!
BATIUK & AYERS

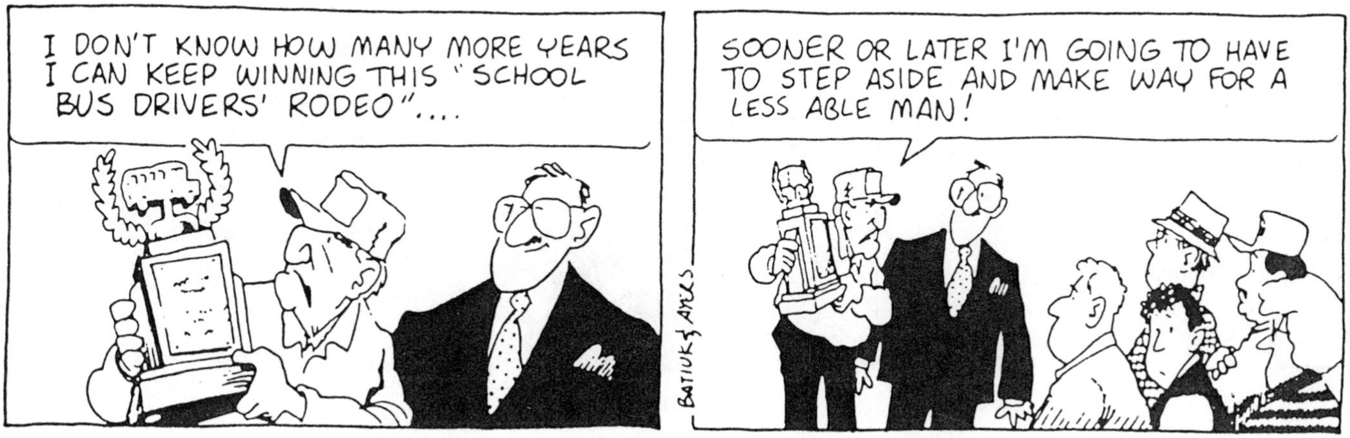
I DON'T KNOW HOW MANY MORE YEARS I CAN KEEP WINNING THIS "SCHOOL BUS DRIVERS' RODEO"....
SOONER OR LATER I'M GOING TO HAVE TO STEP ASIDE AND MAKE WAY FOR A LESS ABLE MAN!
BATIUK & AYERS

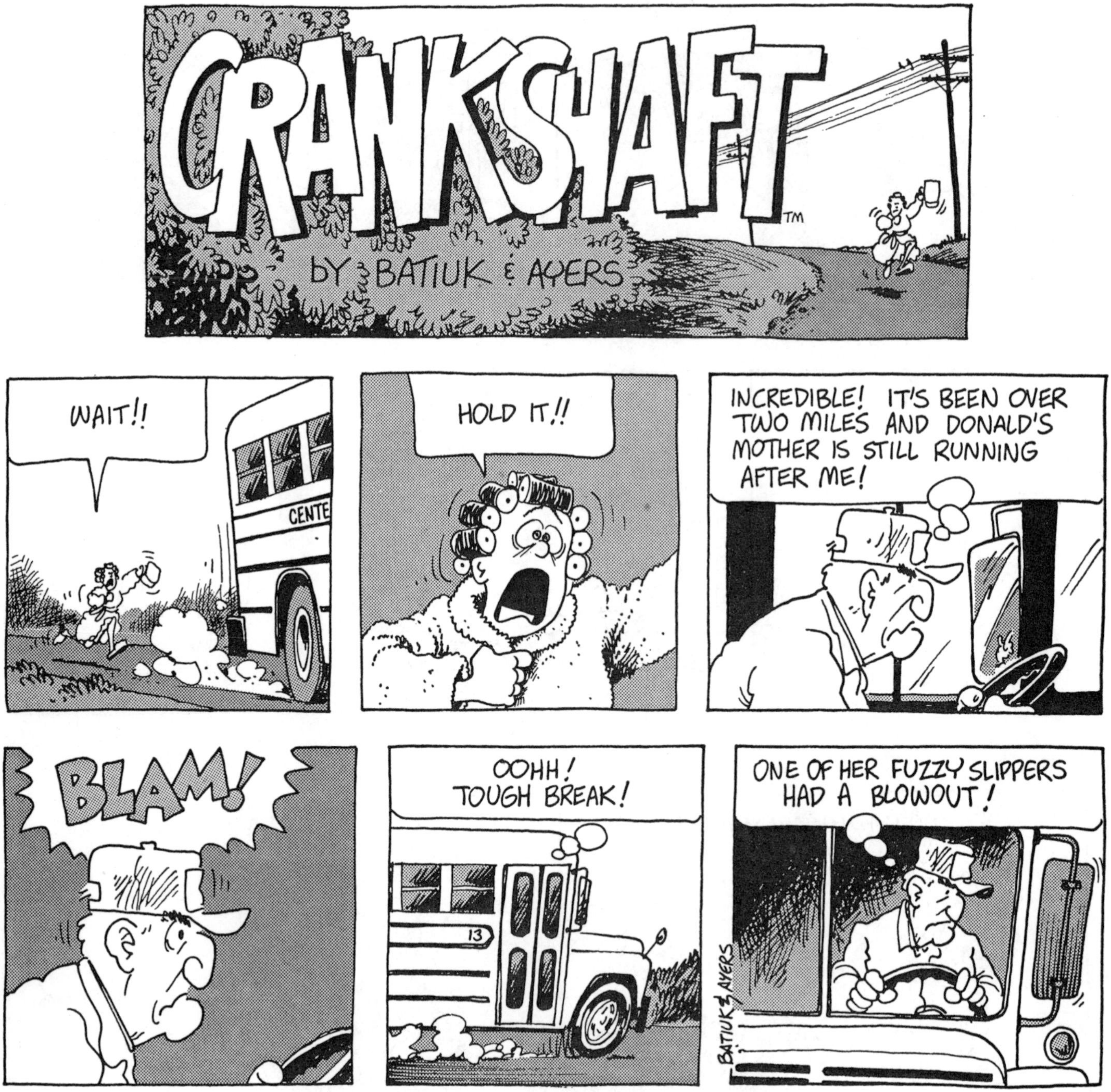
CRANKSHAFT™
BY BATIUK & AYERS
WAIT!!
CENTE
HOLD IT!!
INCREDIBLE! IT'S BEEN OVER TWO MILES AND DONALD'S MOTHER IS STILL RUNNING AFTER ME!
BLAM!
OOHH! TOUGH BREAK!
13
ONE OF HER FUZZY SLIPPERS HAD A BLOWOUT!
BATIUK & AYERS

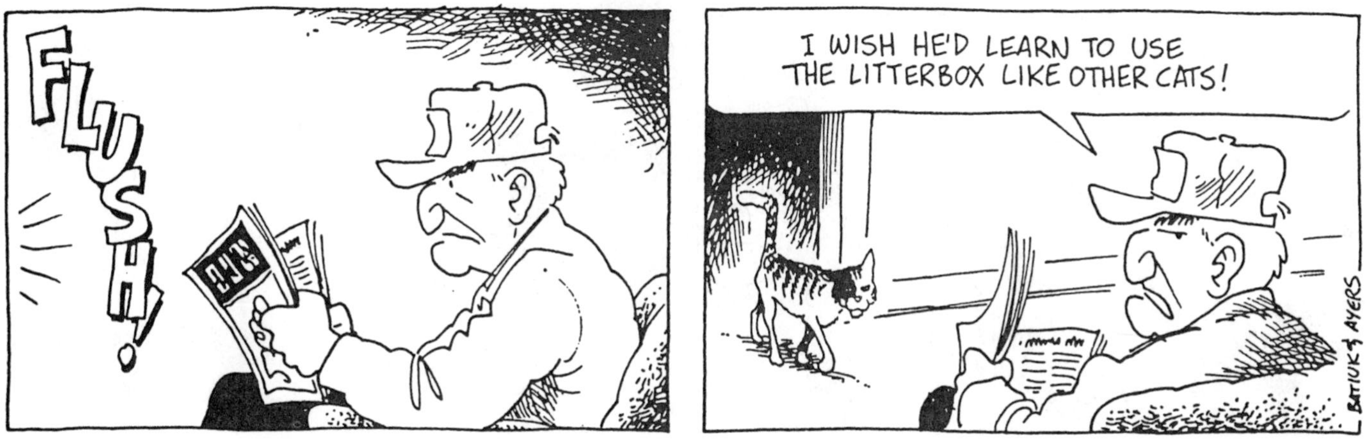
FLUSH!
I WISH HE'D LEARN TO USE THE LITTERBOX LIKE OTHER CATS!
BATIUK & AYERS

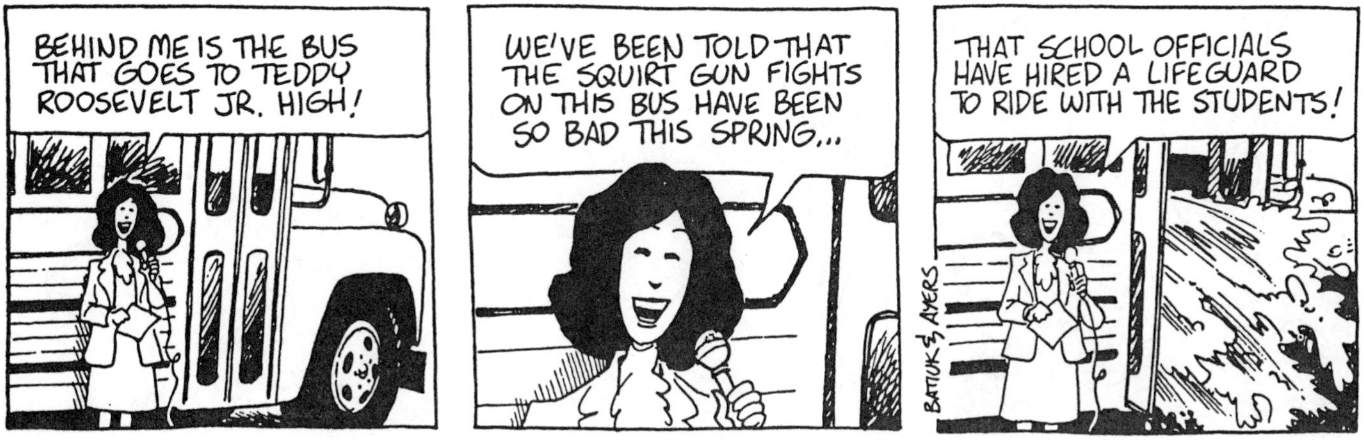
BEHIND ME IS THE BUS THAT GOES TO TEDDY ROOSEVELT JR. HIGH!
WE'VE BEEN TOLD THAT THE SQUIRT GUN FIGHTS ON THIS BUS HAVE BEEN SO BAD THIS SPRING...
THAT SCHOOL OFFICIALS HAVE HIRED A LIFEGUARD TO RIDE WITH THE STUDENTS!
BATIUK & AYERS

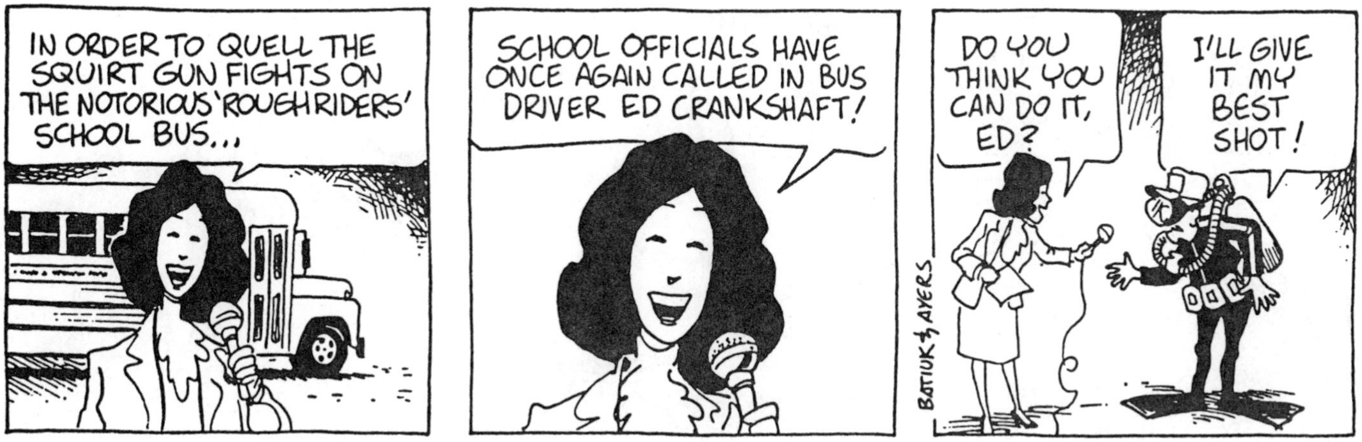
IN ORDER TO QUELL THE SQUIRT GUN FIGHTS ON THE NOTORIOUS 'ROUGHRIDERS' SCHOOL BUS...
SCHOOL OFFICIALS HAVE ONCE AGAIN CALLED IN BUS DRIVER ED CRANKSHAFT!
DO YOU THINK YOU CAN DO IT, ED?
I'LL GIVE IT MY BEST SHOT!
BATIUK & AYERS

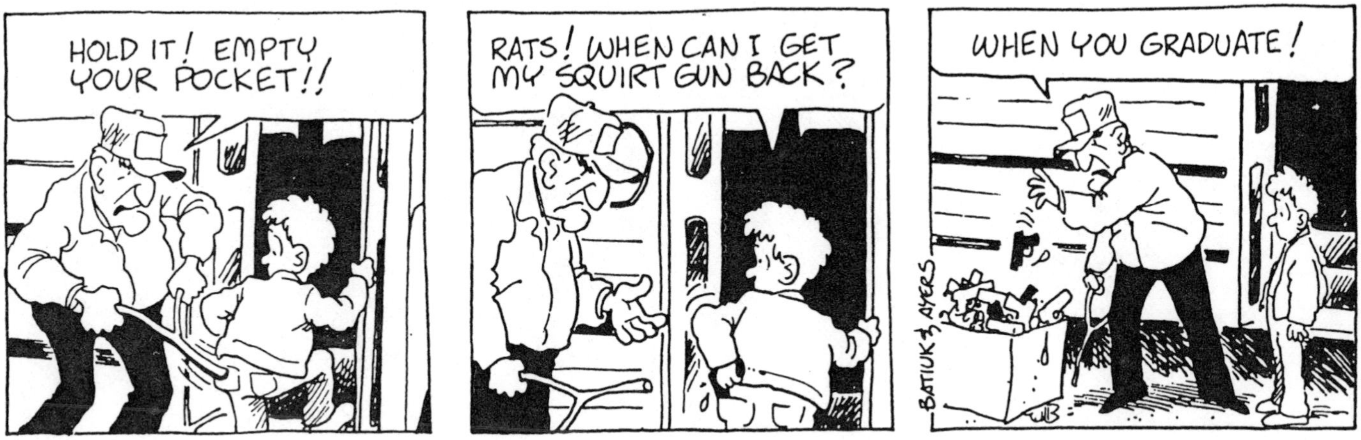
HOLD IT! EMPTY YOUR POCKET!!
RATS! WHEN CAN I GET MY SQUIRT GUN BACK?
WHEN YOU GRADUATE!
BATIUK & AYERS

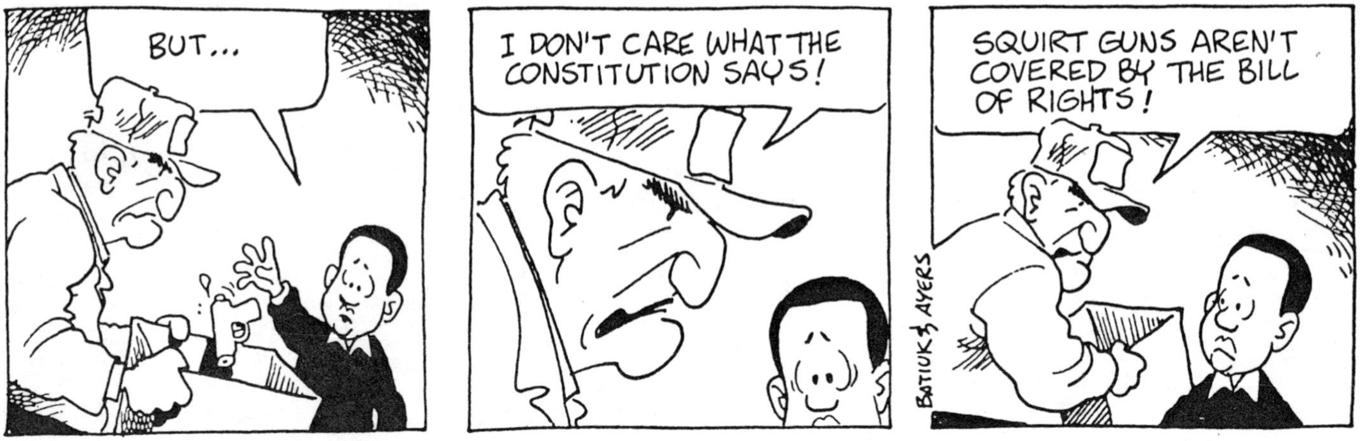
BUT...
I DON'T CARE WHAT THE CONSTITUTION SAYS!
SQUIRT GUNS AREN'T COVERED BY THE BILL OF RIGHTS!
BATIUK & AYERS

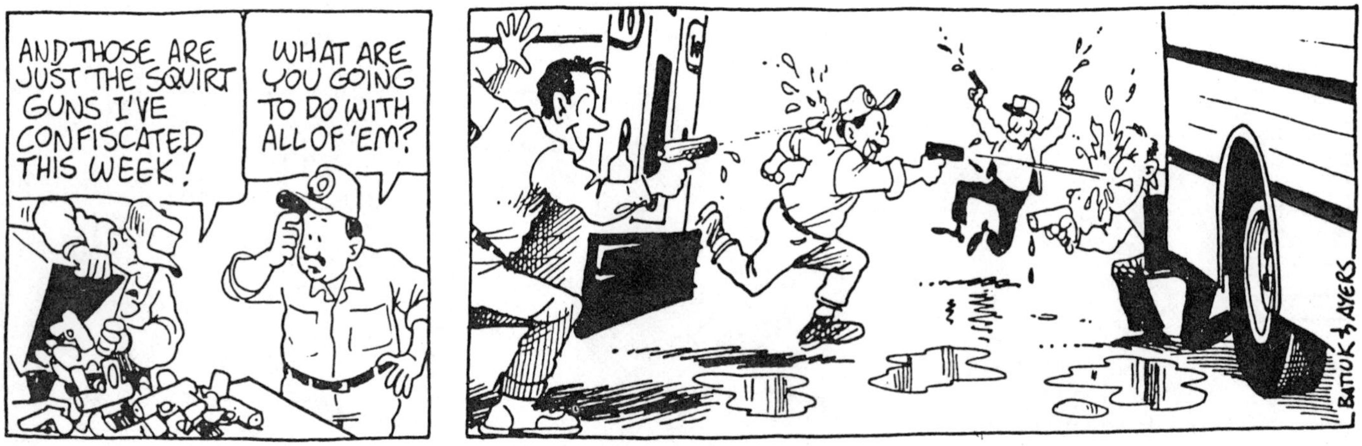
AND THOSE ARE JUST THE SQUIRT GUNS I'VE CONFISCATED THIS WEEK!
WHAT ARE YOU GOING TO DO WITH ALL OF 'EM?
BATIUK & AYERS

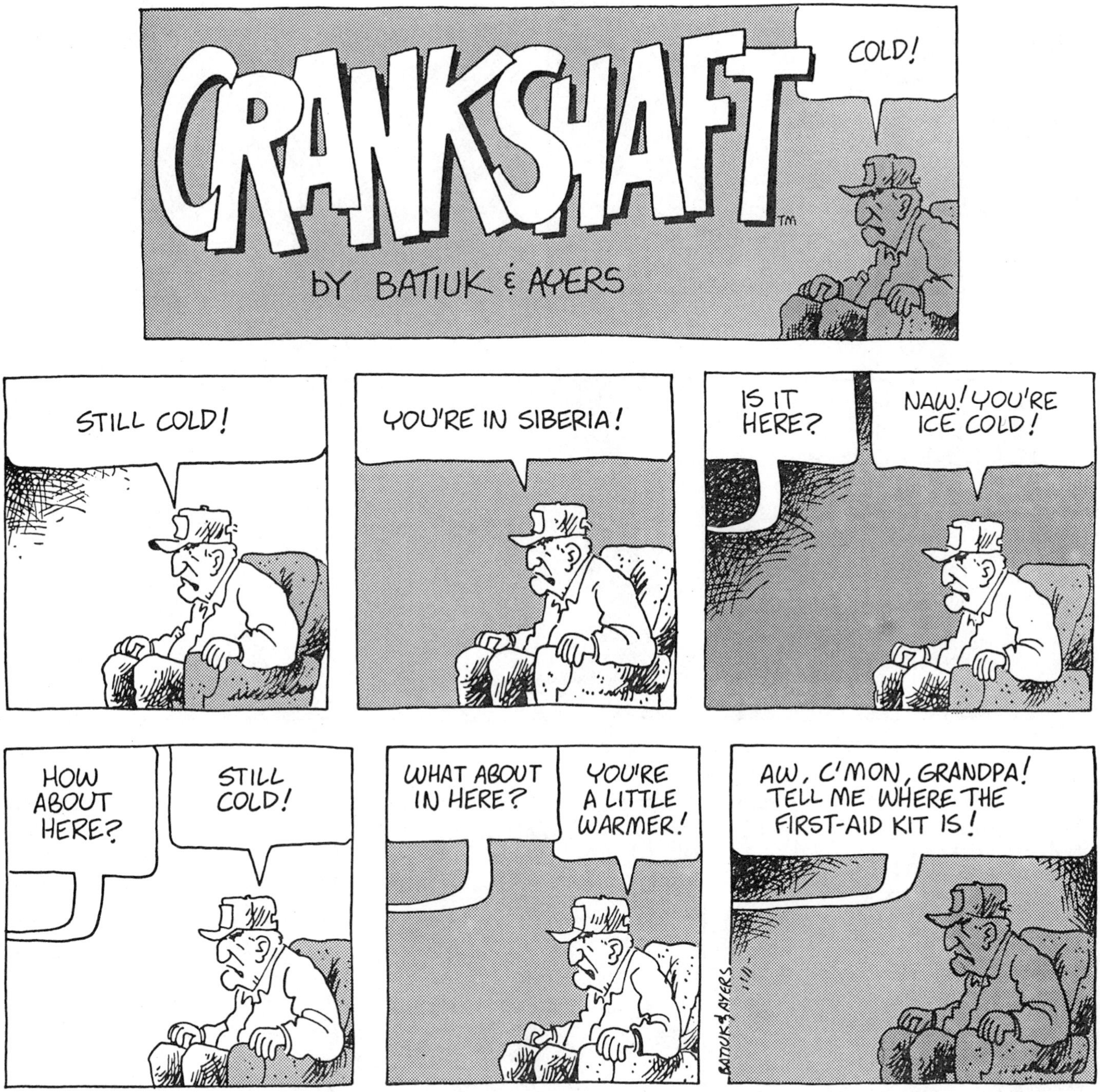
CRANKSHAFT™
BY BATIUK & AYERS
COLD!
STILL COLD!
YOU'RE IN SIBERIA!
IS IT HERE?
NAW! YOU'RE ICE COLD!
HOW ABOUT HERE?
STILL COLD!
WHAT ABOUT IN HERE?
YOU'RE A LITTLE WARMER!
AW, C'MON, GRANDPA! TELL ME WHERE THE FIRST-AID KIT IS!
BATIUK & AYERS

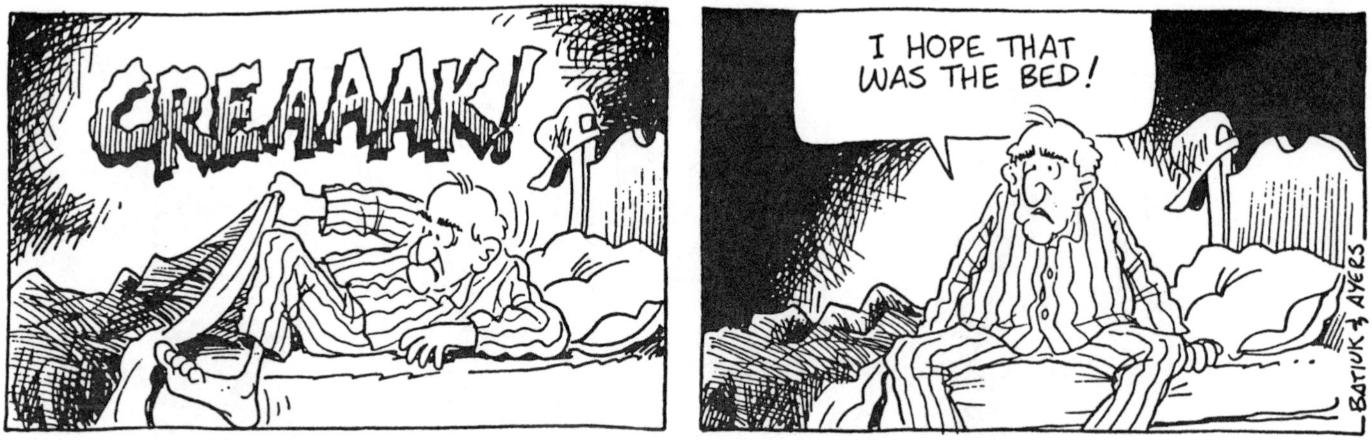
CREAAAK!
I HOPE THAT WAS THE BED!

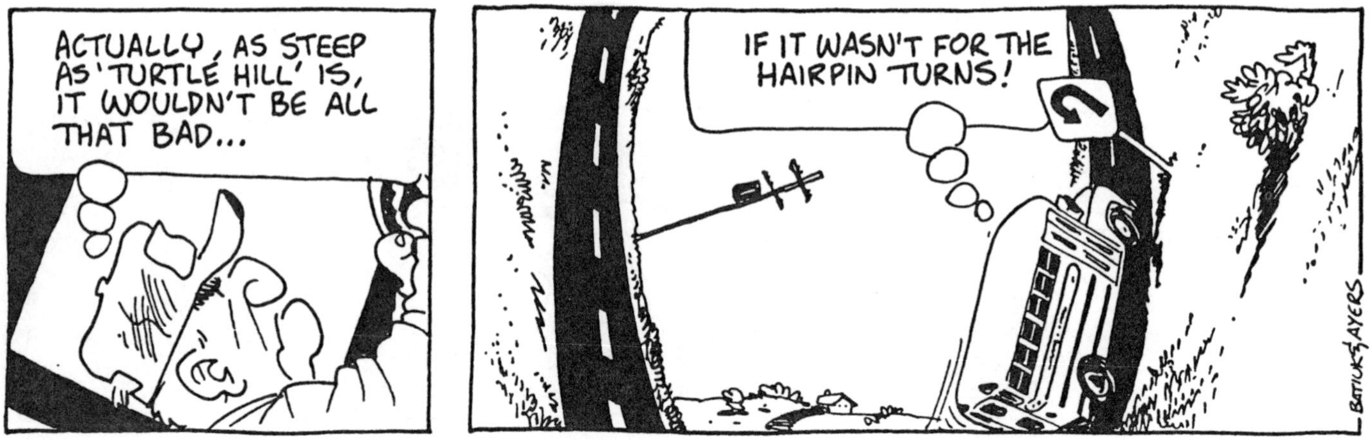
ACTUALLY, AS STEEP AS 'TURTLE HILL' IS, IT WOULDN'T BE ALL THAT BAD...
IF IT WASN'T FOR THE HAIRPIN TURNS!

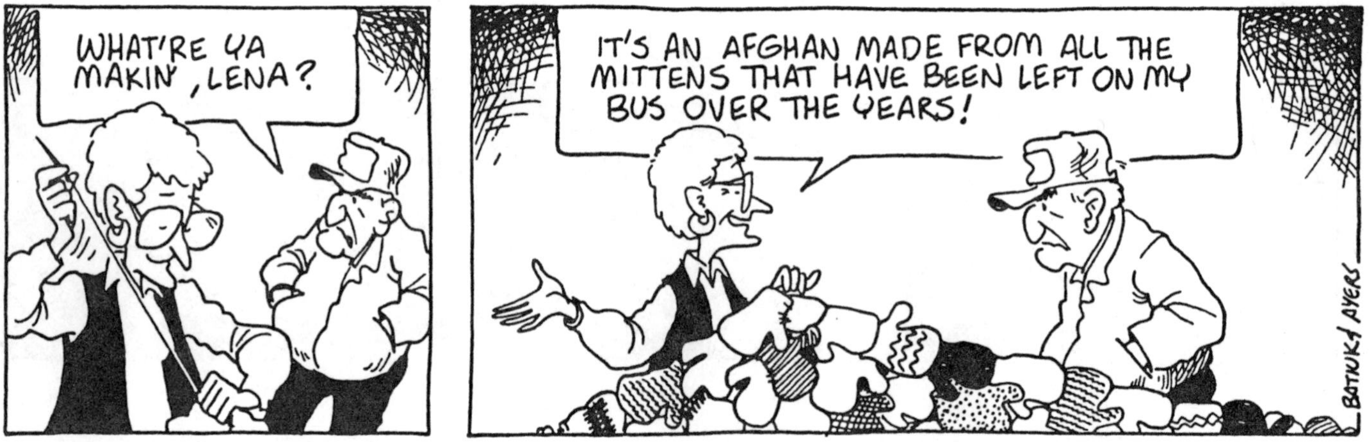
WHAT'RE YA MAKIN', LENA?
IT'S AN AFGHAN MADE FROM ALL THE MITTENS THAT HAVE BEEN LEFT ON MY BUS OVER THE YEARS!

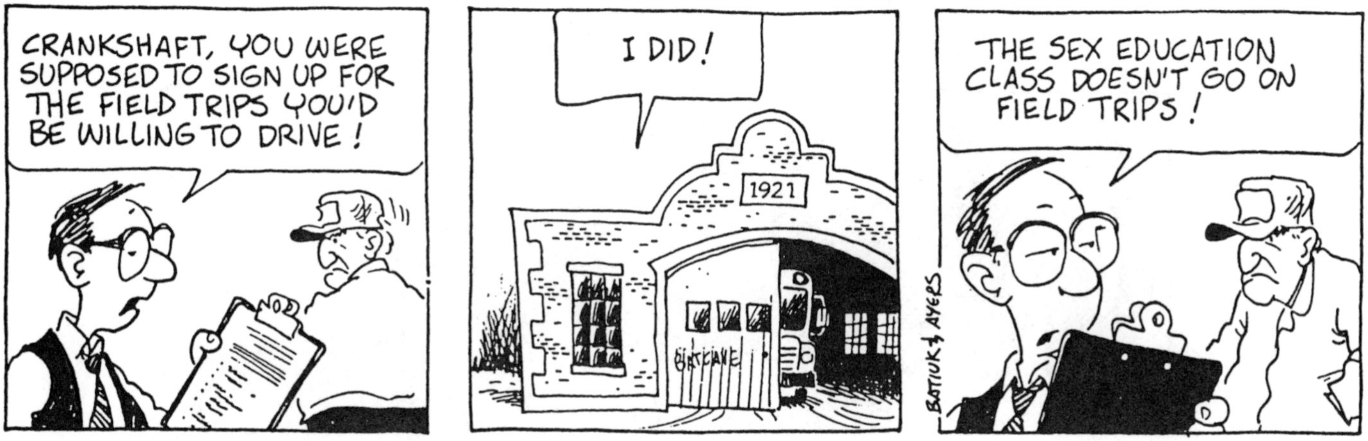
CRANKSHAFT, YOU WERE SUPPOSED TO SIGN UP FOR THE FIELD TRIPS YOU'D BE WILLING TO DRIVE!
I DID!
1921
THE SEX EDUCATION CLASS DOESN'T GO ON FIELD TRIPS!
BATIUK & AYERS

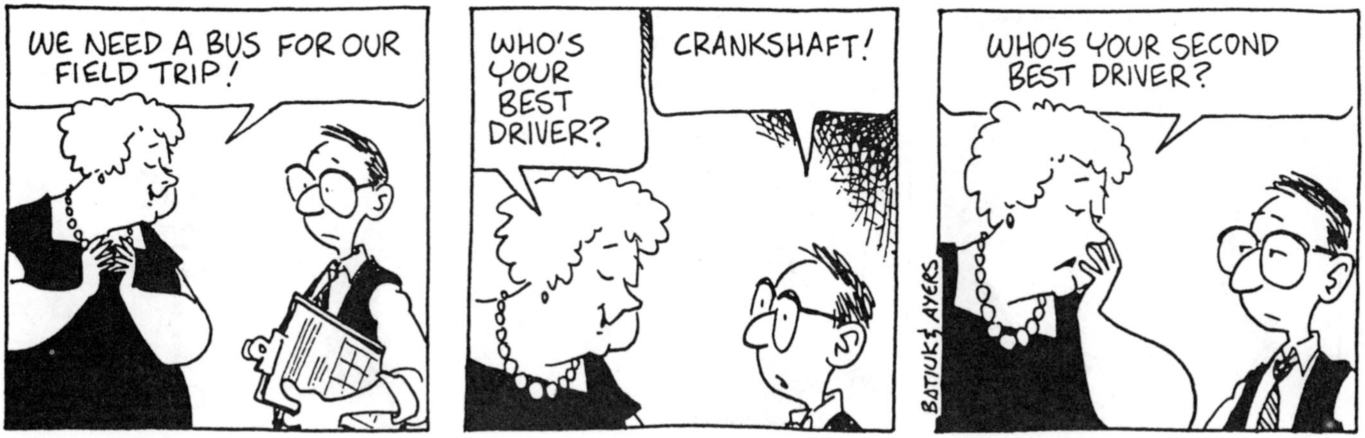
WE NEED A BUS FOR OUR FIELD TRIP!
WHO'S YOUR BEST DRIVER?
CRANKSHAFT!
WHO'S YOUR SECOND BEST DRIVER?
BATIUK & AYERS

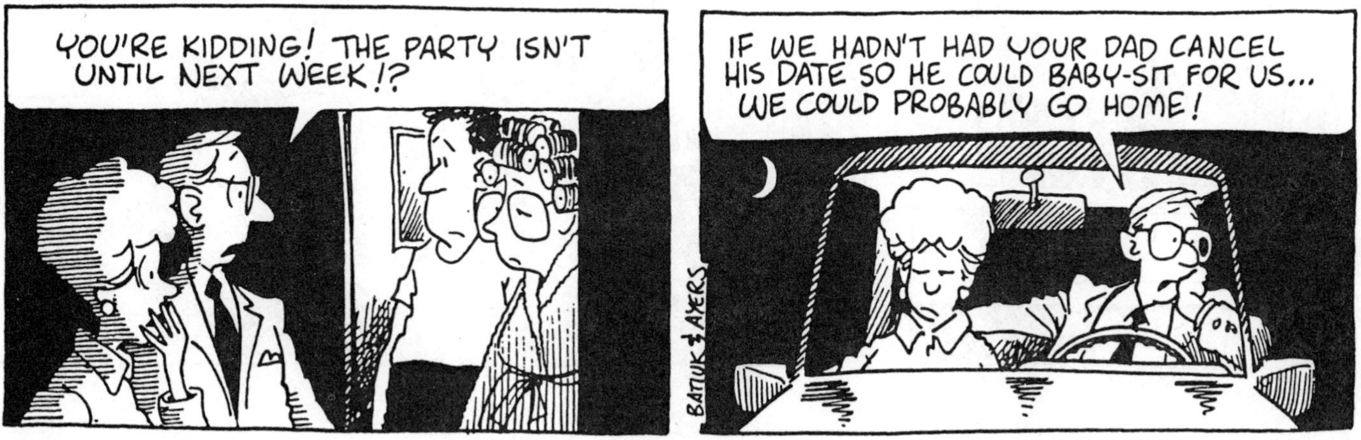
YOU'RE KIDDING! THE PARTY ISN'T UNTIL NEXT WEEK!?
IF WE HADN'T HAD YOUR DAD CANCEL HIS DATE SO HE COULD BABY-SIT FOR US... WE COULD PROBABLY GO HOME!
BATIUK & AYERS

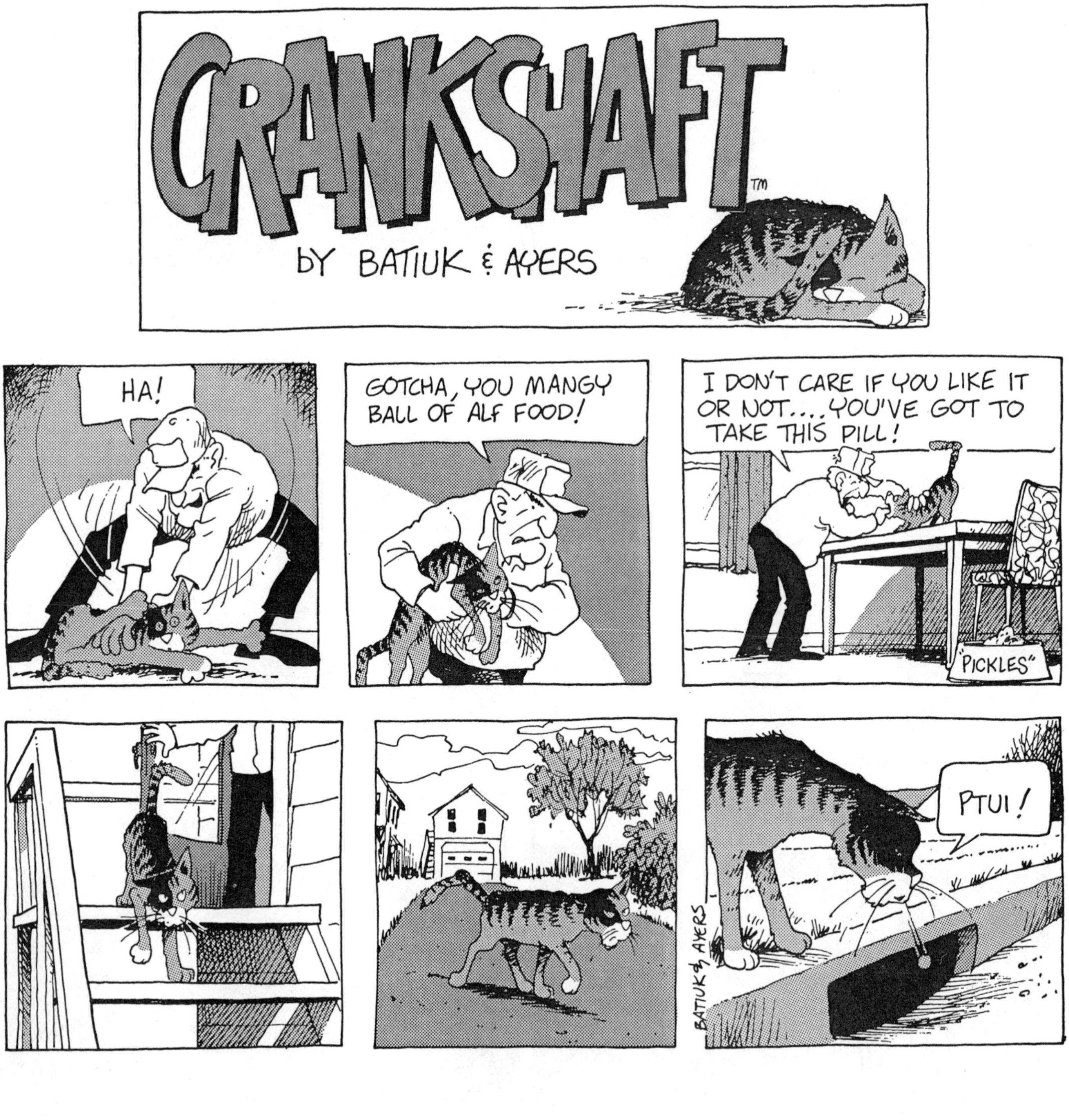
CRANKSHAFT
TM
BY BATIUK & AYERS
HA!
GOTCHA, YOU MANGY BALL OF ALF FOOD!
I DON'T CARE IF YOU LIKE IT OR NOT.... YOU'VE GOT TO TAKE THIS PILL!
"PICKLES"
BATIUK & AYERS
PTUI!

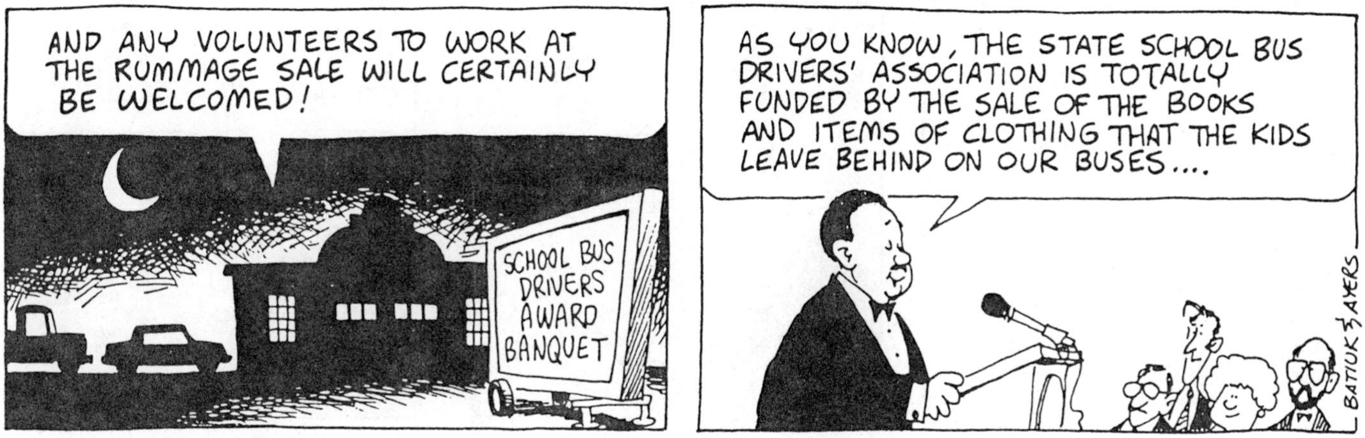
AND ANY VOLUNTEERS TO WORK AT THE RUMMAGE SALE WILL CERTAINLY BE WELCOMED!
SCHOOL BUS DRIVERS AWARD BANQUET
AS YOU KNOW, THE STATE SCHOOL BUS DRIVERS' ASSOCIATION IS TOTALLY FUNDED BY THE SALE OF THE BOOKS AND ITEMS OF CLOTHING THAT THE KIDS LEAVE BEHIND ON OUR BUSES....
BATIUK & AYERS

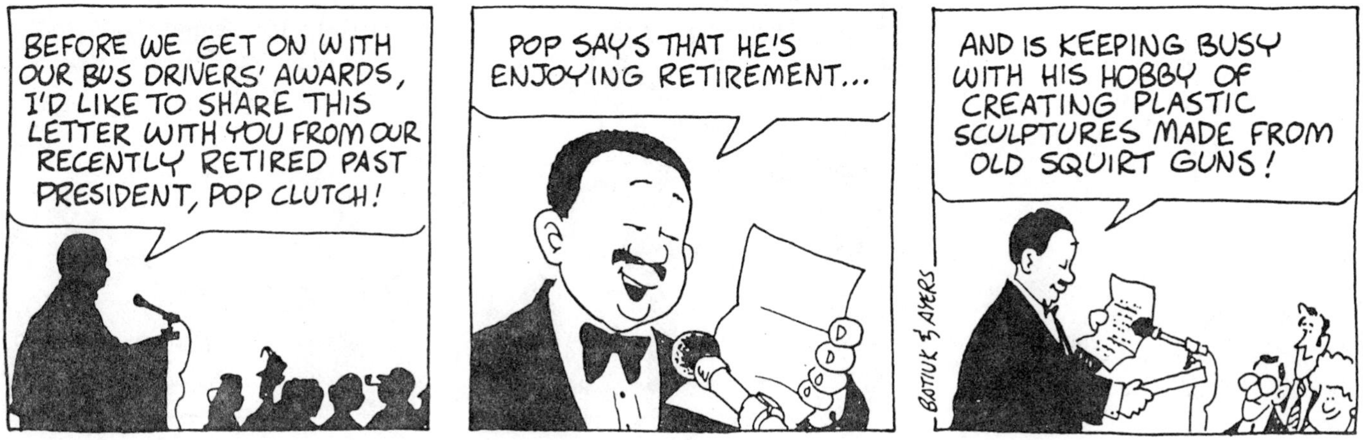
BEFORE WE GET ON WITH OUR BUS DRIVERS' AWARDS, I'D LIKE TO SHARE THIS LETTER WITH YOU FROM OUR RECENTLY RETIRED PAST PRESIDENT, POP CLUTCH!
POP SAYS THAT HE'S ENJOYING RETIREMENT...
AND IS KEEPING BUSY WITH HIS HOBBY OF CREATING PLASTIC SCULPTURES MADE FROM OLD SQUIRT GUNS!
BATIUK & AYERS

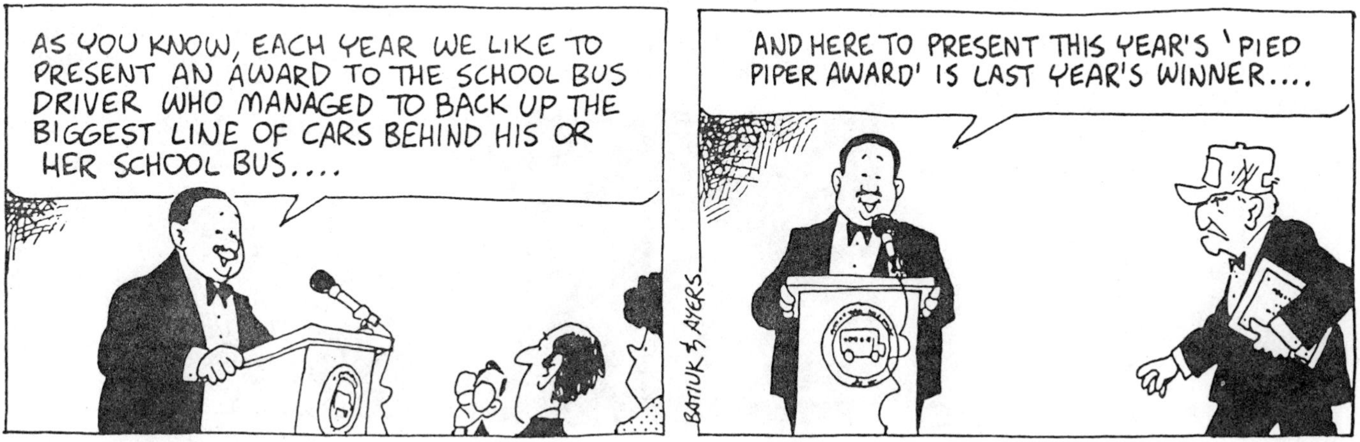
AS YOU KNOW, EACH YEAR WE LIKE TO PRESENT AN AWARD TO THE SCHOOL BUS DRIVER WHO MANAGED TO BACK UP THE BIGGEST LINE OF CARS BEHIND HIS OR HER SCHOOL BUS....
BATIUK & AYERS
AND HERE TO PRESENT THIS YEAR'S 'PIED PIPER AWARD' IS LAST YEAR'S WINNER....

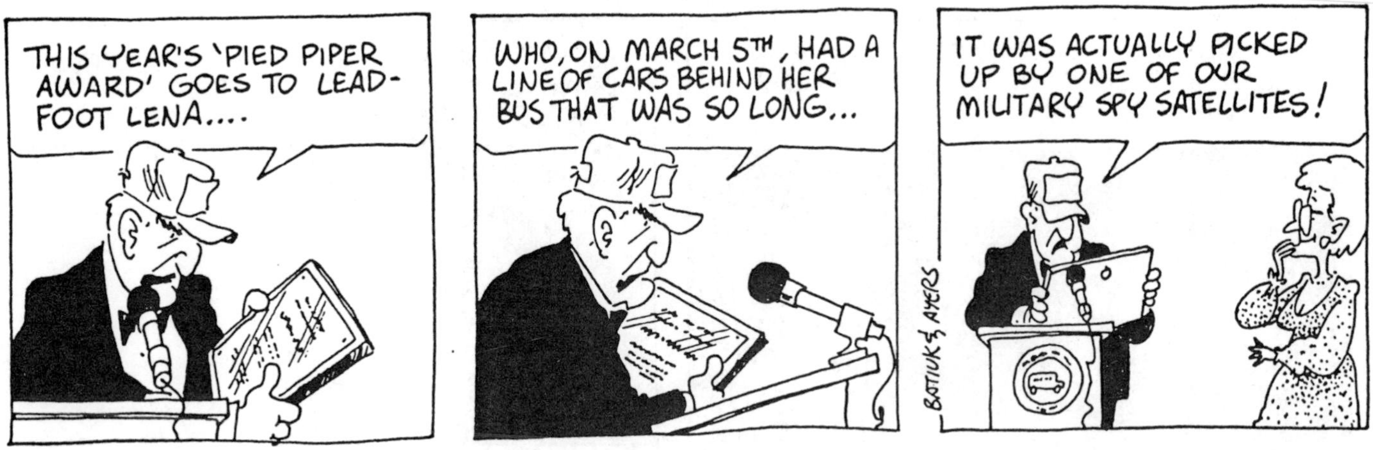
THIS YEAR'S 'PIED PIPER AWARD' GOES TO LEAD-FOOT LENA....
WHO, ON MARCH 5TH, HAD A LINE OF CARS BEHIND HER BUS THAT WAS SO LONG...
IT WAS ACTUALLY PICKED UP BY ONE OF OUR MILITARY SPY SATELLITES!
BATIUK & AYERS

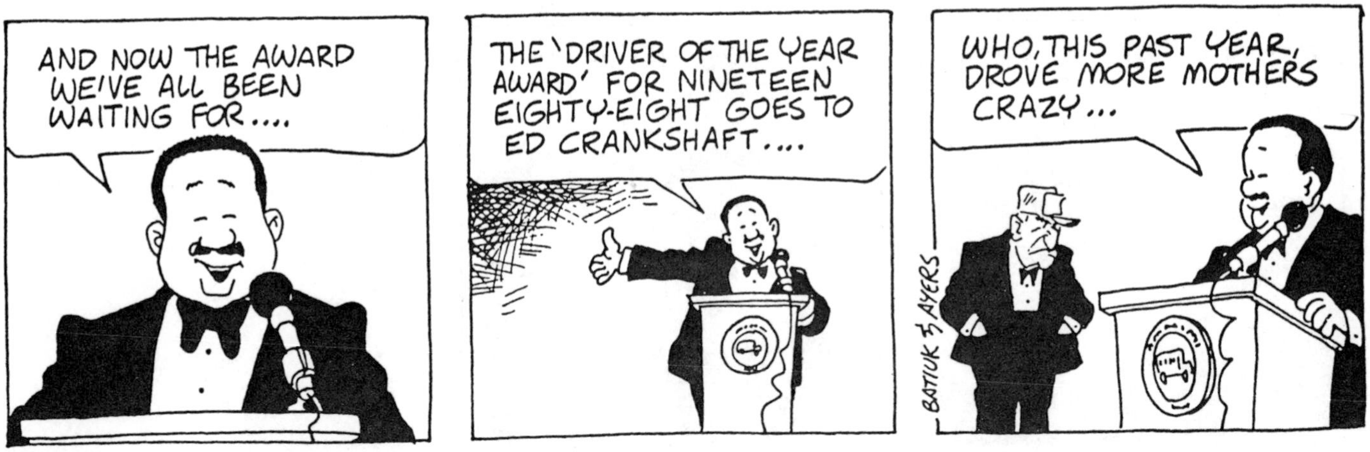
AND NOW THE AWARD WE'VE ALL BEEN WAITING FOR....
THE 'DRIVER OF THE YEAR AWARD' FOR NINETEEN EIGHTY-EIGHT GOES TO ED CRANKSHAFT....
WHO, THIS PAST YEAR, DROVE MORE MOTHERS CRAZY...
BATIUK & AYERS

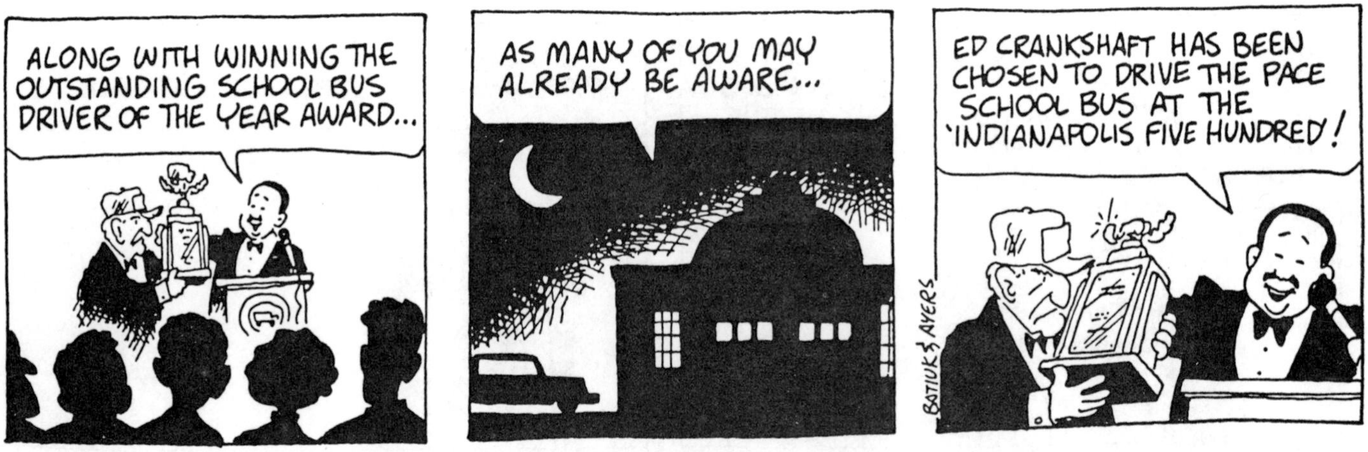
ALONG WITH WINNING THE OUTSTANDING SCHOOL BUS DRIVER OF THE YEAR AWARD...
AS MANY OF YOU MAY ALREADY BE AWARE...
ED CRANKSHAFT HAS BEEN CHOSEN TO DRIVE THE PACE SCHOOL BUS AT THE 'INDIANAPOLIS FIVE HUNDRED'!
BATIUK & AYERS

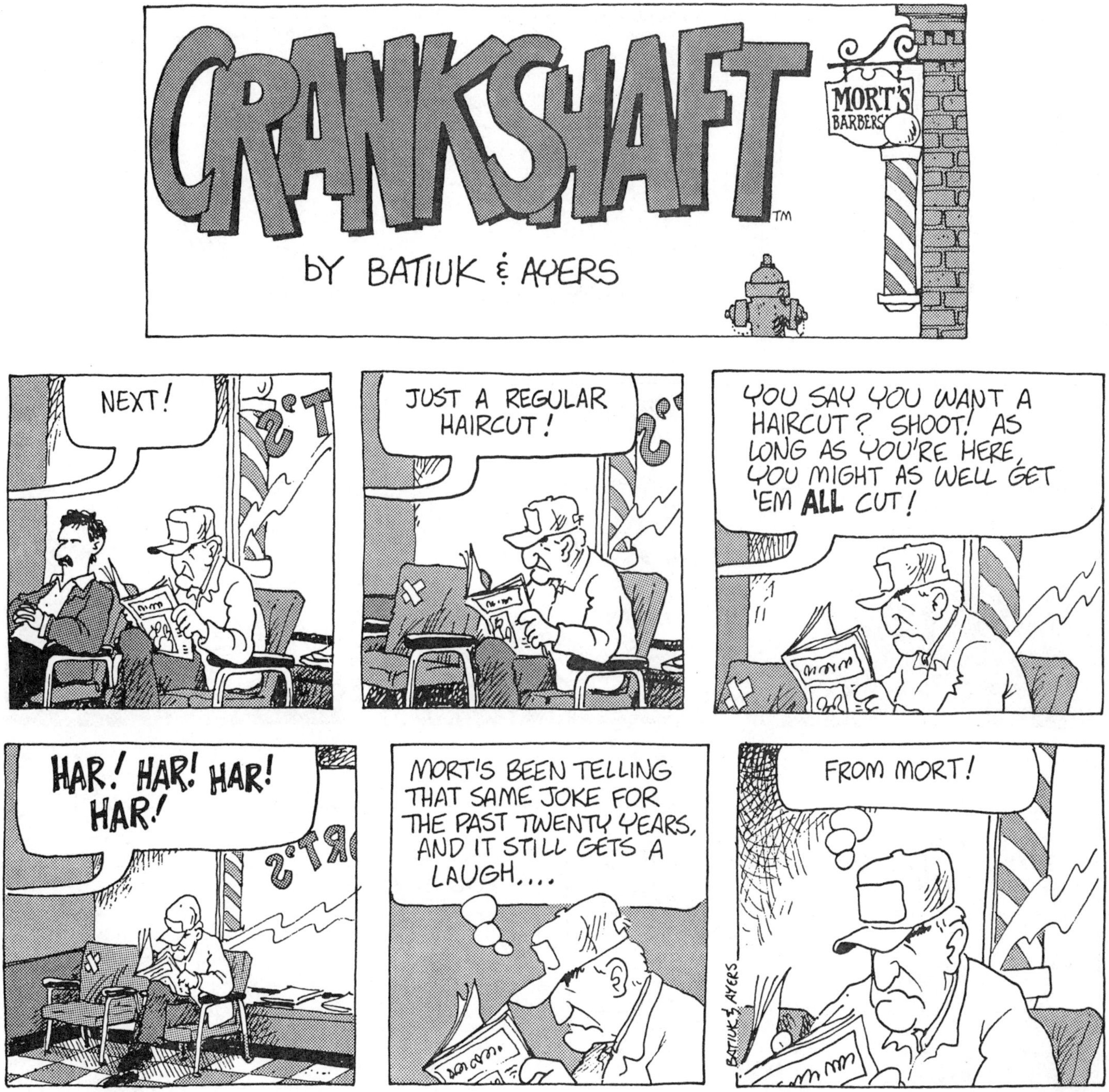
CRANKSHAFT TM
MORT'S BARBERS
BY BATIUK & AYERS
NEXT!
JUST A REGULAR HAIRCUT!
YOU SAY YOU WANT A HAIRCUT? SHOOT! AS LONG AS YOU'RE HERE, YOU MIGHT AS WELL GET 'EM ALL CUT!
HAR! HAR! HAR! HAR!
MORT'S BEEN TELLING THAT SAME JOKE FOR THE PAST TWENTY YEARS, AND IT STILL GETS A LAUGH....
FROM MORT!
BATIUK & AYERS

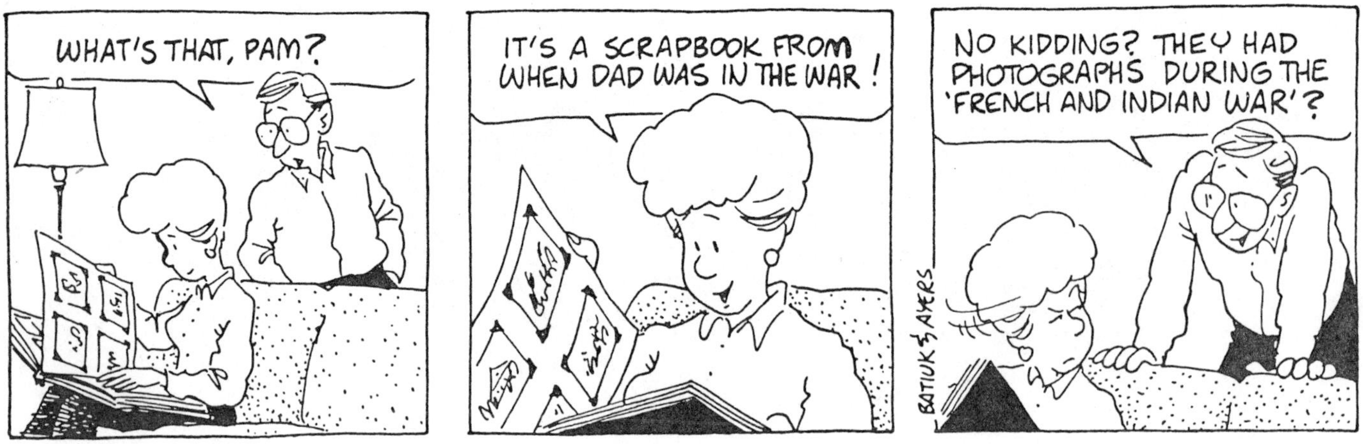
WHAT'S THAT, PAM?
IT'S A SCRAPBOOK FROM WHEN DAD WAS IN THE WAR!
NO KIDDING? THEY HAD PHOTOGRAPHS DURING THE 'FRENCH AND INDIAN WAR'?
BATIUK & AYERS

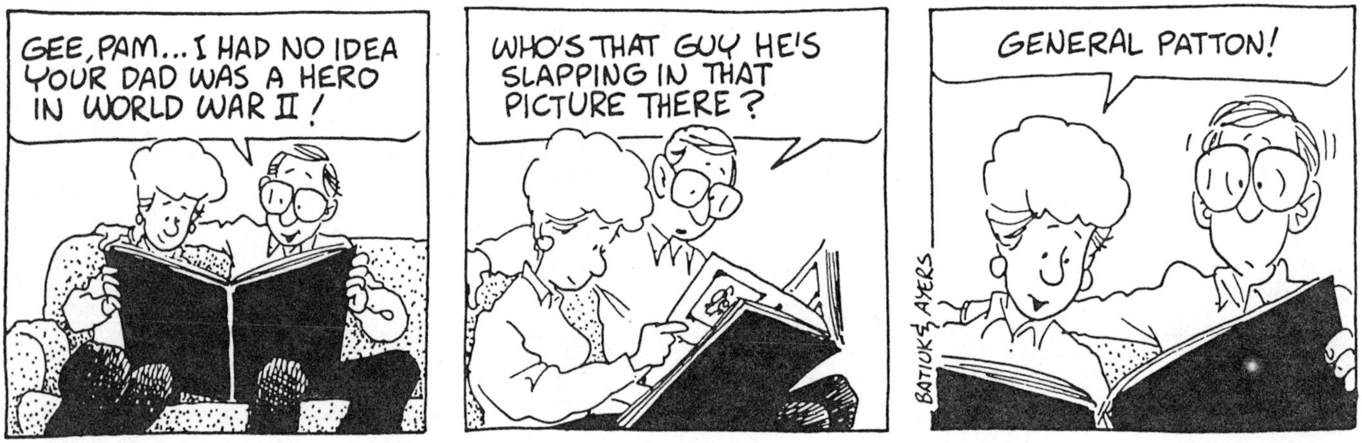
GEE, PAM... I HAD NO IDEA YOUR DAD WAS A HERO IN WORLD WAR II!
WHO'S THAT GUY HE'S SLAPPING IN THAT PICTURE THERE?
GENERAL PATTON!
BATIUK & AYERS

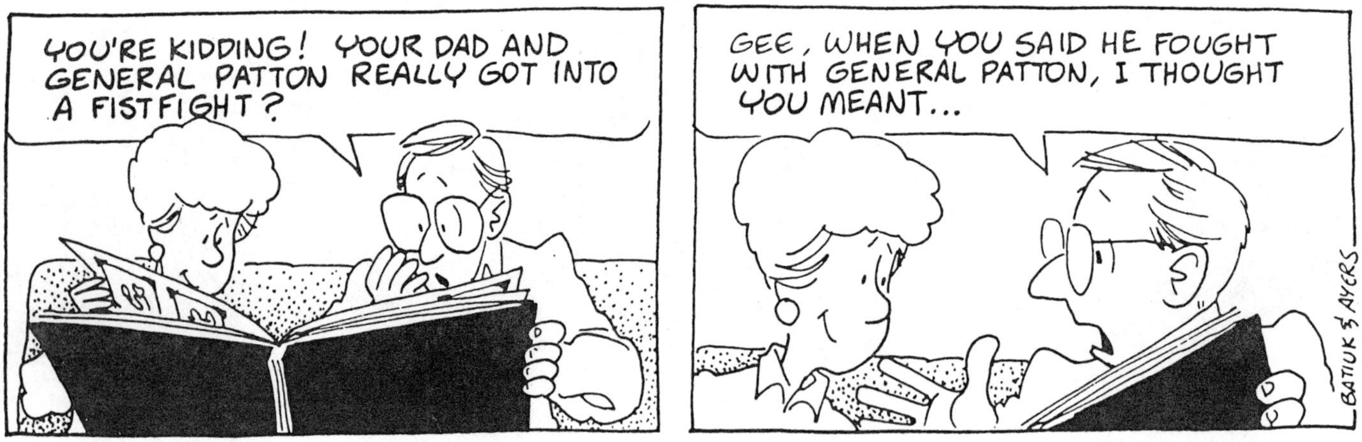
YOU'RE KIDDING! YOUR DAD AND GENERAL PATTON REALLY GOT INTO A FISTFIGHT?
GEE, WHEN YOU SAID HE FOUGHT WITH GENERAL PATTON, I THOUGHT YOU MEANT...
BATIUK & AYERS

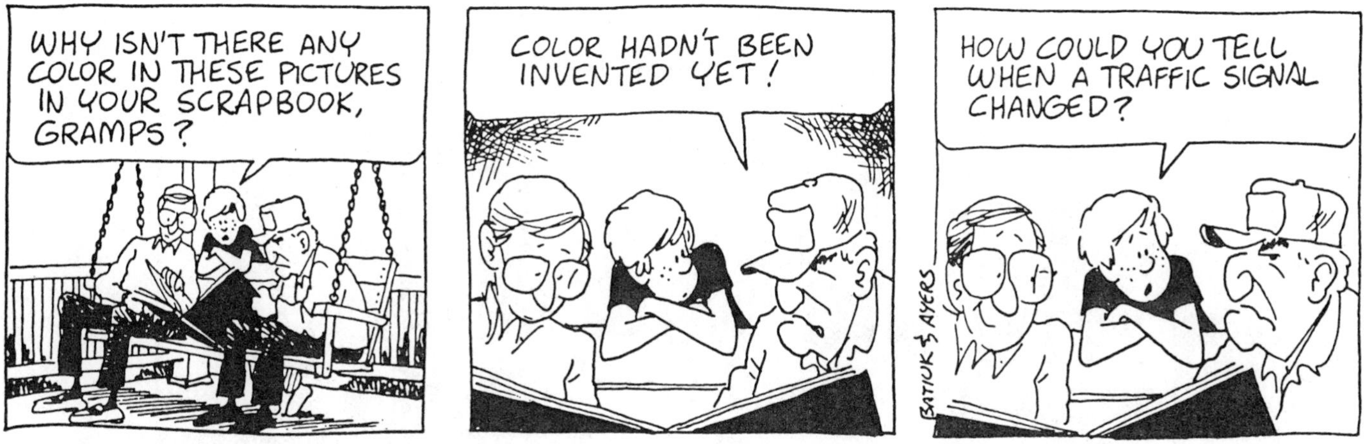
WHY ISN'T THERE ANY COLOR IN THESE PICTURES IN YOUR SCRAPBOOK, GRAMPS?
COLOR HADN'T BEEN INVENTED YET!
HOW COULD YOU TELL WHEN A TRAFFIC SIGNAL CHANGED?
BATIUK & AYERS

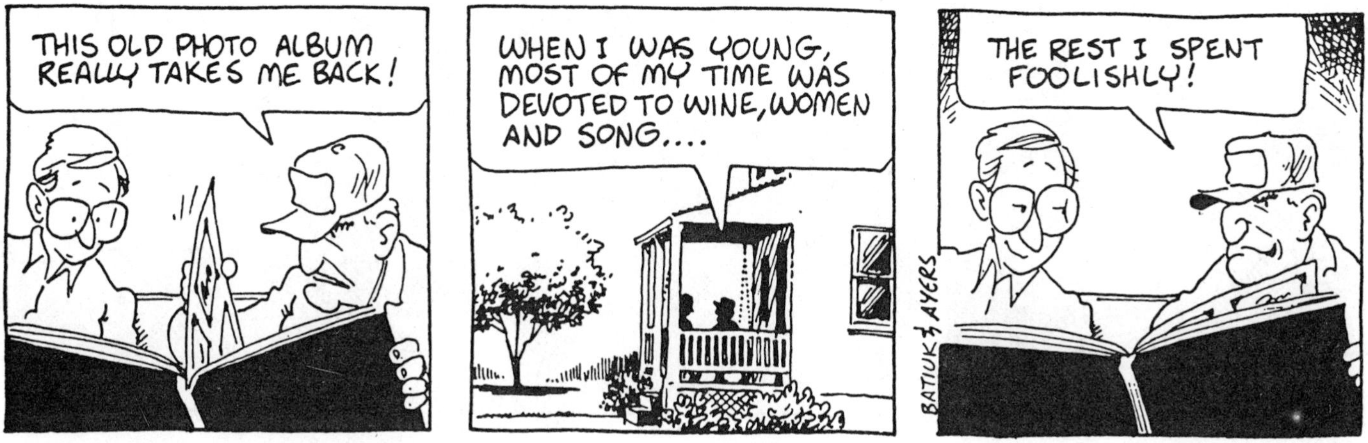
THIS OLD PHOTO ALBUM REALLY TAKES ME BACK!
WHEN I WAS YOUNG, MOST OF MY TIME WAS DEVOTED TO WINE, WOMEN AND SONG....
THE REST I SPENT FOOLISHLY!
BATIUK & AYERS

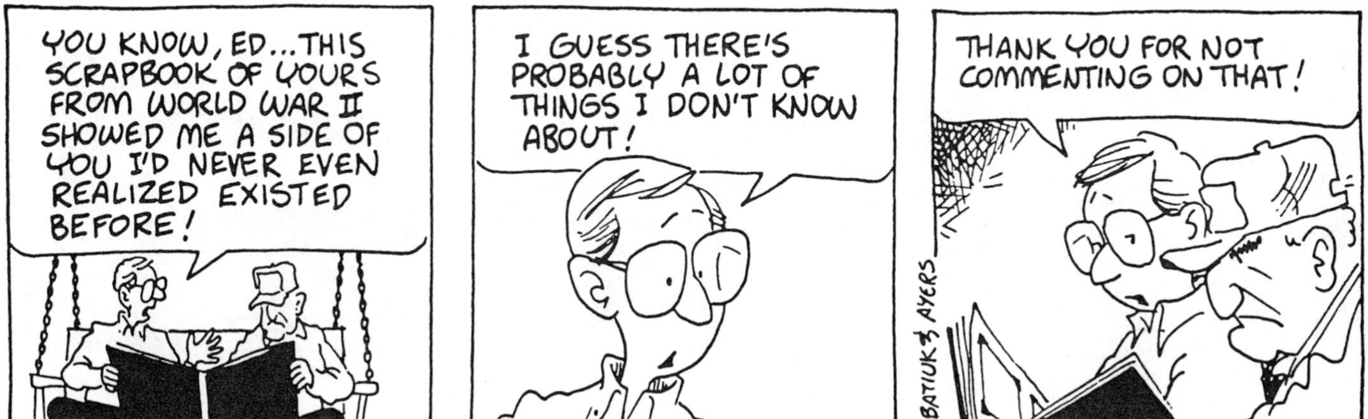
YOU KNOW, ED...THIS SCRAPBOOK OF YOURS FROM WORLD WAR II SHOWED ME A SIDE OF YOU I'D NEVER EVEN REALIZED EXISTED BEFORE!
I GUESS THERE'S PROBABLY A LOT OF THINGS I DON'T KNOW ABOUT!
THANK YOU FOR NOT COMMENTING ON THAT!
BATIUK & AYERS

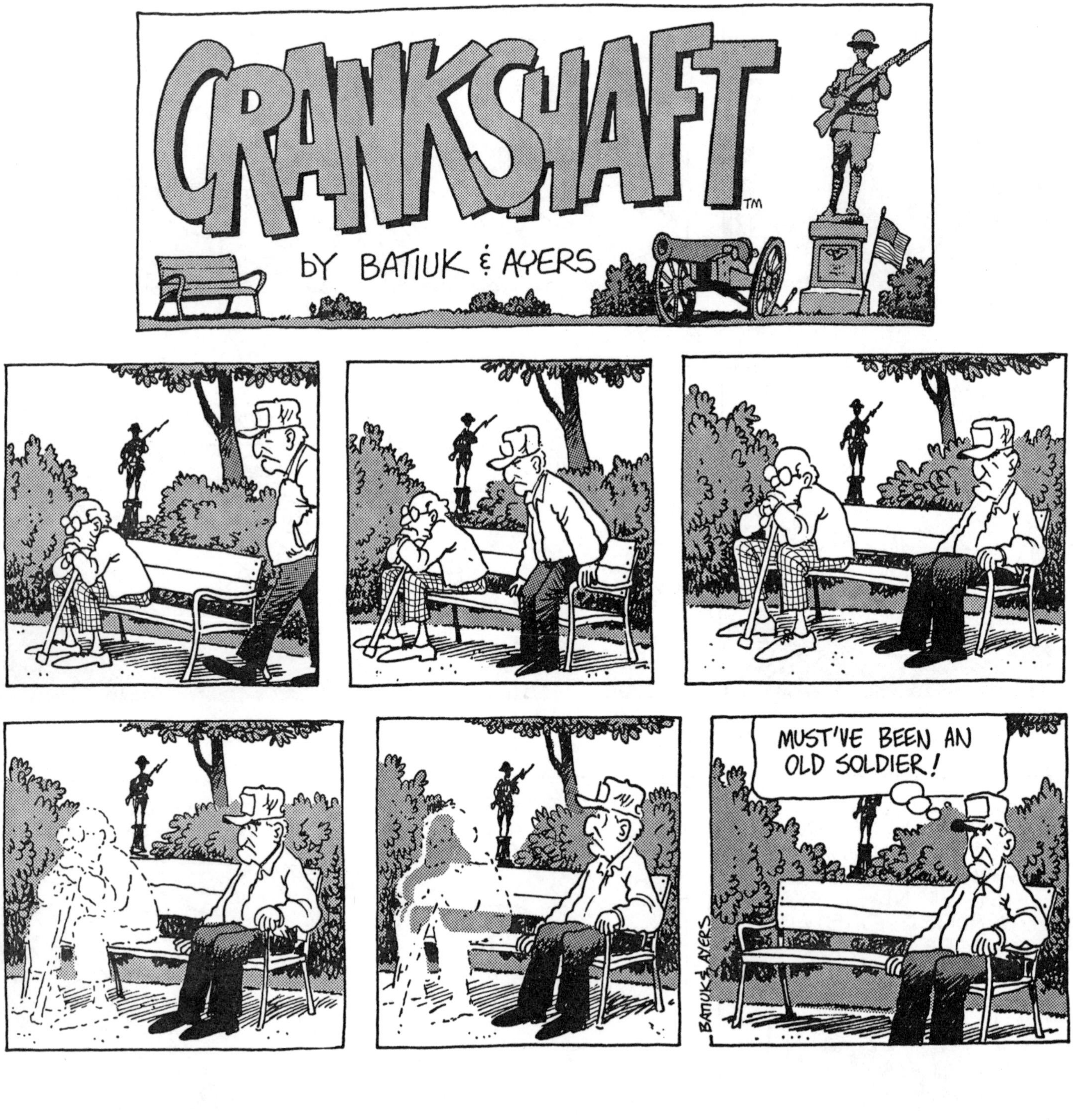
CRANKSHAFT
BY BATIUK & AYERS
MUST'VE BEEN AN OLD SOLDIER!
BATIUK & AYERS

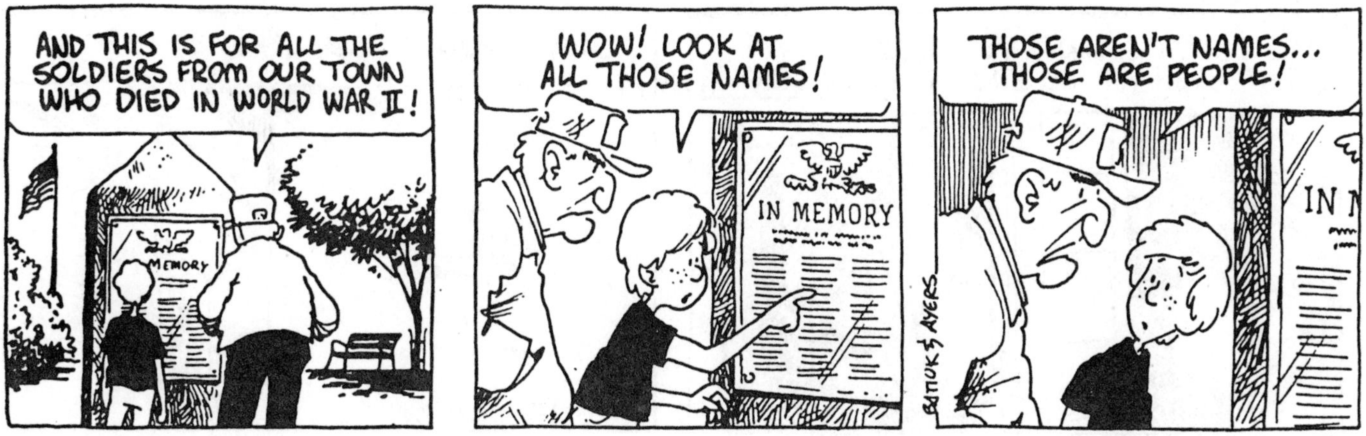
AND THIS IS FOR ALL THE SOLDIERS FROM OUR TOWN WHO DIED IN WORLD WAR II!
IN MEMORY
WOW! LOOK AT ALL THOSE NAMES!
THOSE AREN'T NAMES... THOSE ARE PEOPLE!
BATIUK & AYERS

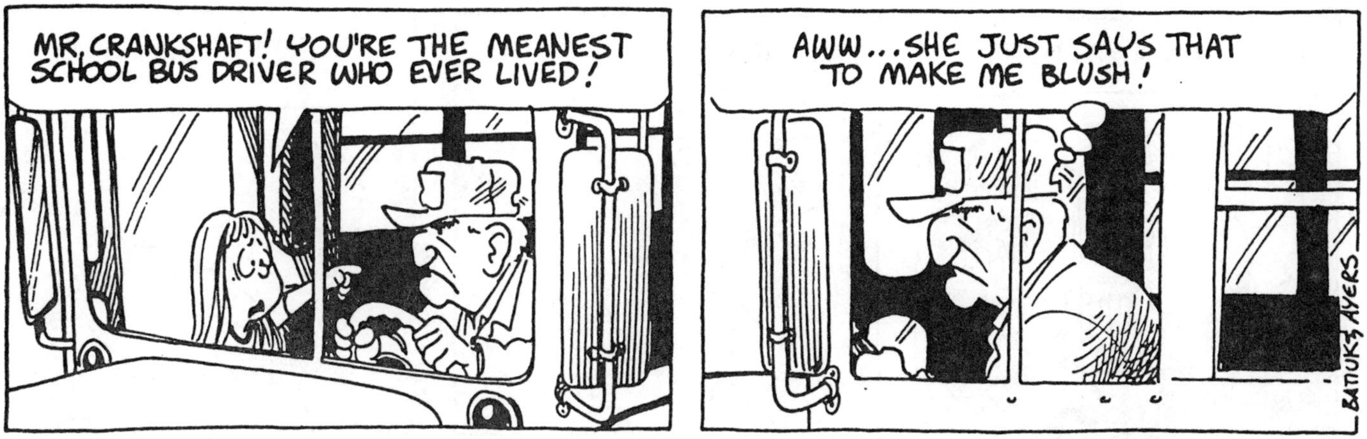
MR. CRANKSHAFT! YOU'RE THE MEANEST SCHOOL BUS DRIVER WHO EVER LIVED!
AWW... SHE JUST SAYS THAT TO MAKE ME BLUSH!
BATIUK & AYERS

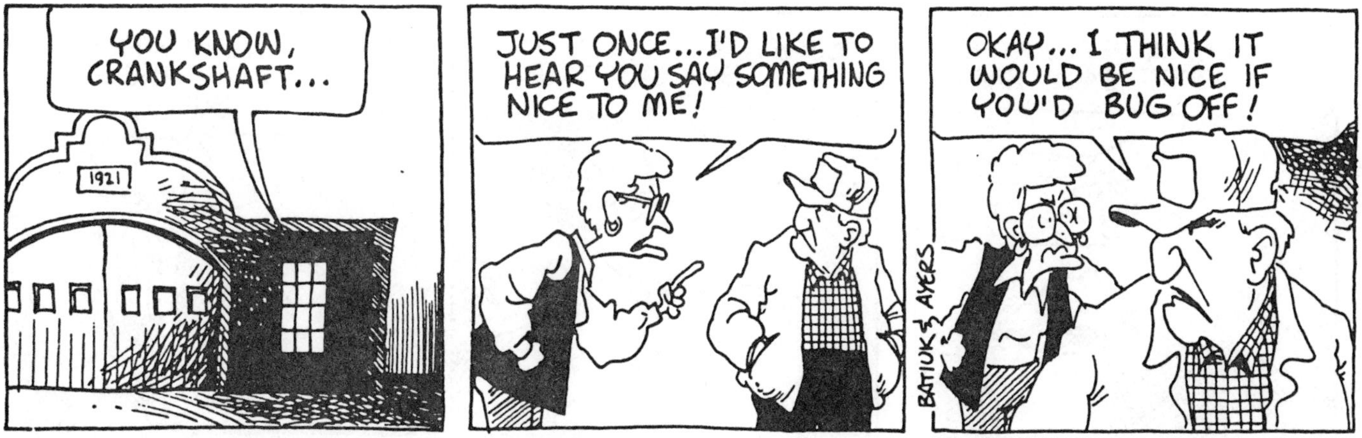
YOU KNOW, CRANKSHAFT...
1921
JUST ONCE... I'D LIKE TO HEAR YOU SAY SOMETHING NICE TO ME!
OKAY... I THINK IT WOULD BE NICE IF YOU'D BUG OFF!
BATIUK & AYERS

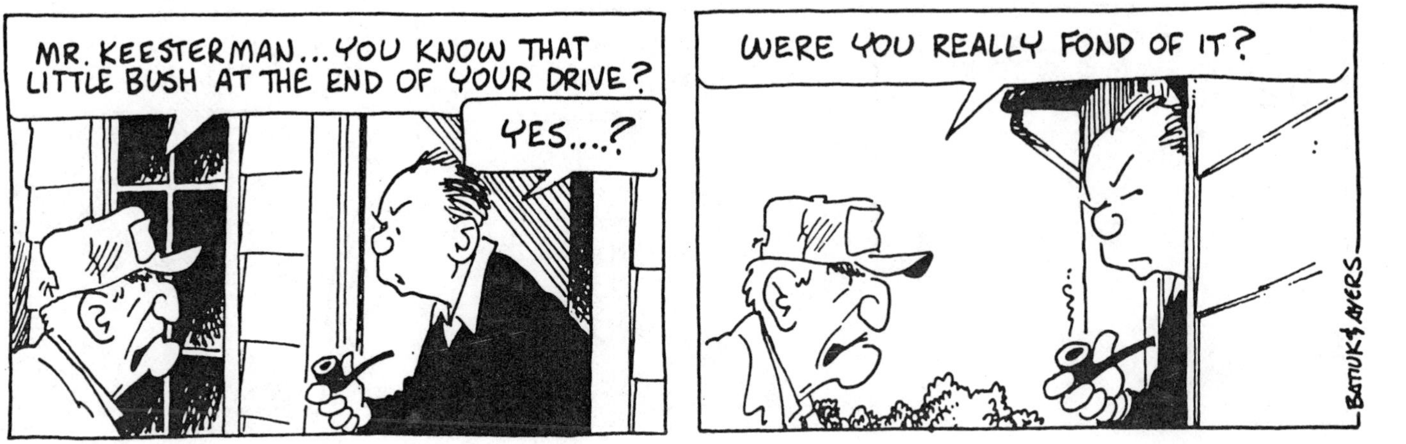
MR. KEESTERMAN... YOU KNOW THAT LITTLE BUSH AT THE END OF YOUR DRIVE?
YES...?
WERE YOU REALLY FOND OF IT?
BATIUK & AYERS

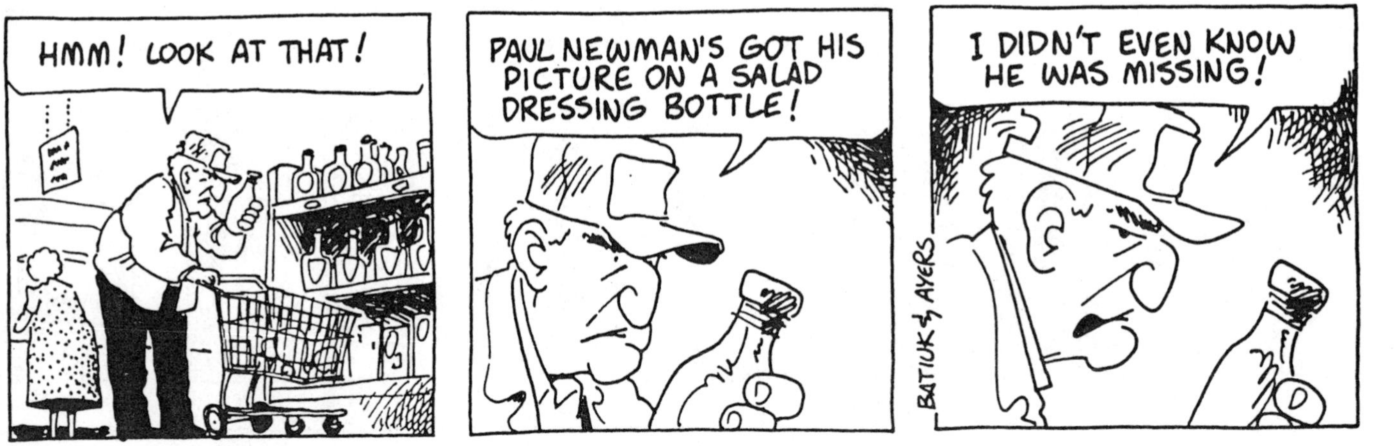
HMM! LOOK AT THAT!
PAUL NEWMAN'S GOT HIS PICTURE ON A SALAD DRESSING BOTTLE!
BATIUK & AYERS
I DIDN'T EVEN KNOW HE WAS MISSING!

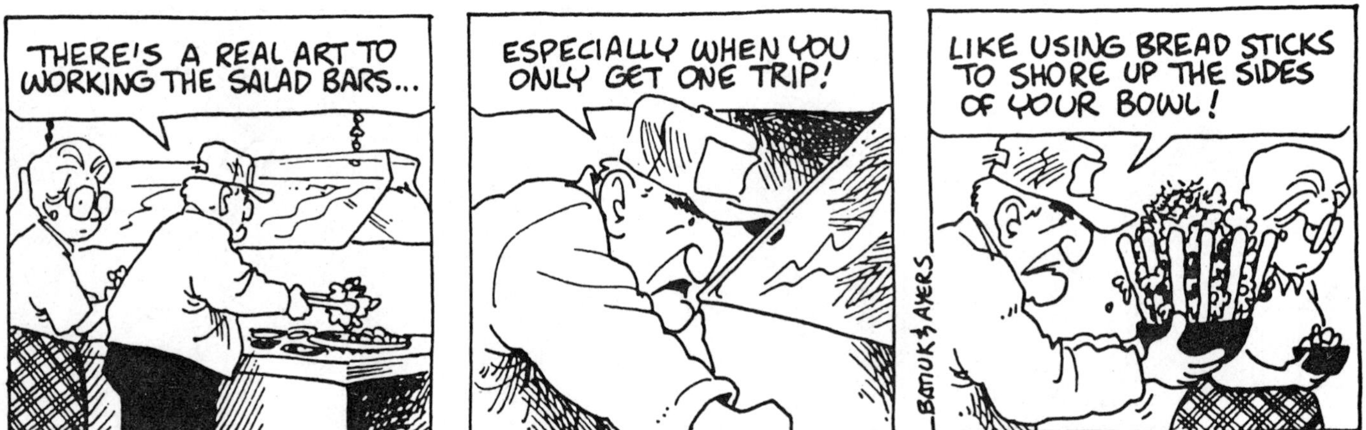
THERE'S A REAL ART TO WORKING THE SALAD BARS...
ESPECIALLY WHEN YOU ONLY GET ONE TRIP!
BATIUK & AYERS
LIKE USING BREAD STICKS TO SHORE UP THE SIDES OF YOUR BOWL!

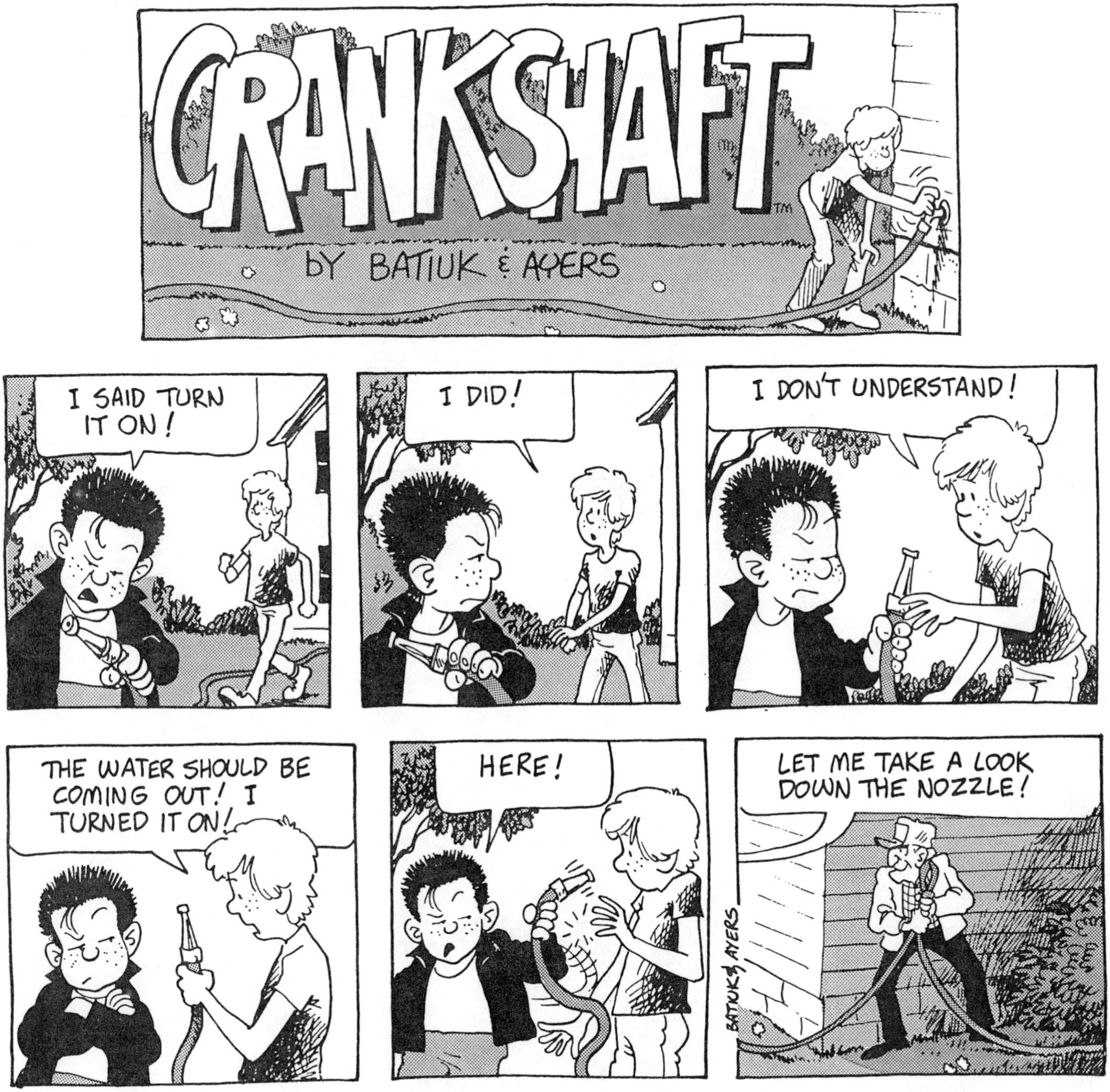
CRANKSHAFT
BY BATIUK & AYERS
I SAID TURN IT ON!
I DID!
I DON'T UNDERSTAND!
THE WATER SHOULD BE COMING OUT! I TURNED IT ON!
HERE!
LET ME TAKE A LOOK DOWN THE NOZZLE!
BATIUK & AYERS

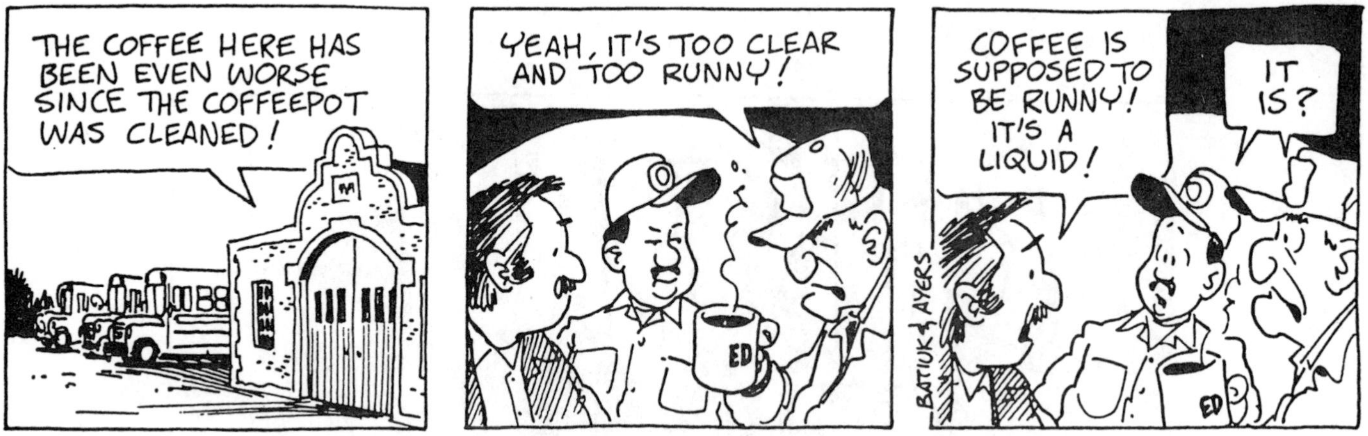
THE COFFEE HERE HAS BEEN EVEN WORSE SINCE THE COFFEEPOT WAS CLEANED!
YEAH, IT'S TOO CLEAR AND TOO RUNNY!
ED
COFFEE IS SUPPOSED TO BE RUNNY! IT'S A LIQUID!
IT IS?
BATIUK & AYERS
ED

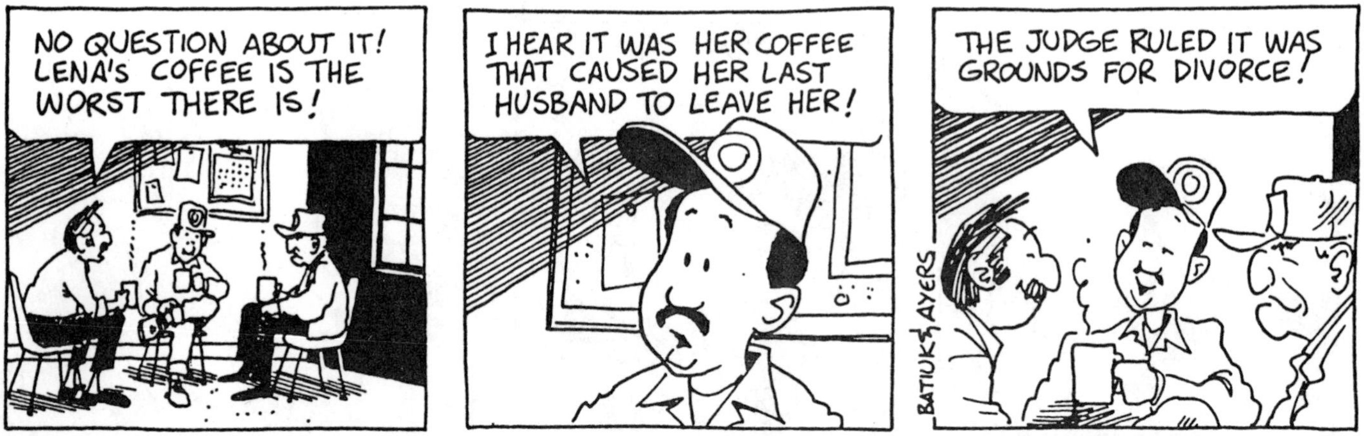
NO QUESTION ABOUT IT! LENA'S COFFEE IS THE WORST THERE IS!
I HEAR IT WAS HER COFFEE THAT CAUSED HER LAST HUSBAND TO LEAVE HER!
THE JUDGE RULED IT WAS GROUNDS FOR DIVORCE!
BATIUK & AYERS

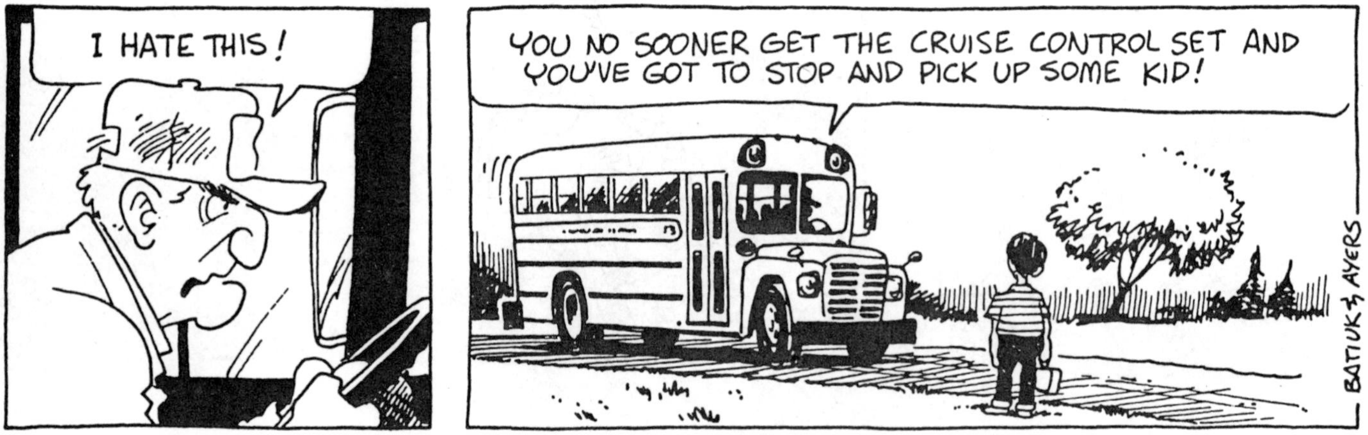
I HATE THIS!
YOU NO SOONER GET THE CRUISE CONTROL SET AND YOU'VE GOT TO STOP AND PICK UP SOME KID!
BATIUK & AYERS

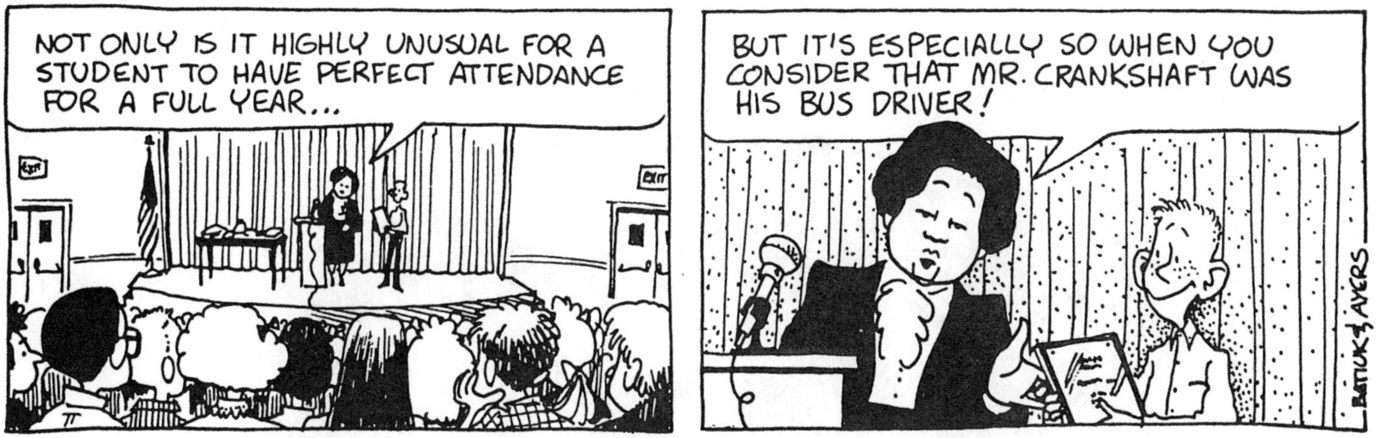
NOT ONLY IS IT HIGHLY UNUSUAL FOR A STUDENT TO HAVE PERFECT ATTENDANCE FOR A FULL YEAR...
BUT IT'S ESPECIALLY SO WHEN YOU CONSIDER THAT MR. CRANKSHAFT WAS HIS BUS DRIVER!
BATIUK & AYERS

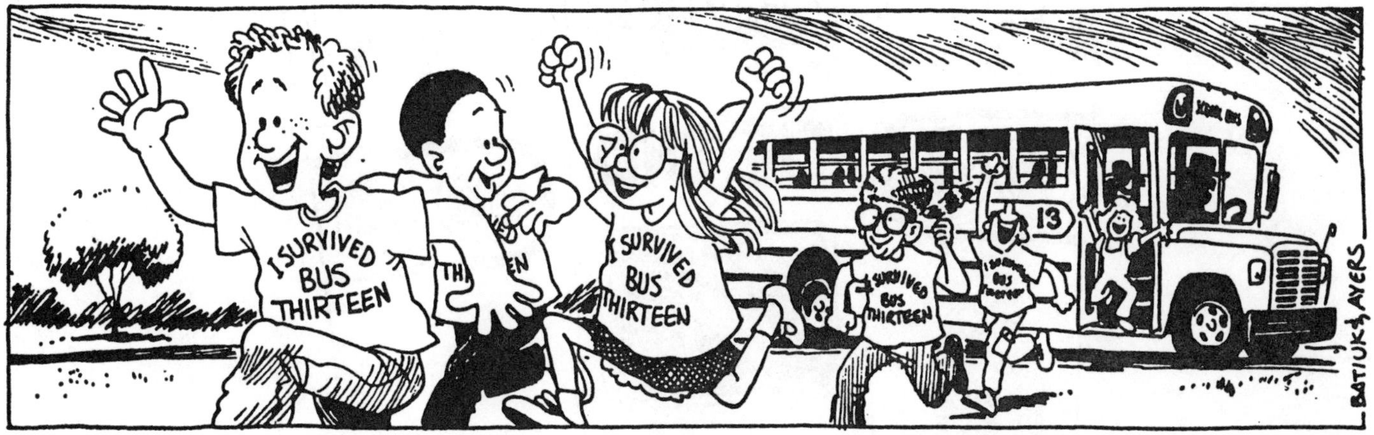
I SURVIVED BUS THIRTEEN
I SURVIVED BUS THIRTEEN
I SURVIVED BUS THIRTEEN
13
BATIUK & AYERS

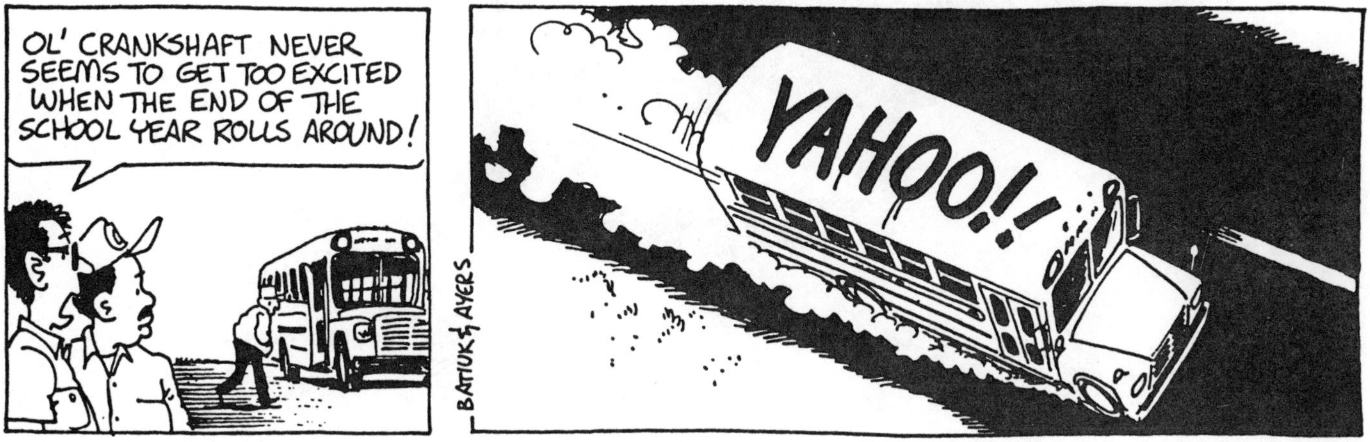
OL' CRANKSHAFT NEVER SEEMS TO GET TOO EXCITED WHEN THE END OF THE SCHOOL YEAR ROLLS AROUND!
BATIUK & AYERS
YAHOO!!

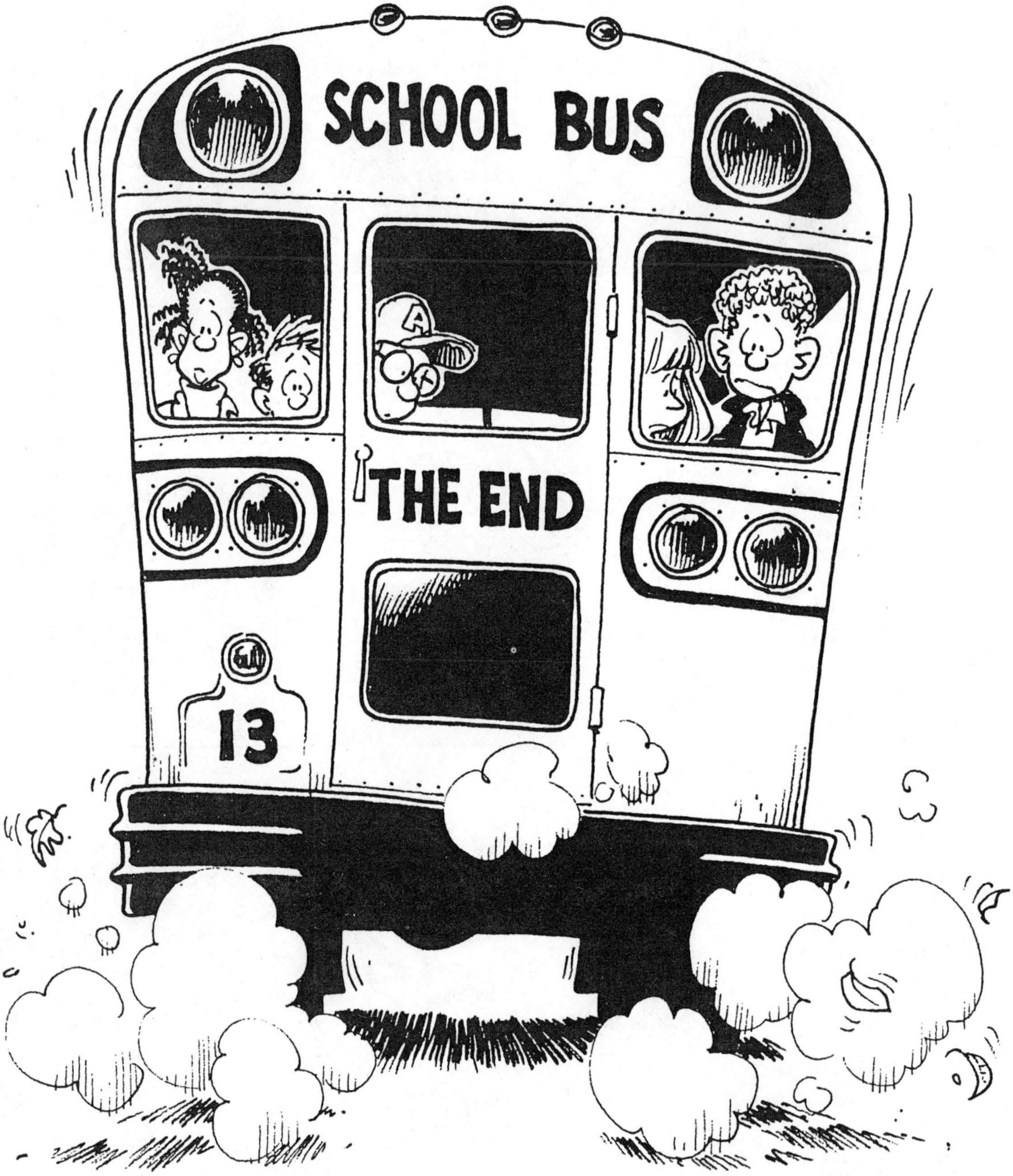
SCHOOL BUS
THE END
13